MW01625661

GEORGIA O'KEEFFE

Edited by

**Sarah Kelly Oehler
and Annelise K. Madsen**

With essays by
Adrienne Brown
Annelise K. Madsen
Sarah Kelly Oehler
Sascha T. Scott
and Lisa Volpe

The Art Institute of Chicago

Distributed by Yale University Press,
New Haven and London

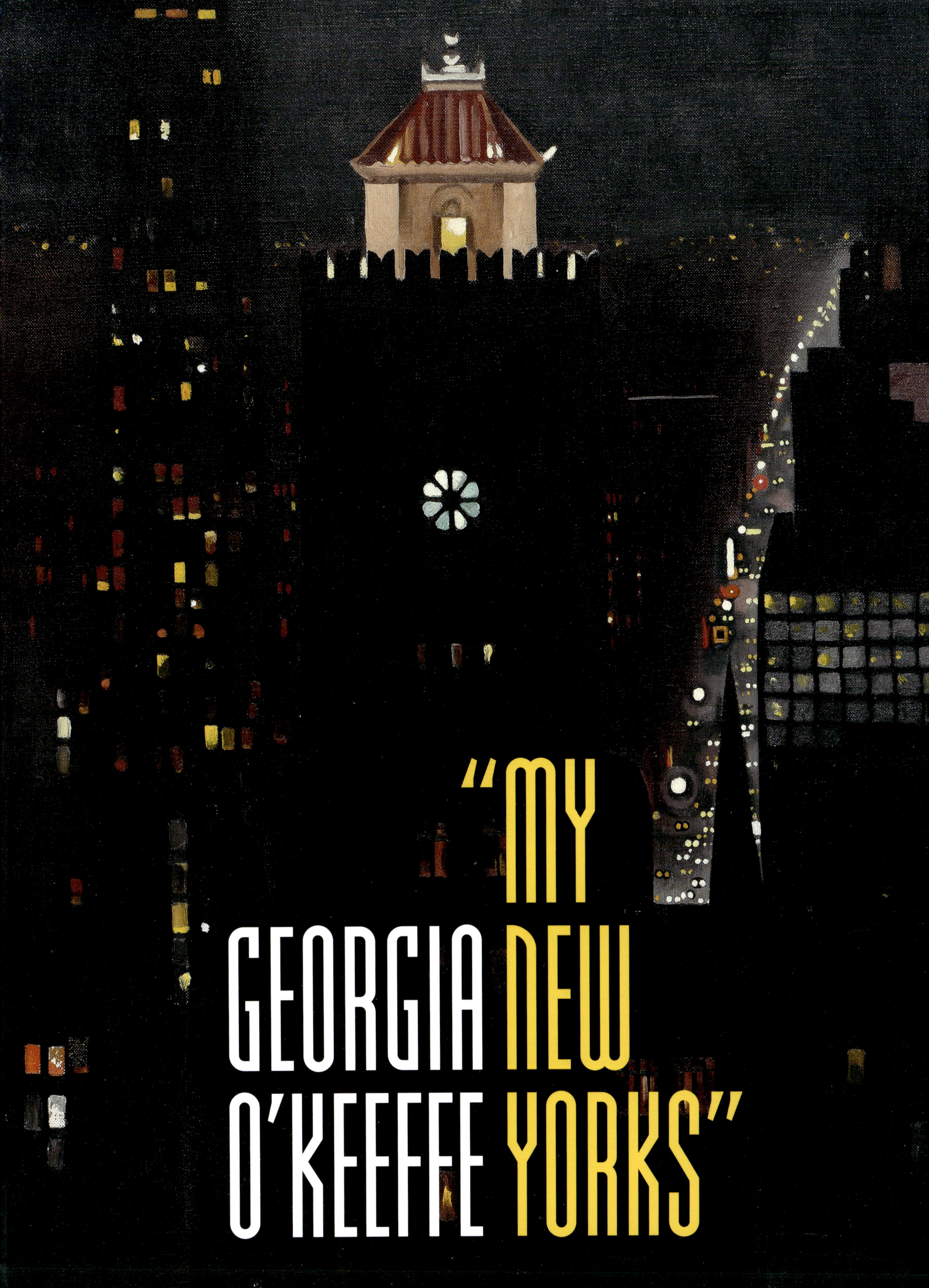
"MY
GEORGIA NEW
O'KEEFFE YORKS"

Georgia O'Keeffe: "My New Yorks" was published in conjunction with an exhibition of the same title organized by the Art Institute of Chicago, on view from June 2 to September 22, 2024, and at the High Museum of Art, Atlanta, from October 25, 2024, to February 16, 2025.

Georgia O'Keeffe: "My New Yorks"
Corporate Sponsor

BANK OF AMERICA

Major support is provided by the Harris Family Foundation in memory of Bette and Neison Harris, an anonymous donor, Richard F. and Christine F. Karger, the Shure Charitable Trust, Richard and Ann Carr, Pam Conant, Constance and David Coolidge, Mr. and Mrs. John T. Golitz, the Jentes Family, Loretta and Allan Kaplan, and Margot Levin Schiff and the Harold Schiff Foundation.

Additional funding is provided by the Jack and Peggy Crowe Fund, the Suzanne and Wesley M. Dixon Exhibition Fund, and The Regenstein Foundation Fund.

Members of the Luminary Trust provide annual leadership support for the museum's operations, including exhibition development, conservation and collection care, and educational programming. The Luminary Trust includes an anonymous donor, Karen Gray-Krehbiel and John Krehbiel, Jr., Kenneth C. Griffin, the Harris Family Foundation in memory of Bette and Neison Harris, Josef and Margot Lakonishok, Ann and Samuel M. Mencoff, Sylvia Neil and Dan Fischel, Cari and Michael J. Sacks, and the Earl and Brenda Shapiro Foundation.

Additional support is provided by

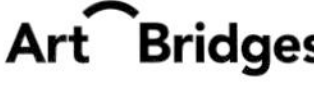

First edition
Printed in Spain

ISBN: 978-0-300-27575-9
(hardcover)

Library of Congress Control Number:
2023952083

Published by
The Art Institute of Chicago
111 South Michigan Avenue
Chicago, IL 60603-6404
artic.edu

Distributed by
Yale University Press
302 Temple Street
P. O. Box 209040
New Haven, CT 06520-9040
yalebooks.com/art

Edited by Sheila Majumdar

Production by Lauren Makholm and Ben Bertin

Photography research by Josephine Yanasak-Leszczynski

Proofreading by Sarah E. Robinson

Indexing by Lee Gable

Photography by Juan Molina Hernández and Robert Lifson

Postproduction by Hayley Hinsberger

Design and typesetting by Roy Brooks, Fold Four, Inc.

Separations by Professional Graphics, Rockford, Illinois

Printing and binding by Brizzolis, arte en gráficas, Madrid

Publishing, the Art Institute of Chicago

Katie Reilly, Associate Vice President

Lisa Meyerowitz, Editorial Director

Lauren Makholm, Director of Production

Imaging, the Art Institute of Chicago

Bonnie Rosenberg, Director of Imaging

Nathan Keay, Associate Director, Photography

Elyse Allen, Assistant Director of Production

Details
Jacket cover: *The Shelton with Sunspots, N.Y.* (pl. 12); jacket back cover: *Manhattan* (pl. 19); jacket interior: *East River from the Shelton, No. III* (pl. 55); p. 3: *New York, Night* (pl. 62); pp. 14–15: *East River from the Shelton (East River No. 1)* (pl. 60); pp. 34–35: *Pink Dish and Green Leaves* (pl. 59); pp. 54–55: *From the Lake No. 3* (pl. 3); pp. 72–73: *New York Street with Moon* (pl. 1); pp. 88–89: *Shelton Hotel, N.Y., No. I* (pl. 11); pp. 104–5: *Brooklyn Bridge* (pl. 37); p. 126: *Radiator Building—Night, New York* (pl. 16); p. 166: *East River from the 30th Story of the Shelton Hotel* (pl. 57); p. 180: *Taos Pueblo* (pl. 66).

CONTENTS

Georgia O'Keeffe: "My New Yorks" Corporate Sponsor

BANK OF AMERICA

Major support is provided by the Harris Family Foundation in memory of Bette and Neison Harris, an anonymous donor, Richard F. and Christine F. Karger, the Shure Charitable Trust, Richard and Ann Carr, Pam Conant, Constance and David Coolidge, Mr. and Mrs. John T. Golitz, the Jentes Family, Loretta and Allan Kaplan, and Margot Levin Schiff and the Harold Schiff Foundation.

Additional funding is provided by the Jack and Peggy Crowe Fund, the Suzanne and Wesley M. Dixon Exhibition Fund, and The Regenstein Foundation Fund.

Members of the Luminary Trust provide annual leadership support for the museum's operations, including exhibition development, conservation and collection care, and educational programming. The Luminary Trust includes an anonymous donor, Karen Gray-Krehbiel and John Krehbiel, Jr., Kenneth C. Griffin, the Harris Family Foundation in memory of Bette and Neison Harris, Josef and Margot Lakonishok, Ann and Samuel M. Mencoff, Sylvia Neil and Dan Fischel, Cari and Michael J. Sacks, and the Earl and Brenda Shapiro Foundation.

Additional support is provided by

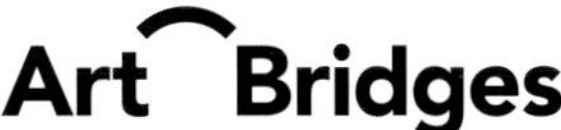

FOREWORD

Between 1925 and 1930, Georgia O'Keeffe made New York City the subject of intense artistic investigation, producing a small but compelling group of paintings and drawings she called "my New Yorks." Through them she explored the expressive potential of the urban skyline, then undergoing dramatic transformation through the construction of towering skyscrapers. Even as many of her contemporaries championed the city as a site of modern dynamism, a triumph of industry over nature, O'Keeffe asserted her artistic independence by portraying the city as an amalgamation of the organic and the inorganic, the natural and the constructed. This reflected her perception of the city, a radically new lived experience as she moved horizontally on the streets of midtown Manhattan and vertically within her skyscraper home in the Shelton Hotel. But more broadly, her New Yorks exemplified O'Keeffe's belief that her paintings needed to manifest her thoughts and feelings rather than simply transcribe facts. Indeed, as she stated in 1926, "One can't paint New York as it is, but rather as it is felt." This conviction shaped her work in New York and beyond as she transitioned in 1929 to depicting the Southwestern landscape with which she became closely associated. This exhibition showcases O'Keeffe's New Yorks, exploring their complexity and situating them within the broader range of her creative production in the late 1920s, a key developmental moment in her career as she achieved widespread recognition and attained financial stability.

Sarah Kelly Oehler, Field-McCormick Chair and Curator, Arts of the Americas, and Vice President of Curatorial Strategy; and Annelise K. Madsen, Gilda and Henry Buchbinder Associate Curator, Arts of the Americas, have done an exemplary job in bringing this catalogue and exhibition to fruition, which dually serve as the first serious investigations into O'Keeffe's substantial body of work exploring New York City's built environment. We are pleased to be joined in this endeavor by the High Museum of Art in Atlanta, led by Rand Suffolk, Nancy and Holcombe T. Green, Jr., Director, who early on embraced the project. Special recognition is due to the private and institutional lenders who entrusted us with the care and display of their artworks. In particular, the exhibition could not have been realized without the research facilities and crucial loan support of the Georgia O'Keeffe Museum, under the leadership of director Cody Hartley.

In Chicago, Bank of America was our corporate sponsor. Major support was provided by the Harris Family Foundation in memory of Bette and Neison Harris, an anonymous donor, Richard F. and Christine F. Karger, the Shure Charitable Trust, Richard and Ann Carr, Pam Conant, Constance and David Coolidge, Mr. and Mrs. John T. Golitz, the Jentes Family, Loretta and Allan Kaplan, and Margot Levin Schiff and the Harold Schiff Foundation. Additional funding was provided by the Jack and Peggy Crowe Fund, the Suzanne and Wesley M. Dixon Exhibition Fund, and The Regenstein Foundation Fund. Members of the Luminary Trust provide annual leadership support for the museum's operations, including exhibition development, conservation and collection care, and educational programming. The Luminary Trust includes an anonymous donor, Karen Gray-Krehbiel and John Krehbiel, Jr., Kenneth C. Griffin, the Harris Family Foundation in memory of Bette and Neison Harris, Josef and Margot Lakonishok, Ann and Samuel M. Mencoff, Sylvia Neil and Dan Fischel, Cari and Michael J. Sacks, and the Earl and Brenda Shapiro Foundation. Additional support was provided by Art Bridges, Bentonville, Arkansas.

The Art Institute of Chicago is proud of its long history with Georgia O'Keeffe, which started in the early decades of her life when she enrolled at the School of the Art Institute of Chicago in 1905. The museum hosted her first large-scale retrospective in 1943, and then-director Daniel Catton Rich became a close confidant of the artist, in 1949 helping her in the monumental task of dividing the Alfred Stieglitz Collection among several institutions across the country, including the Art Institute. The museum hosted subsequent retrospectives in 1971 and 1988, building substantial holdings of her works along the way, many of which were gifts from the artist. Inspired by *The Shelton with Sunspots, N.Y.*, a stunning cityscape that entered the collection in 1985, we are delighted to once again display O'Keeffe's innovative, exquisite, and enduring art.

James Rondeau
President and Eloise W. Martin Director
The Art Institute of Chicago

ACKNOWLEDGMENTS

As curators, we have the honor of showcasing in our galleries *The Shelton with Sunspots, N.Y.*—a distinctive and dynamic painting by Georgia O'Keeffe that has long captivated us. It is with great pleasure that we unite this work with others by the artist likewise inspired by Manhattan in this catalogue and the exhibition *Georgia O'Keeffe: "My New Yorks."* The project benefited from the stalwart support of James Rondeau, President and Eloise W. Martin Director. The enthusiastic guidance of Sarah Guernsey, Deputy Director and Senior Vice President for Curatorial Affairs; Eve Jeffers, Chief Operating Officer; Hilary Branch, Vice President, Planning and Strategy; and Aaron Andersen, Associate Vice President, Financial Planning and Analysis, has been equally crucial.

We are grateful to catalogue authors Adrienne Brown, Sascha T. Scott, and Lisa Volpe for their smart contributions to this volume, which add depth and nuance to our understandings of O'Keeffe by considering the complex narratives that shaped her art making and its reception. For their research and other critical assistance, we are indebted to Phil Alexandre and Marie Evans, Alexandre Gallery, New York; Brooke Anderson; Jonathan Boos; Abigail Bisbee and Kate Drake, Christie's, New York; the Tyson Scholars of American Art Program, Crystal Bridges Museum of American Art, Bentonville, Arkansas; Alice Duncan, Gerald Peters Gallery; Evelyn Hankins, Hannah Green, and Julia Murphy, Hirshhorn Museum, Smithsonian Institution, Washington, DC; Barbara Buhler Lynes; Ellery Foutch, Middlebury College, Vermont; Marta Ruiz del Arbol, Museo Nacional Thyssen-Bornemisza, Madrid; Yesenia Castro and Tal Nadan, New York Public Library; Andrew Schoelkopf and Alana Ricca, Schoelkopf Gallery, New York; Kayla Carlsen, Sotheby's, New York; Lauren Kroiz, University of California, Berkeley; Derrick Cartwright, University of San Diego; and Rebecca Maguire and Matthew Rowe, Beinecke Rare Book and Manuscript Library, Yale University, New Haven, Connecticut.

The museum's exceedingly capable Publishing and Imaging teams, led by Katie Reilly and Bonnie Rosenberg, respectively, and including Elyse Allen, Ben Bertin, Hayley Hinsberger, Nathan Keay, Robert Lifson, Lauren Makholm, Lisa Meyerowitz, Joseph Mohan, Juan Molina Hernández, Isella V. Sandoval, and Josephine Yanasak-Leszczynski, ensured that this catalogue was both conceptually sound and beautifully produced. Sheila Majumdar expertly edited the texts, attending to both the small details and the cohesive whole. Roy Brooks, Fold Four, Inc., created the sensitive and refined book design. Sarah E. Robinson keenly proofread the catalogue, and Lee Gable compiled the index. Mapping Specialists created the base map of midtown Manhattan on page 22.

Across the museum, our colleagues deserve recognition for their far-reaching talents and tremendous dedication to the Art Institute. An endeavor of this scope and complexity cannot succeed without the skills, acumen, and care of so many. Our departmental colleagues in Arts of the Americas are a stellar team, offering expertise, advice, and assistance at all the right moments. We thank especially Chris Shepherd and Tim Roby for their able handling of the artworks, thoughtful planning, and calm demeanor throughout; Kate Weinstein and Julie Warchol, whose keen organization helped move the project along; Elizabeth Pope, former Mellon Fellow Kayleigh Doyen, and former Lunder Consortium intern Molly George for valuable research assistance; Esther Espino for her unflappable resourcefulness; Tess Smith for tackling many tasks; and Elizabeth McGoey for her insights and conversation throughout the project's development.

We extend our particular appreciation to Jennifer Oberhauser, whose feats of coordination and steady guidance ensured that the exhibition's many moving parts would coalesce in the end, Richard Ferrer for his elegant exhibition design, and Vitalii Emelianov for his inspiring visual design. Their partnership was essential during the energetic process of figuring out how walls, galleries, and various material elements could bring the show's artworks and ideas to life.

We also thank current and former staff at the Art Institute: Abby Lewis in Accounting/Controller; Alison Fisher in Architecture and Design; Rosa Berland, Timothy Campos, Leslie Carlson, Cayetana Castillo, Erin Gordon, Michael Kaysen, Julia Loughlin, Joyce Penn, Natasha Perine, Ariana Webber, and the great team of specialists in Collections and Loans; Milan Bobysud, Mary Broadway, Christopher H. Brooks, Francesca Casadio, Christine Fabian, kelly keegan, Allison Langley, Sylvie Penichon, and Kirk Vuillemot in Conservation and Science; Amanda Block, Claire Burdulis, Kate Tierney Powell, and Maureen Ryan in the Director's Office; Amy Allen, Katie Dyson, Stephanie Henderson, Joe Iverson, Miguel Perez, Jenny

Sturrock Petkovic, and the expansive team in Engagement; Leticia Pardo Rojo and Joseph Vatinno in Exhibition Design; Megan Hurlbert and Becca Schlossberg in Exhibitions; Logan Chappe, Devin Davis, Gina Giambalvo, Kirill Mazor, Kari McCluskey, Michael Neault, Alex Quintanilla, and Christine Zavesky in Experience Design; Robert Ciesla, Matthew Rift, Tom Ryan, and the fantastic team of carpenters, electricians, and painters in Facilities and Logistics; Jessica Applebee and Dawn Koster in Financial Planning and Analysis; Marielle Epstein, Emily Fry, Sam Ramos, and Ginia Sweeney in Interpretation; Troy Klyber in Legal; Shannon Burke, Elizabeth L. Dudgeon, Nora Gainer, Paul Jones, Megan Michienzi, Jen Nelson, Katie Rahn, Nadine Schneller, Lauren Schultz, Robby Sexton, and Salina Tsegai in Marketing and Communications; Jennifer Evanoff, Heather Reinholtz, and the dedicated team in the Museum Shop; James Allan, Anna Maria Carvallo VanMeter, Mary Elizabeth DeYoe, Erika Lowe, George Martin, David Nacol, and Jen Oatess in Philanthropy; Barbara Diener, Elizabeth Siegel, Jamie Vaught, and Matthew S. Witkovsky in Photography and Media; Corey Burrage, Lucio Ventura, and the adept security team in Protection Services; and Jill Bugajski, Anna Feuer, Violet Jaffe, Autumn L. Mather, Nathaniel Parks, Bart Ryckbosch, and Leslie M. Wilson in the Research Center and Ryerson and Burnham Libraries and Archives.

Our colleagues at the High Museum of Art, including Nancy and Holcombe T. Green, Jr., Director Rand Suffolk, Frances Francis, Stephanie Mayer Heydt, Kyle Mancuso, Amy Simon, and Kevin Tucker, are responsible for the superb presentation of the exhibition in Atlanta.

The generosity of the lenders to the exhibition ensured that *Georgia O'Keeffe: "My New Yorks"* would shine in the galleries. A heartfelt thank you for agreeing to temporarily part with such important works for the sake of this project. At the Art Institute of Chicago, the department of Photography and Media and the Ryerson and Burnham Libraries and Archives graciously supported the show with key loans and research assistance. We likewise thank Andrew Walker, Amon Carter Museum of American Art, Fort Worth, Texas; Ashley Holland, Monica Ros, and Megan Valentine, Art Bridges, Bentonville, Arkansas; Stephan Jost, Art Gallery of Ontario, Toronto; Louis Bacon; Veronica Roberts and Katie Clifford, Cantor Arts Center, Stanford, California; William M. Griswold and Mark Cole, Cleveland Museum of Art; Michael Christiano, Colorado Springs Fine Arts Center; Rod Bigelow and Jennifer Padgett, Crystal Bridges Museum of American Art; Jeff Fleming, Des Moines Art Center; Johanna Blume, April Knauber, and John Vanausdall, Eiteljorg Museum; Thomas Campbell, Karin Breuer, and Furio Rinaldi, Fine Arts Museums of San Francisco; Jamaal Sheats, Fisk University Galleries, Nashville, Tennessee; T. Barton Thurber, Mary-Kay Lombino, John Murphy, and Kelly Reynolds, Frances Lehman Loeb Art Center, Vassar College, Poughkeepsie, New York; Cody Hartley, Tori Duggan, Dale Kronkright, Yaritza Martinez, Liz Neely, Liz O'Brien, Ariel Plotek, Judy Chiba Smith, and Sherri Sorensen-Clem, Georgia O'Keeffe Museum, Santa Fe, New Mexico; Elie and Sarah Hirschfeld; Max Hollein, David Breslin, and Sylvia Yount, Metropolitan Museum of Art, New York; Katherine Crawford and Robert Cozzolino, Minneapolis Institute of Art; Matthew Teitelbaum and Erica Hirshler, Museum of Fine Arts, Boston; Anne-Marie Russell, Museum of Fine Arts, St. Petersburg, Florida; Glenn Lowry, Samantha Friedman, Emily Olek, and Ann Temkin, The Museum of Modern Art, New York; Jenny Sponberg, Myron Kunin Collection of American Art, Minneapolis; Kaywin Feldman, Harry Cooper, and Sarah Greenough, National Gallery of Art, Washington, DC; Brett Abbott, Keith Gervase, and Lisa Williams, New Britain Museum of American Art, Connecticut; Margaret M. O'Reilly and Sarah Vogelman, New Jersey State Museum, Trenton; Mark White, Petra Brown, Ruth LaNore, and Christian Waguespack, New Mexico Museum of Art, Santa Fe; Louise Mirrer, Emily Croll, Margaret Hofer, and Wendy Nālani E. Ikemoto, New-York Historical Society; Gail Kern Paster, Sarah Boyd Alvarez, and Will Hansen, Newberry Library, Chicago; Sasha Suda, Peter Barberie, Molly Kalkstein, and Jessica Todd Smith, Philadelphia Museum of Art; Jonathan P. Binstock, Dorothy Kosinski, Michele De Shazo, and Elsa Smithgall, Phillips Collection, Washington, DC; Min Jung Kim and Melissa Wolfe, Saint Louis Art Museum; Amada Cruz and Theresa Papanikolas, Seattle Art Museum; Susan Longhenry and Stacey Walsh, Sheldon Museum of Art, University of Nebraska-Lincoln; Stephanie Stebich, Randy Griffey, and Virginia Mecklenburg, Smithsonian American Art Museum, Washington, DC; Baroness Carmen Thyssen-Bornemisza; Matthew Hargraves, Brandy Culp, and Erin Monroe, Wadsworth Atheneum

Museum of Art, Hartford, Connecticut; Mary Ceruti, Walker Art Center, Minneapolis; David Warnock and Michele Speaks; Adam Weinberg and Barbara Haskell, Whitney Museum of American Art, New York; Anne Kraybill, Tera Hedrick, and Patricia McConnell, Wichita Art Museum, Kansas; and multiple anonymous lenders.

The financial support of numerous donors ensured that the exhibition would be thoroughly researched and splendidly presented in the galleries. The corporate sponsor for *Georgia O'Keeffe: "My New Yorks"* was Bank of America. Major support was provided by the Harris Family Foundation in memory of Bette and Neison Harris, an anonymous donor, Richard F. and Christine F. Karger, the Shure Charitable Trust, Richard and Ann Carr, Pam Conant, Constance and David Coolidge, Mr. and Mrs. John T. Golitz, the Jentes Family, Loretta and Allan Kaplan, and Margot Levin Schiff and the Harold Schiff Foundation. Additional funding was provided by the Jack and Peggy Crowe Fund, the Suzanne and Wesley M. Dixon Exhibition Fund, and The Regenstein Foundation Fund. Members of the Luminary Trust provide annual leadership support for the museum's operations, including exhibition development, conservation and collection care, and educational programming. The Luminary Trust includes an anonymous donor, Karen Gray-Krehbiel and John Krehbiel, Jr., Kenneth C. Griffin, the Harris Family Foundation in memory of Bette and Neison Harris, Josef and Margot Lakonishok, Ann and Samuel M. Mencoff, Sylvia Neil and Dan Fischel, Cari and Michael J. Sacks, and the Earl and Brenda Shapiro Foundation. Art Bridges, Bentonville, Arkansas, provided additional support.

Finally, we are deeply grateful to our families, who have offered steady support and encouragement for our endeavors, art historical and otherwise. Your part is essential.

Sarah Kelly Oehler
Field-McCormick Chair and Curator, Arts of the Americas, and Vice President of Curatorial Strategy
The Art Institute of Chicago

Annelise K. Madsen
Gilda and Henry Buchbinder Associate Curator, Arts of the Americas
The Art Institute of Chicago

NOTE TO THE READER

Artworks

In O'Keeffe's artwork titles, her variable uses of internal commas, dashes, punctuation for state acronyms, and Roman and Arabic numerals are retained.

The following conventions are used for dating works:
1920s: executed sometime within 1920 and 1929
1921: executed in 1921
c. 1921: executed sometime around 1921
1921–23: begun in 1921 and completed in 1923 or executed sometime within or around the period 1921 to 1923
June 5, 1936: date photographed

In dimensions, height precedes width. The dimensions for paintings, works on paper, and photographs indicate the size of the image alone unless otherwise noted.

The plates are organized thematically and include O'Keeffe's paintings, works on paper, and photographs, as well as photographs by Alfred Stieglitz and Carl Van Vechten. The List of Plates (pp. 200–203) provides full tombstone information.

Correspondence

When quoting letters by Georgia O'Keeffe or Alfred Stieglitz, our approach to their nontraditional punctuation and capitalization is informed by the style used in Sarah Greenough, ed., *My Faraway One: Selected Letters of Georgia O'Keeffe and Alfred Stieglitz*, vol. 1, *1915–1933* (New Haven, CT: Yale University Press, 2011). Square brackets indicate our editorial corrections and clarifications.

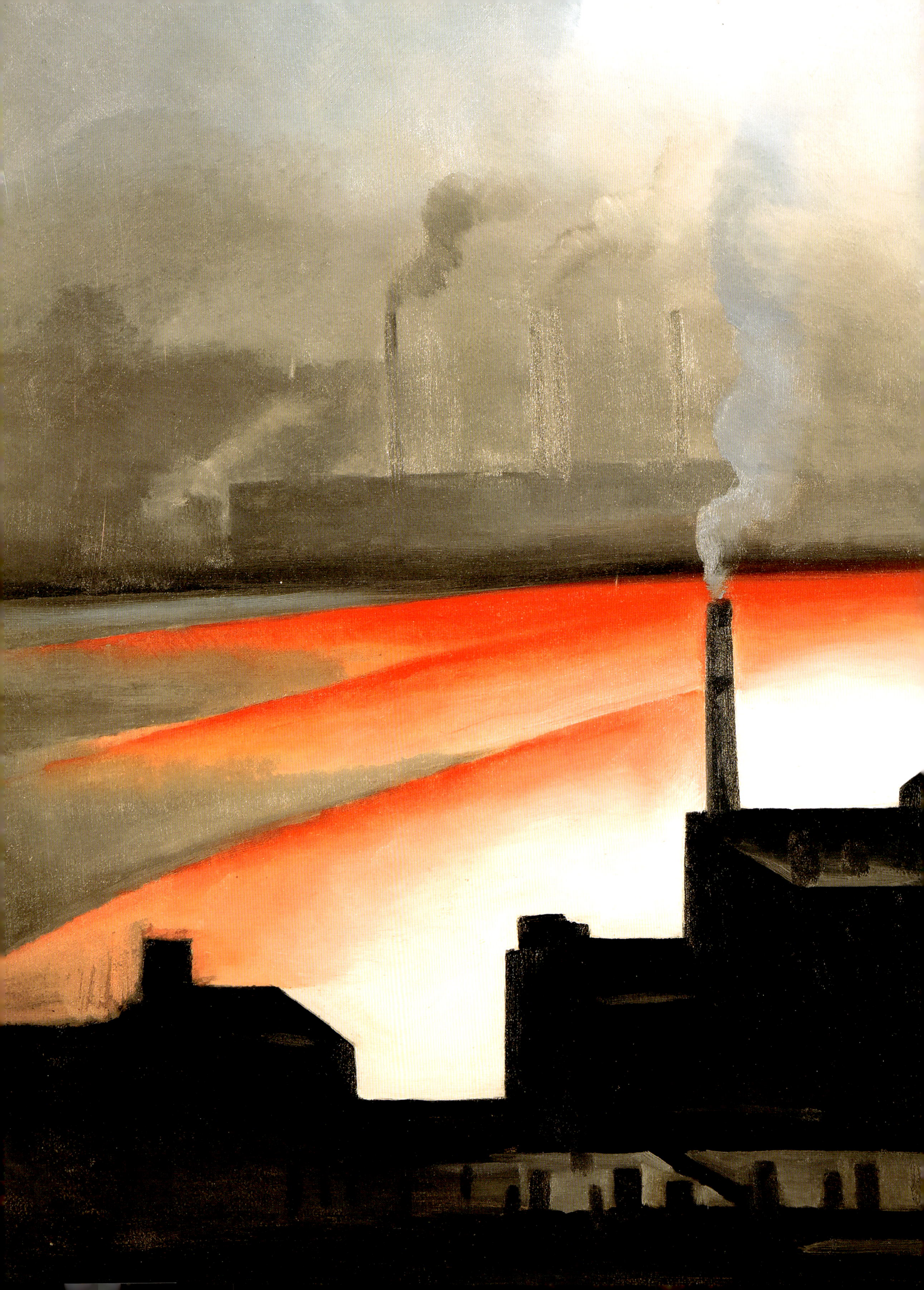

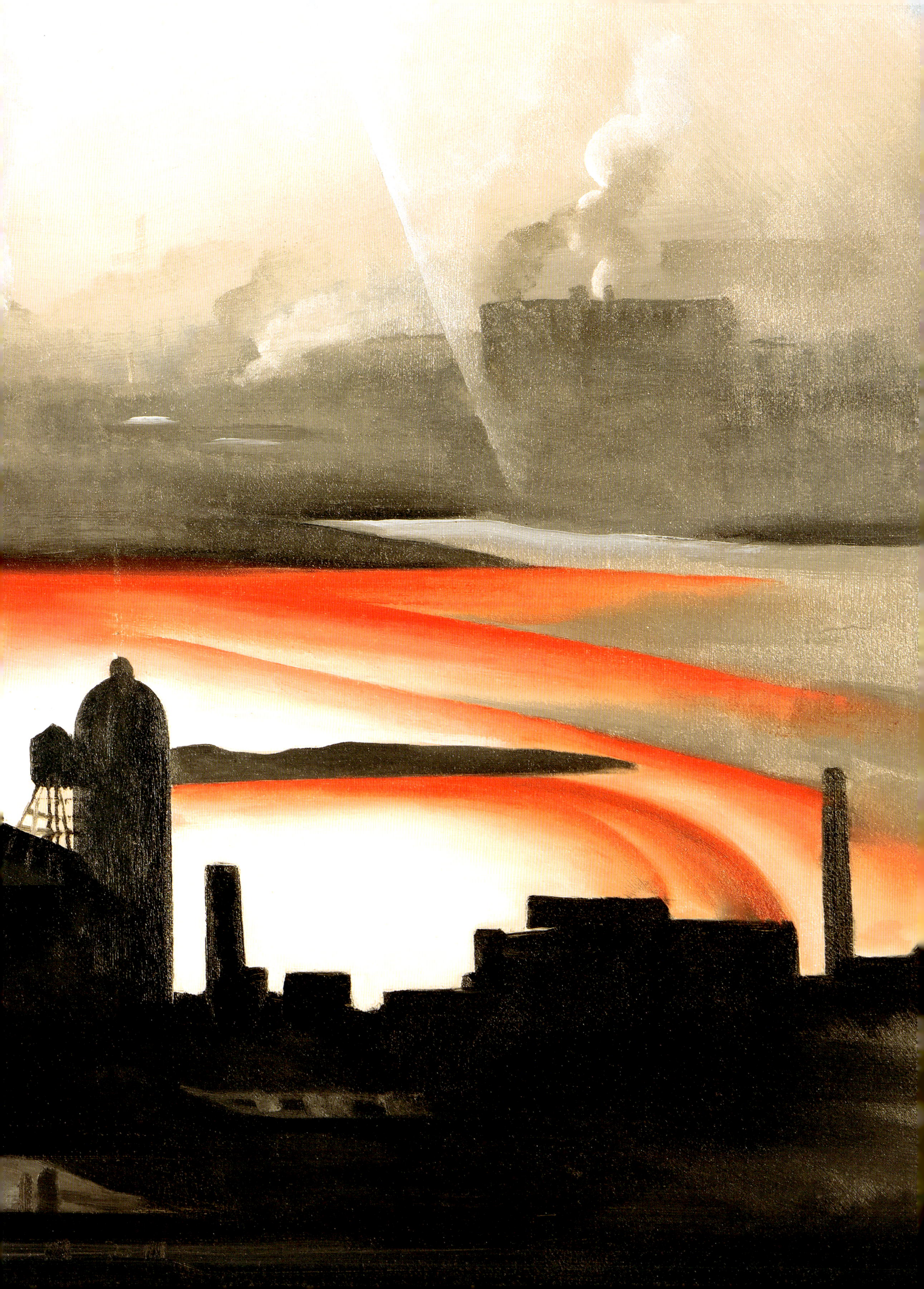

TURNING THE WORLD OVER

GEORGIA O'KEEFFE PAINTS MANHATTAN

Sarah Kelly Oehler

Surrounded by looming buildings, with a haze of steam rising in the cold air, the towering building appears gouged by the glow of the sun, its brilliant rays obscuring vision and eradicating form. Georgia O'Keeffe later recalled, "I went out one morning to look at [the Shelton Hotel] and there was the optical illusion of a bite out of one side of the tower made by the sun, with sunspots against the building and against the sky."[1] This memorable scene resulted in *The Shelton with Sunspots, N.Y.* (pl. 12), one in a powerful group of paintings and drawings the artist made of New York City during a concentrated period from 1925 into the 1930s. She called these works "my New Yorks" and through them explored the dynamic potential of the New York skyline, then undergoing radical transformation through the construction of modern skyscrapers.[2] The paintings reveal her interest in two types of compositions: humbling views directed up at these new urban monoliths and sprawling observations looking down onto the city. O'Keeffe resisted the popular approach of contemporaries such as Charles Sheeler, who celebrated New York as a streamlined, impersonal series of geometric canyons in works such as *Skyscrapers* (fig. 1). Instead, as *The Shelton with Sunspots, N.Y.* so dazzlingly demonstrates, O'Keeffe asserted her artistic independence by portraying the city as an amalgamation of the organic and the inorganic, the natural and the constructed. This reflected her personal perception of the city—and more broadly, her belief that her paintings needed to manifest her thoughts and feelings rather than simply transcribe facts. Indeed, as she stated in 1926, "One can't paint New York as it is, but rather as it is felt."[3]

O'Keeffe's New York subjects emerged from her lived experience—the views and buildings that she saw on a daily basis—and her intuitive approach resulted in a surprising aesthetic range. In some, she explored atmospheric effects and changing weather conditions, others dramatize the city at night, and still others connected to her concurrent practice in abstraction. To express these various ideas, O'Keeffe selected a range of canvas or sheet sizes and proportions; such decisions were integral to her work. Working in series further enabled the artist to develop a complex modernist language in which she transitioned between hard-edged and soft forms with ease. This essay explores these choices and analyzes the breadth of O'Keeffe's New York subjects.[4]

AN IMPOSSIBLE IDEA

O'Keeffe's decision to paint the city was not a foregone conclusion, for she lived in the city far longer than she painted it. Nor was it one made in isolation from concerns of gender, class, and race, all of which shaped her life and career in the urban environment. In 1976, some fifty years after she began this work in earnest, she recounted how her decision to move into the Shelton Hotel (then the tallest residential hotel in New York) had prompted an intense eagerness to paint the city: "I had never lived up so high before and was so excited that I began talking about trying to paint New York. Of course, I was told that it was an impossible idea—even the men hadn't done too well with it."[5] O'Keeffe's

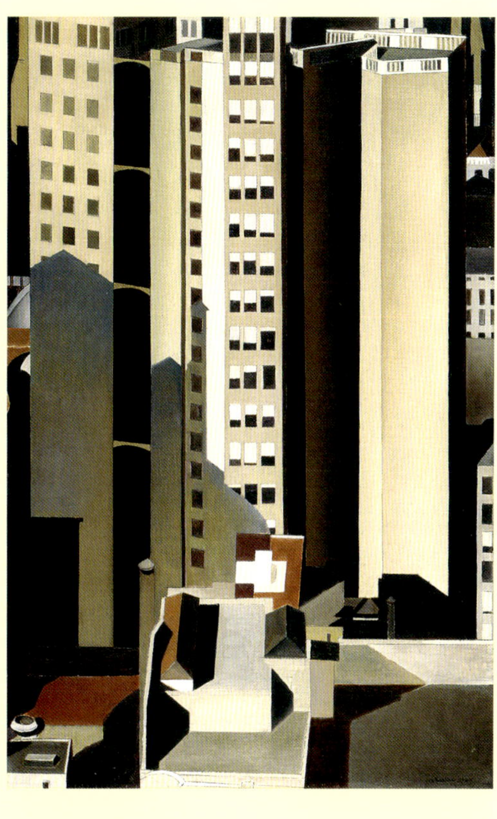

retrospective words must be taken with a note of caution, for she penned them late in life with the purpose of fashioning her legacy through a book combining lavish images and brief anecdotes.[6] But the vividness of her recollections regarding her New York paintings, and the space they are provided in an otherwise pithy publication, point to their significance in her oeuvre. They also offer important insights into her turn toward this new subject matter.

The "impossible idea"—that a woman might successfully visualize the skyscrapers and canyons of Manhattan—reflected the perception of many of her contemporaries that the city and its soaring buildings were encoded as masculine and were thus both inconceivable and undesirable as a subject for a woman. Although O'Keeffe phrased this recollection passively ("I was told"), it was likely framed this way by Alfred Stieglitz, the famed photographer and O'Keeffe's art dealer and husband, who was deeply invested in promoting her work as quintessentially feminine.[7] O'Keeffe's determination to paint the city must therefore also be seen as part of a calculated campaign to redirect the course of her career following several years of intensely sexualized critical rhetoric after the 1921 exhibition *Georgia O'Keeffe: A Portrait*, which featured Stieglitz's monumental photographic series of the artist (see pls. 73–76). Stieglitz took more than three hundred photographs of O'Keeffe over the course of their early relationship: some clothed, many nude, moving between body parts (hands, feet, torso) and her entire being, and occasionally portraying her in front of her own works.[8] This exhibition of photographs shaped the critical reception of her paintings for several years to come; the primarily (but not exclusively) male critics of the era could only respond to her paintings through the lens of her gender and sexuality.[9] O'Keeffe attempted to shift the focus of criticism with her exhibitions of 1923 and 1924 and was frustrated by its persistence even as she turned away from abstraction and toward more naturalistic imagery. O'Keeffe's decision to paint the "masculine" forms of the city in 1925 cannot be understood without reference to this history.

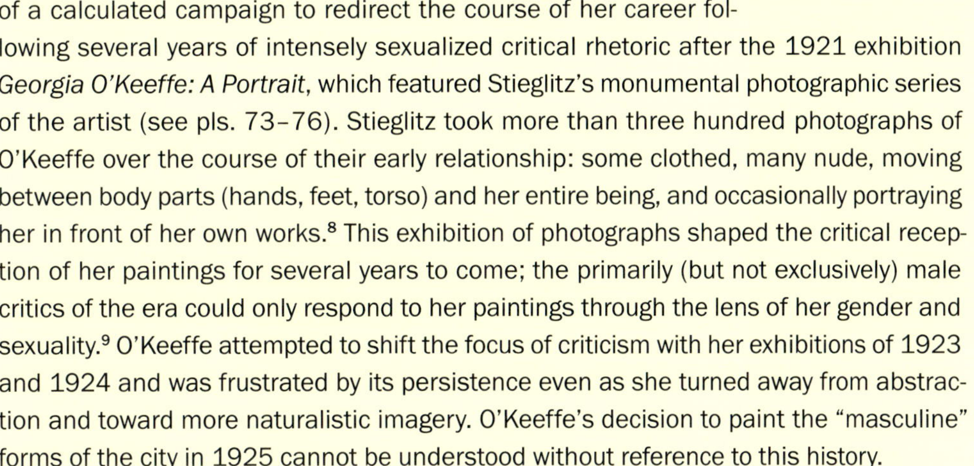

In her 1976 memory, O'Keeffe then faced further setbacks when she tried to exhibit her first major urban composition, *New York Street with Moon* (pl. 1), in a group exhibition at Stieglitz's gallery in March 1925. Despite there being, in her opinion, a perfect place for the painting, she recalled, "But the 'New York' wasn't hung—much to my disappointment."[10] Stieglitz's refusal to show the painting was likely due to his ongoing investment in promoting a feminized ideal of O'Keeffe's work. But she persevered, not allowing this to hinder her aesthetic exploration as she produced further New York compositions. In a triumphant conclusion, she dryly noted that at her annual show at Stieglitz's gallery the following year, "my large 'New York' was sold the first afternoon. No one ever objected to my painting New York after that."[11] Indeed, she sold a number of her New York paintings shortly after exhibiting them in the late 1920s: *New York Street with Moon* went to Mr. and Mrs. Adolph Meyer in 1926, and out of her 1927 exhibition, the collector Alma Wertheim purchased *The Shelton with Sunspots, N.Y.* (for the then-significant sum of six thousand dollars) and the author Edna Bryner Schwab bought *East River from the Shelton, No. III* (pl. 55). These sales would give O'Keeffe greater financial security at a crucial moment of her career; in fact, she later identified 1927 as the year she began to make a living from her art.[12]

FIG. 1
Charles Sheeler (American, 1883–1965). *Skyscrapers*, 1922. Oil on canvas; 50.8 × 33 cm (20 × 13 in.). Phillips Collection, Washington, DC, Acquired 1926.

A CITY DWELLER

Despite her close identification with the Southwest, where she resided year-round starting in 1949, O'Keeffe was no stranger to large cities. Born in Sun Prairie, Wisconsin, she dwelled in Chicago twice between 1905 and 1910, a key moment in that city's skyscraper construction, and first moved to New York in the fall of 1907.[13] She lived in Manhattan intermittently until 1918, when her deepening relationship with Stieglitz brought her back to the city on a more permanent basis. The couple lived at several addresses between 1918 and 1924, generally spending the winter season in Manhattan at properties owned by Stieglitz's family and in the summer season staying at the Stieglitz family house at Lake George, New York.[14] They first moved into a studio owned by his niece Elizabeth Stieglitz at 114 East Fifty-Ninth Street, which O'Keeffe commemorated in *59th Street Studio* (pl. 10).[15] East Fifty-Ninth was their Manhattan home until spring 1920, when, with the building scheduled for demolition, they went to Lake George for the summer. Upon their return to the city that November, they moved into Stieglitz's brother Leopold's home at 60 East Sixty-Fifth Street, where they stayed seasonally until the spring of 1924.

O'Keeffe, however, did not make the city the subject of concerted investigation during these early years in New York. Instead, her fascination with New York skyscrapers can be directly tied to her move into the Shelton Hotel. Designed by Arthur Loomis Harmon, the Shelton was built on Lexington Avenue between Forty-Eighth and Forty-Ninth Streets.[16] Although it has long been believed that O'Keeffe and Stieglitz moved there first in the fall of 1925, they actually lived there briefly a full year earlier, from around November 19 to December 17, 1924, during which time the couple married.[17] Unable to live with Leopold Stieglitz upon returning to Manhattan in the fall of 1924, they planned on renting a top-floor studio in a brownstone at 38 East Fifty-Eighth Street, but renovation efforts delayed the move. The Shelton, which had originally opened as a men's club in fall 1923, began allowing women residents only one month before O'Keeffe's arrival.[18] This first room at the Shelton in November 1924 was small but comfortable; Stieglitz described it in a letter to Sherwood Anderson: "We like the room here. . . . It's a tiny room with marvellously [*sic*] comfortable beds—two exposures—a luxurious bathroom . . . If it weren't that it's too expensive & we do need more space to work in we'd stay here a while. The quiet too is quite unusual."[19] Although their precise location in the building is unknown, photographs of the Shelton indicate that no matter where their room was located, they would have experienced extraordinary views in any direction given the skyscraper's height against what was then a backdrop of shorter buildings (see fig. 2).[20] This means that *prior* to creating her first major New York paintings, O'Keeffe had already briefly lived in a skyscraper, and the experience had an immediate and tremendous impact. Probably in March 1925, she wrote of her "New Yorks" to Henry McBride, acknowledging, "And that New York business goes round in my head—I am sure I wouldn't have such a hard time to get hold of it if I had always lived up here looking out at it."[21]

In November 1925 they returned to the Shelton for the winter, likely moving into an eleventh-floor suite; they were certainly there by April 1926.[22] O'Keeffe described their accommodations to her sister Ida, paying particular attention to the exposures: "We have two rooms here—the bedroom is tiny . . . but it faces north—east and south so we have lots of sun and air . . . the sitting room . . . has a good light so I

FIG. 2
The Shelton Hotel, New York. View from west. Reproduced in Oliver Reagan, ed., *American Architecture of the Twentieth Century*, vol. 1 (New York: Architectural Book Publishing Co., 1927), pl. 1.

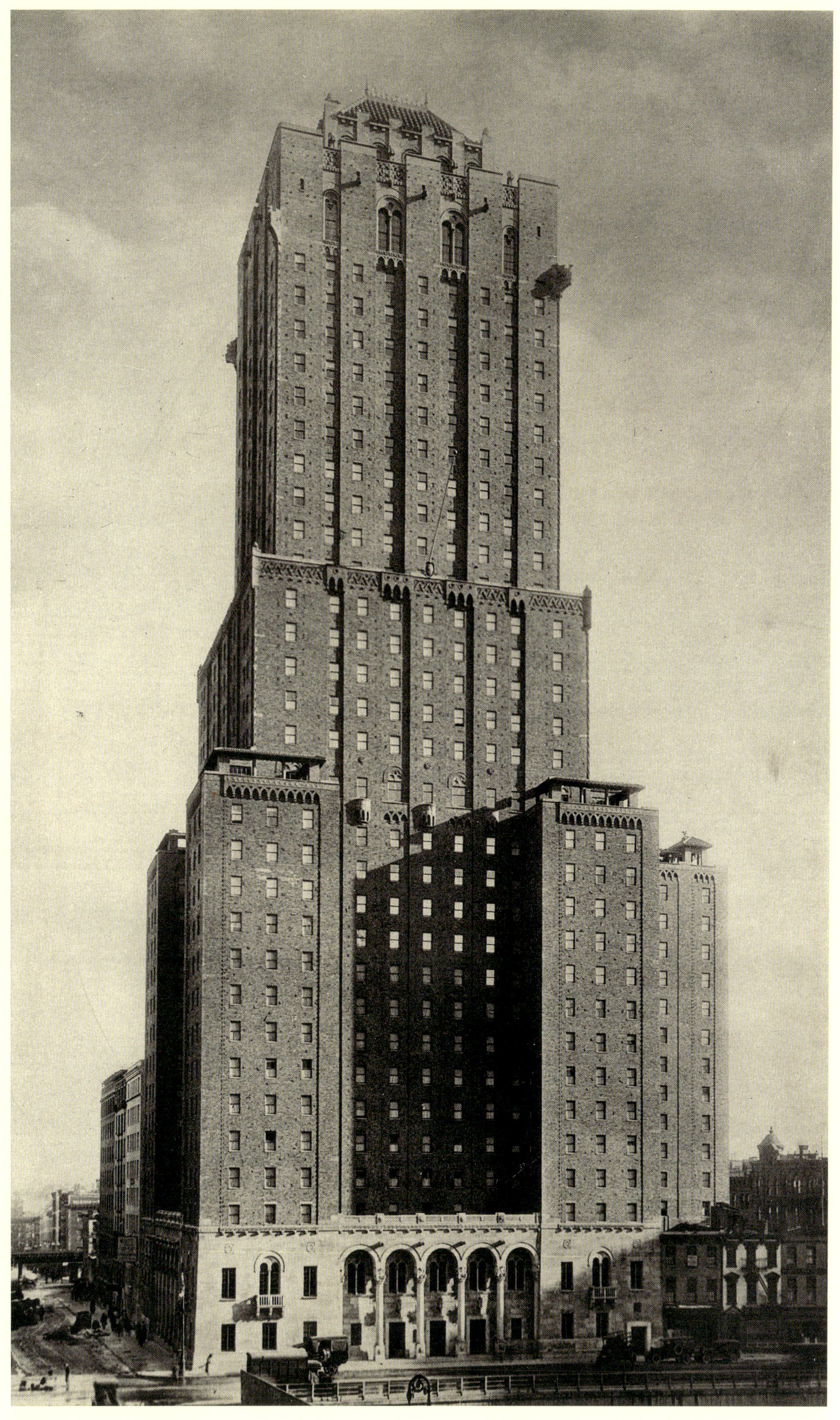

We have two rooms here — the bedroom is tiny — just room for the beds and a path to the bath room and a bureau — but it faces north — east and south so we have lots of sun and air. The sitting room is large enough for our purposes — and has a good light so I can work if I want to — faces north and south — and taking the two for a month it costs the same as the room we had last year cost by the day. — There is a cafeteria on the sixteenth floor where we can go for breakfast and supper at night — the food is excellent and cheaper than the sort of places we usually eat — So for the present we are very comfortable as far as living goes and that helps a lot — We have

can work if I want to—faces north and south" (see fig. 3).[23] The following winter season, between November 1926 and May 1927, they lived in unit 2803, on the east side of the building. O'Keeffe noted the exhilaration of the experience in a letter to another sister, Catherine: "I am living very high up in the world this year on the 28th floor—It is very grand looking out over the city."[24] Finally, in November 1927, they moved to the Shelton's highest residential floor, into unit 3003, which would become their preferred home for the next several winter seasons.[25]

The Shelton offered spaces that were light and airy, with views that were radically new to the vast majority of Americans at that early moment of residential skyscrapers. As one critic noted of O'Keeffe's unit, "It seemed all windows—windows overlooking housetops, steel framework, chimneys; windows to the east through which the panorama of the river and the bridge came flooding."[26] Indeed, the Shelton marketed itself as an excellent home for artistically inclined women and men (see fig. 4). It offered its privileged residents—who were white and sufficiently affluent to afford the space—a peaceful life above the whirlwind of Manhattan, as their advertising noted: "Here, high above the bustling city are quiet, comfortable rooms and suites, charmingly furnished, and flooded with soft north light—an ideal

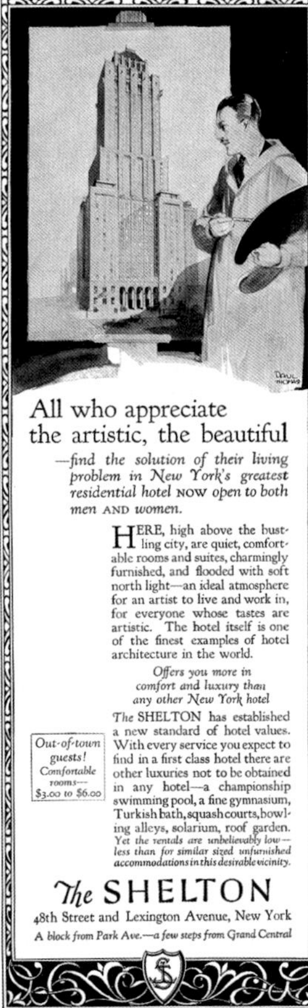

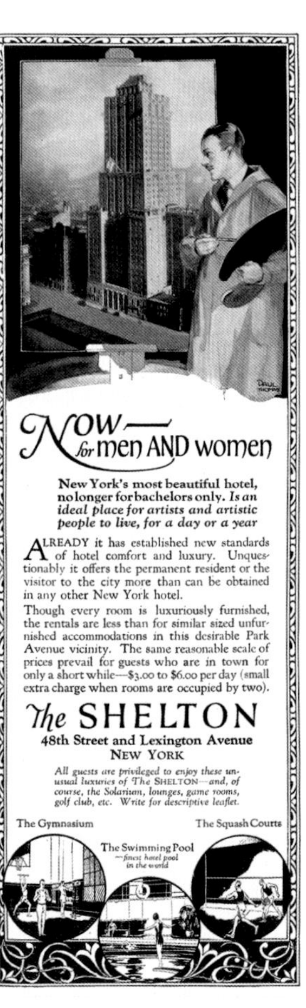

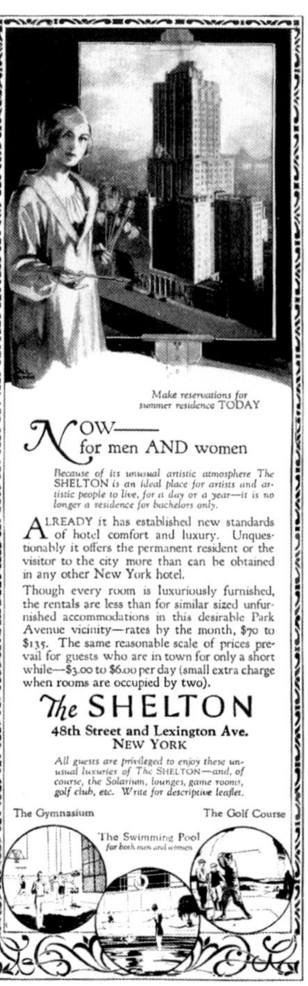

FIG. 3
Letter from Georgia O'Keeffe and Alfred Stieglitz to Ida O'Keeffe, Nov. 1925. Alfred Stieglitz / Georgia O'Keeffe Archive, Yale Collection of American Literature, Beinecke Rare Book and Manuscript Library, Yale University, New Haven, CT.

FIG. 4
Advertisements for the Shelton Hotel. Published in *International Studio* 80, nos. 332–34 (Jan. 1925, Feb. 1925, and Mar. 1925).

atmosphere for an artist to live and work in."[27] Certainly, this tranquility appealed to Stieglitz, who wrote to their friend Sherwood Anderson, "New York is madder than ever. The pace ever increasing.—But Georgia & I somehow don't seem to be of New York—nor of anywhere. We live high up in the Shelton Hotel. . . . We feel as if we were out at mid-ocean—All is so quiet except the wind."[28] O'Keeffe likewise needed the distance for her mind to process her experiences: "Yes I realize it's unusual for an artist to want to work way up near the roof of a big hotel in the heart of the roaring city but I think that's just what the artist of today needs for stimulus. He has to have a place where he can behold the city as a unit before his eyes but at the same time have enough space left to work."[29]

WALKING THE CITY: THE SKY SHAPE TAKES FORM

Although she would soon turn to painting views from her windows, O'Keeffe first painted the city in ways that reflected her practice—continued decades later in New Mexico—of walking her environment in search of inspiration. Indeed, her ambulatory experiences around midtown Manhattan (see fig. 5) shaped her first major paintings, all of which feature street-level views looking up at soaring buildings. O'Keeffe based the works on specific buildings but rarely transcribed them directly; these were not intended as faithful representations but as artistic translations of the experience of seeing them. *New York Street with Moon* (pl. 1), for example, depicts the streets around the Hotel Chatham, a thirteen-story edifice that opened in 1918 and was located on Vanderbilt Avenue between Forty-Eighth and Forty-Ninth Streets.[30] Comparing the painting with a photograph of the building (see fig. 6) demonstrates just a few of her artistic choices and her modernist emphasis on the cityscape as a site for two-dimensional experimentation. O'Keeffe depicted the relatively short building at a sharp upward angle, slimming down its blocky mass and rendering it as a single abstract form. She eliminated its ornamentation but emphasized the flaring cornice at the top. And to further foreground the experience of being an urban explorer in a shifting world of forms, she deliberately framed the hotel with geometric slivers of other buildings at the top and sides of the composition. They crowd the Hotel Chatham, enclosing and constraining it to represent the constant visual boundaries of street-level Manhattan.

Indeed, O'Keeffe described the inspiration for the canvas in her perception of essential contours: "I saw a sky shape near the Chatham Hotel where buildings were going up. It was the buildings that made this fine shape, so I sketched it and then painted it."[31] O'Keeffe's dual emphasis here is key: although the "sky shape" captured her interest as a subject, she recognized that the built environment—these architectural monoliths that loomed, constrained, and inspired her vision—was entirely necessary to afford such curious angles and viewpoints. As a city undergoing tremendous change, street-level Manhattan in the mid-1920s was not uniformly developed; there were numerous height differences and gaps between buildings, and O'Keeffe seems to have gravitated toward subjects that resulted from these absences. Walking the city offered her a constantly changing panorama of abstracted form—sky shapes and skyscrapers that shifted block by block as she moved through Midtown. In two geometric cityscapes of 1926, *City Night* (pl. 21) and *A Street* (pl. 15), her brush captured the feeling of being dwarfed by forms that cannot be easily comprehended due to spatial constraints on seeing. Monumental buildings crowd the canvas, leaving only the thinnest slice of sky, touched by the moon or clouds, to orient the viewer. And in at least one painting, *New*

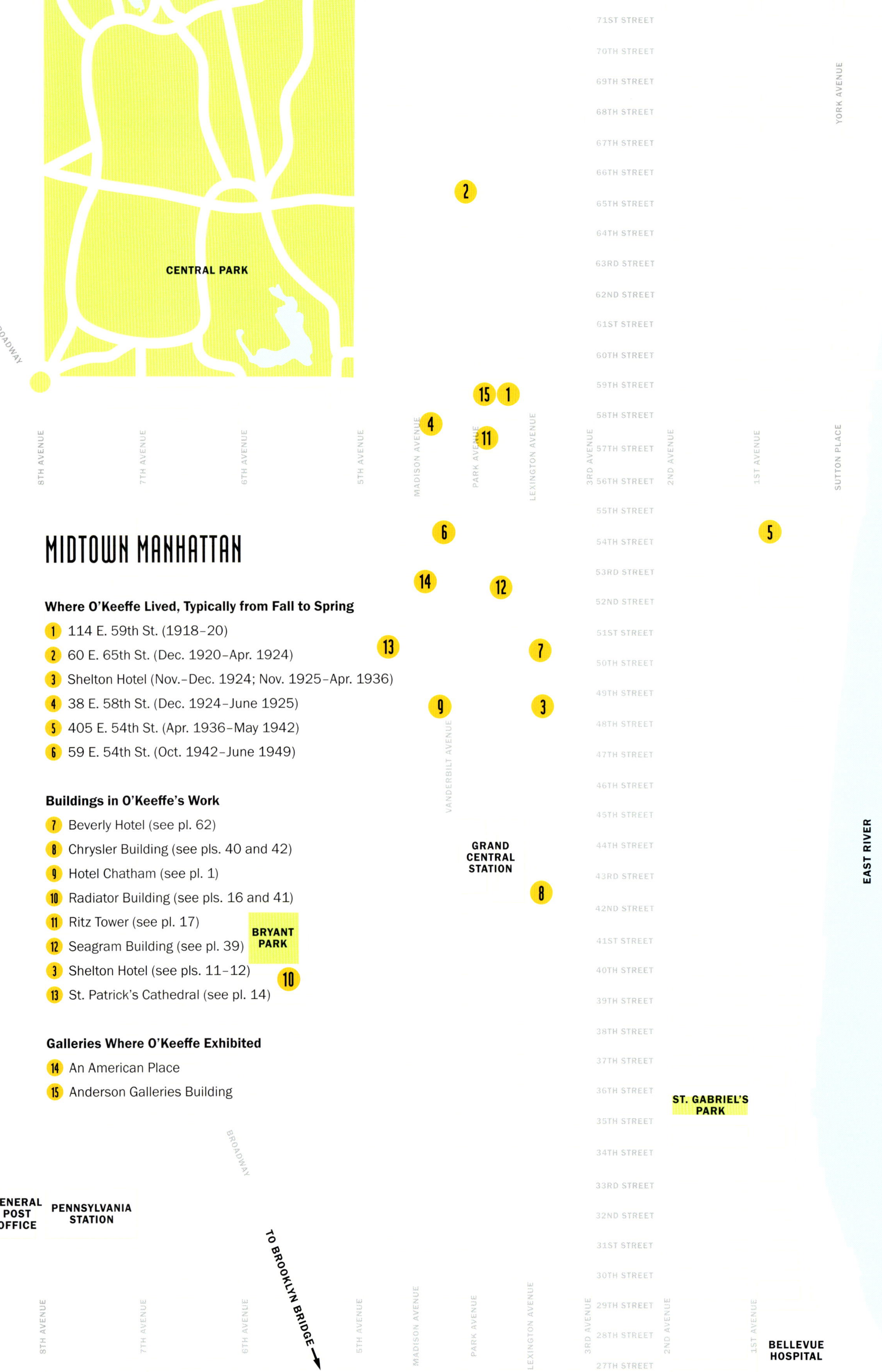
MIDTOWN MANHATTAN
Where O'Keeffe Lived, Typically from Fall to Spring
1 114 E. 59th St. (1918–20)
2 60 E. 65th St. (Dec. 1920–Apr. 1924)
3 Shelton Hotel (Nov.–Dec. 1924; Nov. 1925–Apr. 1936)
4 38 E. 58th St. (Dec. 1924–June 1925)
5 405 E. 54th St. (Apr. 1936–May 1942)
6 59 E. 54th St. (Oct. 1942–June 1949)
Buildings in O'Keeffe's Work
7 Beverly Hotel (see pl. 62)
8 Chrysler Building (see pls. 40 and 42)
9 Hotel Chatham (see pl. 1)
10 Radiator Building (see pls. 16 and 41)
11 Ritz Tower (see pl. 17)
12 Seagram Building (see pl. 39)
3 Shelton Hotel (see pls. 11–12)
13 St. Patrick's Cathedral (see pl. 14)
Galleries Where O'Keeffe Exhibited
14 An American Place
15 Anderson Galleries Building
CENTRAL PARK
BROADWAY
GRAND CENTRAL STATION
BRYANT PARK
ST. GABRIEL'S PARK
EAST RIVER
GENERAL POST OFFICE
PENNSYLVANIA STATION
TO BROOKLYN BRIDGE
BELLEVUE HOSPITAL
8TH AVENUE
7TH AVENUE
6TH AVENUE
5TH AVENUE
MADISON AVENUE
PARK AVENUE
LEXINGTON AVENUE
3RD AVENUE
2ND AVENUE
1ST AVENUE
SUTTON PLACE
YORK AVENUE
VANDERBILT AVENUE
71ST STREET
70TH STREET
69TH STREET
68TH STREET
67TH STREET
66TH STREET
65TH STREET
64TH STREET
63RD STREET
62ND STREET
61ST STREET
60TH STREET
59TH STREET
58TH STREET
57TH STREET
56TH STREET
55TH STREET
54TH STREET
53RD STREET
52ND STREET
51ST STREET
50TH STREET
49TH STREET
48TH STREET
47TH STREET
46TH STREET
45TH STREET
44TH STREET
43RD STREET
42ND STREET
41ST STREET
40TH STREET
39TH STREET
38TH STREET
37TH STREET
36TH STREET
35TH STREET
34TH STREET
33RD STREET
32ND STREET
31ST STREET
30TH STREET
29TH STREET
28TH STREET
27TH STREET

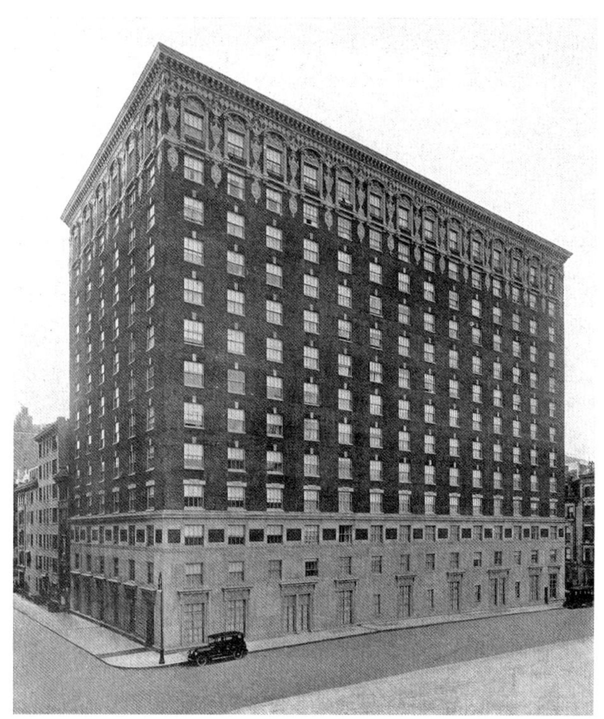

York – Night (Madison Avenue) (pl. 26), she rendered the experience in completely non-objective terms, reveling in seeing the city's intersecting lines as pure form.

It is all the more telling, then, that O'Keeffe balanced these visual constraints in *New York Street with Moon* and other street-level compositions with soaring elements of sky and light, aligning these works with her other depictions of the natural world. The moon shines forth among wispy clouds, their wavy rhythms contrasting with the hard, straight lines of the building's corner. The natural elements are echoed by the haloed streetlight that swoops and curls at street level, its radiance disrupting perception of the building behind, not unlike the sun glare in *The Shelton with Sunspots, N.Y.*[32] This deliberate imposition and interruption was noted by critics when at last O'Keeffe exhibited *New York Street with Moon* at Stieglitz's Intimate Gallery in her annual exhibition in February 1926: "a roof projected into the sky (framed by other roofs and made immaterial by the very heart of the light of changing traffic signals)."[33] The painting gives concrete form to O'Keeffe's perceptual abilities, evoking the ephemeral quality of nature's effects against the permanence of concrete and steel.

O'Keeffe's series of Shelton paintings likewise originated with a fleeting glimpse through a gap in the streetscape: "There was a large opening between 46th and 47th streets and across this, as I walked down Park Avenue, I saw the Shelton being built on Lexington Avenue."[34] This glimpse presumably would have occurred prior to her arrival in November 1924, but her repeated walks in, out, and around the Shelton as a resident soon thereafter resulted in her painting it as a series: she produced at least four Shelton canvases, and very likely more, between late 1925 and 1927.[35] This repeated exposure to the skyscraper from the street led her to experiment with presenting the building at different times of day and with varying perceptual effects of natural phenomena.

O'Keeffe employed the Shelton's soaring form as a vehicle for experimenting with geometries of varying proportions and the impact of natural effects upon those visualizations. In *Shelton Hotel, N.Y., No. I* (pl. 11), she presented the building largely unadorned and awash in an even light, emphasizing the rectilinear grid of windows that marks the rising floors. But although the painting presents almost as a portrait, O'Keeffe did not portray the skyscraper's architecture faithfully. She indicated the two setbacks, at the sixteenth and twenty-first stories, which distinguish the Shelton—the result of New York's adoption of the 1916 Zoning Resolution that dictated setbacks in relation to building height—and also delineated the wing that juts out to the south, but she modified the street-level entrance bays, reducing them from five to three, and she eliminated approximately five floors from the two upper levels, truncating the building.[36] The latter decision in particular accentuates its solid, massive form in notable contrast to her next two Shelton paintings, all three of which she framed with peeks of other buildings on either side, suggesting the ongoing importance of this compositional element. In *The Shelton with Sunspots, N.Y.*, O'Keeffe only barely hinted at the setbacks and overlaid the southern wing with an obscuring haze of mist, portraying the central tower as slender

FIG. 5
Map of midtown Manhattan plotting the locations where O'Keeffe lived and exhibited work as well as the buildings she depicted in her work.

FIG. 6
Hotel Chatham, Vanderbilt Ave., Forty-Eighth to Forty-Ninth Streets, New York, 1917. Halftone photomechanical print; 28 × 20 cm (11 × 7¾ in.). The Miriam and Ira D. Wallach Division of Art, Prints and Photographs, New York Public Library.

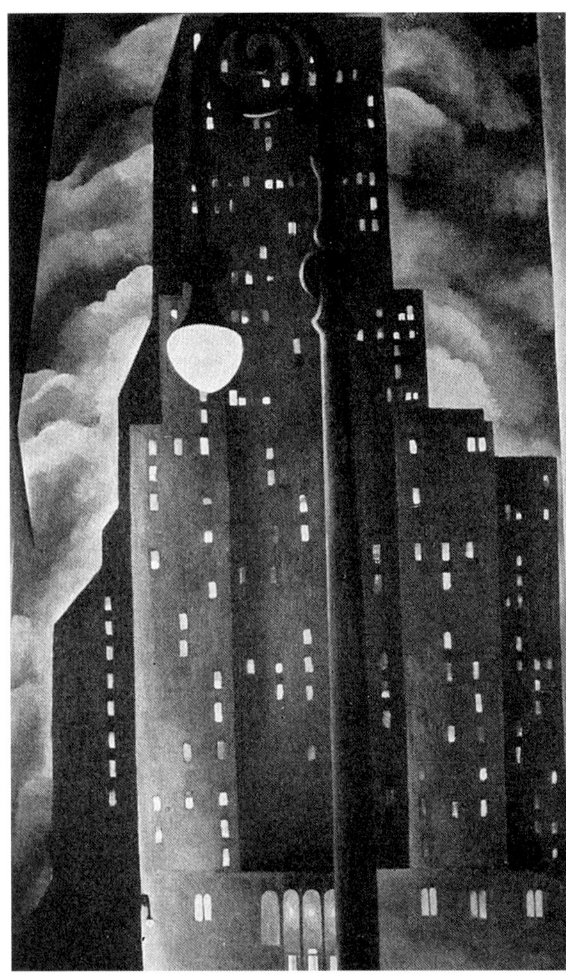

and soaring. In *The Shelton at Night* (fig. 7) O'Keeffe cropped the top of the skyscraper, further accentuating its height. In the foreground she depicted an arching streetlight, superimposing it against the more distant tower of the skyscraper. Although O'Keeffe clearly disliked this painting in the long run (she destroyed it despite probably exhibiting it at least twice), the composition creates a play of near and far that speaks to her fascination with scale and connects the piece with her other works of the period.[37]

Critical response to the Shelton paintings, although positive, ranged widely in tone. Some, such as the critic Louis Kalonyme, went to great rhetorical lengths to frame them—and her other works from this period—as feminine, even motherly: "[In her] glittering golden and night-blue skyscrapers (the Shelton from unbelievably beautiful angles), drawn inexorably upward by brassy suns and white, hard, hypnotic moons, O'Keeffe plays a grand, maternal music, which reveals the shape of the world as a woman sees it and feels affirmatively toward it."[38] Others noted the tension between the architectural and the organic; for example, Henry McBride wrote that "she likes to shave off her gradations until the tall buildings in her pictures, such as the Shelton Hotel, appear to endanger the moon."[39] But for McBride, the paintings provided an important counterpoint in her oeuvre—he differentiated them as "intellectual rather than emotional"—and balanced the myriad of floral and other subjects that typified her work at the time.[40] (This pleased O'Keeffe, who thanked McBride for turning off "the emotional faucet."[41]) Despite these varying critical agendas, however, the circulation of O'Keeffe's paintings as reproductions in mass media introduced other purposes and enabled them to convey very different messages. *The Shelton with Sunspots, N.Y.*, for example, appeared as the frontispiece for an article on unemployment by Leo Wolman entitled "Shadows of Prosperity" in *The Survey (Graphic Number)* (fig. 8), tying O'Keeffe's vision of New York to crucial social questions about the built environment and the economy.

In addition to the Shelton, O'Keeffe painted two other specific buildings from street level: the Ritz Tower and the American Radiator Company Building. Both were located within easy walking distance of the Shelton at Lexington and Forty-Eighth Street, and O'Keeffe likely witnessed their construction as well. Erected between 1925 and 1926, the Ritz Tower sits at the northeast corner of Park Avenue and Fifty-Seventh Street (465 Park Avenue), and it supplanted the Shelton briefly as the tallest apartment hotel in the world. Like O'Keeffe's home, the Ritz Tower was then surrounded by shorter buildings and thus dominated the skyline, as one architectural critic noted: "The effect of the whole design from Park Avenue is perfect, since it is the only tower yet built in that street."[42] This was undoubtedly the draw for O'Keeffe, who would have walked by it constantly on her way to and from the Intimate Gallery, located just two blocks north in the Anderson Galleries Building at 489 Park Avenue. In *Ritz Tower* (pl. 17), she selected a vantage point on the west side of Park Avenue—an especially wide thoroughfare in Manhattan—that allowed her an unobstructed view of the entire edifice. Unlike the

FIG. 7
Georgia O'Keeffe (American, 1887–1986). *The Shelton at Night*, by 1927. Oil on canvas; 121.9 × 76.2 cm (48 × 30 in.). Destroyed by O'Keeffe. Reproduced in Louis Kalonyme, "Scaling the Peak of the Art Season," *Arts and Decoration* 26 (Mar. 1927): 57.

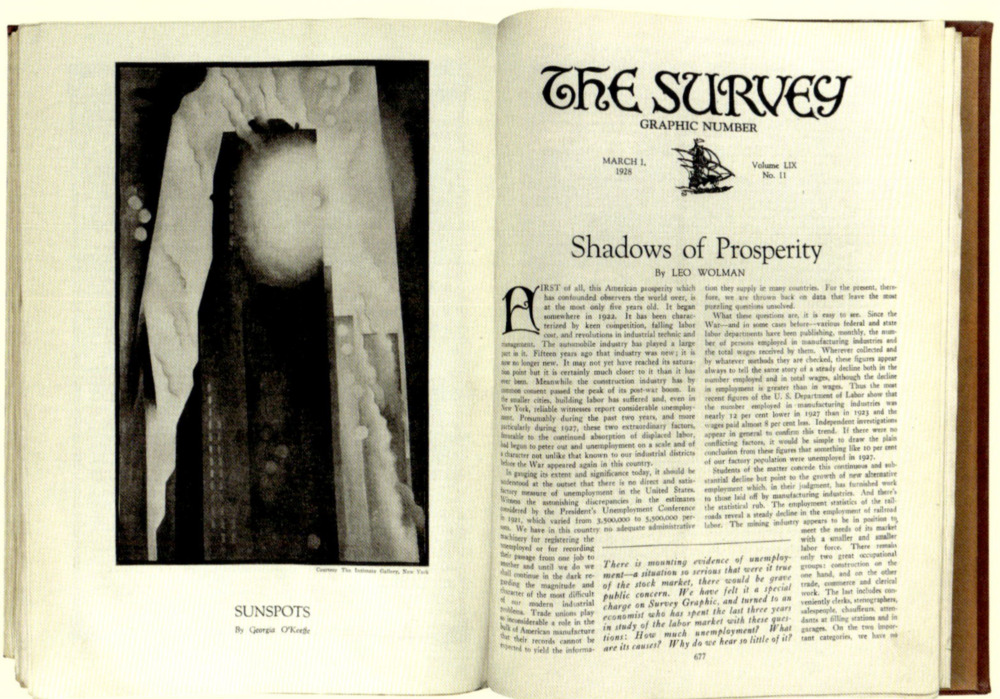

SUNSPOTS
By Georgia O'Keeffe

THE SURVEY
GRAPHIC NUMBER

MARCH 1, 1928 — Volume LIX, No. 11

Shadows of Prosperity

By LEO WOLMAN

FIRST of all, this American prosperity which has confounded observers the world over, is at the most only five years old. It began somewhere in 1922. It has been characterized by keen competition, falling labor cost, and revolutions in industrial technic and management. The automobile industry has played a large part in it. Fifteen years ago that industry was new; it is now no longer new. It may not yet have reached its saturation point but it is certainly much closer to it than it has ever been. Meanwhile the construction industry has by common consent passed the peak of its post-war boom. In the smaller cities, building labor has suffered and, even in New York, reliable witnesses report considerable unemployment. Presumably during the past two years, and more particularly during 1927, these two extraordinary factors, favorable to the continued absorption of displaced labor, had begun to peter out and unemployment on a scale and of a character not unlike that known to our industrial districts before the War appeared again in this country.

In gauging its extent and significance today, it should be understood at the outset that there is no direct and satisfactory measure of unemployment in the United States. Witness the astonishing discrepancies in the estimates considered by the President's Unemployment Conference in 1921, which varied from 3,500,000 to 5,500,000 persons. We have in this country no adequate administrative machinery for registering the unemployed or for recording their passage from one job to another and until we do we shall continue in the dark regarding the magnitude and character of the most difficult of our modern industrial problems. Trade unions play so inconsiderable a role in the bulk of American manufacture that their records cannot be expected to yield the information they supply in many countries. For the present, therefore, we are thrown back on data that leave the most puzzling questions unsolved.

What these questions are, it is easy to see. Since the War—and in some cases before—various federal and state labor departments have been publishing, monthly, the number of persons employed in manufacturing industries and the total wages received by them. Wherever collected and by whatever methods they are checked, these figures appear always to tell the same story of a steady decline both in the number employed and in total wages, although the decline in employment is greater than in wages. Thus the most recent figures of the U. S. Department of Labor show that the number employed in manufacturing industries was nearly 12 per cent lower in 1927 than in 1923 and the wages paid almost 8 per cent less. Independent investigations appear in general to confirm this trend. If there were no conflicting factors, it would be simple to draw the plain conclusion from these figures that something like 10 per cent of our factory population were unemployed in 1927.

Students of the matter concede this continuous and substantial decline but point to the growth of new alternative employment which, in their judgment, has furnished work to those laid off by manufacturing industries. And there's the statistical rub. The employment statistics of the railroads reveal a steady decline in the employment of railroad labor. The mining industry appears to be in position to meet the needs of its market with a smaller and smaller labor force. There remain only two great occupational groups: construction on the one hand, and on the other trade, commerce and clerical work. The last includes conveniently clerks, stenographers, salespeople, chauffeurs, attendants at filling stations and in garages. On the two important categories, we have no

There is mounting evidence of unemployment—a situation so serious that were it true of the stock market, there would be grave public concern. We have felt it a special charge on Survey Graphic, and turned to an economist who has spent the last three years in study of the labor market with these questions: How much unemployment? What are its causes? Why do we hear so little of it?

677

Shelton series, she painted the Ritz Tower in isolation: she did not repeat her compositional strategy of enclosing it within looming buildings at the side. Instead she depicted it against a sweeping array of clouds and the emerging moon, which add dynamism to the nighttime scene. O'Keeffe once again created a dialogue between nature and the manmade, with her artistic mind acting as the mediator.

In *Radiator Building—Night, New York* (pl. 16) O'Keeffe created a dramatic play of artificial light and abstracted form that speaks to the extraordinary experience of seeing this 1924 skyscraper, designed by architect Raymond Hood. Given the artist's preference for seeking out unexpected vistas amid the city's canyons, it is telling that the Radiator Building, of the three specific buildings she painted from street level, is the only one located in the middle of a block: sited at 40 West Fortieth Street between Fifth and Sixth Avenues, it fronts Bryant Park (see fig. 9). This position offered O'Keeffe a view of the Radiator Building from directly across the park, unencumbered by other visual constraints. Her compositional choices thus differed significantly from her other street-level views, for here she could portray the building frontally, centered in the canvas, and in a horizontal relationship to the surrounding, notably shorter, buildings. Indeed, this unfettered access was crucial for Hood's design, who declared that "unlike most skyscrapers that can only be viewed by a sharp craning of the neck . . . there is a long uninterrupted view of the building that gives the most satisfactory opportunity to observe the effect of color and the proportions of its silhouette."[43]

Late in life, O'Keeffe recalled, "I walked across 42nd Street many times at night when the black Radiator Building was new—so that had to be painted, too."[44] This recollection—so casual and off the cuff—downplays O'Keeffe's agency in selecting as her subject one of the most radical and controversial buildings of the mid-1920s. The Radiator Building became the talk of the town thanks to its distinctive architectural features: its black cladding and shimmering gold ornament, especially visible at the crown. To enhance its prominence, Hood orchestrated a brilliant lighting campaign designed to draw attention to the structure and serve as large-scale advertising for its owners, the American Radiator Company (see fig. 10). "The effect," the lighting designer Bassett Jones gushed, "is almost that of pouring over the structure a great volume of spectral-hued incandescent material which streams down the perpendicular surfaces, cooling as

FIG. 8
O'Keeffe. *The Shelton with Sunspots, N.Y.*, 1926 (pl. 12). Reproduced to accompany Leo Wolman, "Shadows of Prosperity," *The Survey (Graphic Number)*, Mar. 1, 1928, 676–77.

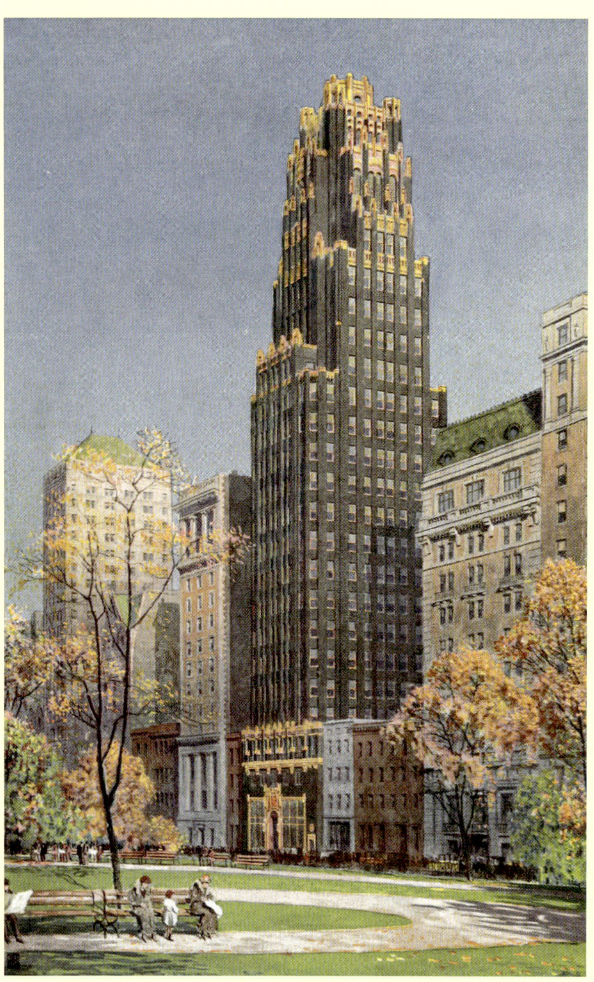

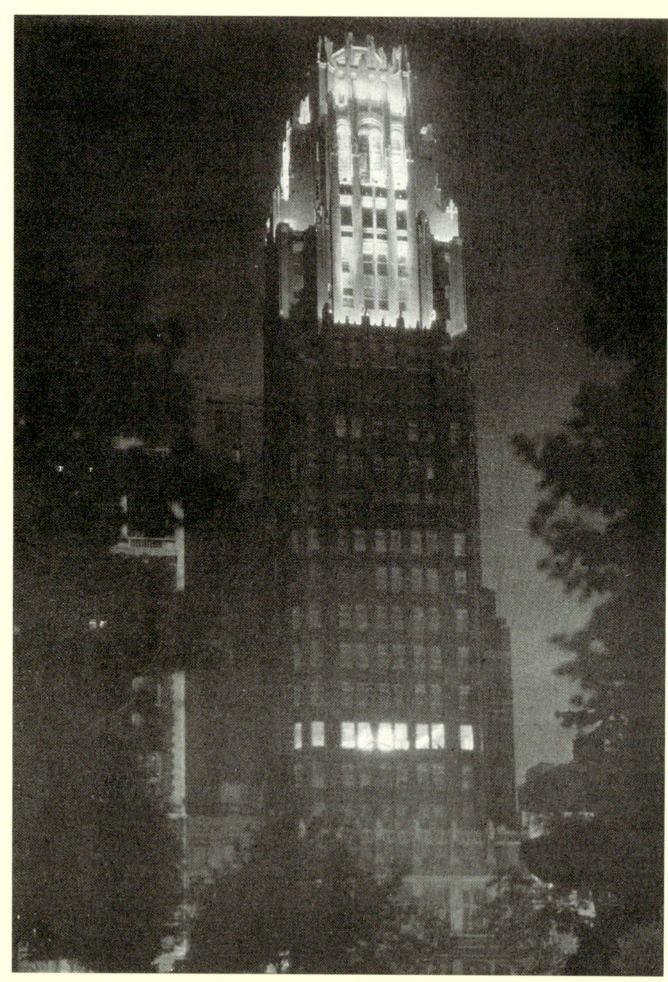

FIG. 9
American Radiator Company Building, New York. Lithograph by Birch Burdette Long. Reproduced in *Architectural Record* 55, no. 5 (May 1924): frontispiece.

FIG. 10
American Radiator Company Building, New York. Reproduced in Bassett Jones, "Illuminating the Exterior of Buildings," *Architectural Forum* 42, no. 2 (Feb. 1925): 94.

it falls and collecting like molten lava."[45] The ploy was successful: "The vast throngs that crowd this district at night are blocking traffic as they stand to contemplate the lacy effect as shown in the brilliantly lighted gilded top."[46]

It is tempting to think of O'Keeffe, the inveterate walker, being in these crowds. She was clearly drawn to the spectacle of light sweeping the black surface, and she amplified its presence in the work, casting the lit crown in a cool white glow that reads as an immaterial rendition of ghostly parapets. Window illumination and street lights dot the surface, suggesting an abstract tapestry of glowing forms. Searchlights stream from behind in broad swathes of deep blue and green, formally connecting her New York paintings to her works of pure abstraction across the decade, from the early *Blue and Green Music* (fig. 11) to *Black and White* (pl. 22) and *Black White and Blue* (pl. 20). Finally, O'Keeffe included blazing red letters of a neon sign spelling the name of her husband Alfred Stieglitz. Four buildings further west, at 24 West Fortieth Street, the Scientific American Building advertised its name in glowing lights. O'Keeffe deliberately compressed space, eliminating at least two buildings between the Radiator Building and the Scientific American Building, to insert Stieglitz into her composition.[47]

Imagining O'Keeffe among the throngs in front of the Radiator Building invites consideration of the vast and racially diverse city in which she lived, one that she otherwise escaped by residing high up in the Shelton. Indeed, by painting the Radiator Building, O'Keeffe—perhaps inadvertently—also engaged with the complex racial politics of the era. The black cladding, or skin, was not only noted for its dramatic nature but was clearly framed by architectural critics of the era in racial terms. Making reference to the color line, a phrase for race differentiation and segregation popularized by W. E. B. Du Bois, Orrick Johns wrote for the *New York Times*, "Raymond M. Hood of

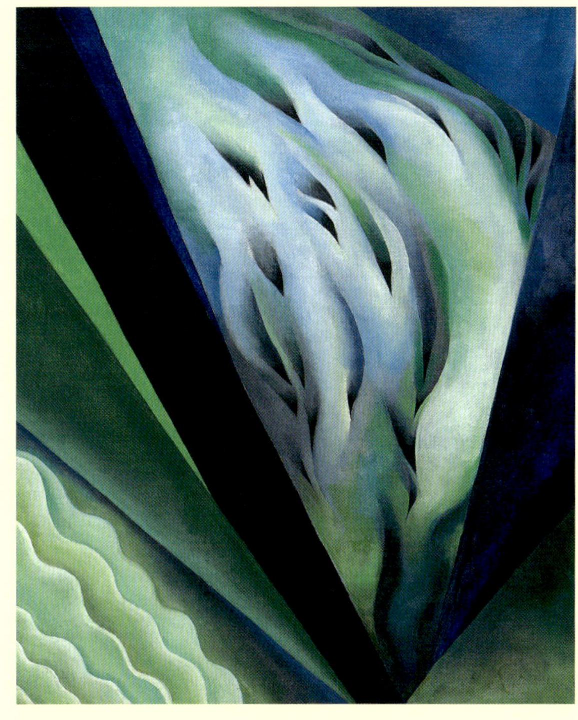

Howells & Hood, architects of the American Radiator building on Fortieth Street, has broken through the color line."[48] Lest his meaning be unclear, Johns continued, "His black and gold peak has no dainty flapper insouciance, however. Here is a barbaric note. You think of tom-toms and gleaming spearpoints. Someone has called it Jack Johnson's golden smile. It certainly is something new and tremendous, but, like jazz and the Ku Klux, hard to place." His racially loaded language stands in direct contrast to his glowingly gendered and notably deracialized characterization of O'Keeffe's home in the same article: "that suave, athletic, well-groomed young fellow, the Shelton Hotel. His type is the essence of masculinity and good form."

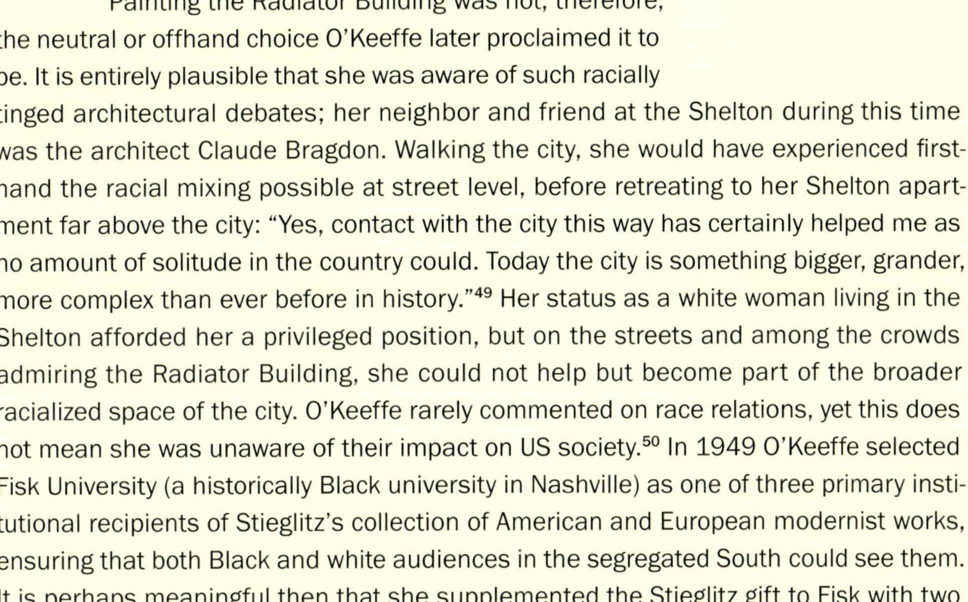

Painting the Radiator Building was not, therefore, the neutral or offhand choice O'Keeffe later proclaimed it to be. It is entirely plausible that she was aware of such racially tinged architectural debates; her neighbor and friend at the Shelton during this time was the architect Claude Bragdon. Walking the city, she would have experienced first-hand the racial mixing possible at street level, before retreating to her Shelton apartment far above the city: "Yes, contact with the city this way has certainly helped me as no amount of solitude in the country could. Today the city is something bigger, grander, more complex than ever before in history."[49] Her status as a white woman living in the Shelton afforded her a privileged position, but on the streets and among the crowds admiring the Radiator Building, she could not help but become part of the broader racialized space of the city. O'Keeffe rarely commented on race relations, yet this does not mean she was unaware of their impact on US society.[50] In 1949 O'Keeffe selected Fisk University (a historically Black university in Nashville) as one of three primary institutional recipients of Stieglitz's collection of American and European modernist works, ensuring that both Black and white audiences in the segregated South could see them. It is perhaps meaningful then that she supplemented the Stieglitz gift to Fisk with two paintings of her own, one of which was *Radiator Building—Night, New York*.[51]

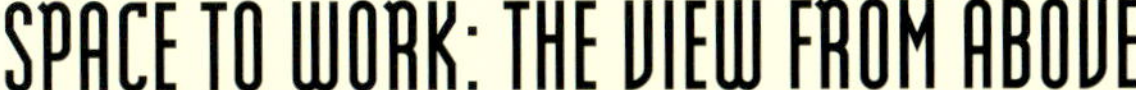

SPACE TO WORK: THE VIEW FROM ABOVE

If O'Keeffe's experiences walking the neighborhood around the Shelton inspired her upward artistic responses (both serial and individual) to the monumental nature of the new skyscrapers, her life in the Shelton was equally stimulating. Her panoramic vista looking east across Manhattan rooftops toward the East River and the distant borough of Queens resulted in a tremendous group of six paintings and three pastels, as well as related drawings in charcoal and graphite, that reveal her interest in capturing the fleeting experiences of seeing a fixed view on a daily basis.[52] It was precisely this fixity that led O'Keeffe to a tremendous range of experimentation using a limited number of compositional elements: an elevated view and a panorama of buildings, seen through a range of seasonal and atmospheric changes. She further varied scale and medium, choosing between large and small, pastel and oil, paper and canvas, to work through her impressions. The breadth of O'Keeffe's engagement with the view from above reaffirms its generative intensity.

FIG. 11
O'Keeffe. *Blue and Green Music*, 1919–21. Oil on canvas; 58.4 × 48.3 cm (23 × 19 in.). The Art Institute of Chicago, Alfred Stieglitz Collection, gift of Georgia O'Keeffe, 1969.835.

The East River series and related elevated views give some indication of her practice as an artist. In preparation, O'Keeffe sought to record her experiences of seeing the city. Small sketches, some still bound in notebooks and others ripped from sketchbooks, give evidence of her habit of making quick visual notes as aide-memoires (see pls. 41–50). Not intended for exhibition, the works delineate the crowns of buildings, the spiky forms of construction cranes, and boats on the East River. On some she jotted notes: "light," "dark," "white." The diversity of views indicates that she did not create them all from her apartment; instead, one can envision her walking the Shelton's public spaces—for example, the sixteenth-floor terrace (see p. 39, fig. 4)—notepad in hand.

O'Keeffe then translated some views into compositions that echo the canyon-like experience of the streets far below—the dark crevices formed by tall buildings. Some are highly abstract compositions in charcoal (see pl. 13), while others retain a specificity that places her in relationship to a known panorama. *Untitled (New York)* (pl. 14), a view looking west from the Shelton toward the spires of St. Patrick's Cathedral, positions her above Lexington Avenue. She later said of this drawing, "This is what I saw out a window where I lived for a short time."[53] Here O'Keeffe abstracted the masses of buildings, using the silky charcoal medium to render them as geometric, planar forms. Despite this overall lack of detail, however, O'Keeffe carefully differentiated buildings through the adroit layering of darker and lighter black tones, creating a recession into space. This is further enhanced by the diagonal thrust of a street, either Forty-Ninth or Fiftieth Street, which cleaves the buildings and harmonizes with the spires of the church. And on one occasion, in *New York, Night* (pl. 62), she painted a panoramic nighttime view looking north from the very top of the Shelton toward the Beverly Hotel, identified by its distinctive rose window, located one block away at Lexington and Fiftieth.[54] The vista down into a dark crevice of a street once again drew her attention, as she recalled, "There was a painting of Lexington Avenue as I saw it out the window at night. Lexington Avenue looked, in the night, like a very tall thin bottle with colored things going up and down inside it."[55]

Before committing oil to canvas, or pastel to paper, O'Keeffe made initial decisions revolving around format and medium.[56] The East River series includes four 12-by-32-inch canvases—a proportion that she frequently used in vertical orientation for still lifes and other subjects—and two pastels were similarly sized at 11 by 28 inches, demonstrating how this low-slung proportion appealed to O'Keeffe in her quest to depict a panoramic view.[57] She also expanded the scale of works in both media, selecting significantly larger supports for the pastel *Pink Dish and Green Leaves* (pl. 59) and *East River from the 30th Story of the Shelton Hotel* (pl. 57), a 30-by-48-inch canvas that was the largest format she had used by that time. Finally, O'Keeffe turned one 26-by-22-inch canvas vertically to create *East River from the Shelton (East River No. 1)* (pl. 60).

These choices facilitated a surprising range of aesthetics that defy any easy labeling of O'Keeffe's style and demonstrate her experimental prowess. With the East River always as her distant anchor, she varied her perspective and horizon line, showcasing more or less of the foreground buildings some thirty stories below. As with her upward views of the Shelton, nature is always present, inserting itself into the built fabric of Manhattan. She based these works on visual observation, adjusting elements as the seasons changed. In one, she depicted a cold winter morning, snow covering a wide expanse of rooftops to create an abstract checkerboard of rectilinear shapes (see pl. 55), while in another, pink and green tones signal the coming of spring (see pl. 57).

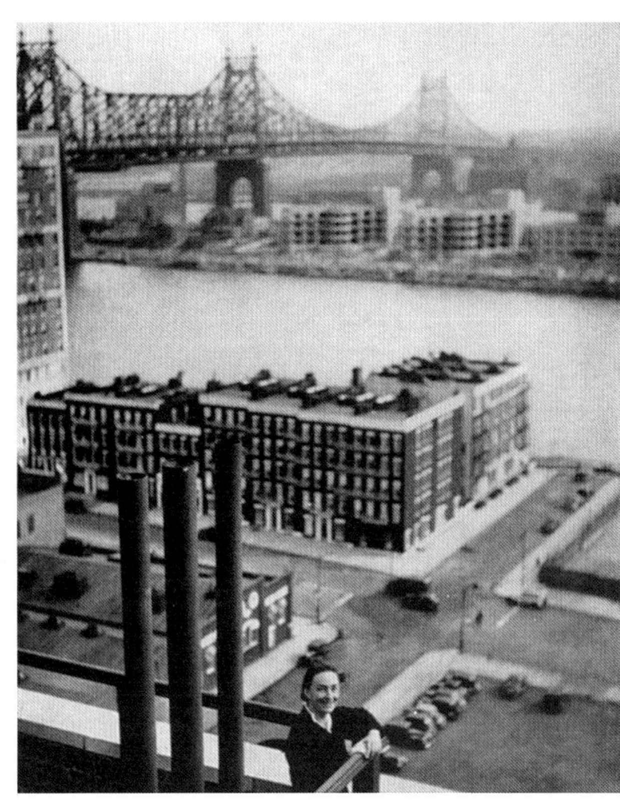

O'Keeffe explored more atmospheric effects in several other works (see pls. 52–54), suffusing the compositions with misty effects that recall the works of James McNeill Whistler, an early influence thanks to the teachings of Arthur Wesley Dow and Alon Bement. *Pink Dish and Green Leaves* is a hybrid—part landscape, part still life—that situates a delicate compote containing natural forms on the windowsill of her Shelton apartment, evoking the raison d'etre of the entire series: her life in a skyscraper.

But it is the vertically oriented *East River from the Shelton (East River No. 1)* that offers the greatest compositional and stylistic surprises, as O'Keeffe tilted her perspective radically upward, minimizing the shadowy buildings below. Instead the sun holds center stage, as rays of light emanate from the haloed orb. It bathes the river in rich red tones, capturing an abstract play of shapes and pigments that evokes her work across all subjects, from flowers to pure abstractions. *East River from the Shelton (East River No. 1)*, and indeed all of the East River works, reinforces O'Keeffe's recognition that all of her paintings were first and foremost exercises in color and form on a two-dimensional surface. A few years prior to starting the series, O'Keeffe voiced her thoughts on the complex relationship between observation and artistic representation: "Nothing is less real than realism. . . . It is only by selection, by elimination, by emphasis, that we get at the real meaning of things."[58] The East River—the view she saw every day from her elevated Shelton windows, in rain, snow, sun, and shadow—became the perfect vehicle for translating her experiences and emotions into painted form, revealing the myriad of decisions that underpinned all of her work, giving expression to her new life on the thirtieth floor.

NEW YORK TO NEW MEXICO

In 1929 O'Keeffe spent the summer in New Mexico and returned with a new direction for her art. The great intensity of her engagement with New York City's buildings and views abated. But she did not leave New York behind entirely; she continued to live there with Stieglitz in the winter season for years to come, bringing—literally—parts of the Southwest to the city, as evidenced by the cow's skull she mounted and photographed on the roof of the Arno Building at 405 East Fifty-Fourth Street, where she moved in 1936 (see fig. 12 and pls. 89 and 91–93). Moreover, she brought her knowledge of the city with her as she herself traveled between the Northeast and the Southwest. In numerous paintings, among them *Dead Tree Bear Lake Taos* (pl. 64) and *After a Walk Back of Mabel's* (pl. 63), both created in 1929, O'Keeffe echoed the monumental forms of skyscrapers in the natural forms of the Southwestern landscape, as towering trees and massive boulders replaced tall buildings. Instead of selecting views across city roofs, she explored the low adobe architecture of Taos Pueblo (see pls. 66 and 68–69), finding abstract form in a different style of construction. She then exhibited New York and New Mexico paintings together (see fig. 13), manifestly demonstrating their shared resonances.

FIG. 12
O'Keeffe in New York. Reproduced in "Alfred Stieglitz Made Georgia O'Keeffe Famous," *Life*, Feb. 14, 1938, 31.

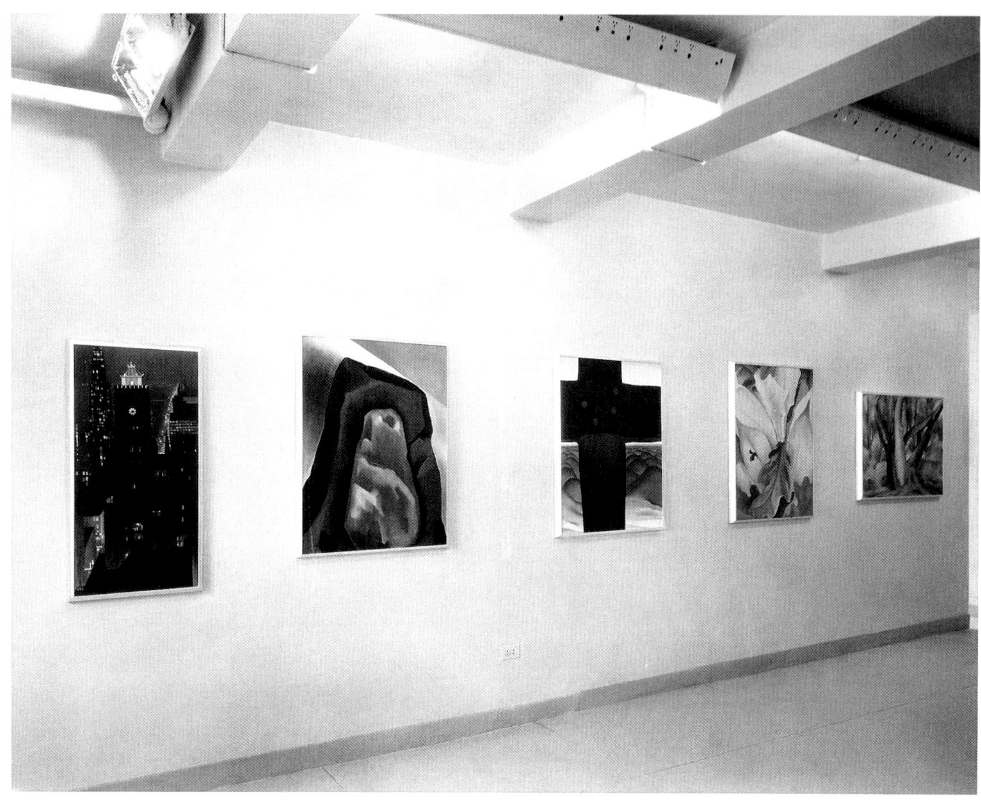

O'Keeffe made occasional forays back into urban subject matter. In 1932 she painted, at a grand scale, the dynamic *Manhattan* (pl. 19), commissioned for a mural exhibition at the Museum of Modern Art, New York.[59] Overtly cubistic in its overlapping forms and jagged lines, *Manhattan* differs notably from her earlier paintings of the city. It unites the two sides of her yearly existence with the inclusion of synthetic flowers, akin to the rose seen in *Cow's Skull with Calico Roses* (pl. 67). With Stieglitz's death in 1946, however, O'Keeffe lost her primary tether to Manhattan. Perhaps in farewell, she focused her sights on the Brooklyn Bridge, as iconic a symbol of the city as the skyscraper. She created several drawings, from fast sketches (see pl. 36) to a large-scale, dynamic rendering that vibrates with energy (see pl. 37). These preliminary works helped O'Keeffe paint her final major New York painting, *Brooklyn Bridge* (pl. 38), in 1949, the year that she finished settling Stieglitz's estate and moved out of New York entirely.

But for five intense years beginning in 1925, New York City was as central to her artistic production as it was to her life. Her Manhattan paintings shifted the tenor of criticism away from the pervasive sexualized rhetoric of the first part of the decade, marked the moment that her paintings began to sell, and brought her financial success. And from the start, O'Keeffe recognized their value, writing boldly and confidently to the critic Henry McBride, "My New Yorks would turn the world over."[60]

FIG. 13
Installation view of *Georgia O'Keeffe: 27 New Paintings, New Mexico, New York, Lake George, Etc.*, An American Place, New York, Feb. 7–Mar. 17, 1930. Photograph by Alfred Stieglitz. Georgia O'Keeffe Museum, Georgia O'Keeffe Foundation Photographs, MS.57.

NOTES

1. Georgia O'Keeffe, *Georgia O'Keeffe* (New York: Viking Press, 1976), n.p., opp. pls. 18–19.
2. Georgia O'Keeffe to Henry McBride, [Mar. 1925?], reprinted in Jack Cowart and Juan Hamilton, with Sarah Greenough, *Georgia O'Keeffe: Art and Letters*, exh. cat. (Washington, DC: National Gallery of Art, in association with Boston: New York Graphic Society Books / Little, Brown, 1987), 179. In the note for the letter (p. 279), Greenough acknowledged that the letter's dating is problematic; she ultimately decided, based on contextual information from McBride's published criticism, that it likely dates to March 1925. If true, the plural ("New Yorks") indicates that by March 1925, O'Keeffe had painted *New York Street with Moon* and at least one other New York composition.
3. Quoted in Blanche C. Matthias, "Georgia O'Keeffe and the Intimate Gallery: Stieglitz Showing Seven Americans," *Chicago Evening Post, Magazine of the Art World*, Mar. 2, 1926, 14.
4. Anna Chave explored the group in an important essay in 1991 but made several factual errors throughout; see p53n36 in this volume. Anna C. Chave, "'Who Will Paint New York?': 'The World's New Art Center' and the Skyscraper Paintings of Georgia O'Keeffe," *American Art* 5, nos. 1–2 (Winter–Spring 1991): 86–107.
5. O'Keeffe, *Georgia O'Keeffe*, n.p., opp. pl. 17.
6. Wanda Corn analyzed the 1976 publication at length, noting that it did not conform to typical memoirs or autobiographies, and while it seemed to fashion a narrative, it is one that withholds far more information than it reveals. See Wanda M. Corn, "Telling Tales: Georgia O'Keeffe on Georgia O'Keeffe," *American Art* 23, no. 2 (Summer 2009): 54–79.
7. See, for instance, Kathleen A. Pyne, *Modernism and the Feminine Voice: O'Keeffe and the Women of the Stieglitz Circle* (Berkeley: University of California Press, 2007).
8. In 1978 O'Keeffe looked retrospectively at Stieglitz's photographic portrait for the exhibition and catalogue *Georgia O'Keeffe: A Portrait by Alfred Stieglitz* (New York: Metropolitan Museum of Art, 1978), featuring an introduction by O'Keeffe. See also the expanded and reprinted 1997 edition, which includes an afterword by Maria Morris Hambourg.
9. For an analysis of the 1920s reception of O'Keeffe's paintings, see Barbara Buhler Lynes, *O'Keeffe, Stieglitz, and the Critics, 1916–1929* (1989; Chicago: University of Chicago Press, 1991).
10. O'Keeffe, *Georgia O'Keeffe*, n.p., opp. pl. 18.
11. Ibid. Although no checklist of O'Keeffe's 1926 exhibition exists, a newspaper review confirms that she did indeed show *New York Street with Moon*, along with a Shelton painting, from February 11 to March 11, 1926. "Foujita's Art Is Seen in Exhibition Here," *New York Times*, Feb. 14, 1926, X12.
12. Mary Lynn Kotz, "A Day with Georgia O'Keeffe," *Art News* 76, no. 10 (Dec. 1977): 44.
13. She attended the School of the Art Institute of Chicago for the 1905–6 academic year, leaving after the spring term due to illness. In the fall of 1907, she enrolled in the Art Students League of New York, studying there for a year. Her finances precluded a second year of enrollment, so she moved back to Chicago in the fall of 1908 to work as a freelance commercial illustrator. In 1910 illness once again caused her to leave that city and return to her family in Virginia.
14. In June 1918 Stieglitz arranged for O'Keeffe to move into Elizabeth Stieglitz's vacant studio; he joined her there after separating from his wife in July 1918.
15. For one analysis of this work, see Bram Dijkstra, *Georgia O'Keeffe and the Eros of Place* (Princeton, NJ: Princeton University Press, 1998), 3–9.
16. The building still exists, although it is currently unoccupied after serving as a Marriott hotel.
17. Letters, including several on Shelton stationery, between O'Keeffe, Stieglitz, and her sister Ida O'Keeffe and their friend Sherwood Anderson, give evidence of their short-term residence in the Shelton. On November 25, 1924, Ida asked Stieglitz, "Are you still at the Shelton?" to which he responded on November 26, 1924, "Don't you think I'd let you know when we leave the Shelton? We'll be here until our place (38 E. 58th) is ready next week." Ida O'Keeffe to Alfred Stieglitz, Nov. 25, 1924; and Stieglitz to Ida O'Keeffe, Nov. 26, 1924, both box 37, folder 889, Alfred Stieglitz / Georgia O'Keeffe Archive, Yale Collection of American Literature, Beinecke Rare Book and Manuscript Library, Yale University (hereafter Stieglitz / O'Keeffe Archive, Yale). Finally, on December 18, 1924, Stieglitz wrote to Sherwood Anderson that they had moved the previous day; Stieglitz to Sherwood Anderson, Nov. 17, 1924, box 29, folder 1496, Sherwood Anderson Papers, Newberry Library, Chicago (hereafter Anderson Papers, Newberry).
18. "Hotel for the Bachelor Opens Its Doors to Women," *New York Times*, Oct. 12, 1924, X11.
19. Alfred Stieglitz to Sherwood Anderson, Nov. 27, 1924, box 29, folder 1496, Anderson Papers, Newberry.
20. Floorplans of the Shelton indicate that most of the corner units with two exposures were two-room suites. Relatively few single rooms had two exposures coupled with what could possibly correlate with Stieglitz's description of a "luxurious bath"—presumably a full bathroom with bathtub rather than a half bath, which would have necessitated them using the shared bathing facilities provided by the Shelton. However, the building featured four tiers of single rooms with two exposures on floors three through fourteen, including two facing Lexington Avenue (westward) and two at the far reaches of the southern wing. Floors sixteen through twenty had several tiers with single rooms and two exposures on the east side of the building, but most had half baths. Floors twenty-one through thirty had one corner tier, facing east and north, with a single room, two exposures, and a full bathroom.
21. O'Keeffe to McBride, [Mar. 1925?], reprinted in Cowart, Hamilton, with Greenough, *Georgia O'Keeffe*, 179. Unaware that O'Keeffe and Stieglitz lived in the Shelton in November 1924, the editors puzzled over this quote, but it makes more sense knowing that she had already experienced high-rise living, and it helps confirm their dating to March 1925. See note 2 above.
22. T. H. R., "Georgia O'Keeffe, Artist," *Shelton Spotlight*, Apr. 24, 1926, n.p., clipping in box 235, folder 4127, Stieglitz / O'Keeffe Archive, Yale.
23. The dash between "north" and "east" is ambiguous in her description of the exposures. It is possible that O'Keeffe meant "north-east and south," but the length and spacing of the dash—as was typical in her correspondence—suggests that the phrase is more likely to mean "north, east, and south." If the latter, a study of the Shelton's floorplans indicates that only one suite in floors three through fourteen fit this description; it was located

in the main tower, at the end of the southern side of the east-facing setback. See Georgia O'Keeffe and Alfred Stieglitz to Ida O'Keeffe, [Nov. 1925], box 37, folder 891, Stieglitz / O'Keeffe Archive, Yale. Although not dated by its authors, this letter contains firm references to John Marin's upcoming exhibition at Stieglitz's new gallery, the Intimate Gallery, which opened on December 7, 1925, demonstrating that the letter was written in late November 1925. Lee Ann Custer, however, dates the letter to November 1926 and therefore posits that the unit she described was apartment 2803, (into which they moved the following year), but this seems less likely. Lee Ann Custer, "Urban 'Voids': Picturing Light, Air, and Open Space in New York, 1890–1935," (PhD diss., University of Pennsylvania, 2021), 155–220. I thank Lee Ann Custer for sharing a copy of her dissertation before its publication.

24. Georgia O'Keeffe to Catherine O'Keeffe Klenert, Dec. 24, 1926, quoted in Roxana Robinson, *Georgia O'Keeffe: A Life*, expand. ed. (New York: Harper and Row, 1989; Waltham, MA: Brandeis University Press, 2020), 288. My thanks to Robinson for her assistance with this quote. This is confirmed by a letter from John Kerfoot to O'Keeffe, written March 22, 1927, and postmarked March 23, 1927. Although Kerfoot only addressed it to O'Keeffe at the Shelton, the envelope bears the handwritten inscription designating "2803" as their unit, presumably added by the building staff to help direct the letter to her. See John Kerfoot to O'Keeffe, Mar. 22, 1927, box 197, folder 3390, Stieglitz / O'Keeffe Archive, Yale. It also bears noting that according to Dorothy Adlow, "Georgia O'Keeffe," *Christian Science Monitor*, June 20, 1927, 11, O'Keeffe was living on the twenty-sixth floor in June 1927, but this is likely an error given the evidence establishing them on the twenty-eighth floor. By June, O'Keeffe and Stieglitz were at Lake George for the summer; Adlow probably visited O'Keeffe at her twenty-eighth-floor unit sometime earlier that spring and simply reported the floor incorrectly.

25. Their thirtieth-floor residence in the winter of 1927–28 was frequently remarked upon in the press; for example, an unidentified author cited this in "Art: On View," *Time*, Feb. 20, 1928, 21–22. This is further confirmed through correspondence; on February 16, 1928, Sherwood Anderson wrote to Stieglitz at the Shelton in unit 3003. See Sherwood Anderson to Alfred Stieglitz, box 13, folder 599, Anderson Papers, Newberry. One outlier is Frances O'Brien, "Americans We Like: Georgia O'Keeffe," *The Nation*, Oct. 12, 1927, 361–62. According to O'Brien, she met with O'Keeffe in her twenty-eighth-floor unit, but it is probable that this meeting occurred the previous spring and that the lead time of the article was several months. O'Keeffe and Stieglitz were still at Lake George on October 20, 1927, according to a letter from Stieglitz to Ida O'Keeffe (Stieglitz to Ida O'Keeffe, Oct. 20, 1927, box 37, folder 891, Stieglitz / O'Keeffe Archive, Yale) and only returned to Manhattan the following month.

26. Lillian Sabine, "Record Price for Living Artist," *Brooklyn Sunday Eagle Magazine*, May 27, 1928, 11.

27. "The Shelton," advertisement in *International Studio* 80, no. 332 (Jan. 1925): xxviii.

28. Alfred Stieglitz to Sherwood Anderson, Dec. 9, 1925, box 29, folder 1498, Anderson Papers, Newberry.

29. Quoted in B. Vladimir Berman, "She Painted the Lily and Got $25,000 and Fame for Doing It!," *New York Evening Graphic Magazine Section*, May 12, 1928, 3-M.

30. O'Keeffe described it as depicting Forty-Seventh Street with "a streetlight in the upper foreground at about the Chatham Hotel." O'Keeffe, *Georgia O'Keeffe*, n.p., opp. pl. 17. The Hotel Chatham was demolished in the 1960s, and Vanderbilt Avenue now ends at Forty-Seventh Street. "Chatham Added to List of Hotels to Be Razed for New Buildings," *New York Times*, July 30, 1965, 14.

31. Katharine Kuh, *The Artist's Voice: Talks with Seventeen Artists* (New York: Harper and Row, 1962), 191.

32. Sarah Whitaker Peters attributed the sunspots and radiant glare to effects of halation, made possible by a camera's lens. O'Keeffe was no stranger to cameras, but she always denied the inclusion of photographic effects (also deliberately distancing herself from Stieglitz's influence). It bears noting that nighttime viewing of streetlights often results in the natural diffraction of light into a perceived halo in the cornea. See Sarah Whitaker Peters, *Becoming O'Keeffe: The Early Years*, 2nd ed. (New York: Abbeville Press, 2001), 277–304.

33. "Foujita's Art," X12.

34. O'Keeffe, *Georgia O'Keeffe*, n.p., opp. pl. 17.

35. This is drawn from her exhibition history. She exhibited at least one Shelton painting in February 1926; by April of 1926, two were seen in her home, including *The Shelton with Sunspots, N.Y.* See note 11 above and T. H. R., "Georgia O'Keeffe, Artist," n.p. She exhibited four together in her February 1927 exhibition, titled *The Shelton I–IV*; these included *Shelton Hotel, N.Y., No. I*; *The Shelton with Sunspots, N.Y.*; almost certainly *The Shelton at Night*; and an additional one, presumably destroyed by O'Keeffe. Finally, in February 1928, she exhibited *The Shelton at Night*, seemingly showing the same canvas as the prior year. *The Shelton at Night* was illustrated in newspapers in 1927 and again in 1928 and was destroyed by O'Keeffe. She later wrote, "There were several other 'Sheltons' that I destroyed because they weren't as good as the 'Sunspots.'" O'Keeffe, *Georgia O'Keeffe*, n.p., opp. pl. 19. Aside from *The Shelton at Night*, there is no record of what the others looked like.

36. The Shelton's setbacks are variously described as being at the fifteenth or sixteenth floor and the twenty-first or twenty-second floor, a discrepancy that stems from the fact that the internal numbering system did not include the thirteenth floor. As a result, the rooftop terrace at the first setback was generally referred to as being on the sixteenth floor. Even the number of floors has been variably reported; throughout this volume we have used thirty-one stories, in line with Gale Harris, *Shelton Hotel*, Landmarks Preservation Commission, Designation List 490, Nov. 22, 2016, s-media.nyc.gov /agencies/lpc/lp/2557.pdf.

37. For more on the destroyed work's exhibition history, see note 35 above.

38. Louis Kalonyme, "In New York Galleries: Georgia O'Keeffe's Arresting Pictures," *New York Times*, Jan. 16, 1927, X10.

39. Henry McBride, "Georgia O'Keefe's [*sic*] Work Shown: Fellow Painters of Little Group Become Fairly Lyrical Over It," *New York Sun*, Jan. 15, 1927, 22B, reprinted in Lynes, *O'Keeffe, Stieglitz, and the Critics*, 258–60.

40. Lynes, *O'Keeffe, Stieglitz, and the Critics*, 259.

41. Georgia O'Keeffe to Henry McBride, Jan. 16, 1927, reprinted in Cowart, Hamilton, with Greenough, *Georgia O'Keeffe*, 185.

42. Howard Robertson, "'Two Splendid Skyscrapers': The Hotel Shelton and the Ritz Tower, New York," *Architect and Building News*, Jan. 21, 1927, 148.
43. Raymond M. Hood, "The American Radiator Company Building, New York," *American Architect and the Architectural Review*, Nov. 19, 1924, 470.
44. O'Keeffe, *Georgia O'Keeffe*, n.p., opp. pl. 20.
45. Bassett Jones, "Illuminating the Exteriors of Buildings," *Architectural Forum* 42, no. 2 (Feb. 1925): 95.
46. "Editorial Comment," *American Architect and the Architectural Review*, Nov. 19, 1924, 487.
47. Of O'Keeffe's New York paintings, *Radiator Building—Night, New York* has generated the greatest art historical interest, and O'Keeffe's inclusion of Stieglitz's name has been the subject of much speculation, from a crisis in their marriage to a gentle poking at Stieglitz's long-heralded distaste for advertising. See Elizabeth Duvert, "Georgia O'Keeffe's *Radiator Building*: Icon of Glamorous Gotham," *Places* 2, no. 2 (Fall 1984): 3–17; Chave, "'Who Will Paint New York?,'" 86–107; and Vivien Green Fryd, "Georgia O'Keeffe's *Radiator Building*: Gender, Sexuality, Modernism, and Urban Imagery," *Winterthur Portfolio* 35, no. 4 (Winter 2000): 269–89.
48. Orrick Johns, "What the Modish Building Will Wear," *New York Times*, Oct. 4, 1925, SM11.
49. O'Keeffe, quoted in Berman, "She Painted the Lily," 3-M.
50. O'Keeffe and Stieglitz's attitudes toward race have been discussed in regards to different aspects of their life and work. See, for instance, Camara Dia Holloway, "Lovechild: Stieglitz, O'Keeffe, and the Birth of American Modernism," *Prospects* 30 (2005): 395–432; Lauren Kroiz, *Creative Composites: Modernism, Race, and the Stieglitz Circle* (Berkeley: University of California Press; Washington, DC: Phillips Collection, 2012); and Tara Kohn, "Elevated: Along the Fringes of 291 Fifth Avenue," *Panorama: Journal of the Association of Historians of American Art* 4, no. 2 (Fall 2018), doi.org/10.24926/24716839.1657.29. For an analysis of the Stieglitz circle and eugenic thinking, see Randall Griffey, "Reconsidering the 'Soil': The Stieglitz Circle, the Regionalists, and Cultural Eugenics in the Twenties," in *Youth and Beauty: Art of the American Twenties*, ed. Teresa A. Carbone, exh. cat. (New York: Brooklyn Museum; New York: Skira Rizzoli, 2011), 245–77. Finally, Amanda Mehsima Licato explores the evidence for an intimate relationship between O'Keeffe and novelist Jean Toomer in their letters; see Amanda Mehsima Licato, "The Shared Journeys of Jean Toomer and Georgia O'Keeffe," *Yale Program in the History of the Book* (blog), bookhistory.yale.edu/blog/shared-journeys-jean-toomer-and-georgia-okeeffe.
51. The other was *Flying Backbone*, then a relatively recent painting of 1944 (Alfred Stieglitz Collection, Co-owned by Fisk University, Nashville, Tennessee, and Crystal Bridges Museum of American Art, Bentonville, Arkansas). This stands in direct contrast to the gifts to the Metropolitan Museum and the Art Institute of Chicago: both museums received significant numbers of her paintings from across the breadth of her career. My thanks to Crystal Bridges Museum of American Art, the Tyson Scholars Program, and particularly curator Jennifer Padgett for supporting my research on *Radiator Building—Night, New York*.
52. Eight of the nine paintings and pastels are catalogued in Barbara Buhler Lynes, *Georgia O'Keeffe: Catalogue Raisonné*, vol. 1 (New Haven, CT: Yale University Press, 1999), nos. 531–33, 576, 614, 619–20, and 654. The ninth, *East River from the Shelton (30th Story)*, was once in the collection of the Art Institute of Chicago and is now missing; see Lynes, *Georgia O'Keeffe: Catalogue Raisonné*, vol. 2 (New Haven, CT: Yale University Press, 1999), 1105, no. 83; and p. 40, fig. 5 in this volume.
53. Georgia O'Keeffe, *Some Memories of Drawings* (New York: Atlantis Editions, 1974), n.p. As Lynes (*Catalogue Raisonné*, 1:no. 525) points out, O'Keeffe could have seen a westward view from the public spaces, but it is more likely she saw the view from her own window.
Lynes suggests that this west-facing unit was on the eleventh floor, per the *Shelton Spotlight* of April 1926 (see note 23), but the eleventh-floor unit was more likely the unit into which they moved in November 1925 and likely stayed through the spring of 1926, and it did not have a western exposure. It stands to reason that O'Keeffe might have completed the drawing in November 1924, the only time when they could have lived on the western side of the building.
54. Chave, "'Who Will Paint New York?,'" 98, misidentified it as the Berkley Hotel. It is now the Benjamin Royal Sonesta Hotel.
55. O'Keeffe, *Georgia O'Keeffe*, n.p., opp. pl. 20.
56. For a discussion of her initial steps in starting a composition, see Bruce Robertson, "Useable Form: O'Keeffe's Materials, Methods, and Motifs," in *Georgia O'Keeffe: Abstraction*, ed. Barbara Haskell, exh. cat. (New York: Whitney Museum of American Art; Washington, DC: Phillips Collection; Santa Fe: Georgia O'Keeffe Museum; New Haven, CT: Yale University Press, 2009), 125–33.
57. The missing East River was also 12 by 32 inches. Lynes, *Catalogue Raisonné*, 2:1105, no. 83.
58. Quoted in "I Can't Sing, So I Paint! Says Ultrarealistic Artist: Art Is not Photography—It Is Expression of Inner Life! Miss Georgia O'Keeffe Explains Subjective Aspect of Her Work," *New York Sun*, Dec. 5, 1922; see Lynes, *O'Keeffe, Stieglitz, and the Critics*, 180.
59. Wanda M. Corn, "Painting Big—O'Keeffe's *Manhattan*," *American Art* 20, no. 2 (Summer 2006): 22–25.
60. O'Keeffe to McBride, [Mar. 1925?], reprinted in Cowart, Hamilton, with Greenough, *Georgia O'Keeffe*, 179.

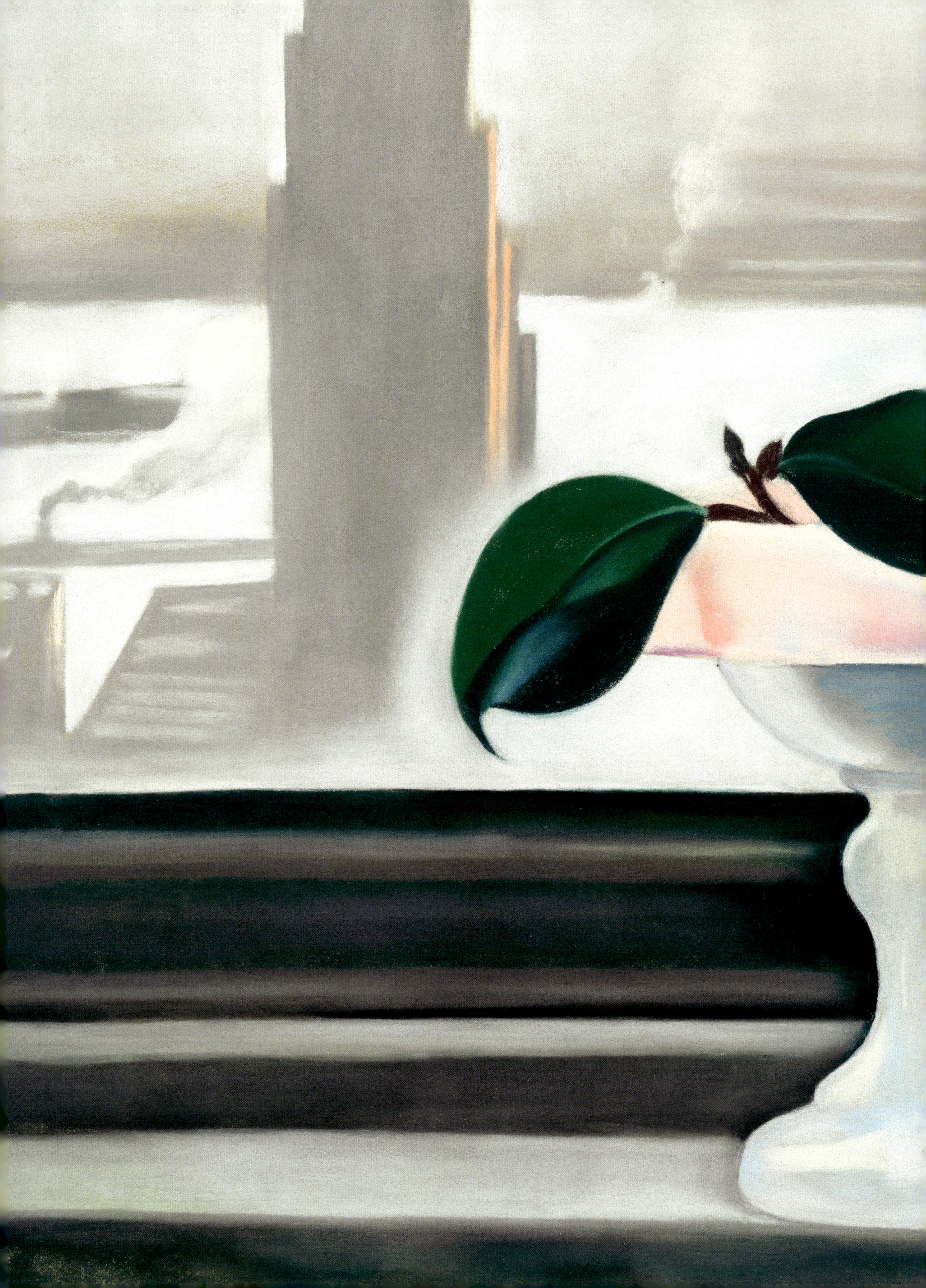

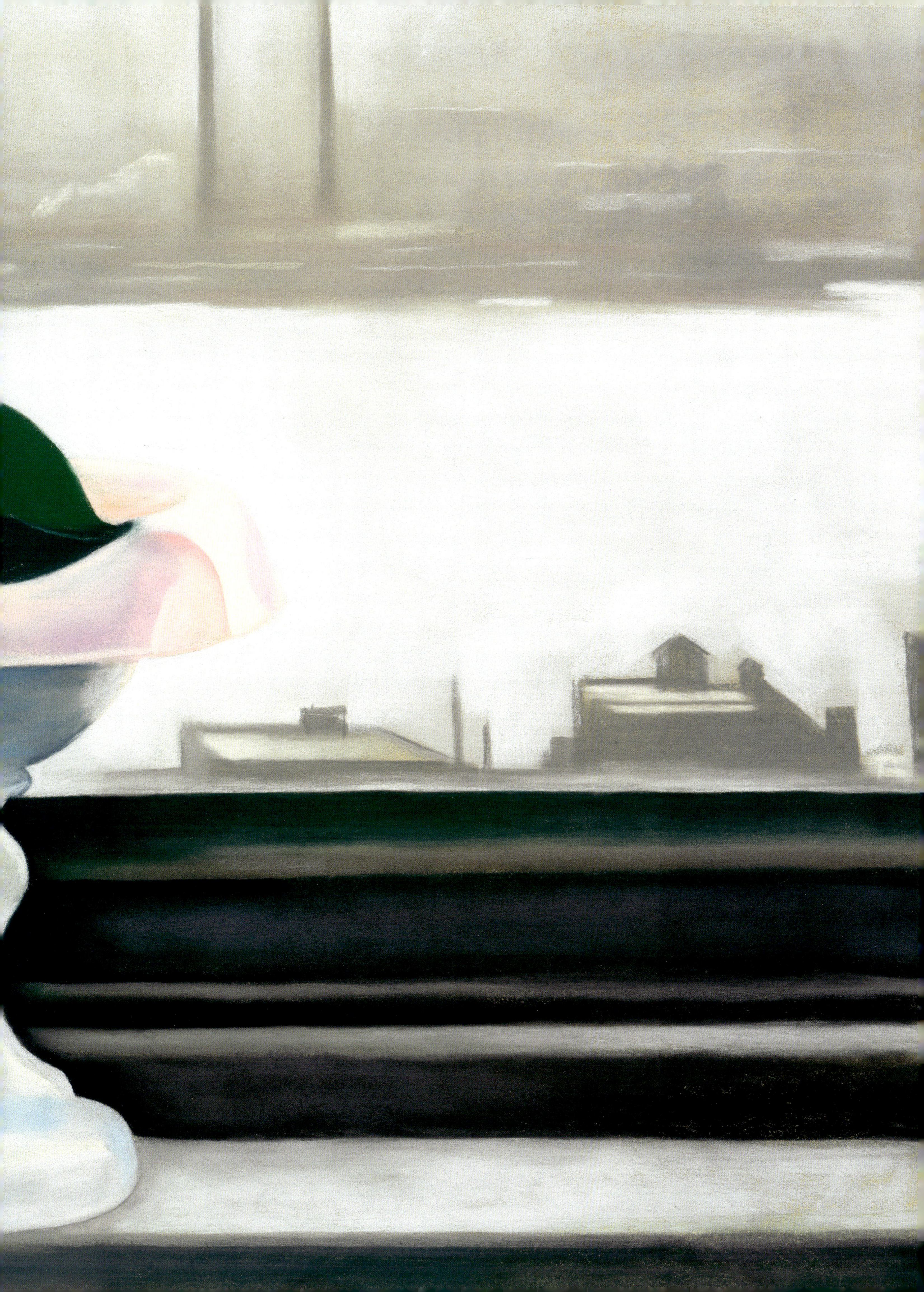

TALL BUILDINGS AND TINY SHELLS

GEORGIA O'KEEFFE, NEW YORK, AND THE SCALE OF THINGS

Annelise K. Madsen

"The pink dish with the city is frankly my foolishness—but I thought to myself—I am that way so here it goes—if I am that way I might as well put it down," quipped Georgia O'Keeffe in a letter to Mitchell Kennerley in January 1929, two weeks before the opening of her annual exhibition at the Intimate Gallery.[1] Kennerley was president of the Anderson Galleries Building at 489 Park Avenue, where the gallery, run by her husband Alfred Stieglitz, was located. O'Keeffe described a number of works in her upcoming show, offering the above assessment of *Pink Dish and Green Leaves* (pl. 59) in a manner at once self-deprecating and assertive. In the large and luminous pastel, the artist centered a glass compote on a windowsill in the foreground, its curvilinear forms in translucent white and pink, along with a sprig of deep green leaves, set against the molding of the window frame and a hazy cityscape beyond. Calling it "foolishness," yet also determined to "put it down," she emphasized the exploratory impulse behind the composition. O'Keeffe was up to something different.

Pink Dish and Green Leaves is indeed distinctive, anchored at the threshold between her apartment in the Shelton Hotel and the industrial vista along the East River outside her window. Its domestic setting, if abbreviated, is nonetheless a rare subject for the artist, whose compositions overwhelmingly frame enlarged, cropped objects at the front of the picture plane or, in the case of the East River series, portray the city from an elevated position void of any signposts revealing location. The work brings together O'Keeffe's things—the handheld objects she gathered and collected throughout her life, from leaves to shells, rocks, flowers, feathers, and bones (see figs. 1 and 2)—and an urban view. It is one of her "New Yorks," as she called her paintings and drawings inspired by the built environs of the city, yet is also part genre picture and still life.[2] The pastel thus offers a perspective on O'Keeffe that encourages us to look broadly at the artist's aesthetic experimentation in the 1920s and to consider how her New Yorks fit into these larger efforts.

The windowsill view represents one exercise among many in which O'Keeffe honed in on the East River as subject matter. This investigation began shortly after she and Stieglitz moved into an apartment in the Shelton Hotel, a novel residential high-rise located in Midtown on Lexington Avenue between Forty-Eighth and Forty-Ninth Streets, and continued over several years. Living and working in apartments on various floors from which she could look out and down at the city catalyzed an intensive period of creation from 1925 into the 1930s. In addition to executing pastels, O'Keeffe rendered compositions in oil and charcoal, creating at least ten depictions of the river between 1926 and 1932.[3] *Pink Dish and Green Leaves* is the only one to include a portion of her domestic space. Among the rest, there is considerable variation. Although four of the paintings are the same canvas size (approximately 12 by 32 inches) and two pastels have similar dimensions, O'Keeffe used different color palettes, achieving a range of atmospheric effects (see fig. 5 and pls. 52–56). A larger-scale panoramic view, *East River from the 30th Story of the Shelton Hotel* (pl. 57), lends a certain weight to the subject with its more extensive depiction of the built environment on both sides of the river. Further, the vertical work *East River from the Shelton (East River No. 1)* (pl. 60) stands out as organic and ethereal in feeling, with its radiating sun, fiery oranges along the water, and silhouetted skyline.

O'Keeffe unveiled her East River series to the public over several years, including two or three works from the growing set in her exhibitions at Stieglitz's gallery in 1927, 1928, and 1929. From descriptions in press accounts, it is clear that *Pink Dish and Green Leaves* was one of two East River views exhibited at the Intimate Gallery in February–March 1929.[4] Sometime after she composed the pastel, she worked on a painting featuring the same compote, *3 Eggs in Pink Dish* (pl. 58).[5] She again centered the glass vessel in the composition, now pictured from above, with eggs nestled inside. Undulating white drapery, reflecting soft hues of pink and gray, surrounds the dish. We can imagine that O'Keeffe moved the compote from the windowsill to another space in her apartment, perhaps onto a chair covered with the fabric. The painting, then, offers important context as we think through the East River pictures. Executing compositions that are recognizably her New Yorks, O'Keeffe all the while attended to the various objects that she brought into her interior world for other avenues of aesthetic exploration. Skyscrapers and things, hung together.

This essay offers an integrative view of O'Keeffe's New York works, examining her skyscrapers and cityscapes alongside the still lifes, flowers, and natural abstractions that likewise date to this moment of experimentation. After visiting the artist at the Shelton in 1927, critic Frances O'Brien captured the breadth of O'Keeffe's practice: "Paintings of flowers and leaves and the music of flowers and leaves. Paintings also of tall buildings, of tiny shells, of Lexington Avenue."[6] Rather than seeing O'Keeffe's New Yorks as a discrete body of work in her career, I contend that they are a constitutive element of her formal explorations of the 1920s. Manipulating scale, paring down or abstracting forms, keying color, and working serially, she approached tall buildings and tiny shells—and numerous subjects in between—similarly and concurrently. At her annual exhibitions at Stieglitz's galleries in the 1920s and early 1930s, O'Keeffe displayed such varied works together, offering visitors, critics, and potential patrons an expansive view of her distinctive aesthetics.

The artist's move into the Shelton Hotel (see fig. 3) must have been a revelation to the senses. Rising more than thirty stories in midtown Manhattan, the newly constructed skyscraper was the first of its kind, offering the "highest, airiest residence floors in the world" and plentiful amenities (see p. 20, fig. 4).[7] Architect Arthur Loomis Harmon designed innovative setbacks at the sixteenth and twenty-second floors, which

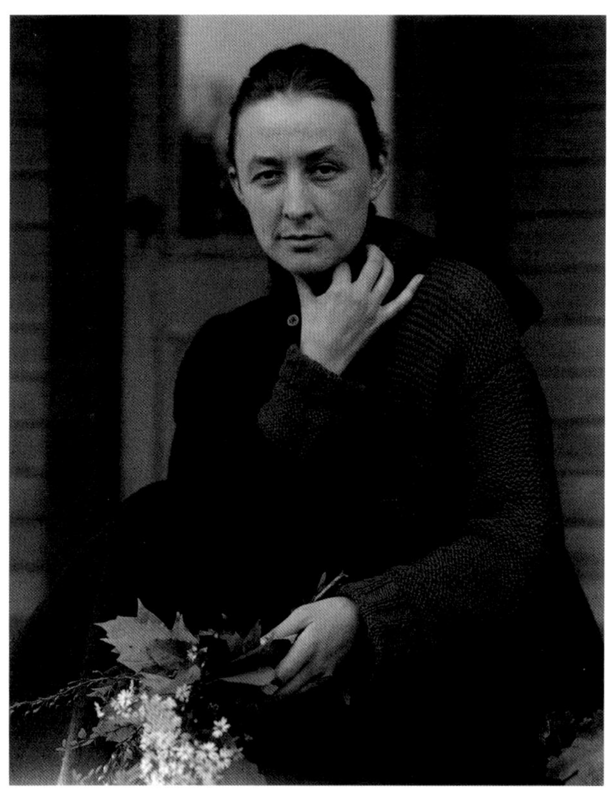

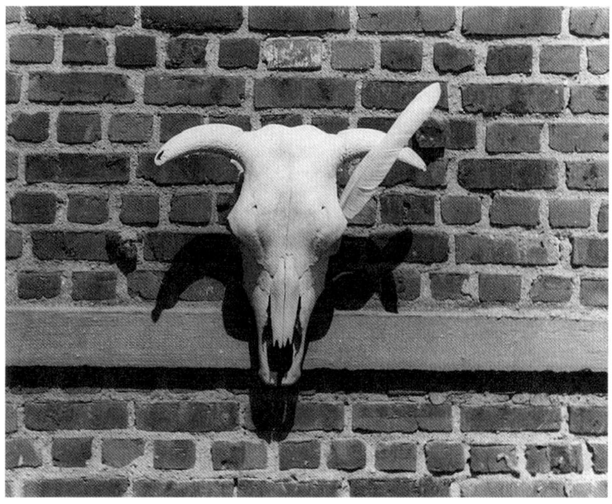

FIG. 1
Alfred Stieglitz (American, 1864–1946). *Georgia O'Keeffe*, 1918, printed 1918–34. Gelatin silver print; sheet (trimmed to image): 11.4 × 9.1 cm (4 1/2 × 3 9/16 in.). National Gallery of Art, Washington, Alfred Stieglitz Collection, 1980.70.81.

FIG. 2
Carl Van Vechten (American, 1880–1964). *Georgia O'Keeffe*, June 5, 1936. Gelatin silver print; image and sheet: 19.8 × 25 cm (7 13/16 × 9 13/16 in.). Philadelphia Museum of Art: Gift of John Mark Lutz, 1965.

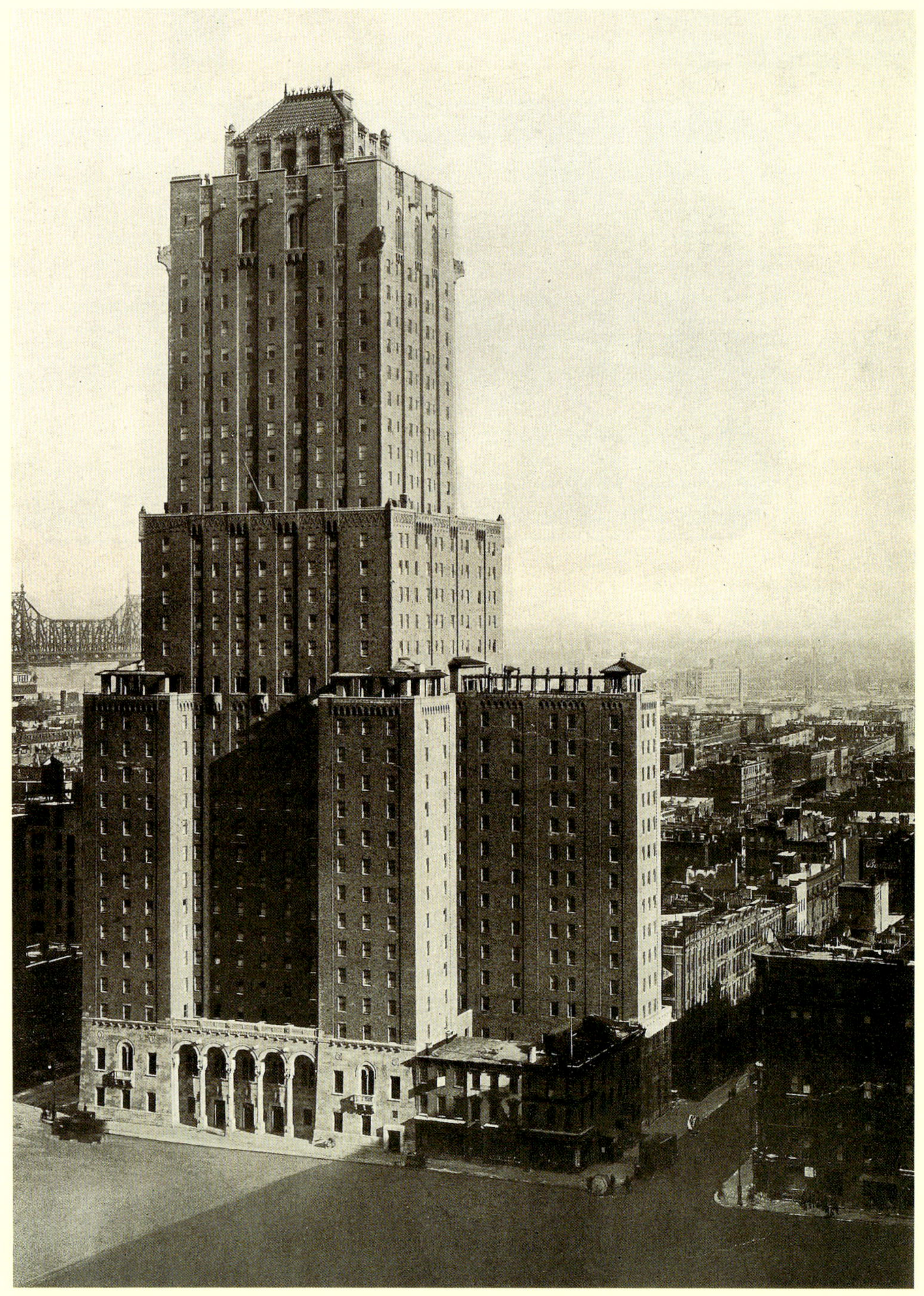

allowed more light to descend into the street canyons below; created multiple rooftop terraces; and granted panoramic views to the apartments, whose windows faced as many as three directions.[8] Conceived as "a residence for men" when it opened its doors in fall 1923, the policy changed the following year and women were permitted to live in the hotel.[9] O'Keeffe became one of the Shelton's earliest female residents when she and Stieglitz first stayed in an apartment there for about a month in November–December 1924.[10]

FIG. 3
The Shelton Hotel, Lexington Avenue between Forty-Eighth and Forty-Ninth Streets, New York. Reproduced in "The Shelton, Arthur Loomis Harmon, Architect," *Architecture* 49, no. 4 (Apr. 1924): 100.

After O'Keeffe relocated to New York City from Texas in 1918, the couple's lifestyle was marked by seasonal moves. Late fall, winter, and part of spring were spent in Manhattan. Then they packed up their belongings, vacated their living quarters, and headed to the Stieglitz family home at Lake George in upstate New York for the summer. During the fall, they moved back to the city. From late 1920 to April 1924, their New York City address was 60 East Sixty-Fifth Street, the home of Alfred's brother Leopold.[11] After the 1924 season at Lake George, O'Keeffe and Stieglitz got their first taste of Shelton

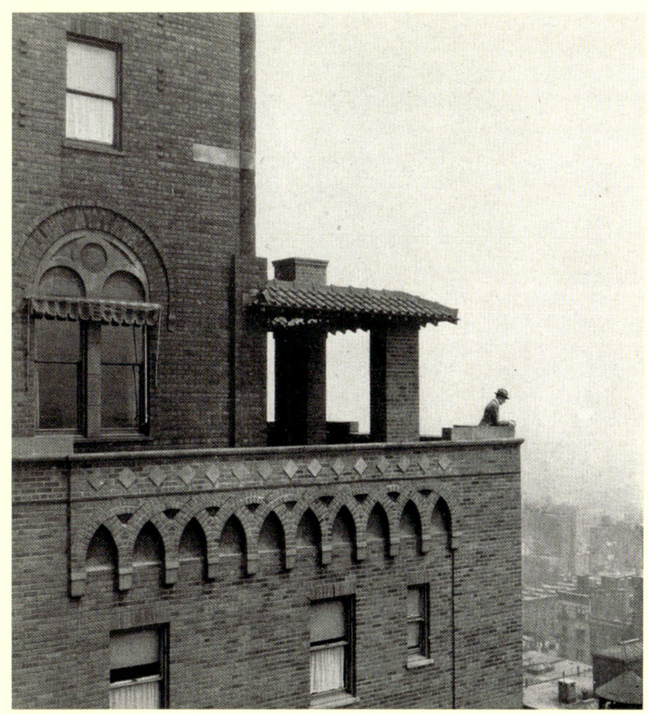

living for a few short weeks as they readied an apartment on the top floor of a four-story brownstone at 38 East Fifty-Eighth Street, a short walk from the Anderson Galleries Building. Yet when they headed to Lake George six months later in June 1925, they were not able to secure the apartment for the fall.[12] And so plans took shape for a move to the Shelton Hotel, which would become their urban home base for the next decade.

On December 9, 1925, Stieglitz wrote to author Sherwood Anderson, "New York is madder than ever. The pace ever increasing.—But Georgia & I somehow don't seem to be of New York—nor of anywhere. We live high up in the Shelton Hotel. . . . We feel as if we were out at midocean—All is so quiet except the wind."[13] Residing in various apartments on the eleventh, twenty-eighth, twenty-ninth, and thirtieth floors (and possibly others), O'Keeffe and Stieglitz found themselves immersed in the city yet also far removed from the crowds, noises, grit, and cadences of an urban existence.[14] Writer and architect Claude Bragdon credited the new building's success to its "escape . . . into the vertical dimension" (see fig. 4).[15] It was a privileged position—affording rare views—and an overwhelmingly white space. As a Shelton resident, O'Keeffe gained a field of vision accessible to few New Yorkers.[16] In a 1928 interview, she described the advantages of her high-rise apartment: "When I came to live at the Shelton about three years ago . . . I couldn't afford it. But I can now, so of course I'm going to stay. Yes I realize it's unusual for an artist to want to work way up near the roof of a big hotel in the heart of the roaring city but I think that's just what the artist of today needs for stimulus. He has to have a place where he can behold the city as a unit before his eyes but at the same time have enough space left to work."[17]

Through O'Keeffe's paintings and works on paper from 1925 onward, we can envision her movements in and around the spaces of the Shelton. She and Stieglitz kept their apartment spare, the only notes of color being a painting on her easel or a small number of artworks on the wall. Describing the artists' thirtieth-floor apartment (3003, their preferred location over the years), journalist Lillian Sabine wrote, "So austere it was, with its cold gray walls, and its white covers over dull upholstery."[18] But the room did impress: "It seemed all windows—windows overlooking housetops, steel framework, chimneys; windows to the east through which the panorama of the river and the bridge came flooding."[19] O'Keeffe gazed through these windows to compose *Pink Dish and Green Leaves* and the rest of her East River pictures. It was her daily view over several years. She captured the river and its surroundings in changing light and seasons, from overcast or smoky skies (see fig. 5 and pl. 52) and snowy rooftops (see pl. 55) to crisp sunlight and the first flourishes of green in spring (see pl. 57). From an elevated position in the Shelton, she also trained her eye upon the Beverly Hotel (see pl. 62), another newly built skyscraper located a block north on Lexington Avenue, rendering it against the night sky. Always one to take long walks, O'Keeffe exited the Shelton and perambulated the neighborhood. Her street-level views of Midtown's engineered monoliths must have taken shape during these outings, including paintings of the Shelton Hotel itself

FIG. 4
Corner pavilion on the sixteenth floor, Shelton Hotel, New York. Reproduced in Claude Bragdon, "The Shelton Hotel, New York, Arthur Loomis Harmon, Architect," *Architectural Record* 58, no. 1 (July 1925): 9.

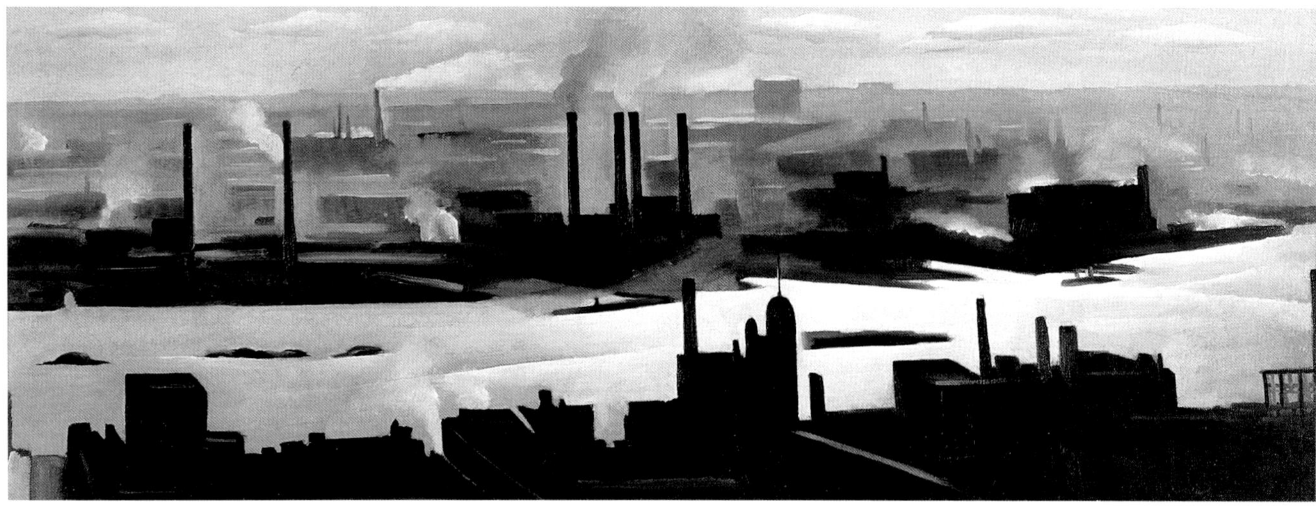

FIG. 5
Georgia O'Keeffe (American, 1887–1986). *East River from the Shelton (30th Story)*, 1926. Oil on canvas; 30.5 × 81.3 cm (12 × 32 in.). The Art Institute of Chicago, Alfred Stieglitz Collection, gift of Georgia O'Keeffe, 1955.1222 (now missing).

FIG. 6
Georgia O'Keeffe with collection of shells at a window of her apartment at 405 East Fifty-Fourth Street, New York, c. 1937. Photograph by Kurt Severin (American, born Germany, 1902–1982). Library of Congress, Prints and Photographs Division.

FIG. 7
"Georgia O'Keeffe Turns Dead Bones to Live Art," *Life*, Feb. 14, 1938, 28–29.

(see pls. 11–12) and of unknown structures and locales in compositions of heightened abstraction, such as *City Night* (pl. 21) and *A Street* (pl. 15).

As in the city, O'Keeffe took solitary walks wherever she found herself, whether at Lake George, along the Atlantic coast, across the arid landscapes of New Mexico, or elsewhere. During these outings, she spotted, selected, and collected an assortment of things. At York Beach, Maine, in September 1926, for instance, O'Keeffe wrote to Stieglitz, "After breakfast I looked over all my shells that I have been picking up since I am here—sorted out the ones I wanted. . . . At about a quarter to ten I started for the lighthouse—walking—alone—I had a very good time all by myself."[20] She carried with her these shells from Maine; leaves, flowers, and even shingles from an old barn at Lake George; rocks; and more. Ephemeral items might only move a short distance—such as from the environs of the lake to her studio there—but other found objects traveled much further. A photograph of O'Keeffe at her windowsill in the penthouse apartment at 405 East Fifty-Fourth Street (fig. 6), where she and Stieglitz moved in 1936, shows her arranging shells and things—presumably gathered from other places and then assembled in New York. In July 1931 O'Keeffe shipped animal bones from New Mexico back to Lake George, and the "barrels and boxes of bones" soon made their way to her apartment at the Shelton.[21] Five years later, a steer's skull hung in the rooftop terrace of the Fifty-Fourth Street building, captured by photographer Carl Van Vechten (pls. 91 and 93) and O'Keeffe herself (pl. 89). The artist's collected bones were prominently featured in a *Life* article in February 1938 (fig. 7), including one of Van Vechten's rooftop photographs.

The myriad of objects O'Keeffe kept within arm's reach, combined with the stimulating sightlines of skyscraper living (see p. 29, fig. 12), provided rich source material for artistic exploration during the mid-1920s into the 1930s and beyond. The range of O'Keeffe's output in these years is stunning: leaves, carefully arranged and enlarged (see fig. 8 and pl. 4); shells and shingles, solitary or in combination, detailed (see pl. 29) or pared down (see pl. 27); landscapes, some energetic and visionary (see pls. 2–3), some minimal (see fig. 9), others monumental (see pls. 6, 61, and 69); cityscapes, some recognizable (see pl. 16), others coded (see pl. 26); New Yorks that combine hard lines with organic forms evocative of sun flares, moonlight, or streetlights (see pls. 1, 12, and 17); still lifes and natural abstractions on elongated canvases, stretching upward like urban structures (see pls. 5, 7, and 64), others compact and jewel-like (see pl. 35); larger-than-life flowers, celebrating singular details (see fig. 14 and pls. 30 and 34) or reworked into novel forms (see pl. 31 and fig. 10); geometric plays of line, shape, and color (see pls. 20 and 25); dried bones adorned with flowers (see pl. 67); and more.

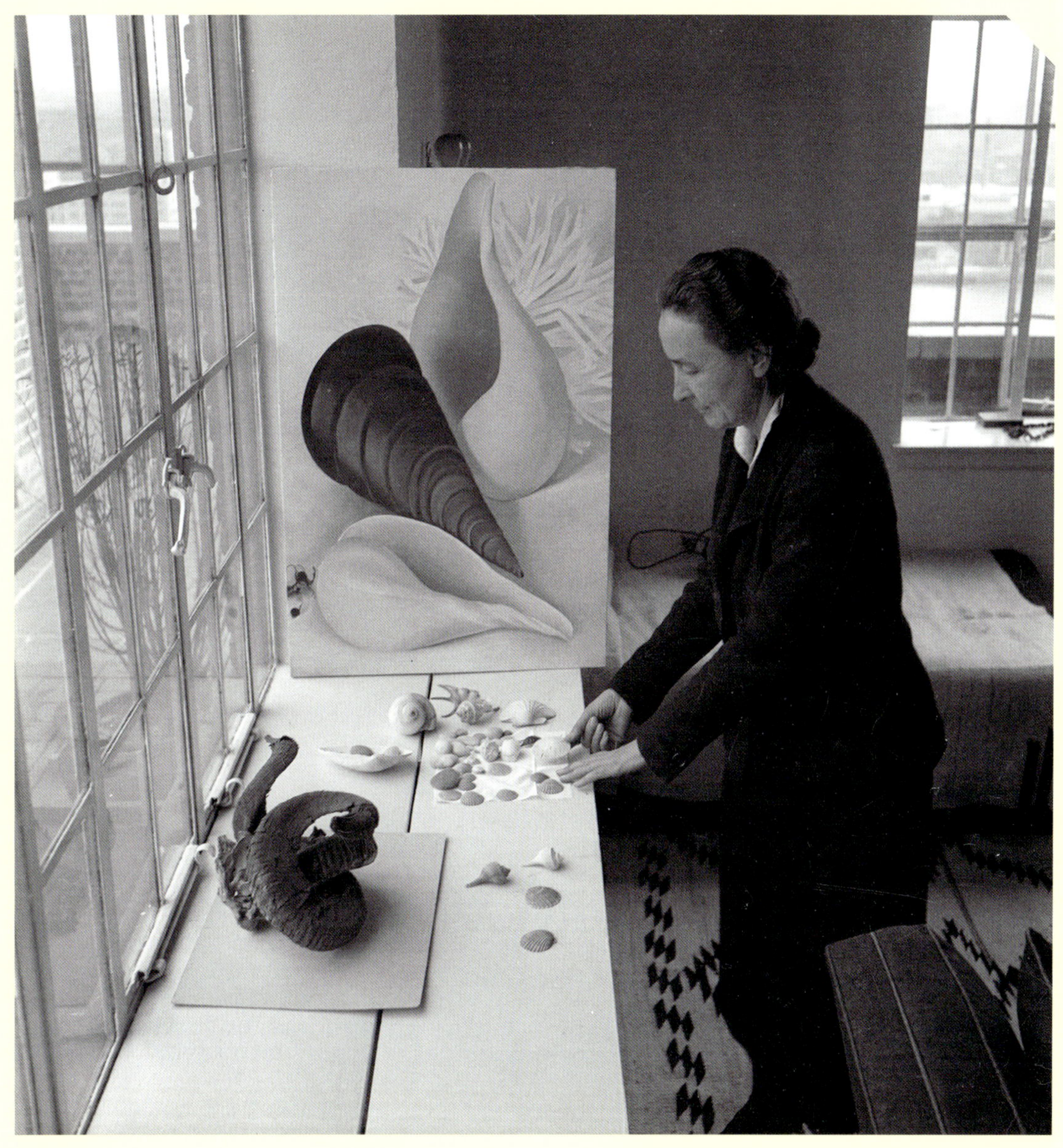

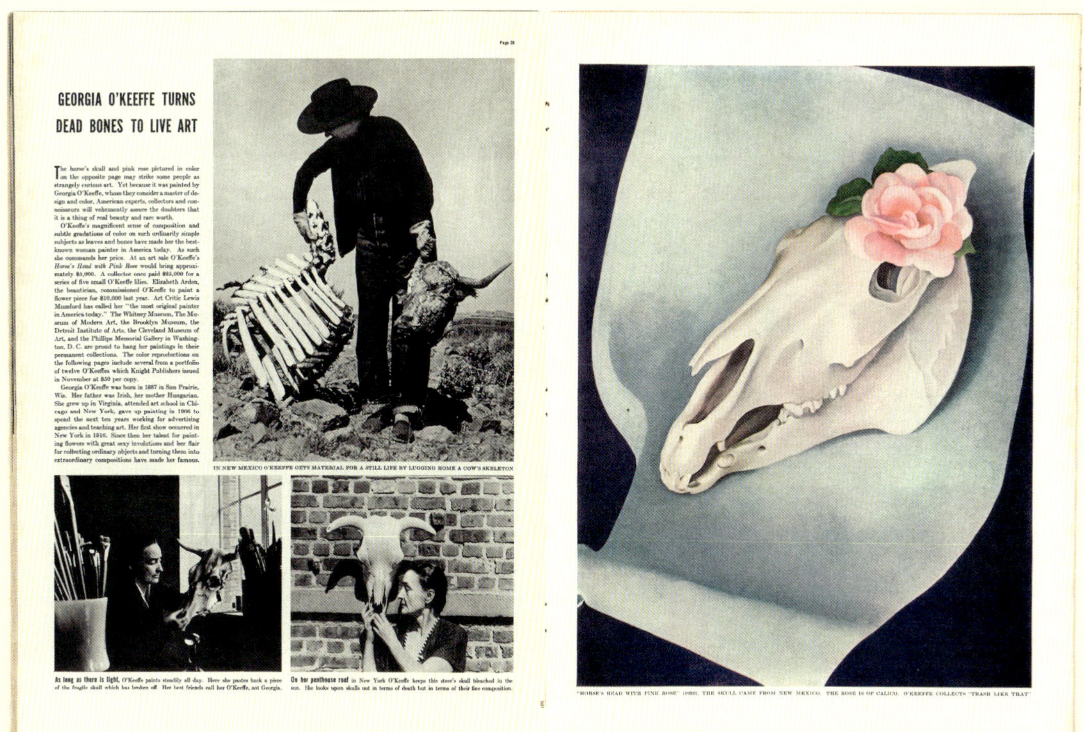

GEORGIA O'KEEFFE TURNS DEAD BONES TO LIVE ART

The horse's skull and pink rose pictured in color on the opposite page may strike some people as strangely curious art. Yet because it was painted by Georgia O'Keeffe, whom they consider a master of design and color, American experts, collectors and connoisseurs will vehemently assure the doubters that it is a thing of real beauty and rare worth.

O'Keeffe's magnificent sense of composition and subtle gradations of color on such ordinarily simple subjects as leaves and bones have made her the best-known woman painter in America today. As such she commands her price. At an art sale O'Keeffe's *Horse's Head with Pink Rose* would bring approximately $3,000. A collector once paid $25,000 for a series of five small O'Keeffe lilies. Elizabeth Arden, the beautician, commissioned O'Keeffe to paint a flower piece for $10,000 last year. Art Critic Lewis Mumford has called her "the most original painter in America today." The Whitney Museum, The Museum of Modern Art, the Brooklyn Museum, the Detroit Institute of Arts, the Cleveland Museum of Art, and the Phillips Memorial Gallery in Washington, D. C. are proud to hang her paintings in their permanent collections. The color reproductions on the following pages include several from a portfolio of twelve O'Keeffes which Knight Publishers issued in November at $50 per copy.

Georgia O'Keeffe was born in 1887 in Sun Prairie, Wis. Her father was Irish, her mother Hungarian. She grew up in Virginia, attended art school in Chicago and New York, gave up painting in 1906 to spend the next ten years working for advertising agencies and teaching art. Her first show occurred in New York in 1916. Since then her talent for painting flowers with great sexy involutions and her flair for collecting ordinary objects and turning them into extraordinary compositions have made her famous.

IN NEW MEXICO O'KEEFFE GETS MATERIAL FOR A STILL LIFE BY LUGGING HOME A COW'S SKELETON

As long as there is light, O'Keeffe paints steadily all day. Here she pastes back a piece of the fragile skull which has broken off. Her best friends call her O'Keeffe, not Georgia.

On her penthouse roof in New York O'Keeffe keeps this steer's skull bleached in the sun. She looks upon skulls not in terms of death but in terms of their fine composition.

"HORSE'S HEAD WITH PINK ROSE" (1930). THE SKULL CAME FROM NEW MEXICO. THE ROSE IS OF CALICO. O'KEEFFE COLLECTS "TRASH LIKE THAT"

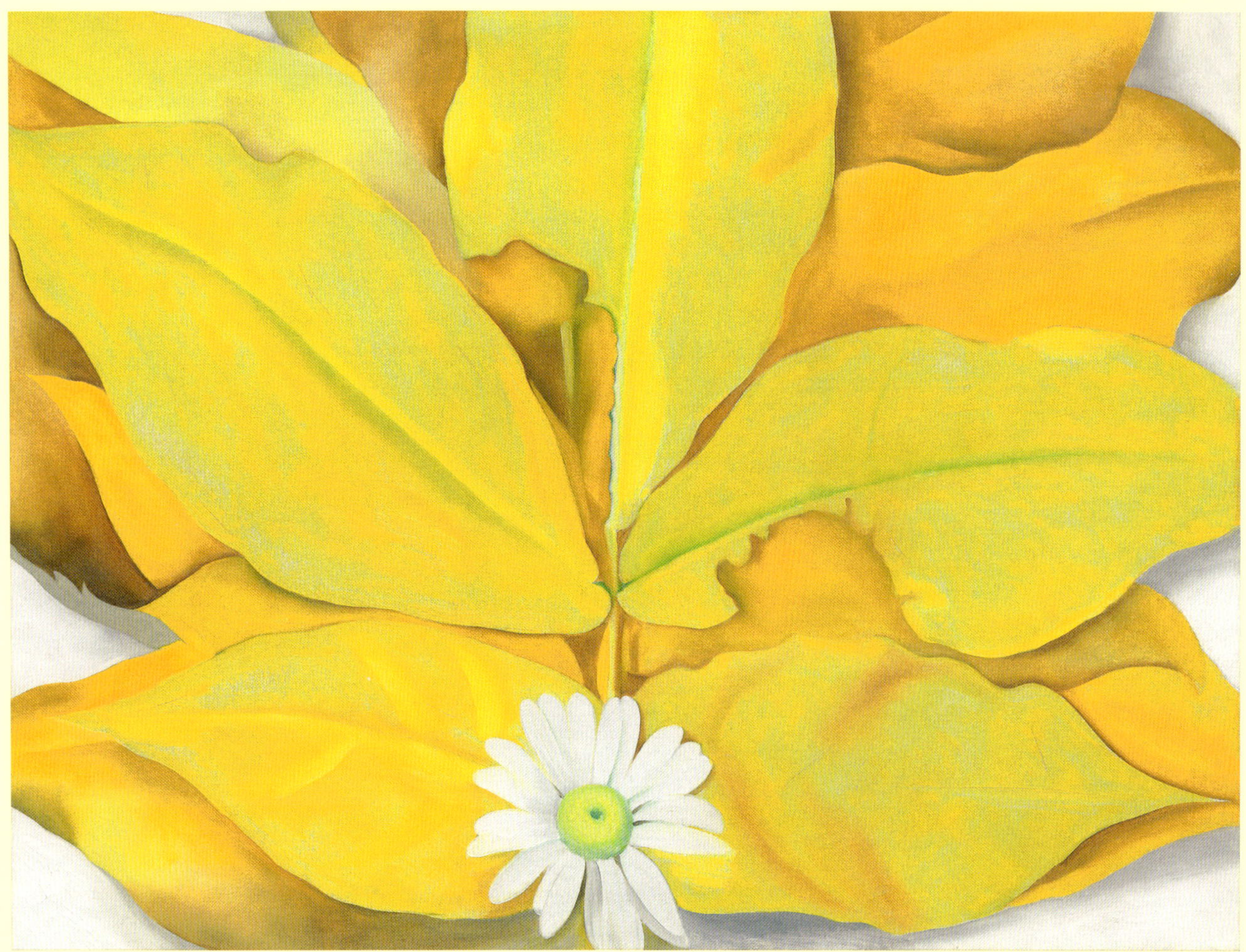

In contemporary press accounts, critics called out this great assortment. In the sweeping words of one journalist, "Roofs of New York buildings, a barn, an arc-light, innumerable windows, lilies, poppies, a pepper, some grapes, some plums, a daisy, a variety of leaves, a shell—these are a few of the objects which give O'Keeffe her starting-point."[22] Declaring that "her color is like no one else's," critic Louis Kalonyme pointed to the artist's skillful manipulation of a diverse palette across subject matter, from the "cold fresh green of blue seas to orange and red and purple and white . . . flowers" to "glittering golden and night-blue skyscrapers."[23] Color served as connective tissue in her work. Embracing an organic metaphor, historian and critic Lewis Mumford stated plainly, "The point is that all these paintings come from a central stem; and it is because the stem is so well grounded in the earth and the plant itself so lusty, that it keeps on producing new shoots and efflorescences, now through the medium of apples, pears, eggplants, now through leaves and stalks, now in high buildings and sky-scapes, all intensified by abstraction into symbols of quite different significance."[24]

At her exhibitions at Stieglitz's galleries, O'Keeffe brought such varied compositions together year after year, convincingly demonstrating that her practice was anything but narrow in scope. Her 1927 installation at the Intimate Gallery, entitled *Georgia O'Keeffe: Paintings, 1926*, was exemplary of her approach, with a checklist showcasing the variety and depth of the artist's production. Notably, the range of works on display included a critical mass of O'Keeffe's New Yorks for the first time.[25] The year marked an assured moment in her career, a turning point in several respects. First, Henry McBride voiced a shift in the criticism, characterizing the artist's work as "intellectual rather than emotional," a declaration that elated O'Keeffe, who resisted the language of sexuality and the unconscious (rooted in the theories of Sigmund Freud) that critics had

FIG. 8
O'Keeffe. *Yellow Hickory Leaves with Daisy*, 1928. Oil on canvas; 76.5 × 101.6 cm (29 7/8 × 39 7/8 in.). The Art Institute of Chicago, Alfred Stieglitz Collection, gift of Georgia O'Keeffe, 1965.1180.

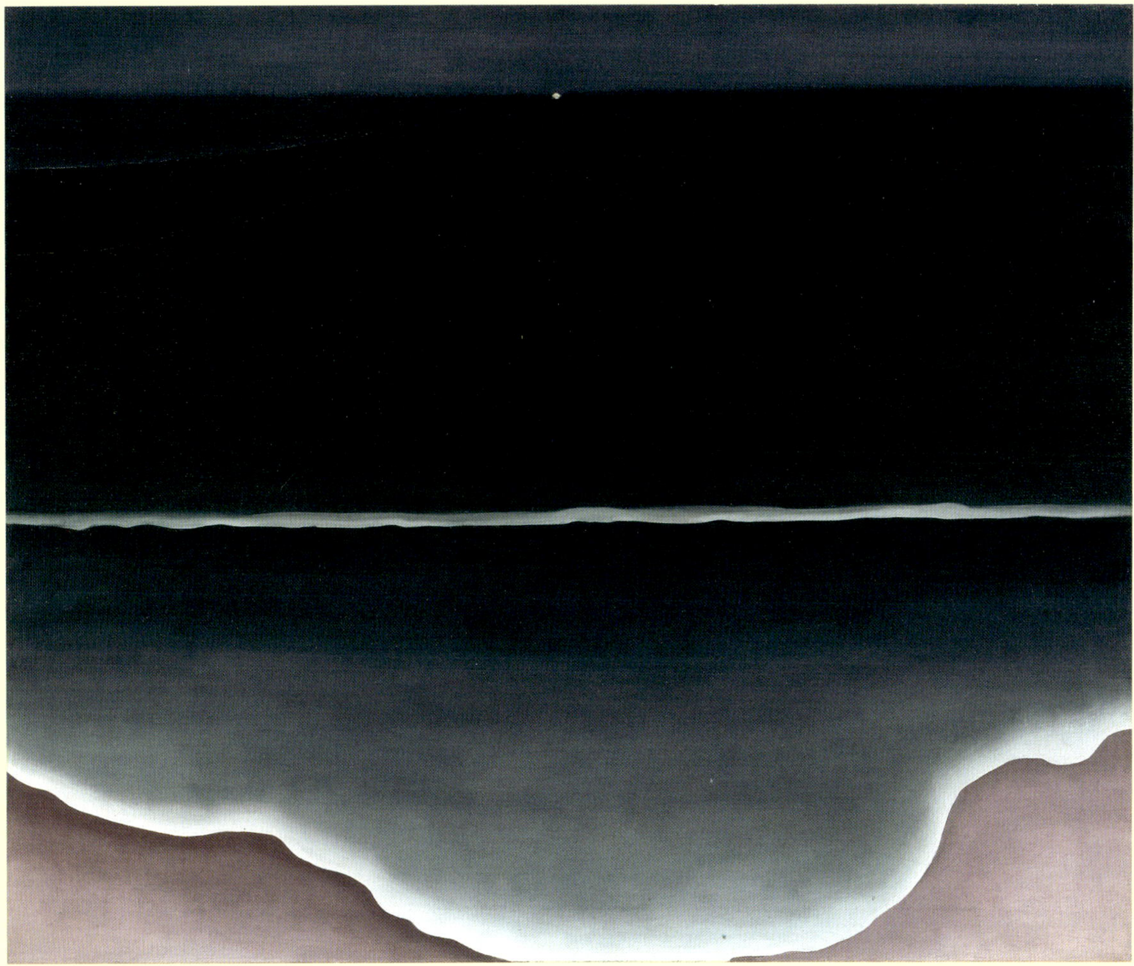

persistently imposed on her paintings for more than a decade.[26] "I am particularly amused and pleased to have the emotional faucet turned off—no matter what other one you turn on. It is grand," she penned to McBride that January after reading his review.[27] Further, the exhibition drew crowds and O'Keeffe realized strong sales of her works, most important among them *The Shelton with Sunspots, N.Y.* (pl. 12), which sold for an impressive six thousand dollars, as well as *East River from the Shelton, No. III* (pl. 55).[28] Alongside private collectors, museums made their first acquisitions: in 1926 the Phillips Memorial Art Gallery (now the Phillips Collection), Washington, DC, purchased two works, including *Pattern of Leaves* (pl. 4); accessions at the Brooklyn Museum, New York, and the Cleveland Museum of Art (see pl. 30) followed in the coming years.[29] Decades later, O'Keeffe linked the period to her financial independence: "I've made my living selling my paintings since 1927."[30]

Before looking closely at the 1927 Intimate Gallery exhibition, it is helpful to consider O'Keeffe's output and ambitions in the prior couple years, as this backstory set the stage for the successes to come. As she saw it, her first New York should have debuted at her 1925 exhibition at the Anderson Galleries, part of a group show Stieglitz organized called *Seven Americans*. O'Keeffe was keen to paint the city and make the subject matter her own. *New York Street with Moon* (pl. 1) was ready in time for the exhibition, but Stieglitz did not hang it. "My New Yorks would turn the world over," she asserted to McBride, likely in March 1925, and expressed her frustration, adding, "And that New York business goes round in my head."[31] Decades later, O'Keeffe recalled what happened: "The men decided they didn't want me to paint New York. . . . They wouldn't let me [hang the picture]. They told me to 'leave New York to the men.' I was furious!"[32] She intended to show this New York composition alongside another novel effort, that of

FIG. 9
O'Keeffe. *Wave, Night*, 1928. Oil on canvas; 76.2 × 91.4 cm (30 × 36 in.). Addison Gallery of American Art, Purchased as the gift of Charles L. Stillman (PA 1922), 1947.33.

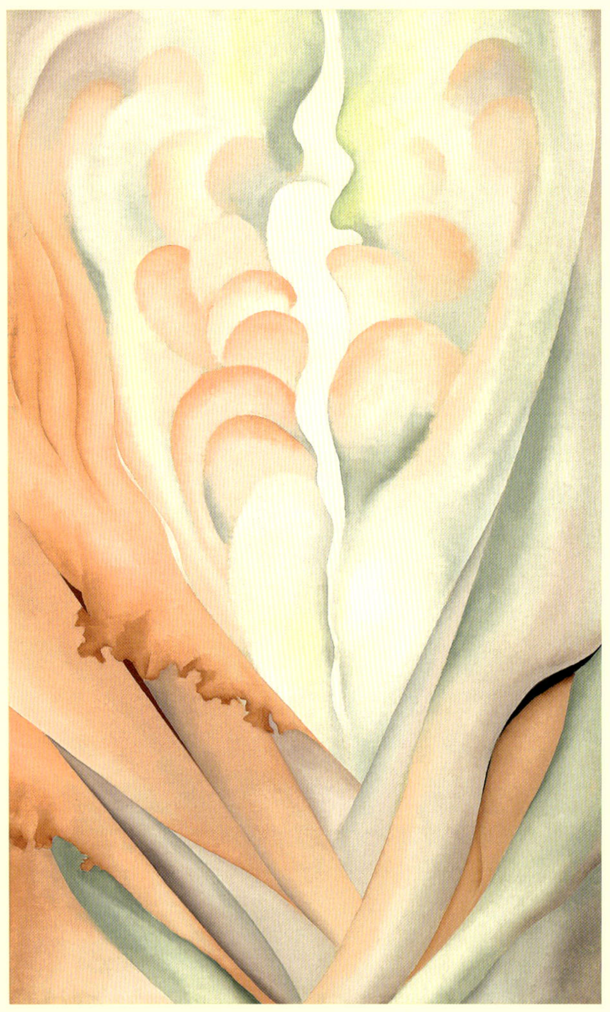

her grandly scaled flowers, including *Flower Abstraction* (fig. 10).[33] The opportunity to demonstrate this aesthetic range would have to wait.

Redemption came soon enough. The artist included *New York Street with Moon* in her solo exhibition at the Intimate Gallery the following year. "It sold on the very first day of the show: the very first picture sold. From then on they *let* me paint New York," O'Keeffe wryly recounted in 1965.[34] The full checklist of the 1926 exhibition is not known, but we can glean details from press accounts and other archives about which works, and what kinds of works, were on view. A *New York Times* review described *New York Street with Moon*, a rendering of the Hotel Chatham at Vanderbilt Avenue and Forty-Eighth Street: "a roof projected into the sky (framed by other roofs and made immaterial by the very heart of the light of changing traffic signals)."[35] The reviewer also called out the Shelton Hotel by name as another painting's subject, confirming that O'Keeffe displayed at least two New Yorks in 1926.[36] Indeed, on the heels of the exhibition's close, the artist executed others. In a letter that March to critic Blanche Matthias, who had published an extensive review in the *Chicago Evening Post*, the artist confided, "I have two new paintings of New York that I think are probably my best paintings. They seem to surprise everyone."[37] In April a feature on O'Keeffe in the *Shelton Spotlight* (see fig. 11), a weekly publication for the "guests of the Shelton," revealed that she had three recently completed oils hanging in her eleventh-floor apartment—two of the Shelton, one of which was certainly *The Shelton with Sunspots, N.Y.*, and the third very possibly *A Street*. On the former, the author stated, "The views of the Shelton exercise a certain magnetism in that they almost force a close study of the play of light and shade. In one painting, the Shelton skyscraper is shown with the sun peeping around the upper turret and the optical illusion of a dozen or more miniature suns scattered over the whole thing. The total effect is one of strange colorful suspense."[38] By spring 1926, O'Keeffe had hit her stride. Her New Yorks were a growing body of work among multiple aesthetic pursuits. And in January 1927, she staged her most important exhibition yet.

The paintings and pastels featured in the exhibition represented an enticing variation of subject matter and form across the artist's range of expression: New Yorks, flowers, things and still lifes, landscapes, and abstractions, some natural, others geometric. A principal throughline of the show was O'Keeffe's approach to material in multiple takes; the checklist reads as a set of series.[39] In this written record of the 1927 exhibition, she front-loaded her serial New Yorks: the Shelton Hotel followed by street-level views and the East River. Then came several series of flowers: dark irises, white and yellow calla lilies, petunias and morning glories, cannas, and other blooms. Next were two still-life series featuring found objects: shells and shingles (with a Maine seascape in between). Views of a Lake George barn and nearby trees followed. Last came a group of formal abstractions. It is unlikely that O'Keeffe hung the

FIG. 10
O'Keeffe. *Flower Abstraction*, 1924. Oil on canvas; 122.2 × 76.2 cm (48 1/8 × 30 in.). Whitney Museum of American Art, New York; 50th Anniversary Gift of Sandra Payson, 85.47.

FIG. 11
T. H. R., "Georgia O'Keeffe, Artist," *Shelton Spotlight*, Apr. 24, 1926. Alfred Stieglitz / Georgia O'Keeffe Archive, Yale Collection of American Literature, Beinecke Rare Book and Manuscript Library, Yale University, New Haven, CT.

THE SHELTON SPOTLIGHT

Published Every Saturday for the Guests of the Shelton.

NEW YORK CITY APRIL 24, 1926

GEORGIA O'KEEFFE, ARTIST

THAT witty, ironic and caustic chronicler of current affairs, *The New Yorker,* said in a recent issue:

"If ever there were a raging, blazing soul mounting to the skies it is that of Georgia O'Keeffe. . . . One O'Keeffe hung in the Grand Central Station would even halt the home-going commuters.

Coming upon an O'Keeffe for the first time, one must feel that it is some sort of phantasy or dream. It seems not to be real because it is so joyous. Surely if the authorities knew, they would pass laws against Georgia O'Keeffe, take away her magic tubes and brushes. America with its eyes on success, must not be dazed by the unproductive glory of unmoral beauty."

Georgia O'Keeffe is considered the foremost modern woman painter of America. She is one of the group of painters sponsored by Alfred Stieglitz at the famous "291," who now have their headquarters in Room 303 at the Anderson Galleries. Her first work to attract attention was a series of black and white abstractions exhibited in 1916. Since then there have been paintings of landscapes, trees, still life, much wondered about abstractions and flowers.

Louis Kalonyme in a recent number of *Arts and Decoration* made the following comment on Miss O'Keeffe's work:

"Though there are greater painters, no one in America can paint the living quality of flowers and branches and leaves as Georgia O'Keeffe does. On her chromatic color scale, whose tones are individual and inimitable and range from the cold fresh green of the sea's mountains of ice to the orange and red moment before the advent of summer twilight, O'Keeffe plays a grand, maternal music which reveals the shape of the world as a woman sees and feels affirmatively toward it. She strips it bare of the defensive veils of false, feminine sentiments and exposes woman as an elementary being, closer to the earth than man."

In her suite on the eleventh floor of the Shelton, that commands a wide sweep of the shifting panorama of the city, Miss O'Keeffe has hung three recently completed paintings which have attracted admiring comment from the few persons privileged to see them. Two of the paintings are of the Shelton itself—but what remarkable studies —athrob with a color, verve (one might almost say a hidden dynamo) that has not been in the power of any other current in-

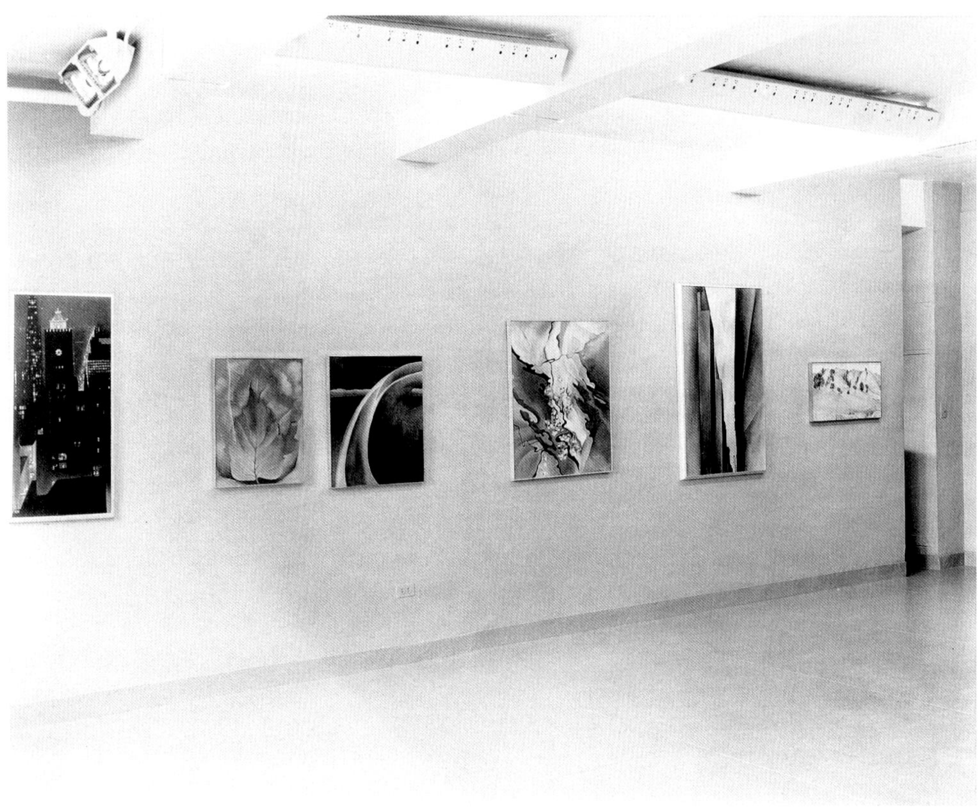

exhibition series by series, based on extant installation views from other shows in the 1920s and 1930s (see fig. 12 and p. 30, fig. 13), opting instead to present visitors with expansive views and distinctive juxtapositions of compositions across categories. But the ordering of the checklist did emphasize that a serial approach extended across her explorations, the New Yorks among them. And in placing three series of New York works at the top of the list, O'Keeffe signaled the importance of this rapidly developing aesthetic project.[40]

The artist executed a number of exterior views of her skyscraper home, including a painting that she ranked among her best, *The Shelton with Sunspots, N.Y.*, as well as "several other 'Sheltons'" that she later destroyed, suggesting the subject matter was an exhilarating yet difficult one.[41] Of the four Shelton works gathered at the 1927 exhibition, we can identify two or possibly three: the two extant paintings of the series, *Shelton Hotel, N.Y., No. I* (pl. 11) and *The Shelton with Sunspots, N.Y.*, along with two others. It is possible that *The Shelton at Night*, which was photographed and published in *Arts and Decoration* in March 1927 (see p. 24, fig. 7), was among the four that year; it definitely featured in her 1928 exhibition at the Intimate Gallery and was destroyed sometime later.[42] Images of other Sheltons have not survived, yet there were almost certainly more than four in the overall series. O'Keeffe had already shown at least one Shelton in 1926, which may or may not have been on view again the following year. Of the several others she ruined in dissatisfaction, some may never have made the cut for exhibition.

FIG. 12
Installation view of *Georgia O'Keeffe: Exhibition of Paintings, 1919–1935*, An American Place, New York, Jan. 27–Mar. 11, 1935. Photograph by Alfred Stieglitz. Georgia O'Keeffe Museum, Georgia O'Keeffe Foundation Photographs, MS.57.

The three known Shelton compositions demonstrate an ambition to transform the structure with her brush in markedly different ways. In *Shelton Hotel, N.Y., No. I*, O'Keeffe emphasized the geometric plays of form inspired by the skyscraper's repeating windows and multiple setbacks, reinforcing this upward view with two more tall structures encroaching on each side. *The Shelton with Sunspots, N.Y.* reveals a visual field from about the same location on Lexington Avenue, facing east with the mass of the Shelton at center, flanked by other rising forms. In this case, O'Keeffe combined

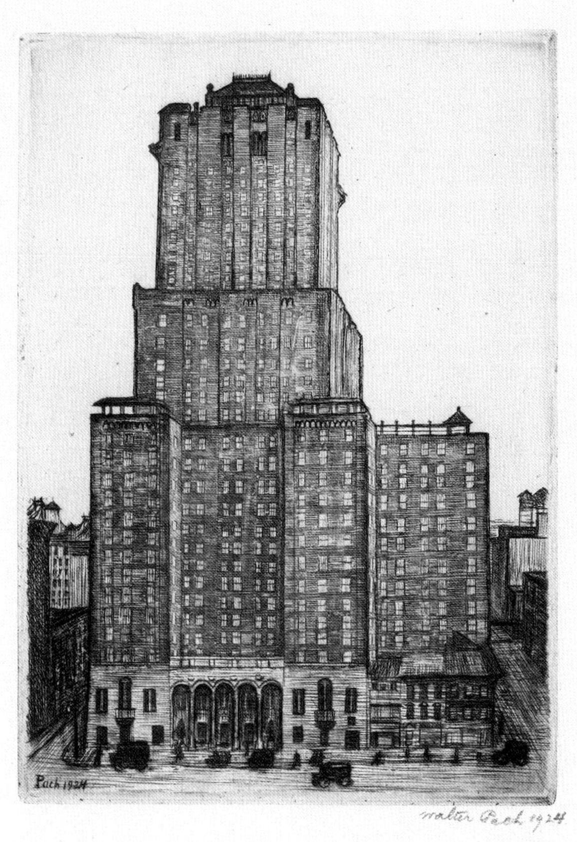

the study of geometric shapes with waves, orbs, and flares of light, softening her hard edges and endowing the composition with a measure of force and movement. *The Shelton at Night* appears to be a study of light—the artificial glow of the streetlight in the foreground; the high-rise's tessellated, illuminated windows; and the natural light of the moon and sky. Compositionally, these three paintings show O'Keeffe working a subject toward innovative modernist ends, quite different from that of her contemporary Walter Pach, for instance, who created an etching of the Shelton Hotel in 1924 (fig. 13) that describes the entire structure in legible detail from an elevated position across the street.

The series on the checklist that followed O'Keeffe's Sheltons, street views, and East River scenes focused on irises, the boldest of these being *Black Iris* (fig. 14). Positioned at the front of the picture plane, the enlarged blossom fills the space, extending beyond the composition's borders. The dark purples and charcoals of the petals comprising the lower half endow the flower, however ephemeral, with a sense of weight and permanence. At the top, the petals and their gentle folds appear translucent, as if illuminated from behind, especially in the modulated soft pinks and grays. The black irises were found objects of a different sort, not collected from nature on walks around Lake George, for instance, but sought out in New York City flower shops during the few weeks of spring when they would bloom.[43] And so we can imagine the artist taking a purposeful walk through her neighborhood to select a specimen, bringing the iris home to her Shelton apartment, and painting the flower in multiple takes, with views of the East River around her as she worked.

Another subject on view in the 1927 exhibition was a seven-painting series featuring a sea shell and an old shingle—two of the artist's things that catalyzed her considerable exploration toward varied ends. O'Keeffe arranged the found objects on a table in her room at Lake George. Some of the compositions read easily as still lifes, such as *Shell and Old Shingle No. II* (fig. 15), in which she rendered details of the shingle as well as those of the underside of the clam shell within the setting's shallow space. The shingle casts a shadow on the wall behind and the flattened form of a leaf at left draws from the room's patterned wallpaper. Other investigations resulted in organic abstractions further removed from the things themselves, as in the lyrical *Shell and Old Shingle VI* (pl. 27). And in one work, O'Keeffe's handheld object transformed into a landscape. In 1976 the artist recalled how *Shell and Old Shingle No. VII* (pl. 28) emerged: "After painting the shell and shingle many times, I did a misty landscape of the mountain across the lake, and the mountain became the shape of the shingle—the mountain I saw out my window, the shingle on the table in my room."[44]

O'Keeffe demonstrated tremendous dexterity when it came to scale. She could make the small monumental, transforming one thing into something else, such as a shingle into a mountain. Or she could reconceive how we see objects in the world—taking flowers from minuscule to magnified. In 1962 O'Keeffe connected this scaling up of flowers with the changes to her New York environs, recollecting: "I'll make them big like the huge buildings going up. People will be startled; they'll *have* to look at them—and

FIG. 13
Walter Pach (American, 1883–1958). *The Shelton, New York*, 1924. Etching and aquatint; 17.9 × 12.9 cm (7 1/16 × 5 1/16 in.). The Metropolitan Museum of Art, New York, gift of Alexander M. Bing, 1928, 28.31.24.

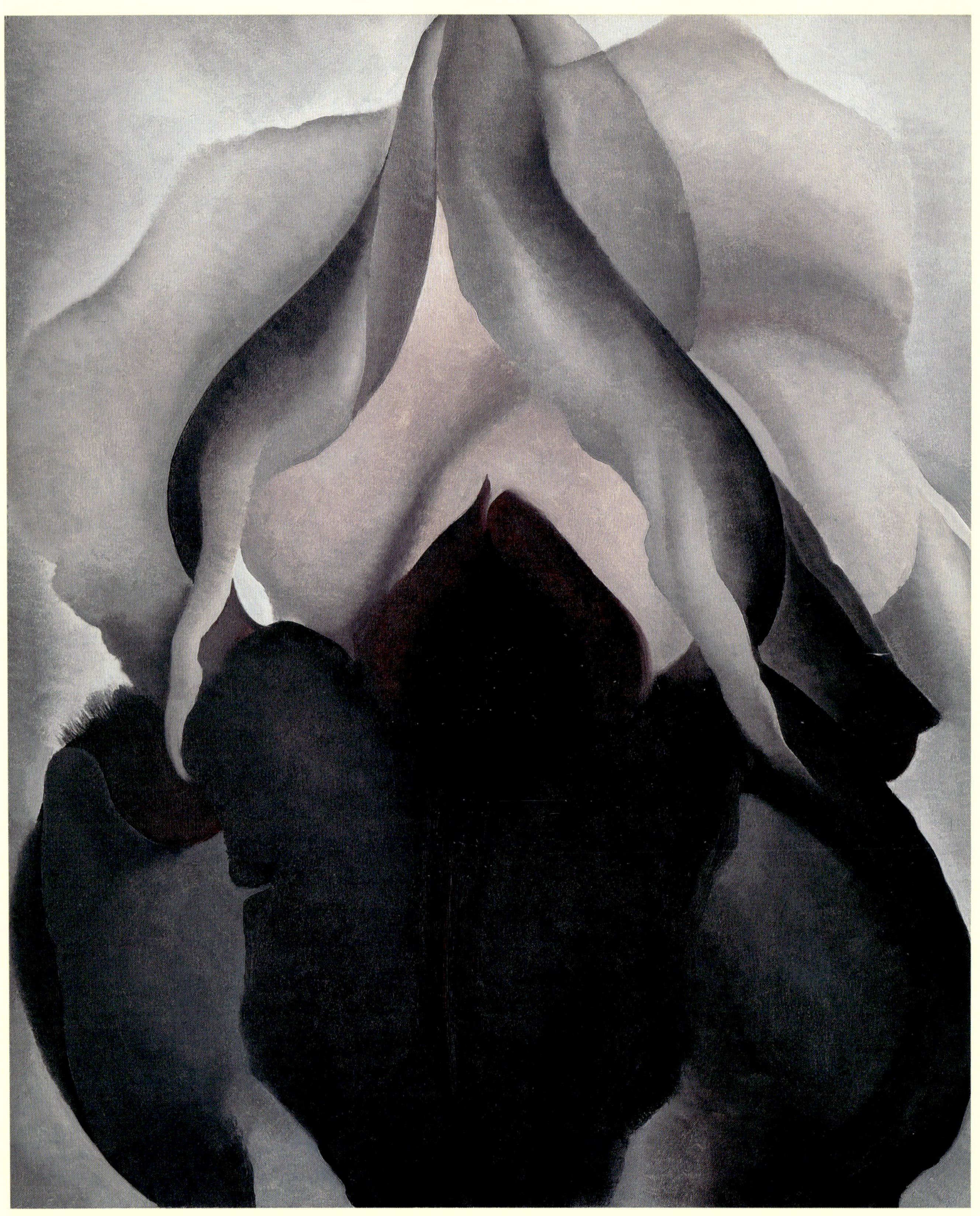

FIG. 14
O'Keeffe. *Black Iris*, 1926. Oil on canvas; 91.4 × 75.9 cm (36 × 29 ⅞ in.). The Metropolitan Museum of Art, New York, Alfred Stieglitz Collection, 1969, 69.278.1.

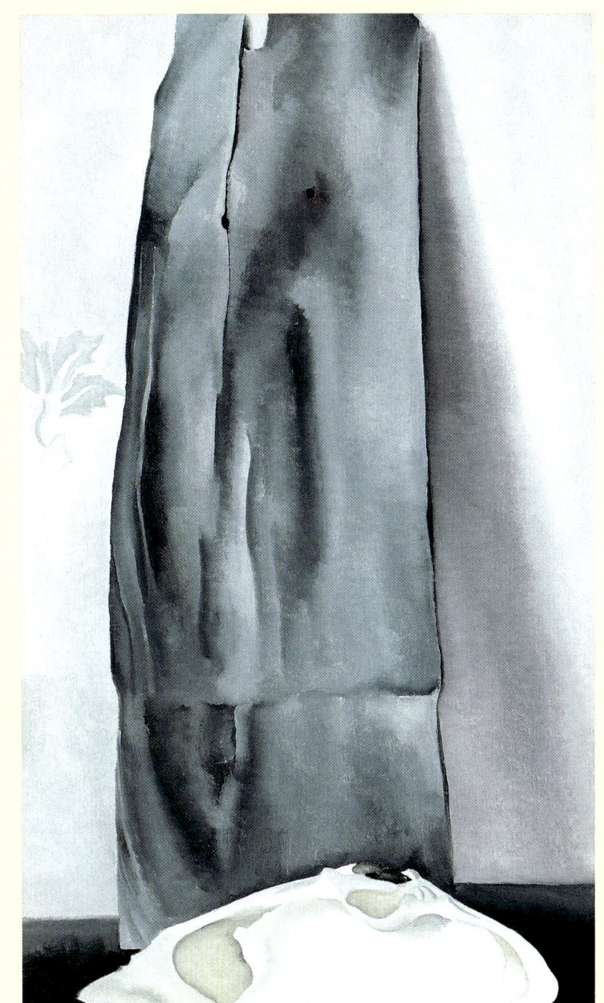

they did."[45] Manipulations of scale likewise worked in the other direction, as with the vast landscapes or cityscapes she contained within her easel-sized canvases. O'Keeffe called this out in the press. In 1946 she told the story of a gallery visitor who asked, "Why do you paint flowers so large?" O'Keeffe explained, "I pointed to a picture of the East River and said, 'You'd never ask me why I make the East River so small.'"[46] Flowers and New Yorks were part and parcel of the same aesthetic project; she labored on one subject in view of the other.

Following the success of the 1927 exhibition, O'Keeffe continued to show the great variety of her work at Stieglitz's gallery and beyond, expanding her field of vision to Southwestern subjects beginning with her 1930 exhibition at An American Place.[47] Harmonizing with the imposing forms of skyscrapers and flowers were crosses, rocks, and adobe structures (see pls. 61, 63, and 69 and p. 30, fig. 13). Like her street-level New Yorks, O'Keeffe painted upward views of trees, including the dizzying and celestial *Lawrence Tree* (fig. 16) and *Dead Tree Bear Lake Taos* (pl. 64). Two years later, in *Manhattan* (pl. 19)—the central panel of a mural triptych she designed for an exhibition at the Museum of Modern Art in New York—the artist floated renderings of three flowers atop an expansive array of flat, geometric skyscrapers. These evoked the artificial flowers fabricated out of paper and cloth that she had encountered in New Mexico.[48] Throughout her career but especially in the 1920s and 1930s, O'Keeffe readily made connections across subject, scale, and site—in artworks themselves and in the exhibitions that showcased them.

From 1925 to the early 1930s, O'Keeffe's New Yorks proved integral to her diverse aesthetic explorations. The intensity of that period—her attempts to paint the city as her own—would not be matched again. Yet the project did not disappear entirely in later years. In 1949, the year O'Keeffe left New York and moved permanently to New Mexico (having finished the immense task of settling Stieglitz's estate), she focused on one of the city's iconic structures, the Brooklyn Bridge. She rendered several drawings, including a large charcoal (see pl. 37), and completed a grandly scaled painting (see pl. 38). In these works, O'Keeffe honed in on the arches of the masonry towers, the cutouts of sky they framed, and the animated network of lines suggested by the suspended cables.[49] Sometime in the 1970s, O'Keeffe, then an octogenarian, revisited a New York picture first shown at the 1927 exhibition, *City Night* (pl. 21). The reprised composition, *Untitled (City Night)* (pl. 72), has grander proportions and the addition of a few stars in the evening sky, but it otherwise follows the formal layout of the earlier painting. What prompted O'Keeffe to (re)make one of her prominent New Yorks decades after she had lived in the city? Perhaps a clue can be found in the large-format publication she produced in 1976, *Georgia O'Keeffe*. More treatise than memoir, and a legacy-shaping endeavor to be sure, the book juxtaposes the artist's own words with color reproductions of more than one hundred works spanning her career.[50] Here, amid key New Yorks—the Hotel Chatham, the Shelton, the East River, the Radiator Building—and the

FIG. 15
O'Keeffe. *Shell and Old Shingle No. II*, 1926. Oil on canvas; 76.8 × 46 cm (30 1/4 × 18 1/8 in.). Museum of Fine Arts, Boston, Alfred Stieglitz Collection—Bequest of Georgia O'Keeffe, 1987.536.

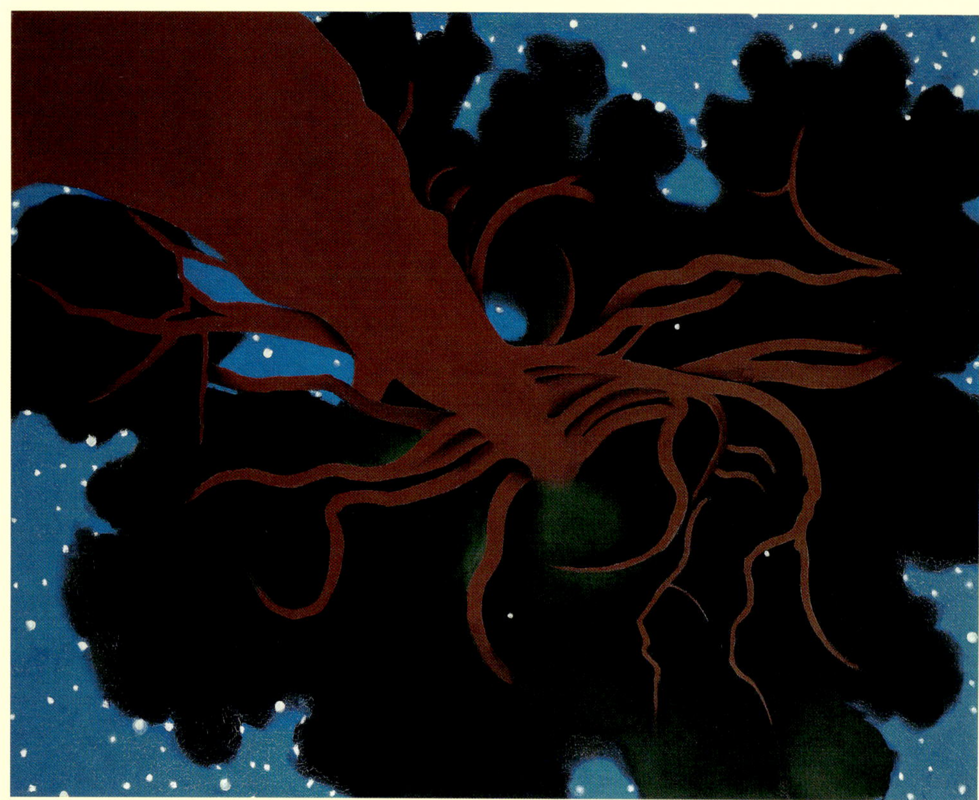

finely tuned stories she shared about them, O'Keeffe signaled that the project of painting New York remained unfinished: "When you live up high, the snow and rain go down and away from you instead of coming toward you from above. I was never able to do anything with that. There were many other things that I meant to paint. I still see them when I am in the Big City."[51]

FIG. 16
O'Keeffe. *The Lawrence Tree*, 1929. Oil on canvas; 78.7 × 101.6 cm (31 × 40 in.). Wadsworth Atheneum Museum of Art, The Ella Gallup Sumner and Mary Catlin Sumner Collection Fund, 1981.23.

NOTES

1. Georgia O'Keeffe to Mitchell Kennerley, Jan. 20, 1929, box 6, Mitchell Kennerley Papers, Archives and Manuscripts Division, New York Public Library.

2. On the term "my New Yorks," see, for example, Georgia O'Keeffe to Henry McBride, [Mar. 1925?]; and O'Keeffe to Dorothy Brett, mid-Feb. 1932, reprinted in Jack Cowart and Juan Hamilton, with Sarah Greenough, *Georgia O'Keeffe: Art and Letters*, exh. cat. (Washington, DC: National Gallery of Art, in association with Boston: New York Graphic Society Books / Little, Brown, 1987), 179, 206. On her collected objects and still lifes, see Elizabeth Hutton Turner, *Georgia O'Keeffe: The Poetry of Things*, exh. cat. (Washington, DC: Phillips Collection; New Haven, CT: Yale University Press, in association with the Dallas Museum of Art, 1999).

3. The series includes a painting once in the collection of the Art Institute of Chicago and now missing, *East River from the Shelton (30th Story)* (p. 40, fig. 5); see Barbara Buhler Lynes, *Georgia O'Keeffe: Catalogue Raisonné*, vol. 2 (New Haven, CT: Yale University Press, 1999), 1105, no. 83.

4. In addition to O'Keeffe's letter to Kennerley, in which she discusses several works in the 1929 Intimate Gallery exhibition (see note 1), at least two press accounts describe a work in the exhibition that matches *Pink Dish and Green Leaves*. One critic wrote, "The latest work from her brush [*sic*], a still life—pink bowl against a window with an urban view is definitely decorative, though nothing that Miss O'Keeffe does could be called decorative in any superficial sense." "Georgia O'Keeffe," *New York Times*, Feb. 10, 1929, 124. Further, there is a typescript of an unsigned Intimate Gallery review that discusses the work in detail. The typescript is dated March 1928, but it must be from the following year as the critic names five other works by their exact titles on the 1929 exhibition checklist. On *Pink Dish and Green Leaves*, the critic wrote: "None the less true but much vaguer, much greyer, is the other painting [*sic*] of the East River. A shadowy haze envelopes everythings [*sic*].... In the greyness ascends a [skyscraper]. Contrasting with this smoky outline of man's mechanistic skill stands on a marble window-sill in front... a glass vase holding two green leaves. The vase is bordered in a delightful rosy pink, fresh and exuberant. The leaves are a rich velvety green." Unsigned Intimate Gallery review, typescript, dated Mar. 1928 [likely 1929], box 222, folder 3965, Alfred Stieglitz / Georgia O'Keeffe Archive, Yale Collection of American Literature, Beinecke Rare Book and Manuscript Library, Yale University, New Haven, CT (hereafter Stieglitz / O'Keeffe Archive, Yale). The other East River composition in the exhibition was *East River from the 30th Story of the Shelton Hotel* (pl. 57), likewise described in detail in the Yale typescript. Presumably, then, these two works are those titled "East River from the Shelton, No. VI" and "East River from the Shelton, No. VII" in "List of Paintings," *Georgia O'Keeffe: Paintings, 1928*, the Intimate Gallery, Feb. 4–Mar. 17, 1929. From the *New York Times* article, it is possible to read the "two more or less literal views of the East River from the Shelton" as distinct from the description of the "pink bowl against a window with an urban view" that follows; in that case, *Pink Dish and Green Leaves* may have been on view but not included on the checklist.

5. O'Keeffe wrote to her sister Catherine O'Keeffe Klenert on May 29, 1929, "My latest is of eggs in a pink dish—three white eggs." Lynes, *Georgia O'Keeffe: Catalogue Raisonné*, vol. 1 (New Haven, CT: Yale University Press, 1999), 386, no. 647. In a review of O'Keeffe's 1930 exhibition at An American Place, a critic wrote, "Among individual paintings in the show, not related to any group, we liked best 'The Portrait of a Farm-house' [pl. 65], with its almost architectural matter-of-factness, and a still life of eggs in a pink compote, set upon a cover of exquisitely painted white." Georgia O'Keeffe: An American Place," *Art News* 28, no. 21 (Feb. 22, 1930): 10, 12. This description suggests that the painting was exhibited in 1930, although it does not appear on the checklist by its title or a similar one; for the checklist, see Lynes, *Catalogue Raisonné*, 2:1118.

6. Frances O'Brien, "Americans We Like: Georgia O'Keeffe," *The Nation*, Oct. 12, 1927, 361.

7. "A Giant Hotel for None But Men," *New York Hotel Record*, Sept. 19, 1923, 30, clipping in "Shelton Hotel" folder, George B. Corsa Hotel Collection, New-York Historical Society.

8. For a period assessment of its architectural features, see Claude Bragdon, "The Shelton Hotel, Arthur Loomis Harmon, Architect," *Architectural Record* 58, no. 1 (July 1925): 1–18. For views and plans, see also Oliver Reagan, ed., *American Architecture of the Twentieth Century*, vol. 1 (New York: Architectural Book Publishing, 1927), pls. 1–6. In various narrative descriptions and plans, the setbacks are designated at either the fifteenth or sixteenth floor, and then at the twenty-first or twenty-second floor. This discrepancy may be due to whether or not authors or publishers accounted for the thirteenth floor in their numbering (see p. 32n36). On the zoning changes that precipitated such architectural innovations as they relate to the Shelton Hotel and O'Keeffe, see Lee Ann Custer, "Urban 'Voids': Picturing Light, Air, and Open Space in New York, 1890–1935" (PhD diss., University of Pennsylvania, 2021), 155–220. I thank Lee Ann Custer for sharing a copy of her dissertation before its publication.

9. "The Shelton, a Residence for Men," *New York Times*, Mar. 2, 1924, RPA8; and "Hotel for the Bachelor Opens Its Doors to Women," *New York Times*, Oct. 12, 1924, X11.

10. They stayed at the Shelton Hotel November 19–December 17, 1924. On November 17, from Lake George, Stieglitz wrote to Sherwood Anderson, "We'll be on the way ourselves day after to-morrow [*sic*]." Alfred Stieglitz to Sherwood Anderson, Nov. 17, 1924, box 29, folder 1496, Sherwood Anderson Papers, Newberry Library, Chicago (hereafter Anderson Papers, Newberry). On November 20, Stieglitz wrote to Ida O'Keeffe on Shelton stationery and she replied a few days later, "Are you still at the Shelton?" Stieglitz to Ida O'Keeffe, Nov. 20, 1924; and Ida O'Keeffe to Stieglitz, Nov. 25, 1924, both box 37, folder 889, Stieglitz / O'Keeffe Archive, Yale. Additional letters written from the Shelton include Stieglitz to Ida O'Keeffe, Nov. 26, 1924, box 37, folder 889, Stieglitz / O'Keeffe Archive, Yale; and Stieglitz to Anderson, Nov. 27 and Dec. 7, 1924, box 29, folder 1496, Anderson Papers, Newberry.

11. Roxana Robinson, *Georgia O'Keeffe: A Life*, expand. ed. (New York: Harper and Row, 1989; Waltham, MA: Brandeis University, 2020), 229; Alfred Stieglitz to Sherwood Anderson, Apr. 9, 1924, box 29, folder 1495, Anderson Papers, Newberry; and Anderson to Stieglitz, Apr. 16, 1924, box 2, folder 38, Stieglitz / O'Keeffe Archive, Yale.

12. In December 1924 Stieglitz wrote to

Anderson, "Since yesterday night Georgia & I are located on the top floor of a brownstone 4 story building." Alfred Stieglitz to Sherwood Anderson, Dec. 18, 1924, box 29, folder 1496, Anderson Papers, Newberry. On June 1, 1925, Stieglitz wrote to Anderson, "We leave for Lake George on the 3rd—We are both glad—still we hate to give up 38 E. 58. It has been clean & quiet—& simple. We can't afford to keep it & not use it for five months. We did make an offer—but the landlord has said nothing." Stieglitz to Anderson, June 1, 1925, box 29, folder 1497, Anderson Papers, Newberry.

13. Alfred Stieglitz to Sherwood Anderson, Dec. 9, 1925, box 29, folder 1498, Anderson Papers, Newberry.

14. The couple likely moved into the Shelton on November 16, 1925; see Alfred Stieglitz to Sherwood Anderson, Nov. 30, 1925, box 29, folder 1498, Anderson Papers, Newberry. It is reasonable to assume that they moved into an apartment on the eleventh floor, as they are recorded as living there in April 1926, which was part of their seasonal stay at the hotel, late 1925–spring 1926; see T. H. R., "Georgia O'Keeffe, Artist," *Shelton Spotlight*, Apr. 24, 1926, n.p., clipping in box 235, folder 4127, Stieglitz / O'Keeffe Archive, Yale. O'Keeffe's description of the apartment's two-room layout and three exposures in a letter to her sister Ida aligns with a particular apartment location on the third through fourteenth floors; see Georgia O'Keeffe and Alfred Stieglitz to Ida O'Keeffe, [Nov. 1925], box 37, folder 891, Stieglitz / O'Keeffe Archive, Yale (for the dating of this letter, see pp31–32n23). The next season, late 1926–spring 1927, they lived on the twenty-eighth floor in apartment 2803; see Georgia O'Keeffe to Catherine O'Keeffe Klenert, Dec. 24, 1926, quoted in Robinson, *Georgia O'Keeffe*, 288; and John Kerfoot to Georgia O'Keeffe, Mar. 23, 1927 ("2803" written on envelope), box 197, folder 3390, Stieglitz / O'Keeffe Archive, Yale. The following season, late 1927–spring 1928, they likely moved directly into apartment 3003 on the thirtieth floor (thereafter their preferred location), as they are recorded there in February 1928; see Sherwood Anderson to Stieglitz, Feb. 16, 1928, box 13, folder 599, Anderson Papers, Newberry. O'Brien's article, "Americans We Like," published in October 1927, located the couple on the twenty-eighth floor, but the interview likely took place in spring 1927—the prior season—when they were living two floors down, since O'Keeffe and Stieglitz were still at Lake George on October 20, 1927; see Stieglitz to Ida O'Keeffe, box 37, folder 891, Stieglitz / O'Keeffe Archive, Yale. In 1934 they lived in apartment 2915 on the twenty-ninth floor; see Jean Toomer to Georgia O'Keeffe, Feb. 20, 1934 ("2915" written on envelope), box 216, folder 3831, Stieglitz / O'Keeffe Archive, Yale.

15. Bragdon, "The Shelton Hotel," 18.

16. The residential experience for O'Keeffe must have been predominantly one of whiteness, yet the skyscraper as a new architectural form in the late nineteenth and early twentieth centuries also destabilized racial perception in urban spaces. Its vantage points, scale, and the patterns of movement it introduced altered the ways in which race was experienced and read by city dwellers. See Adrienne Brown, *The Black Skyscraper: Architecture and the Perception of Race* (Baltimore: Johns Hopkins University Press, 2017).

17. Quoted in B. Vladimir Berman, "She Painted the Lily and Got $25,000 and Fame for Doing It!" *New York Evening Graphic Magazine Section*, May 12, 1928, 3-M.

18. Lillian Sabine, "Record Price for Living Artist," *Brooklyn Sunday Eagle Magazine*, May 27, 1928, 11.

19. Ibid. Sabine noted two paintings on easels during her visit. For an account of the paintings O'Keeffe hung in her apartment, see T. H. R., "Georgia O'Keeffe," n.p.

20. Georgia O'Keeffe to Alfred Stieglitz, Sep. 15, 1926, reprinted in Sarah Greenough, ed., *My Faraway One: Selected Letters of Georgia O'Keeffe and Alfred Stieglitz*, vol. 1, *1915–1933* (New Haven, CT: Yale University Press, 2011), 373.

21. Georgia O'Keeffe to Alfred Stieglitz, July 10, 1931, reprinted in ibid., 596. "When she arrived at her apartment in the Shelton last autumn with barrels and boxes of bones from the New Mexico desert she felt as if she were bringing back some rare treasure." Ishbel Ross, "Bones of Desert Blaze Art Trail of Miss O'Keeffe," *New York Herald Tribune*, Dec. 29, 1931, 3. On O'Keeffe's collected things and the Southwest, see Lauren Kroiz, *Creative Composites: Modernism, Race, and the Stieglitz Circle* (Berkeley: University of California Press; Washington, DC: Phillips Collection, 2012), 173–84.

22. Unsigned Intimate Gallery review, typescript, Stieglitz / O'Keeffe Archive, Yale.

23. Louis Kalonyme, "Scaling the Peak of the Art Season," *Arts and Decoration* 26 (Mar. 1927): 93.

24. Lewis Mumford, "O'Keefe [*sic*] and Matisse," *New Republic*, Mar. 2, 1927, reprinted in Barbara Buhler Lynes, *O'Keeffe, Stieglitz, and the Critics, 1916–1929* (1989; Chicago: University of Chicago Press, 1991), 264.

25. See "List of Paintings," *Georgia O'Keeffe: Paintings, 1926*, the Intimate Gallery, Jan. 11–Feb. 27, 1927.

26. Henry McBride, "Georgia O'Keefe's [*sic*] Work Shown: Fellow Painters of Little Group Become Fairly Lyrical Over It," *New York Sun*, Jan. 15, 1927, reprinted in Lynes, *O'Keeffe, Stieglitz, and the Critics*, 259.

27. Georgia O'Keeffe to Henry McBride, Jan. 16, 1927, reprinted in Cowart, Hamilton, with Greenough, *Georgia O'Keeffe*, 185. Numerous critics placed O'Keeffe's art in a double bind, using essentializing, gendered language to describe and interpret it while also praising and validating it; on the artist's early criticism, see Lynes, *O'Keeffe, Stieglitz, and the Critics*, 3–26.

28. Some nine thousand people visited the exhibition during its more than six-week run; see Greenough, *My Faraway One*, 377–78. On the sale of *The Shelton with Sunspots, N.Y.*, see Alfred Stieglitz to Duncan Phillips, Feb. 2 and Feb. 13, 1927, box 53, folder 2, Directorial Correspondence of Duncan Phillips, Phillips Collection Archives. A first payment for *East River from the Shelton No. III* is discussed in Arthur Schwab to Stieglitz, Apr. 14, 1927, box 8, folder 191, Stieglitz / O'Keeffe Archive, Yale.

29. In 1928 the Brooklyn Museum accessioned the gift of *Black Pansy & Forget-Me-Nots (Pansy)* (1926), which was among the works shown at the Intimate Gallery in 1927 and purchased by Mrs. Alfred S. Rossin; see Lynes, *Catalogue Raisonné*, 1:312, no. 550. In 1930 the Cleveland Museum of Art purchased *White Flower* (pl. 30).

30. Mary Lynn Kotz, "A Day with Georgia O'Keeffe," *Art News* 76, no. 10 (Dec. 1977): 44.

31. Georgia O'Keeffe to Henry McBride, [Mar. 1925?], reprinted in Cowart, Hamilton, with Greenough, *Georgia O'Keeffe*, 179.

32. Ralph Looney, "Georgia O'Keeffe,"

Atlantic Monthly 215, no. 4 (Apr. 1965): 108. For additional retellings, see Katharine Kuh, *The Artist's Voice: Talks with Seventeen Artists* (New York: Harper and Row, 1962), 191; Georgia O'Keeffe, *Georgia O'Keeffe* (New York: Viking Press, 1976), n.p., opp. pls. 17–18; and Kotz, "A Day with Georgia O'Keeffe," 44–45.

33. For O'Keeffe's portion of the 1925 checklist, see Lynes, *Catalogue Raisonné*, 2:1116.

34. Looney, "Georgia O'Keeffe," 108.

35. "Foujita's Art Is Seen in Exhibition Here," *New York Times*, Feb. 14, 1926, X12. Hotel Chatham has since been destroyed.

36. In 1991 Anna Chave published an important essay on O'Keeffe and New York, which has often been cited in the scholarship since then. However, she stated incorrectly the number of New York works shown in 1926, 1927, and 1928 at nine, six, and three, respectively. These numbers align instead with the checklists for the 1927, 1928, and 1929 exhibitions—a mistake likely made because the dates in the title of the exhibitions correspond to when O'Keeffe made the works, the year prior, not to the dates of each exhibition's run. Further, she misnamed the Beverly Hotel, calling it the Berkley Hotel. See Anna C. Chave, "'Who Will Paint New York?': 'The World's New Art Center' and the Skyscraper Paintings of Georgia O'Keeffe," *American Art* 5, nos. 1–2 (Winter–Spring 1991): 98, 100.

37. Georgia O'Keeffe to Blanche Matthias, Mar. 1926, reprinted in Cowart, Hamilton, with Greenough, *Georgia O'Keeffe*, 183. For Matthias's review, see Blanche C. Matthias, "Georgia O'Keeffe and the Intimate Gallery," *Chicago Evening Post, Magazine of the Art World*, Mar. 2, 1926, 1.

38. T. H. R., "Georgia O'Keeffe," n.p.

39. "List of Paintings," *Georgia O'Keeffe: Paintings, 1926*. O'Keeffe employed this serial strategy in numerous exhibitions at Stieglitz's galleries.

40. See Peter R. Kalb, *The New York Cityscapes of Georgia O'Keeffe and Margaret Bourke-White* (New York: Midmarch Arts Press, 2003), 15.

41. "Miss O'Keefe [*sic*] has painted several versions of the Shelton." Henry McBride, "Georgia O'Keefe's [*sic*] Recent Work," *New York Sun*, Jan. 14, 1928, reprinted in Lynes, *O'Keeffe, Stieglitz, and the Critics*, 275. In 1976, O'Keeffe recollected, "There were several other 'Sheltons' that I destroyed because they weren't as good as the 'Sunspots.'" O'Keeffe, *Georgia O'Keeffe*, n.p., opp. pl. 19.

42. Kalonyme, "Scaling the Peak of the Art Season," 57; "List of Paintings—1927," *O'Keeffe Exhibition*, the Intimate Gallery, Jan.–Feb., 1928. See also Lynes, *Catalogue Raisonné*, 2:1105, no. 84.

43. O'Keeffe, *Georgia O'Keeffe*, n.p., opp. pl. 30.

44. Ibid., n.p., opp. pls. 51–52; quote opp. pl. 52.

45. Kuh, *Artist's Voice*, 191.

46. Mary Braggiotti, "Her Worlds Are Many," *New York Post*, May 16, 1946, clipping in box 236, folder 4142, Stieglitz / O'Keeffe Archive, Yale.

47. See announcement *Georgia O'Keeffe: 27 New Paintings, New Mexico, New York, Lake George, Etc.*, An American Place, Feb. 7–Mar. 17, 1930; for the checklist, see Lynes, *Catalogue Raisonné*, 2:1118.

48. See "O'Keeffe," in *Murals by American Painters and Photographers*, exh. cat. (New York: Museum of Modern Art, 1932), n.p.; and Wanda M. Corn, "Painting Big—O'Keeffe's *Manhattan*," *American Art* 20, no. 2 (Summer 2006): 22–25.

49. The painting was exhibited in 1949 at the Downtown Gallery, owned by Edith Halpert (who became O'Keeffe's dealer), and at An American Place in 1950, after which the latter closed its doors for good.

50. On O'Keeffe's undertaking to write, design, and publish this book, see Wanda M. Corn, "Telling Tales: Georgia O'Keeffe on Georgia O'Keeffe," *American Art* 23, no. 2 (Summer 2009): 54–79.

51. O'Keeffe, *Georgia O'Keeffe*, n.p., opp. pl. 20.

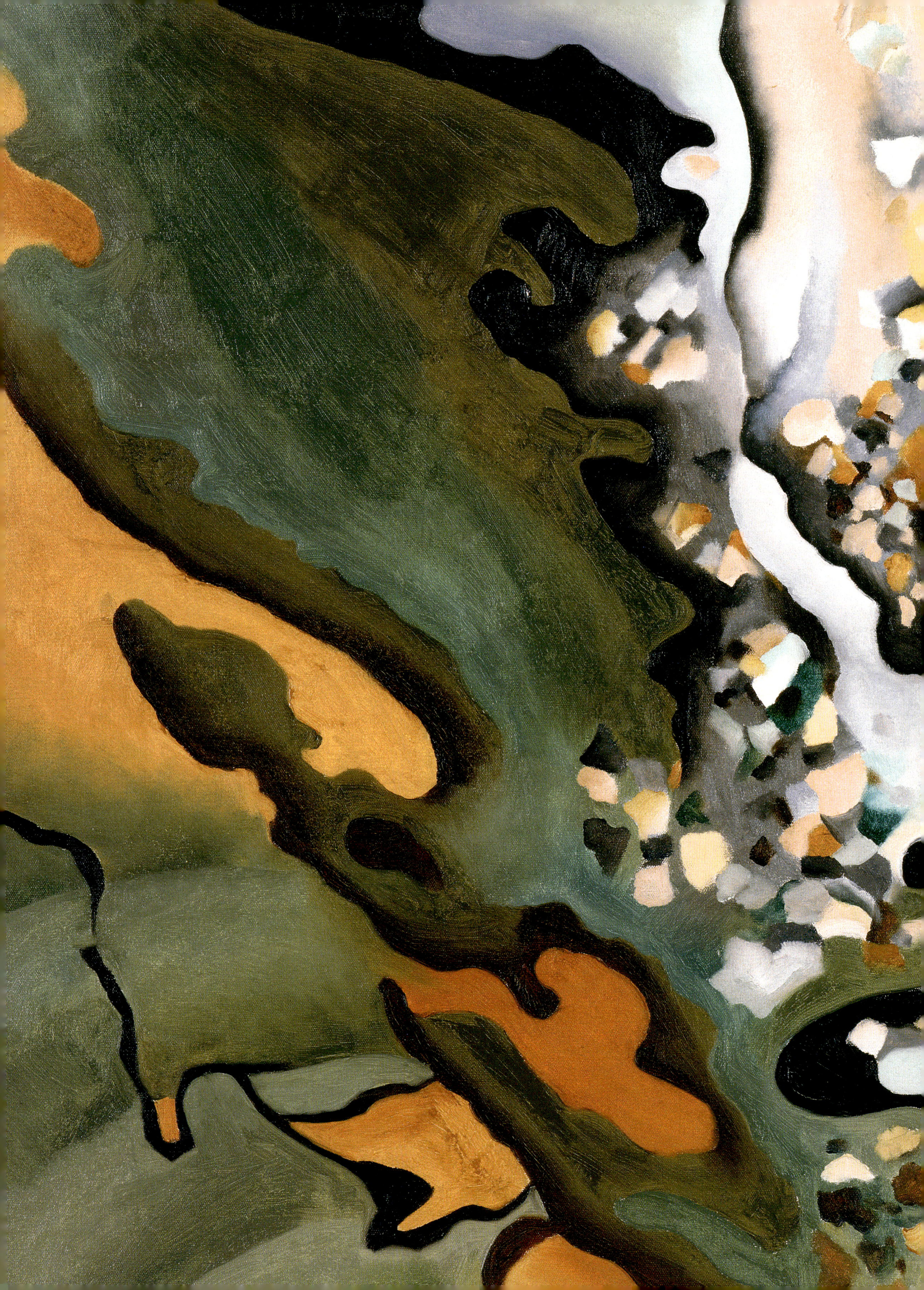

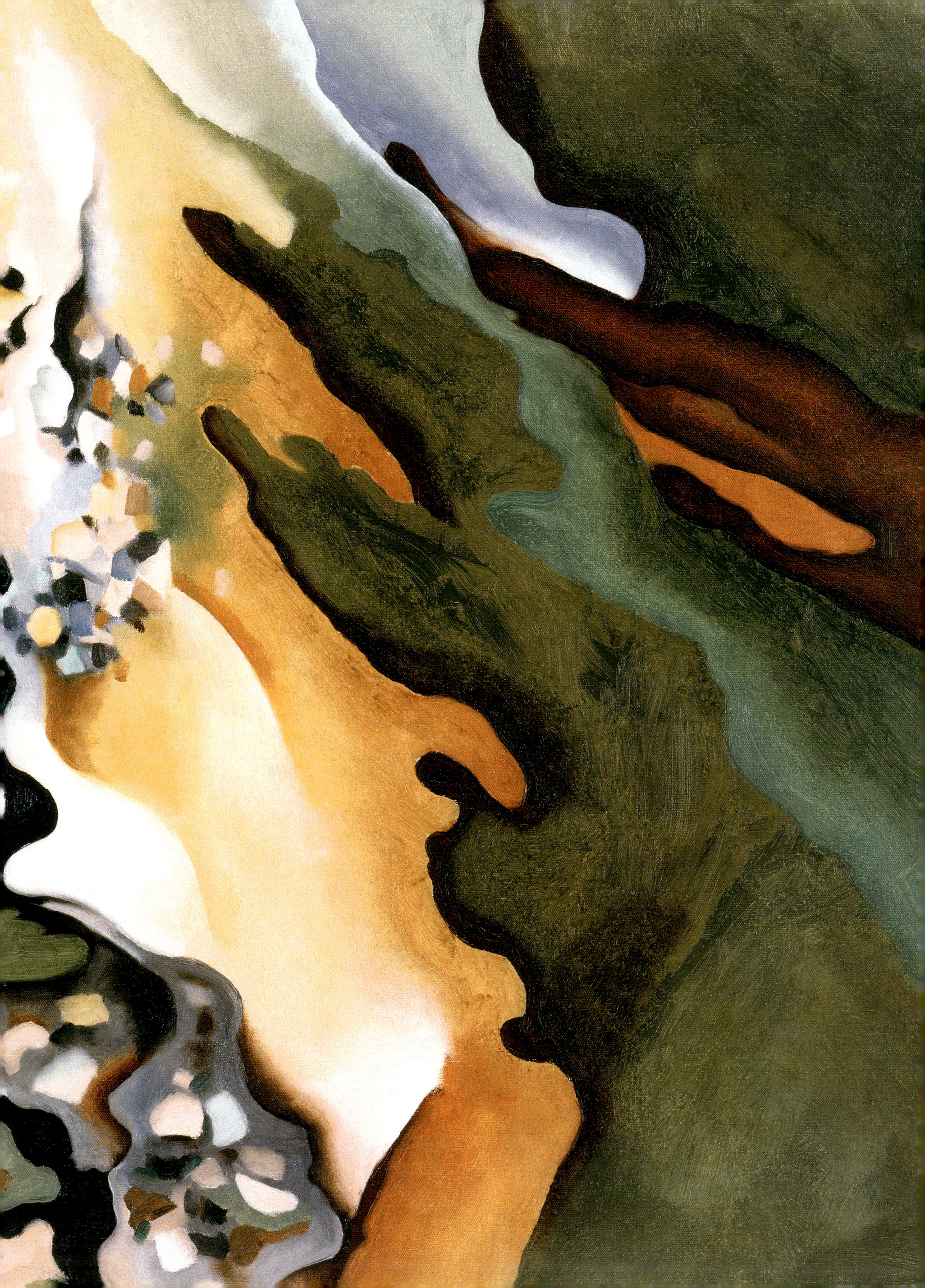

O'KEEFFE AND THE "CITY OF AMNESIA"

US LANDSCAPE PAINTING AND INDIGENOUS ERASURE

Sascha T. Scott

Georgia O'Keeffe's *Shelton with Sunspots, N.Y.* of 1926 (pl. 12) imagines the recently built residential hotel as a magnificent mountain bathed in early morning light. The sun peeks out from behind the tower, cloaking the front in soft shadow. Mist rises from the canyon-like streets of New York City to the sky, where it emanates as waves of atmosphere and light from the resplendent towers. The view is speckled with yellow spots, an effect O'Keeffe recalled seeing: "I went out one morning to look at [the Shelton Hotel] before I started to work and there was the optical illusion of a bite out of one side of the tower made by the sun, with sunspots against the building and against the sky."[1] The painting encourages ascension, as the eye climbs up the dark structure to the brilliant light and cloud-filled sky. O'Keeffe transformed New York City—which by the 1920s was notorious for being cacophonous, congested, and chaotic—into a quiet, empty, and contemplative landscape.

The Shelton with Sunspots, N.Y. is among O'Keeffe's most intriguing New York scenes. Many scholars have noted that the painting naturalizes skyscrapers, transmuting towers of steel into mountains of stone.[2] This visual language echoes how skyscrapers had been characterized since the late nineteenth century, as people sought to make sense of this radical architectural innovation and the social changes it wrought.[3] John Charles Van Dyke, in *The New New York* (1909), praised the picturesque qualities of New York City, likening the skyline to "distant mountain peaks" and the city to the "mountain walls of the Alps."[4] Architectural critic Claude Bragdon—who, like O'Keeffe, lived in the Shelton—saw skyscrapers "as a series of distant diminishing silhouettes and perspectives" receiving "the sun's first rays long before they penetrate into the city canyons," an apt description of *The Shelton with Sunspots, N.Y.*[5]

By the time O'Keeffe painted the Shelton Hotel in 1926, critics understood skyscrapers simultaneously as technological marvels and marvelous mountains, each interpretation seen as testifying to America's exceptionalism. For example, in his illustrated book *The Metropolis of Tomorrow* (1929), Hugh Ferriss presented the Shelton (see fig. 1) as a bastion of progress, rendering it as a stone structure rising from a blaze of ethereal light. This discourse about tall buildings drew on two strong cultural nationalist impulses. Many argued that the United States may not have a long and venerable cultural legacy like Europe but instead offered something better: an abundance of both pristine, contemplative nature and culture-shaping technologies.

Those who focused on nature believed that America's wilderness was the only cultural heritage the new nation needed. The Transcendentalist cultural and philosophical movement, which took hold in the 1830s, first popularized this position. In the early twentieth century, the movement inspired Alfred Stieglitz's circle of modernists, including O'Keeffe, who read Transcendentalist literature and integrated these ideas into their art.[6] Those who celebrated technology argued that the nation required no past at all. This perspective is particularly acute in writings about New York City, praised

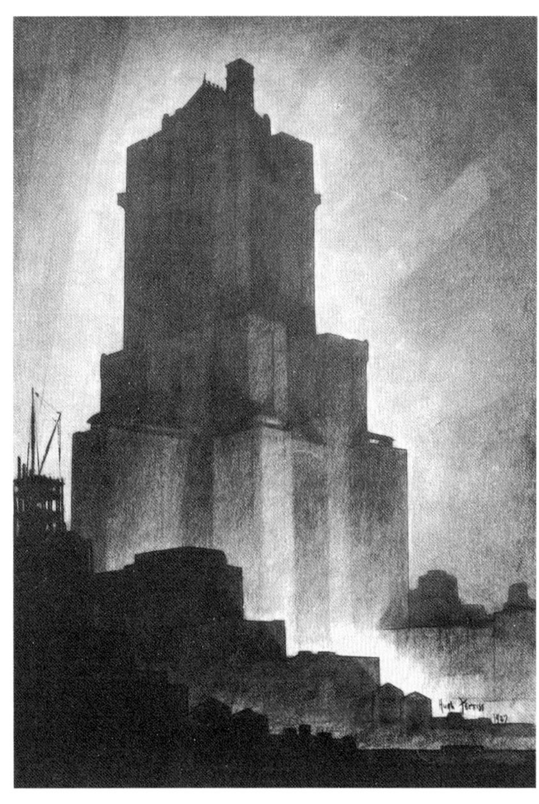

variously as a city with no history, a city of constant change, a city focused on the present, and the city of the future.[7] As Van Dyke wrote, "What has New York to do with romance or the past?"[8] Like many commentators, he argued America should stop looking backward, live intently in the present, and look to the future.

The Shelton with Sunspots, N.Y. articulates these two cultural nationalist positions, fusing the natural and the technological. The painting reflects critical praise of skyscrapers as icons of modernity and of the Shelton Hotel for its tallness and pleasing silhouette (it was an elegant and innovative solution to New York's new setback laws).[9] At the same time, the work is essentially a landscape painting, one that draws from nineteenth-century conceptual and aesthetic traditions that imagined the American wilderness as unpeopled and untouched, as well as a place of transcendence.[10] This way of seeing and knowing the land is structured by, justifies, and naturalizes settler colonialism.

As an art historian who writes about the relationships between US modernism, settler colonialism, and Indigenous peoples, I am interested in how representations of New York City and the surrounding regions transform Indigenous places into American spaces. By 1926 the nation celebrated skyscrapers as *indigenously* American and imagined New York City as having only a present and a future. These assumptions vanished Indigenous people and their histories, leading anthropologist Evan T. Pritchard to dub Manhattan "the city of amnesia."[11] This forgetting is the work of settler colonialism, defined as the process whereby nations conquer and permanently occupy Indigenous lands. Settler colonial states continually assert their dominance through the "logic of elimination," which historian Patrick Wolfe explained includes genocide, removal, disenfranchisement, and other forms of erasure, including cultural and historical.[12] These erasures can be facilitated by how a history of a place is told and how a place is visualized in art.

This essay considers the ways that O'Keeffe's paintings of New York City built on and still amplify settler acts of forgetting by examining three moments and three locations in what has variously been called Lenapehoking (by the Lenape), New Amsterdam (by the Dutch), and New York State (by the United States). The narrative begins in 1920s Manhattan, when Kanien'kehà:ka (Mohawk) ironworkers—who hailed from Kahnawà:ke (a reserve in Quebec) and settled in Brooklyn—were building the very skyscrapers O'Keeffe was painting. This discussion understands New York City as an Indigenous hub, calling attention to both Indigenous presence and its erasure. The narrative then travels to the 1820s, to the development of America's first national aesthetic movement, popularly known as the Hudson River School. Working throughout New York State, including the Catskill Mountains and Lake George regions, artists associated with the movement helped popularize the myth that America is composed of untouched and uncontested spaces ready for settler possession—an aesthetic and ideological legacy that reverberates in O'Keeffe's paintings of New York City and surrounding regions. The final temporal moment dates to the 1620s, when the Dutch claimed Manahatta (the Lenape name for Manhattan) for themselves, a famous episode celebrated by a

FIG. 1
The Shelton Hotel, New York. Arthur Loomis, Harmon, Architect. Drawing by Hugh Ferriss. Reproduced in Hugh Ferriss, *The Metropolis of Tomorrow* (New York: Ives Washburn, 1929), 31.

monument that was erected in Battery Park (now called the Battery) in the same year O'Keeffe first exhibited what she called "my New Yorks."

This expansive temporal and regional scope situates O'Keeffe's *Shelton with Sunspots, N.Y.* within the history and politics of Manhattan while addressing ideas about Native people and national culture that flowed in and out of the city over time. O'Keeffe's romantic vision of New York City, which transformed the densely populated, skyscrapered city into an unpeopled landscape, built on three centuries of settler mythmaking, through which Lenape Manahatta became settler Manhattan, the city of amnesia.

1920S: KANIEN'KEHÀ:KA NEW YORK

The New York skyscrapers O'Keeffe painted were the products of skilled and dangerous labor undertaken by a diverse labor force that included Kanien'kehà:ka ironworkers. Whereas urban realists working in the 1900s and 1910s caused a stir by painting dense working-class and immigrant neighborhoods in New York City, modernist painters working from the 1910s onward tended to deemphasize people, focusing on the city's new and enthralling architecture. This was especially true of artists who gravitated toward the intellectual and artistic circle of O'Keeffe's husband, Alfred Stieglitz.[13] While O'Keeffe and her peers often ignored New York City's workers, laborers frequently were featured in the work of photographers, including Lewis Wickes Hine, who famously photographed the men who built skyscrapers, calling them "sky boys."

One of the most iconic photographs of ironworkers, *Lunch atop a Skyscraper* (fig. 2), was long misattributed to Hine.[14] The *New York Herald Tribune* first published the photograph in 1932, and this version and subsequent reproductions never named the subjects, who came to personify the American spirit: hardworking, courageous, unflappable, and bold. Today members of the Kanien'kehà:ka community—whose ironworkers still build skyscrapers in major metropolises and who preserve a strong living memory of this tradition—believe the shirtless man in the photograph is Rotinonhsión:ni (Haudenosaunee) ironworker Peter Rice.[15]

Well before the photograph was taken, and as early as 1912, Kanien'kehà:ka men were traveling to Manhattan for ironworking jobs, having honed the skill by building bridges near their home at Kahnawà:ke beginning in the late nineteenth century.[16] (This transregional movement was not uncommon for Indigenous peoples then, nor prior to European invasion. What is now Manhattan was a center of Indigenous mobility and exchange long before the Dutch arrived.) With the 1920s skyscraper boom, Kanien'kehà:ka ironworkers realized there was enough work to keep them in New York City. As Kanien'kehà:ka men and women relocated to Brooklyn, they established "Little Caughnawaga" (an anglicization of *Kahnawà:ke*), a neighborhood that thrived until the 1970s.[17] At the time O'Keeffe painted *The Shelton with Sunspots, N.Y.*, Kanien'kehà:ka workers were helping build the city, and the city was simultaneously becoming an important hub of Kanien'kehà:ka culture, community identity, and belonging away from their homeland.[18]

When O'Keeffe embarked on her skyscraper venture, executing more than twenty cityscapes between 1925 and 1932, her friends and peers were interpreting skyscrapers through the lens of nationalism. In 1925 O'Keeffe's friend Claude Bragdon identified the skyscraper as "a symbol of the American Spirit" and the "only truly original development in the field of architecture to which we can lay unchallenged claim."[19] He

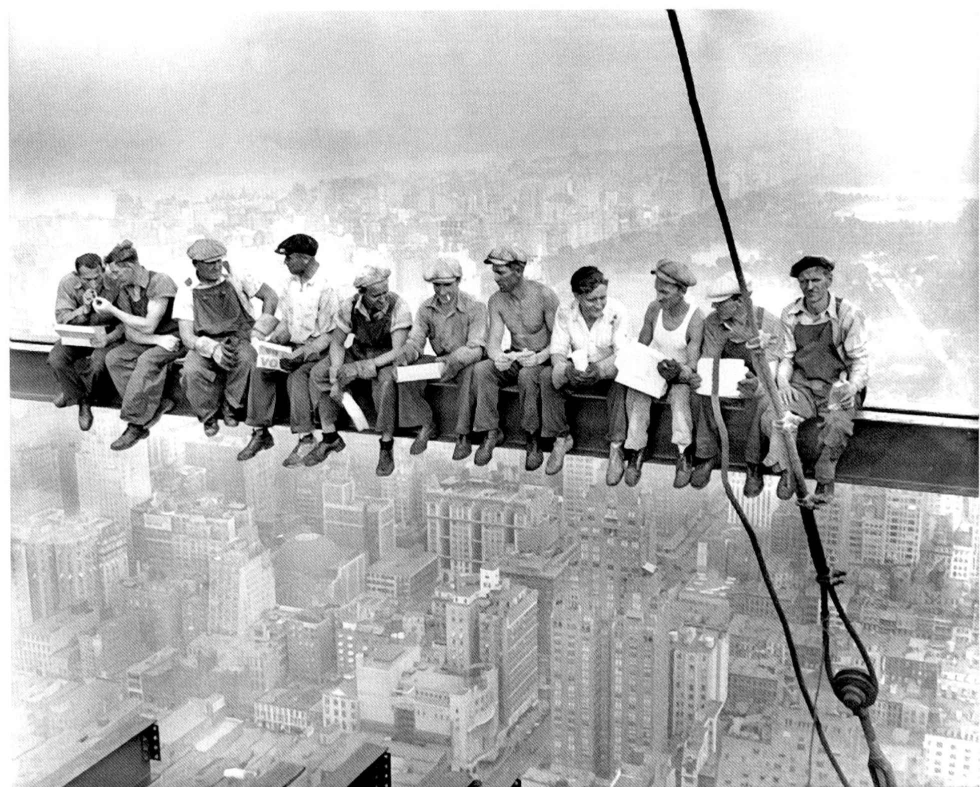

expanded on this idea in his 1932 book *The Frozen Fountain*. Everything else about American culture, he argued, was adapted from Europe, whereas the "skyscraper is a *natural growth*," emphasizing that, "of all our architectural flora, the skyscraper alone is truly indigenous to the American soil."[20] Many shared Bragdon's view, including British architect Alfred Bosson, who declared the skyscraper "as indigenous as the red Indian."[21]

Bosson was not thinking about Kanien'kehà:ka ironworkers, even though they received some media attention at the time. In 1927 the *New York Times* described Kanien'kehà:ka ironworkers as "young braves . . . employed in the construction of New York skyscrapers."[22] It was not until the late 1940s and 1950s, however, that these workers received more widespread and sustained national attention, in magazines such as the *New Yorker*, *Collier's*, and *National Geographic*.[23] Even then, the media dubbed Kanien'kehà:ka ironworkers "cowboys of the skies" and "rough pioneers," presenting them as mythological, deracialized types who represented the essence of American courage and rugged individualism.[24]

This assimilationist rhetoric was in keeping with official federal Indian policy, which encouraged "assimilation" when the article was written in 1927 and then "termination" from the mid-1940s through the 1960s. Both policies attempted to disband tribal communities, making their lands available for settlement and resource extraction. By the mid-twentieth century, settler society widely assumed that Native people had vanished from New York City and the surrounding regions, even as Indigenous people lived among them in cities and on nearby reservations. Period writings not only declared Indians from the area "extinct" but also widely projected that Native people across the United States would soon follow.[25] As novelist and critic Waldo Frank proclaimed in *Our America* (1919), "The Indian is dying and is doomed. There can be no question of this. There need be no sentimentality."[26]

O'Keeffe and her peers could not see what Indigenous people have always known: Indigenous people are native to modernity, which they lived and cocreated, as historian Philip Deloria (Dakota) explained.[27] Indigenous peoples have always lived in and helped build urban centers like New York City. In these Indigenous hubs, they have

FIG. 2
Lunch atop a Skyscraper, 1932. Photographer unknown (possibly Charles Clyde Ebbets, Tom Kelley, or William Leftwich). Reproduced in *New York Herald Tribune*, Oct. 2, 1932.

reimagined their traditions, reaffirmed their nationhood, fought for their sovereignty, and articulated self-determination.[28] As Orvis Diabo, one of the first Kanien'kehà:ka ironworkers to move to Brooklyn, recounted, "When they talk about the men that built this country, one of the men they mean is me."[29]

1820S: THE AESTHETIC OF EMPTINESS

By the 1920s, the long-rehearsed myth of the vanishing Indian had convinced most Americans that contemporary Native people were irrelevant to Manhattan and the surrounding regions. Native people were certainly not on O'Keeffe's mind when she painted New York. O'Keeffe's vision of the city as an unpopulated, contemplative landscape (see pls. 1 and 15) articulates an aesthetic of emptiness—an aesthetic paradigm that builds on and perpetuates long-standing settler practices of cultural and political erasure of Indigenous peoples. Notably, most of O'Keeffe's landscape paintings, including those of Lake George (see pl. 32) and New Mexico (see pl. 70), are defined by this aesthetic of emptiness. Turning to nineteenth-century landscape painting elucidates the cultural foundations of this aesthetic and its relationship to histories of conquest, settler occupation, and Indigenous removal.

During the mid-1820s, Thomas Cole created a series of paintings that offer a romantic vision of untouched nature based on an extensive sketching tour of the Hudson River valley, the Catskill Mountains, and Lake George. *Sunrise in the Catskills* (fig. 3), for example, pictures a backlit mountain with the sun peeking over the top as mist rises from the base toward the early morning sky—compositional features that resonate with O'Keeffe's *Shelton with Sunspots, N.Y.* Hudson River School painting may have been passé by the 1920s, but visual evidence suggests that O'Keeffe and other modernists knew of nineteenth-century aesthetic strategies for picturing the land—strategies with potent ideological meanings.

Cole's *Sunrise in the Catskills* presents a land empty of people, untouched and uncontested. The region was none of these things. The Catskills are the traditional homelands of the Esopus (Lenape) people, who had settled in clearings near water sources and developed diverse agricultural practices by the time the Dutch found their way to the area in the early seventeenth century. In the following decades, the Esopus suffered heavy losses of life and land fighting Dutch incursions into their territory. By the eighteenth century, European settlers pushed the Esopus to western New York, and by the 1830s, they were forcibly relocated to Wisconsin after the Indian Removal Act passed, legislation through which President Andrew Jackson authorized the violent displacement of Indigenous people from the Eastern United States to lands west of the Mississippi River.[30]

Cole's approach to painting the Catskills as empty and uncontested extended to other landscapes in New York State, such as Lake George, located about 130 miles north of the mountains. The artist first visited and painted Lake George in 1826, visualizing the area as a pristine wilderness (see fig. 4). Decades later, John Frederick Kensett, a second-generation Hudson River School painter, popularized this vision. Like Cole, Kensett was transfixed by the region's majestic landforms and waters and often pictured the region as an unpeopled, unspoiled, and spiritual place (see fig. 5). This is also how O'Keeffe often depicted the area around Lake George. During the 1920s, O'Keeffe and Stieglitz escaped New York City by summering at his property in the region. There she

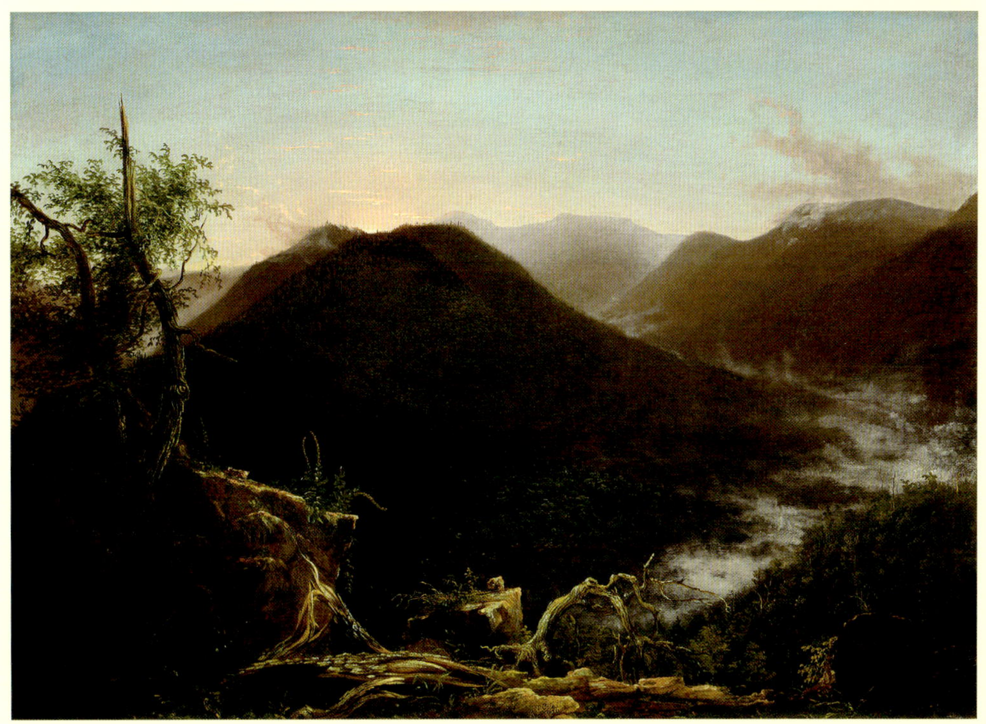

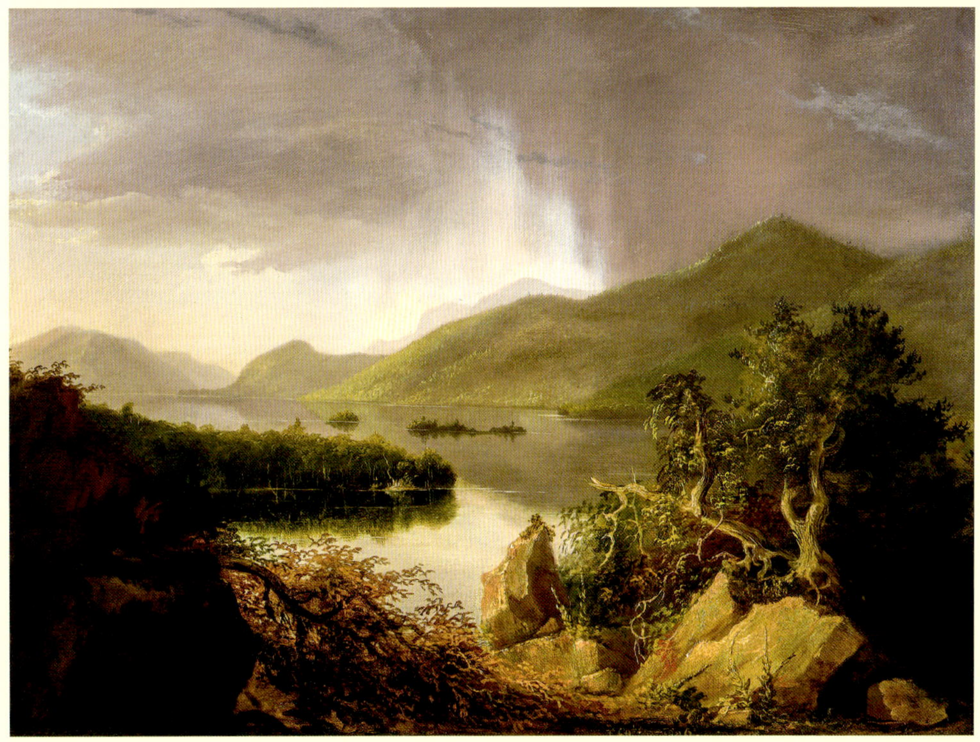

FIG. 3
Thomas Cole (American, born England, 1801–1848). *Sunrise in the Catskills,* 1826. Oil on canvas; 64.8 × 90.1 cm (25 ½ × 35 ½ in.). National Gallery of Art, Washington, gift of Mrs. John D. Rockefeller 3rd, in Honor of the 50th Anniversary of the National Gallery of Art, 1989.24.1.

FIG. 4
Cole. *View on Lake George,* 1826. Oil on wood panel; 46.4 × 62.9 cm (18 ¼ × 24 ¾ in.). Hood Museum of Art, Dartmouth, purchased through a gift from Evelyn A. and William B. Jaffe, Class of 1964H, by exchange, 2017.11.

painted *Red Hills, Lake George* (fig. 6), inspired by the weathered mountains around the lake. O'Keeffe abstracted the form and color of these landforms, smoothing out their contours and painting them in vivid red—perhaps amplifying their autumnal colors. Behind the hills, the brilliant sun radiates circles of light, piercing the darkness at the edges of the canvas.

Cole, Kensett, and O'Keeffe each conveyed the beauty and tranquility of Lake George through an aesthetic of emptiness. To imagine the area as such, however, ignored a great deal. By the time Cole painted Lake George, travel books had already popularized it. Three decades later, when Kensett focused on the area, the lake was home to a popular resort and many luxury hotels that still operated in O'Keeffe's time.

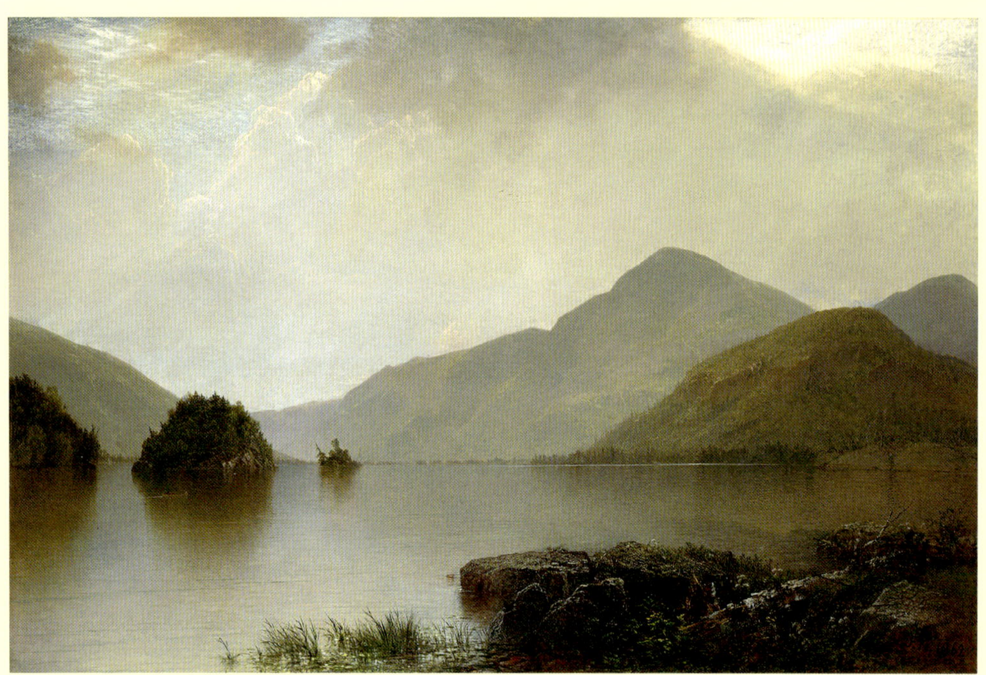

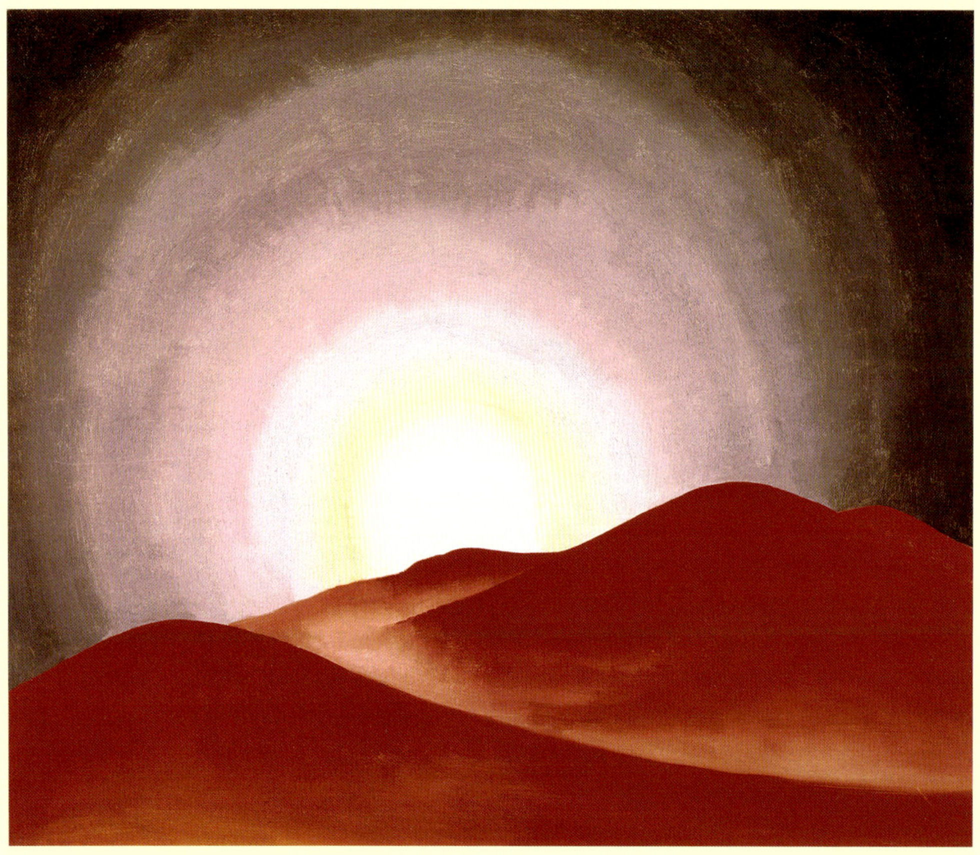

FIG. 5
John Frederick Kensett (American, 1816–1872). *Lake George*, 1869. Oil on canvas; 112.1 × 168.6 cm (44 1/8 × 66 3/8 in.). The Metropolitan Museum of Art, New York, Bequest of Maria DeWitt Jesup, from the collection of her husband, Morris K. Jesup, 1914, 15.30.61.

FIG. 6
Georgia O'Keeffe (American, 1887–1986). *Red Hills, Lake George*, 1927. Oil on canvas; 68.6 × 81.3 cm (27 × 32 in.). Phillips Collection, Washington, DC, Acquired 1945.

During parts of the year, boats would have dotted the lake, especially near the towns along the shore. All three artists often omitted human interventions in order to depict uncontested, untouched nature.[31]

As beautiful as the region was, it was not a foregone conclusion that Lake George and the surrounding landscape naturally invited such representations. During the eighteenth century, the area was a site of settlement and contestation, and artists visualized it as such. During the French and Indian War (1754–63)—the North American theater of the Seven Years' War—the British and French fought each other along the

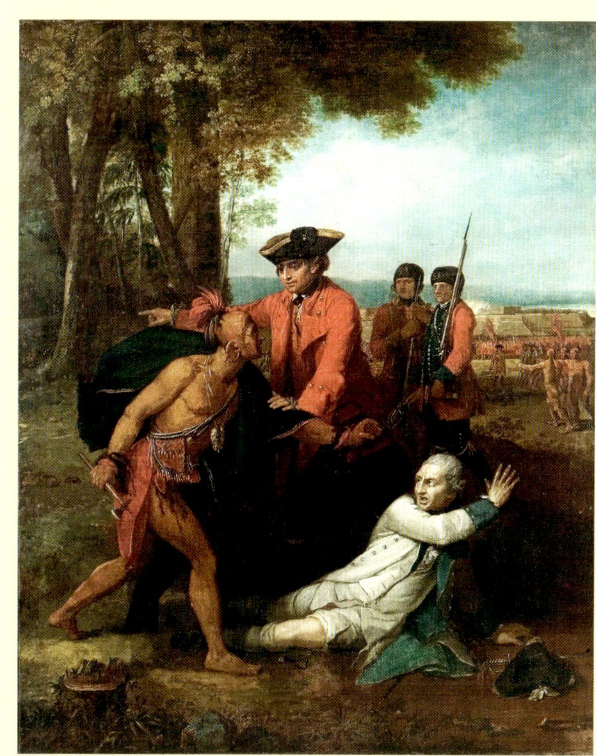

shores of Lake George, called Kanià:taro'kte ("lake end") by the Kanien'kehà:ka. Although far more Indigenous people fought for the French, both sides relied on Indigenous allies. During the Lake George campaign of 1755, the British and their Kanien'kehà:ka allies tried to expel French and Abenaki troops from the region.[32] Benjamin West's *General Johnson Saving a Wounded French Officer from a North American Indian* (fig. 7) memorializes the campaign, depicting British solider Johnson rescuing French commander Baron de Dieskau from being scalped by a Kanien'kehà:ka warrior. Tellingly, West pictured Johnson directing the Native man outside the boundaries of the battle toward the forest beyond.[33] The painting accentuates two common ideas about Native people at the time. First, whether ally or foe, Indians were considered "savages," as coded by the Native figure's semi-nude body and merciless attack. Second, Native people were inextricably tied to the wilderness. In both cases, Indians were understood as foils and impediments to European civilization. Lake George itself, barely visible, serves merely as the setting for the drama of war. Eighteenth-century artists often visualized the region as a contested space, as denoted by military encampments. By the nineteenth century, when Indian Removal became official policy and constructions of US national identity rested on myths about untouched nature, artists' visual strategies for representing places like Lake George shifted to serve dominant ideologies.

Cole's erasures, which his followers repeated and modernists naturalized, stemmed from an ideological program he shared with Transcendentalists. In the 1835 lecture "Essay on American Scenery," he described America's "wild and uncultivated scenery" as "a fitting place to speak to God."[34] Similarly, Ralph Waldo Emerson, in his book-length essay *Nature* (1836), advocated for solitary engagement with nature as a way to connect with God. Both Cole and Emerson argued that the United States' vast areas of pristine nature are what made the new nation exceptional, separating it from Europe.[35] Emerson wrote, "The foregoing generations beheld God and nature face to face. . . . Why should not we also enjoy an original relation to the universe? Why should not we have a poetry and philosophy of insight and not of tradition, and a religion by revelation to us, and not the history of [Europeans]?"[36] America's nature was pitched as a better and more divine source of culture than Europe's long histories and traditions.

In making such claims, Transcendentalists and their followers argued that social and cultural interactions with the American wilderness were relatively new. Cole praised this freshness, declaring that "very few generations have passed away since this vast tract of the American continent, now the United States, rested in the shadow of primaeval forests."[37] By "very few generations" he meant Europeans and their descendants, dismissing Native people as scarcely less savage than beasts. Cole and his Transcendentalist peers claimed America for European Americans, rejecting Native peoples' long histories on, rights to, and sophisticated stewardship of the land.[38]

It comes as little surprise, then, that Cole and his followers did not represent contemporary Indigenous people. When they painted Native figures at all, they depicted mythologized Indians—images that fueled Indigenous dispossession. Most of Cole's

FIG. 7
Benjamin West (American, 1738–1820). *General Johnson Saving a Wounded French Officer from a North American Indian*, 1764–68. Oil on canvas; 129.5 × 106.5 cm (51 × 41 15/16 in.). Derby Museum and Art Galleries, England.

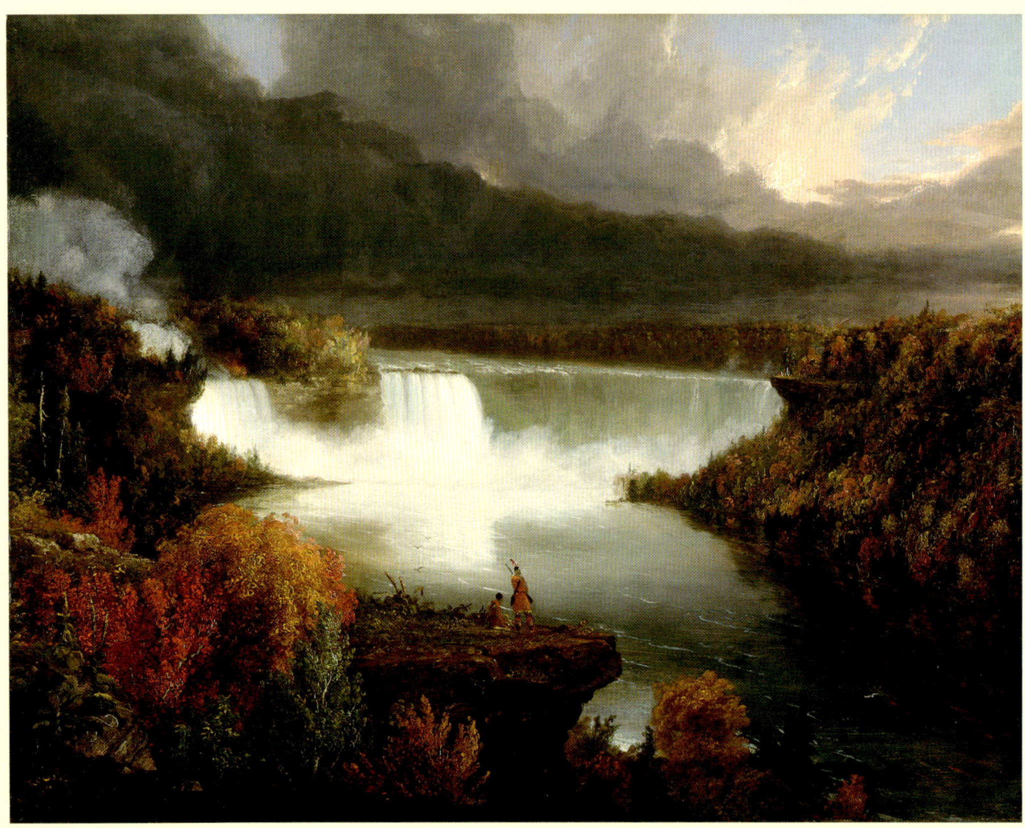

landscapes with Indians explicitly reference the literature of James Fenimore Cooper, who penned a series of widely popular historical novels whose most famous characters include stereotyped Indians. Cole also created a handful of paintings of Native figures who have no obvious literary pretext.[39] Perhaps the most famous of these is *Distant View of Niagara Falls* (fig. 8), which paved the ideological foundations for his later paintings, including *Indian at Sunset* (fig. 9). In these works, Cole's Native figures are inextricably linked to the wilderness (as in West's painting) and doomed to vanish.

In Cole's *Indian at Sunset*, a stereotyped Indian man—signified by the feather on his head, his dark skin, and hints of exoticizing clothing—sits among trees overlooking a body of water lined by thick forest. This landscape could have been inspired by any number of regions Cole visited during his career, including the Catskills and Lake George. Before calm waters the passive Indian contemplates his tragic fate (and the fate of his people), as communicated by the autumnal landscape and setting sun. The painting follows the paradigm of the vanishing Indian, a pervasive trope in US painting and literature by the mid-nineteenth century. Paintings like *Indian at Sunset* were fueled by Cole's own fears about industrial growth. They suggest that America's untouched wilderness, like the wild Indian, would inevitably disappear in the face of progress.

Paintings of vanishing Indians are paradigmatic of what anthropologist Renato Rosaldo terms "imperialist nostalgia," defined as "mourning for what one has destroyed."[40] Cole created *Distant View of Niagara Falls* the same year the Indian Removal Act of 1830 was passed. What followed was a period of aggressive invasions onto Indigenous lands and a notorious ethnic cleansing, including the Trail of Tears (1830–50), when sixty thousand Cherokee, Chickasaw, Choctaw, Muscogee, and Seminole people were removed from their homelands to "Indian Territory."[41] Between 1838 and 1839 alone, at least four thousand Cherokee died during their forced relocation to Oklahoma.[42] By the time Cole painted *Indian at Sunset*, the US government had gone to great lengths to actualize the vanishing of Native peoples.

FIG. 8
Cole. *Distant View of Niagara Falls*, 1830. Oil on panel; 47.9 × 60.6 cm (18 7/8 × 23 7/8 in.). The Art Institute of Chicago, Friends of American Art Collection, 1946.396.

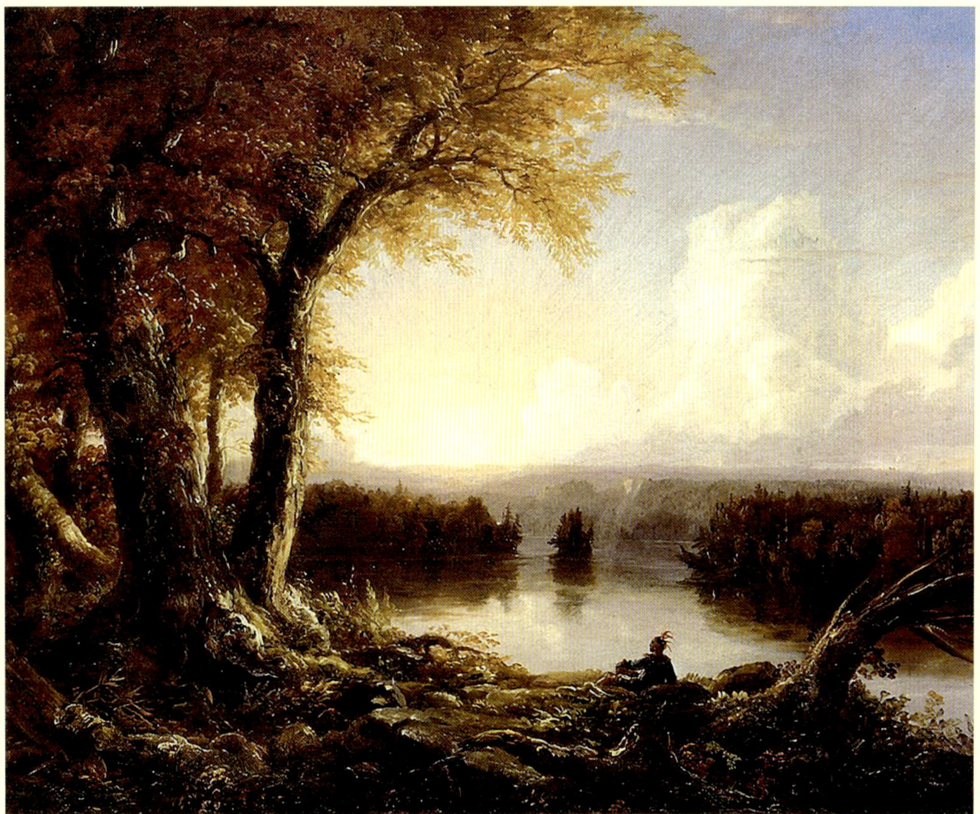

Nineteenth-century landscape paintings that erase Native people (such as Cole's *Sunrise in the Catskills* [fig. 3]) spin land possession as a settler right, while paintings that picture Indians as doomed (see Cole's *Indian at Sunset*) pitch settler possession as an inevitable fact.[43] Such representations denied the ongoing presence, sovereignty, political agency, and land rights of Indigenous peoples. They also contributed to Indigenous erasure by conditioning settler society to forget that Indigenous lands were stolen and to see settler possession of these lands as interminable and divinely ordained. For these reasons, artist and visual historian Jolene Rickard (Tuscarora) views nineteenth-century landscape painting as among the "arts of Indigenous dispossession," "one of the conceptual and visceral tools of colonization."[44]

By the early twentieth century, the erasure of Indigenous presence was all but complete in modernist representations of landscapes.[45] Like *Red Hills, Lake George*, most of O'Keeffe's landscapes, whether created in the Northeast or Southwest, romanticize place, presenting land as empty, neutral, and free of conflict. They picture place as claimed by the settler imagination, as does *The Shelton with Sunspots, N.Y.*

1620S: MANAHATTA

Manhattan—built, like all settler cities, on Indigenous lands—had been claimed for settler needs and desires three hundred years before O'Keeffe painted *The Shelton with Sunspots, N.Y.*[46] In 1626 the Dutch asserted ownership of Manahatta ("place for gathering wood to make bows"), the Lenape name for what is now called Manhattan.[47] The facts of how the Dutch, then the British, and finally the United States came to control this place have been variously twisted, elided, and willfully forgotten. This strategic misremembering is evident in the Netherland Monument, erected in December 1926, the year O'Keeffe first exhibited her New York paintings. To mark the tercentenary of the Dutch purchase of Manahatta from the Lenape, the city installed the monument at the

FIG. 9
Cole. *Indian at Sunset*, c. 1845. Oil on canvas; 35.6 × 43.8 cm (14 × 17 1/4 in.). Private collection.

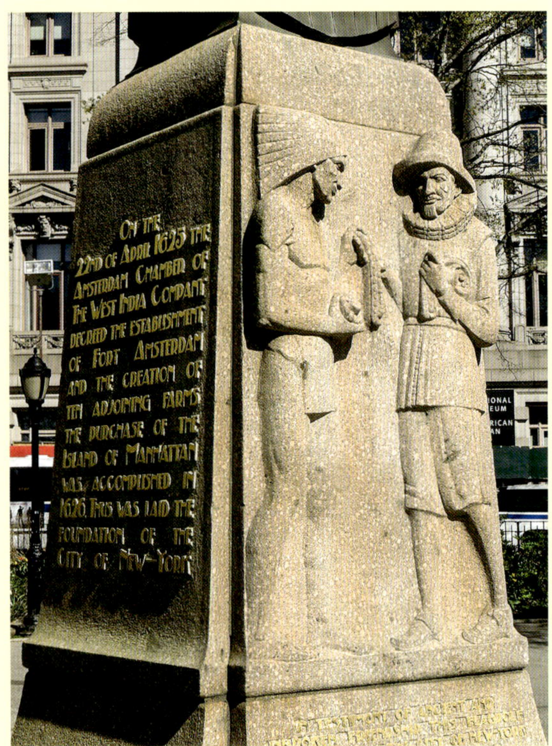

tip of Manhattan where Fort Amsterdam once stood—located four miles due south of O'Keeffe's residence at the Shelton.[48]

Composed of a four-sided stone plinth holding a flagpole, the Netherland Monument was a present from the people of Holland. One side depicts a Native man in a Plains-style feathered headdress accepting beaded gifts from a Dutch official (see fig. 10). The inscription below reads, "In testament of ancient and unbroken friendship this flagpole is presented to the city of New York by the Dutch people, 1926." The monument imagines a peaceful and mutually agreed upon transfer of land from Indians to the Dutch.

There are no Lenape on this monument, only stereotyped Indians, and, even then, they are subsidiary actors in a settler story of righteous land acquisition. Manhattan, the city of amnesia, was built on this myth. The Netherland Monument reflects the logic of elimination through which settler colonial states assert themselves on a territory by replacing the Indigenous peoples they have tried to destroy or erase. Lenape peoples did not passively or willfully leave Manahatta; rather, settler colonial forces facilitated their disappearance through treaties (often dishonestly made or broken), genocide, and political, historical, and cultural eradication.

The 1926 monument perpetuates a myth that began in the 1620s, when Manahatta served as an important center of Lenapehoking ("the land of the people"), encompassing large parts of present-day New York, New Jersey, Pennsylvania, and Delaware. Lenape peoples have had a relationship to their homelands, which they and their ancestors have cared for and cultivated, for over ten thousand years.[49] The Shelton Hotel was built just inland from a place called Sapokahikan ("the canoe landing place"), where nearby Indigenous people came ashore to trade with the Lenape living on the island.[50] Lenapehoking was never a static place, but the transformations that came with the arrival of Europeans starting in 1524 were radical. The most profound disruptions occurred after English captain Henry Hudson made his way to Manahatta's shores on behalf of the Dutch East India Company in 1609. In the years that followed, European explorers, traders, and settlers pressed Lenape peoples into a constant state of negotiation, drawing them into a market-based economy. Nevertheless, during the early years of contact, Lenape peoples maintained control of their lands, a difficult task as Europeans tried to impose foreign concepts regarding land and land ownership.[51] Whereas Indigenous relationships to land emphasize balance, coexistence, and stewardship, the Dutch focused on the land's extractable commodities.[52]

To achieve the latter, the Dutch West India Company, founded by the Dutch Republic in 1621, was given control of New Netherland, a territory that included Lenapehoking and present-day Connecticut and parts of Rhode Island. The company was charged with challenging Spanish dominance in the Atlantic, and, to do so, it established the settlement New Amsterdam.[53] The small port city's directive was to maintain a peaceful relationship with Indigenous peoples in order to protect the settlement, a necessity given that the significant Lenape population was already engaged in the European fur trade.[54] What it meant to maintain peace for the Dutch, however, did not exclude treacherous manipulations of the Lenape.

FIG. 10
Hendrick Albertus van den Eijnde (Dutch, 1869–1939). Detail of the Netherland Monument, dedicated Dec. 6, 1926. The granite and bronze sculpture was first erected at the tip of Manhattan, near Fort Amsterdam, and was later relocated to the northeast entrance of the Battery.

As the Dutch sought to develop New Amsterdam into a strategic port, they encountered a problem: how to claim land they had no legal right to. So, they created a legal pretense to defraud the Lenape. In 1626 the governor of New Amsterdam, Peter Minuit, reportedly purchased Manahatta for a sum of goods valued at sixty guilders. The only evidence of this transaction is a 1626 letter written by Peter Schaghen, representative of the States General for the Dutch West India Company.[55] Settlers used the fabricated sale of Manahatta thereafter to claim a peaceful transfer of land, as communicated in the 1926 Netherland Monument, as well as to suggest the simple-mindedness, greed, and gullibility of Indians.

It is now widely understood that the Lenape did not intend to sell their land, a concept foreign to them, and that the Dutch knew the Lenape were not transferring title.[56] The Creator granted the Lenape their homelands; as stewards of this land, they could neither sell nor individually own it.[57] What they "exchanged" was not the land itself, but rather use rights, for things like settlement, hunting, and fishing. The Dutch could *share* the territory in exchange for gifts, while Indigenous communities continued to live on and care for their homelands. The Lenape likely assumed more gifts would follow as the Dutch sought to renew the agreement. Accordingly, the Lenape did not leave after the "purchase," a refusal that led to bloodshed as New Amsterdam became the primary port into New Netherland.[58]

Over the next four decades, the Dutch committed brutal violence against Indigenous peoples in Lenapehoking. Owing to this violence and other factors—including epidemics, the Dutch destroying Lenape environmental infrastructures, and a quick rise in the population of New Amsterdam—by the end of the seventeenth century, Europeans outnumbered Lenape one hundred to one.[59] This demographic shift led to profound changes in land use. The Dutch emphasized livestock and crops, rendering the Lenape's traditional ways of interacting with the land increasingly impossible.[60]

The situation did not improve after New Amsterdam fell to the British in August 1664. By this time, Lenape peoples had already lost political control over the region, and many had been forced westward. Some Lenape continued to live in the port city, taking employment as laborers, tenant farmers, field hands, servants, sailors, and sellers of handmade goods. Some Lenape moved to parts of New York and New Jersey that remained more isolated.[61] Still, within one hundred years of the Dutch's arrival, most of the original Indigenous inhabitants of Manahatta had been removed and dispersed.[62]

Despite these removals, the story of Lenapehoking is neither simply about the past nor about passive Lenape victimization. In the face of terrible oppression, Lenape peoples resisted and have been resilient. Many Lenape continue to live in Lenapehoking. Those who were dispersed to Delaware, Indiana, New Jersey, Ohio, Oklahoma, Ontario, and Wisconsin—many of whom call themselves the Delaware—may live far from Lenapehoking, but they have not forgotten their homelands. No matter where they live today, Lenape peoples and descendants of the Lenape continue to revitalize their communities and the traditions of their ancestors.[63]

REMEMBERING

Settler artists' representations of land helped transform and claim Indigenous places as American spaces. This perspective is reinforced by the possessive language O'Keeffe used to describe places, language that has been replicated by those who have written about her.[64] Whereas O'Keeffe used possessive language to describe her *artworks* of New York City, calling them "my New Yorks," when she painted places settler society deemed "exotic," she often used possessive language to describe the place itself.[65] After O'Keeffe began summering in New Mexico in 1929, she called Cerro Pedernal "my private mountain," and upon visiting Hawai'i in 1939, she referred to 'Īao Valley as "my green valley."[66] In using "my," O'Keeffe meant to convey her personal connection to place. Yet, as Aileen Moreton-Robinson (Quandamooka First Nation) has convincingly argued, the assumption that one has the right to possess land—literally or metaphorically—is a settler perspective and part of the colonial project. The language of settler possession is at odds with Indigenous ways of understanding land. It also denies Indigenous stewardship of and belonging in their homelands, and thus facilitates, justifies, and naturalizes Indigenous dispossession and erasure.[67]

Writings about O'Keeffe published around the time she created her New York paintings operate in a similar way. Just as skyscrapers were being praised as authentically indigenous innovations, O'Keeffe was being spotlighted as a truly indigenous painter. In 1927, after interviewing O'Keeffe in her Shelton apartment for *The Nation*, Frances O'Brien declared, "O'Keeffe is America's. Its own exclusive product."[68] O'Keeffe herself fueled such nationalist rhetoric. Meditating on what it took to be an authentically American painter, she proclaimed, "It is necessary to feel America, live America, love America, and then work."[69] To feel, live, love, and work was to create America. As Waldo Frank put it: "We [cultural producers] go forth all to seek America. And in the seeking we create her. In the quality of our search shall be the nature of the America that we create."[70] O'Keeffe's *The Shelton with Sunspots, N.Y.* helped "create America," envisioning the urban center the artist lived and worked in as a contemplative mountainous landscape that is, was, and has always been defined and occupied by settlers.

When O'Keeffe painted New York, "America" was a partial concept whose limited scope omitted much. The composition of *The Shelton with Sunspots, N.Y.* is an apt metaphor for this tunnel vision. From one's position on the street, the towering buildings close in on both sides. To escape this constriction, the eye must move back and up the idealized and abstracted Shelton. In the painting, New York is no longer a place; it is an idea. It is "America" as abstracted by erasure and historical amnesia. To be sure, in 1926, this vision was *the* American vision, one that had been structured by settler colonialism. It was rare for most people, especially those living in the East, to have any accurate or in-depth knowledge about the Indigenous places they occupied. This settler way of seeing and knowing is a fact of history. It cannot be undone. And still, it is important to recognize and reckon with the cognitive and cultural impacts of settler constructions of history and place, which reverberate today and continue to vanish Indigenous pasts, presents, and presence. Historical amnesia—willful forgetting—is a settler colonial strategy, one that can be disrupted by holding space to remember.

NOTES

1. Georgia O'Keeffe, *Georgia O'Keeffe* (New York: Viking Press, 1976), n.p., opp. pls. 18–19. For a discussion of photography with respect to this painting, see Anna C. Chave, "'Who Will Paint New York?': 'The World's New Art Center' and the Skyscraper Paintings of Georgia O'Keeffe," *American Art* 5, nos. 1–2 (Winter–Spring 1991): 92; and Wanda M. Corn, "Painting Big—O'Keeffe's *Manhattan*," *American Art* 20, no. 2 (Summer 2006): 23.
2. On O'Keeffe's naturalizing vision, see Elizabeth Dean, "Georgia O'Keeffe's *Radiator Building*: Icon of Glamorous Gotham," *Revue française d'études américaines*, no. 11 (Apr. 1981): 83; and Chave, "'Who Will Paint New York?,'" 95–97.
3. On language naturalizing skyscrapers, see Mike Wallace, *Greater Gotham: A History of New York City from 1898 to 1919* (New York: Oxford University Press, 2017), 152–53; and Merrill Schleier, *The Skyscraper in American Art, 1890–1931* (Ann Arbor: UMI Research Press, 1986), 36. On romantic representations of New York City and their escapist function, see Wanda M. Corn, "The New New York," *Art in America* 61, no. 4 (1973): 58–65; and Alan Trachtenberg, "Image and Ideology: New York in the Photographer's Eye," *Journal of Urban History* 10, no. 4 (Aug. 1984): 462–63.
4. John Charles Van Dyke, *The New New York: A Commentary on the Place and the People* (New York: Macmillan Company, 1909), 6.
5. Claude Bragdon, "The Shelton Hotel, New York: Arthur Loomis Harmon, Architect," *Architectural Record* 58, no. 1 (July 1925): 18. Similar language is used in Hugh Ferriss, *The Metropolis of Tomorrow* (New York: Ives Washburn, 1929), 30.
6. On Transcendentalism and the Stieglitz circle, see Charles C. Eldredge, *Georgia O'Keeffe: American and Modern* (New Haven, CT: Yale University Press, in association with InterCultura and the Georgia O'Keeffe Foundation, 1993), 194; and Wanda M. Corn, *The Great American Thing: Modern Art and National Identity, 1915–1935* (Berkeley: University of California Press, 1999), 250.
7. Corn, *Great American Thing*, 24, 43–89. On skyscrapers and cultural nationalist discourse, see Corn, "New New York," 64; Schleier, *Skyscraper in American Art*, 6, 13–17; and Corn, *Great American Thing*, xv.
8. Van Dyke, *New New York*, 146.
9. Bragdon, "Shelton Hotel," 1–18.
10. Similarly, Corn, "New New York," 60, interprets the romantic imagery and describes the city as drawing from these nineteenth-century ideas.
11. Evan T. Pritchard, *Native New Yorkers: The Legacy of the Algonquin People of New York* (San Francisco: Council Oak Books, 2002), 19.
12. Patrick Wolfe, "Settler Colonialism and the Elimination of the Native," *Journal of Genocide Research* 8, no. 4 (Dec. 2006): 387–409.
13. This shift is well examined in the art historical literature; see Schleier, *Skyscraper in American Art*, 26; and David Peters Corbett, "The Problematic Past in the Work of Charles Sheeler, 1917–1927," *Journal of American Studies* 45, no. 3 (Aug. 2011): 561–62.
14. Many now believe the photographer was Charles Ebbets, Thomas Kelley, or William Leftwich.
15. Allan Downey, "Indigenous Brooklyn: Ironworking, Little Caughnawaga, and Kanien'keha:ka Nationhood in the Twentieth Century," *American Quarterly* 75, no. 1 (Mar. 2023): 33. The photograph appeared in the Sunday supplement of the *New York Herald Tribune*, Oct. 2, 1932.
16. David Weitzman, *Skywalkers: Mohawk Ironworkers Build the City* (New York: Roaring Book Press, 2010), 58.
17. Downey, "Indigenous Brooklyn," 28.
18. Ibid., 34, 37. On Native hubs, see Renya K. Ramirez, *Native Hubs: Culture, Community, and Belonging in Silicon Valley and Beyond* (Durham, NC: Duke University Press, 2007), 1–4.
19. Bragdon, "Shelton Hotel," 1. For similar claims, see also Claude Fayette Bragdon, *The Frozen Fountain: Being Essays on Architecture and the Art of Design in Space* (New York: Alfred A. Knopf, 1932), 25.
20. Bragdon, *Frozen Fountain*, 25. Italics in the original. This text relies on cultural national rhetoric common among modernists, who frequently evoked "soil," "spirit," and Americanness in their art and writing; see Corn, *Great American Thing*, 31.
21. Quoted in Jim Rasenberger, *High Steel: The Daring Men Who Built the World's Greatest Skyline, 1881–Present*, 1st ed. (New York: HarperCollins, 2004), 37.
22. "New York Indian Colony Now Has Its Own Club," *New York Times*, Feb. 6, 1927, X15.
23. Rasenberger, *High Steel*, 160–61; and Weitzman, *Skywalkers*, 91.
24. Schleier, *Skyscraper in American Art*, 27.
25. Clark Wissler, introduction to *The Indians of Greater New York and the Lower Hudson*, ed. Clark Wissler (New York: Hudson-Fulton Publication, 1909), xv, declares the Mohegans in the area "extinct."
26. Waldo Frank, *Our America* (New York: Boni and Liveright, 1919), 115.
27. Philip J. Deloria, *Becoming Mary Sully: Toward an American Indian Abstract* (Seattle: University of Washington Press, 2019), 22–23.
28. Downey, "Indigenous Brooklyn," 27–50; and Ramirez, *Native Hubs*.
29. Quoted in Weitzman, *Skywalkers*, 67.
30. The Esopus—sometimes referred to as the Munsee Esopus—are a Lenape people who speak Munsee, an Algonquin dialect. Their descendants are the Stockbridge-Munsee; see Stockbridge-Munsee Community Band of Mohican Indians, mohican.com; and James Warren Oberly, *A Nation of Statesmen: The Political Culture of the Stockbridge-Munsee Mohicans, 1815–1972* (Norman: University of Oklahoma Press, 2005). On the Esopus and the Dutch, see Robert S. Grumet, *First Manhattans: A History of the Indians of Greater New York* (Norman: University of Oklahoma Press, 2011), 49–55; and Paul Otto, *The Dutch-Munsee Encounter in America: The Struggle for Sovereignty in the Hudson Valley* (New York: Berghahn Books, 2006), 153–55.
31. When Cole visited Lake George in 1826, at least four books about the region had been published; Kevin J. Avery, "Selling the Sublime and the Beautiful: New York Landscape Painting and Tourism," in *Art and the Empire City: New York, 1825–1861*, ed. Catherine Hoover Voorsanger and John K. Howat, exh. cat. (New York: Metropolitian Museum of Art, in association with New Haven, CT: Yale University Press, 2000), 113. By the 1860s, Lake George was a well-known resort town; Sally E. Svenson, *Blacks in the Adirondacks* (Syracuse, NY: Syracuse University Press, 2017), 83. Like all Hudson River School painters, Kensett did not omit human presence from all of his work; see Angela Miller, *The Empire of the Eye: Landscape Representation and American Cultural Politics, 1825–1875* (Ithaca, NY: Cornell University Press, 1993), 245–47.

32. On the Battle of Lake George, see Fred Anderson, *Crucible of War: The Seven Years' War and the Fate of Empire in British North America, 1754–1766* (New York: Knopf Doubleday, 2007), 114–23.
33. On West's painting, see Gail D. MacLeitch, *Imperial Entanglements: Iroquois Change and Persistence on the Frontiers of Empire* (Philadelphia: University of Pennsylvania Press, 2012), 45–47.
34. Thomas Cole, "Essay on American Scenery, 1835," in *American Art, 1700–1960: Sources and Documents*, ed. John W. McCoubrey (Englewood Cliffs, NJ: Prentice-Hall, 1965), 100. This essay was first published in 1836.
35. On the cultural nationalist impulses in Transcendentalism and nineteenth-century landscape painting, respectively, see William H. Truettner, "Ideology and Image: Justifying Westward Expansion," in *The West as America: Reinterpreting Images of the Frontier, 1820–1920*, ed. William H. Truettner, exh. cat. (Washington, DC: National Museum of American Art by the Smithsonian Institution Press, 1991), 34–36; and Miller, *Empire of the Eye*.
36. Emerson, *Nature*, 5.
37. Cole, "Essay on American Scenery," 101–2.
38. Both Cole and Emerson evoked the concept of *terra nullius*, defined as "no one's land" or "land without a master," a concept that first came into widespread use during the nineteenth century; see Merete Borch, "Rethinking the Origins of Terra Nullius," *Australian Historical Studies* 32, no. 117 (2001): 222–39.
39. Cole knew Cooper personally; see Elizabeth Mankin Kornhauser and Tim Barringer, eds., *Thomas Cole's Journey: Atlantic Crossings*, exh. cat. (New York: Metropolitan Museum of Art, 2018), 136–37.
40. Renato Rosaldo, "Imperialist Nostalgia," *Representations*, no. 26, special issue, Memory and Counter-Memory (Spring 1989): 107.
41. For more on this decades-long period of removal, see Jeffery Ostler, *Surviving Genocide: Native Nations and the United States from the American Revolution to Bleeding Kansas* (New Haven, CT: Yale University Press, 2019), 247–326.
42. There are various estimations of how many Cherokee died. At least four thousand is commonly given.
43. On how Cole's *Distant View of Niagara Falls* erases histories of colonialism, violence, and exploitation, see Linda L. Revie, *The Niagara Companion: Explorers, Artists, and Writers at the Falls, from Discovery through the Twentieth Century* (Waterloo, Ontario: Wilfrid Laurier University Press, 2003), 47. On how nineteenth-century landscape paintings simulate possession, see Miller, *Empire of the Eye*, 245. On how visual constructs of nature and Indians justified US expansion into Indigenous lands, see Elizabeth Johns, "Settlement and Development: Claiming the West," in *West as America*, 191.
44. Jolene Rickard, "Arts of Dispossession," in *Picturing the Americas: Landscape Painting from Tierra del Fuego to the Arctic*, ed. Peter John Brownlee, Valéria Piccoli, and Georgiana Uhlyarik (New Haven, CT: Yale University Press, 2015), 116.
45. Notable exceptions include some interpretations of the Southwest by modernists who began to awaken to vibrant Indigenous cultures in the late 1910s; see Sascha T. Scott, *A Strange Mixture: The Art and Politics of Painting Pueblo Indians* (Norman: University of Oklahoma Press, 2015). O'Keeffe began summering in New Mexico in 1929, painting very few works that reference Native peoples. Those that do, tend to focus on her impressions of ceremonial dances and objects.
46. Julie Tomiak et al., "Introduction: Settler City Limits," in *Settler City Limits: Indigenous Resurgence and Colonial Violence in the Urban Prairie West*, ed. Heather Dorries et al. (East Lansing: Michigan State University Press, 2019), 4.
47. This translation of the word *Manahatta* was offered in the exhibition *Native New York*, at the National Museum of the American Indian (NMAI), New York, viewed May 4, 2023. Ives Goddard gave a similar translation in "The Origin and Meaning of the Name 'Manhattan,'" *New York History* 91, no. 4 (Fall 2010): 289. Goddard (ibid., 270–93) explained that Europeans long mistranslated *Manahatta* in a way that perpetuated calculated misinformation and reveals racial bias (e.g., "place of intoxication"). This is also discussed in Joanne Barker, "Territory as Analytic: The Dispossession of Lenapehoking and the Subprime Crisis," *Social Text* 36, no. 2 (June 2018): 27.
48. The monument was moved to its current location, nearby the original site, sometime between 1940 and 1952; see "The Battery: Netherland Monument," NYC Parks, accessed May 10, 2023, nycgovparks.org/parks/battery-park/monuments/1092.
49. The Delaware Tribe of Indians explains, "The name by which we call ourselves is Lenape," which roughly translates to "The People" or "The Original People"; Delaware Tribe of Indians, delawaretribe.org/blog/2013/06/26/faqs/. On Lenape languages and history, see "Our Tribal history," The Nanticoke Lenni-Lenape, nanticoke-lenape.info/history.htm; and Pritchard, *Native New Yorkers*, 14. On the Lenape's relationship to their homelands, see "About Us," Nanticoke Lenni-Lenape Tribal Nation, accessed Mar. 14, 2023, nlltribe.com/about-us/.
50. Wall text from *Native New York*, NMAI, viewed May 4, 2023. On the process of curating this exhibition, see Gabrielle Tayac, "Authoring Indigenous Studies in Three Dimensions: An Approach to Museum Curation," in *Sources and Methods in Indigenous Studies*, ed. Chris Andersen and Jean M. O'Brien (London: Routledge, Taylor and Francis, 2016), 230–38.
51. Otto, *Dutch-Munsee Encounter*, 164–65.
52. Anne-Marie Cantwell and Diana diZerega Wall, *Unearthing Gotham: The Archaeology of New York City* (New Haven, CT: Yale University Press, 2001), 298.
53. Grumet, *First Manhattans*, 25; and Otto, *Dutch-Munsee Encounter*, 79.
54. Otto, *Dutch-Munsee Encounter*, 83; and Cantwell and diZerega Wall, *Unearthing Gotham*, 167.
55. Notably, there are few documents, and no deed or bill of sale, that chronicle this fated purchase. Peter Schaghen only reported the "sale," not identifying the Lenape who participated in the agreement. On the "sale" as fraud, see Grumet, *First Manhattans*, 25–26; Otto, *Dutch-Munsee Encounter*, 93–98; Cantwell and diZerega Wall, *Unearthing Gotham*, 143–45, 188; and Barker, "Territory as Analytic," 27.
56. Some of the earliest deeds to land near Manhattan obtained by the Dutch West India Company confirm this hypothesis; see Grumet, *First Manhattans*, 30. These "misunderstandings" and manipulations were not unique to the Dutch; on British "remarkable indifference" to Native understandings of land and land tenure, see William Cronon, *Changes in the Land: Indians, Colonists, and the Ecology of New*

England (New York: Hill and Wang, 1983), 58–69.
57. Cantwell and diZerega Wall, *Unearthing Gotham*, 144–45.
58. Howard B. Rock and Deborah Dash Moore, *Cityscapes: A History of New York in Images* (New York: Columbia University Press, 2001), 6–7.
59. Between 1640 and 1645, thousands of Lenape men, women, and children were slaughtered, including during Kieft's War, also called the Wappinger War (1643–45); see, Grumet, *First Manhattans*, 17, 33–43; and Otto, *Dutch-Munsee Encounter*, 106–26. This violence continued under Director General of New Netherland Peter Stuyvesant, who governed the colony from 1647 to 1664, when the Dutch lost control to the British; Grumet, *First Manhattans*, 45–58. On population decline owing to epidemics, see also Grumet, *First Manhattans*, 17, 56, 107, 126–27, 137. On the destruction of Indigenous environmental infrastructures, see Emmanuel Kreike, *Scorched Earth: Environmental Warfare as a Crime against Humanity and Nature* (Princeton, NJ: Princeton University Press, 2021), 8–10.
60. Cantwell and diZerega Wall, *Unearthing Gotham*, 145–47, 167–68.
61. Otto, *Dutch-Munsee Encounter*, 163–64; and Cantwell and diZerega Wall, *Unearthing Gotham*, 147–48.
62. Cantwell and diZerega Wall, *Unearthing Gotham*, 147–48; and Otto, *Dutch-Munsee Encounter*, 176.
63. See the official websites for the Lenape Center, Delaware Nation, Nanticoke Lenni-Lenape Indians of New Jersey, Ramapough Lenape Indian Nation, Delaware First Nation/Moravian of the Thames First Nation, and Delaware Tribe of Indians. During Dutch occupation during the 1700s, the term *Delaware* was used to refer to Lenape along the Delaware River. Many Native communities who call themselves "Delaware" today are descendants of displaced Lenape peoples.
64. I discuss this issue at length in Sascha T. Scott, "Georgia O'Keeffe's Hawaiʻi?: Decolonizing the History of American Modernism," *American Art* 34, no. 2 (Summer 2020): 26–53.
65. Georgia O'Keeffe to Henry McBride, [Mar. 1925?]; and O'Keeffe to Dorothy Brett, mid-February 1932, reprinted in Jack Cowart and Juan Hamilton, with Sarah Greenough, *Georgia O'Keeffe: Art and Letters*, exh. cat. (Washington, DC: National Gallery of Art, in association with Boston: New York Graphic Society Books / Little, Brown, 1987), 179 and 205.
66. On these statements, see Amei Wallach, "Georgia O'Keeffe," *Newsday*, Oct. 30, 1977, 5; and Georgia O'Keeffe to Alfred Stieglitz, Mar. 25–27, 1939, box 91, folder 1798, Alfred Stieglitz / Georgia O'Keeffe Archive, Yale Collection of American Literature, Beinecke Rare Book and Manuscript Library, Yale University, New Haven, CT.
67. Aileen Moreton-Robinson, *The White Possessive: Property, Power, and Indigenous Sovereignty* (Minneapolis: University of Minnesota Press, 2015), 1–4.
68. Frances O'Brien, "Americans We Like: Georgia O'Keeffe," *The Nation*, Oct. 12, 1927, 361.
69. Quoted in Blanche C. Matthias, "Georgia O'Keeffe and the Intimate Gallery: Stieglitz Showing *Seven Americans*," *Chicago Evening Post, Magazine of the Art World*, Mar. 2, 1926, 14.
70. Frank, *Our America*, 10.

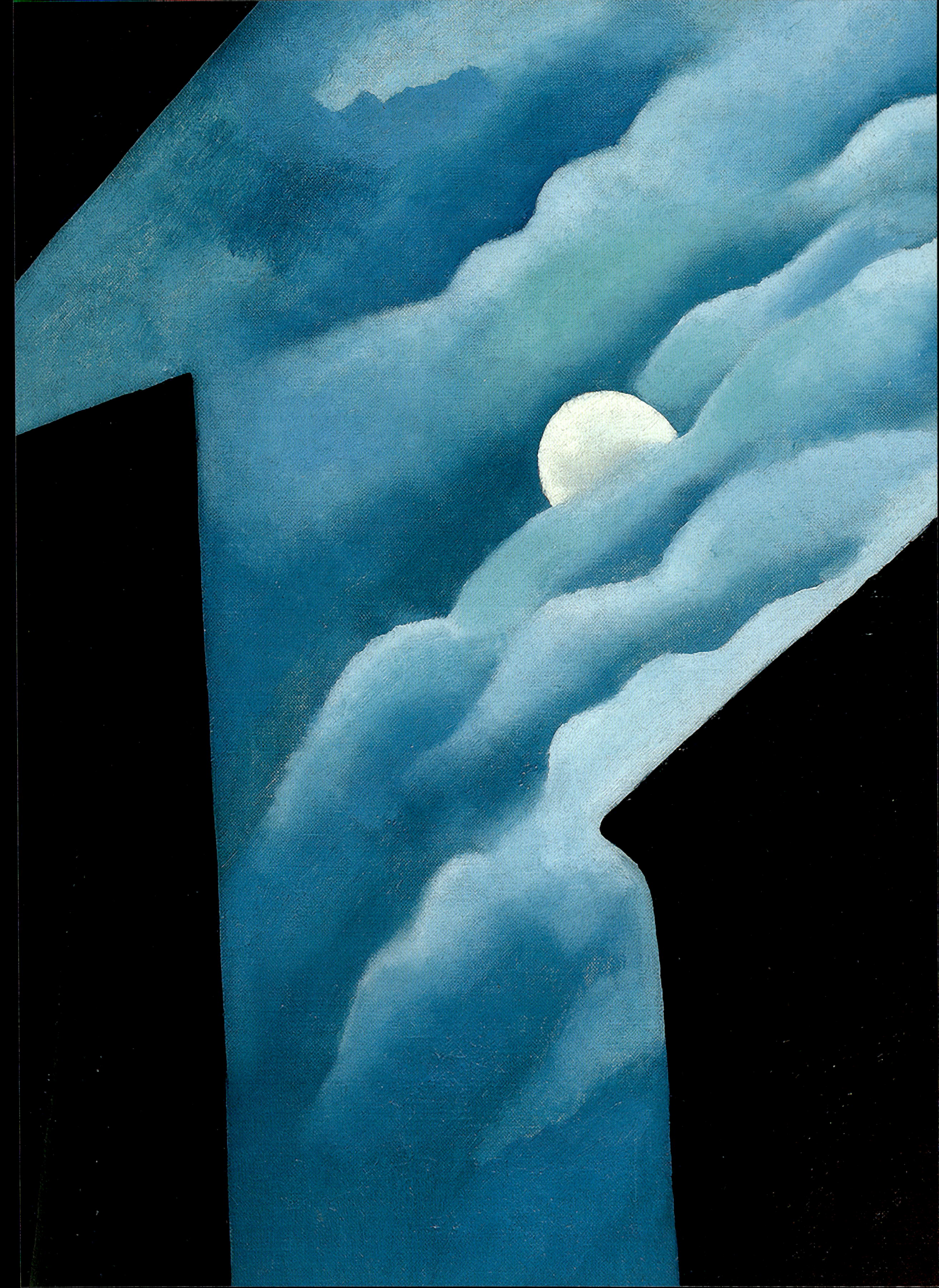

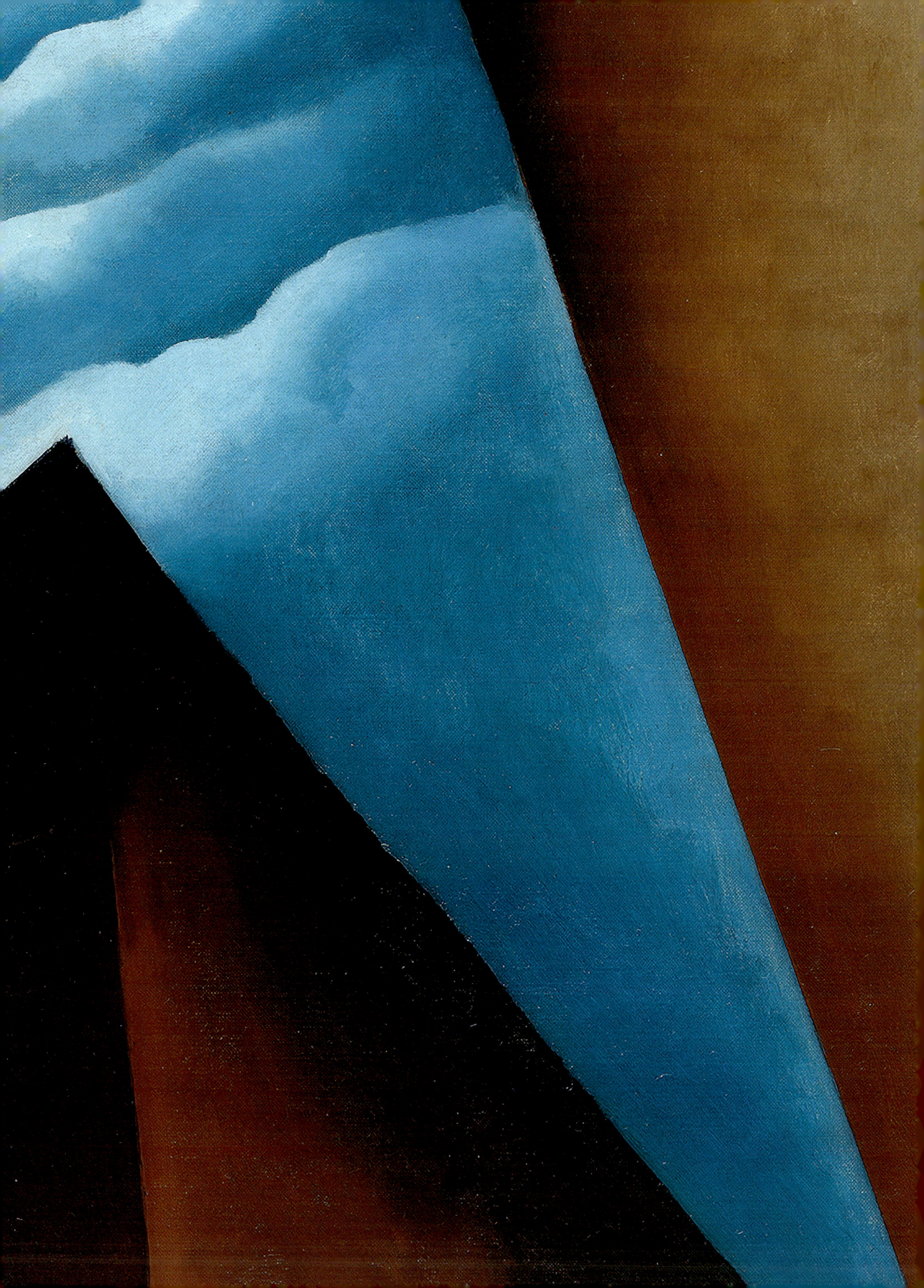

IMPOSSIBLE IDEAS

SEEING THE CITY WITH GEORGIA O'KEEFFE AND AARON DOUGLAS

Adrienne Brown

Renting an apartment on the upper floors of the thirty-one-story Shelton Hotel in the 1920s, as Georgia O'Keeffe later recalled, inspired her to start "talking about trying to paint New York."[1] "Of course," she noted, "I was told that it was an impossible idea—even the men hadn't done too well with it."[2] But O'Keeffe persisted and painted her first cityscape, *New York Street with Moon* (pl. 1), in 1925. Although Alfred Stieglitz did not include this work in his next show, when he finally exhibited the work a year later, it sold the afternoon of opening day. "No one ever objected to my painting New York after that," she wryly concluded.[3]

O'Keeffe's triumphalist account of besting "the men" has gained traction ever since. Scholarship since the 1970s has often replicated O'Keeffe's framework when contextualizing her work, situating her early cityscapes in relation to those produced by men in Stieglitz's circle who similarly sought a pictorial language for capturing the changing metropolis, as well as by the artists with whom they were engaging, studying, and rebutting. Common touchpoints for comparison include Stieglitz's urban photography and modernist works by George Ault, Charles Demuth, Walker Evans, Hugh Ferriss, Edward Hopper, John Marin, Charles Sheeler, Joseph Stella, and Edward Weston; the regionalist paintings of Thomas Hart Benton, John Steuart Curry, and Grant Wood; and occasional nods to the artwork of female contemporaries including Margaret Bourke-White, Imogen Cunningham, and Elsie Driggs.[4]

Such juxtapositions have occluded other ways of parsing O'Keeffe's approach to the "impossible idea" of urban capture. By the 1920s, the question of how to represent New York was decades old, plaguing not just artists but also statisticians and social scientists, politicians and revolutionaries. New York was increasing exponentially in size, scale, density, variety of vantage points, and population as its rapid infrastructural and demographic changes, in turn, transformed what it meant to see and be seen within the metropolis. The perceptual changes occasioned by cities expanding spatially and demographically remade seeing, knowing, and reading on multiple scales, from the individual body to the collective abstraction of the body politic. It is within this milieu of the city's growing masses of bodies and buildings—each of which stood accused of disrupting preexisting hierarchies—that I interrogate O'Keeffe's early efforts to depict New York.

Resituating O'Keeffe's early cityscapes beyond her immediate sphere of midtown Manhattan opens up her New York paintings for comparison with works by artists elsewhere in the city who were similarly perceived as less capable of producing "impossible" artistic feats. The air of patriarchal dismissal that suffuses O'Keeffe's account of first painting New York in the 1920s gestures toward the prevailing sense among her peers and critics that the work of urban representation was best left to male artists.[5] But the skepticism O'Keeffe recalled facing also hints at the yoked gendered *and* racial anxieties about metropolitan prowess, indexed by criticisms of her work in this period. Ever-taller buildings—with their effect on scale and density—coupled with the growing masses of racial and ethnic "others" together stood accused of diminishing the distinctive physical and mental characteristics of white urbanites by purportedly making their pedigree increasingly harder to spot and, by extension, preserve. Take, for example, the warnings of eugenicist Lothrop Stoddard in his 1920 bestseller, *The Rising Tide of Color against White World-Supremacy*, about the supposed decline of white urban populations worldwide—but especially in the United States—since the end of the nineteenth century. "The Nordic native American has been crowded out with amazing rapidity by these swarming, prolific aliens," Stoddard claimed, "and after two short generations he has in many of our urban areas become almost extinct."[6] The "crowding out" of urban whiteness Stoddard feared was as much an effect of a changing built environment as it was of immigration and birthrates, each troubling the purported ability to distinguish the "Nordic native" from the "alien" masses.[7] The popularity of race science and eugenics in America peaked in the 1920s, as did concerns about "race suicide" stemming from the relatively lower birth rates of native-born Anglo-Americans compared to other populations, further speaking to prevalent desires to reestablish a biological ordering to control a public and city deemed more unruly and incapable of being represented than ever before.[8] How might we consider O'Keeffe's "impossible idea" of urban representation, then, in relation to the work of contemporaries across the color line who—faced with the trenchant patriarchy and white nativism alike—were committed to "trying to paint New York," not only interrogating who and what belonged in the city but also imagining new ways to see and live within it?

This essay hazards a response by placing O'Keeffe's cityscapes in conversation with the oeuvre of another artist who began making images of New York in the late 1920s: Aaron Douglas, a figure most associated with the Harlem Renaissance. Although there is no conclusive record that Douglas and O'Keeffe ever met in the 1920s, they moved in overlapping social circles.[9] In the twenties, O'Keeffe could have seen the mural Douglas created to adorn a bathroom in her friend Carl Van Vechten's New York apartment, encountered his illustrations circulating in the city's broader print culture (see fig. 1), or bumped into him at an artist salon. Douglas, likewise, may have seen works by O'Keeffe at one of Stieglitz's galleries. If he failed to see her artwork in person, Douglas likely read about it in the many news stories covering her and her exhibitions in the local and national press.[10] Regardless of whether they met, Douglas and O'Keeffe offer a compelling artistic comparison: each used their work to interrogate what it meant to see and be seen in New York when the question of how bodies should appear and be made comprehensible within the ever-growing city was a matter of both aesthetic and social urgency.

In placing the work of Douglas and O'Keeffe in conversation, I take my lead from scholarship that centers Douglas—particularly the writing of Richard Powell, who has keenly argued that Douglas was "especially implicated in making city images that confront rather than acquiesce to" the skyscraper's "soaring, impersonal edifices."[11] Powell resituated Douglas's work alongside "a broad swathe of 'skyscraper painters,'" including O'Keeffe, whose works similarly sought "a spiritual yet constitutive understanding of two-dimensional monumentality."[12] O'Keeffe and Douglas pursued different, yet conversant, strategies for capturing the feel or spirit of the city in ways that exceeded the mimetic but were no less grounded in the concrete materiality of urban space. Focusing on their approaches to dimensionality, darkness, and the role of the human figure will illuminate the investments Douglas and O'Keeffe shared by shifting our perspective to better see each of them within the same urban scene.

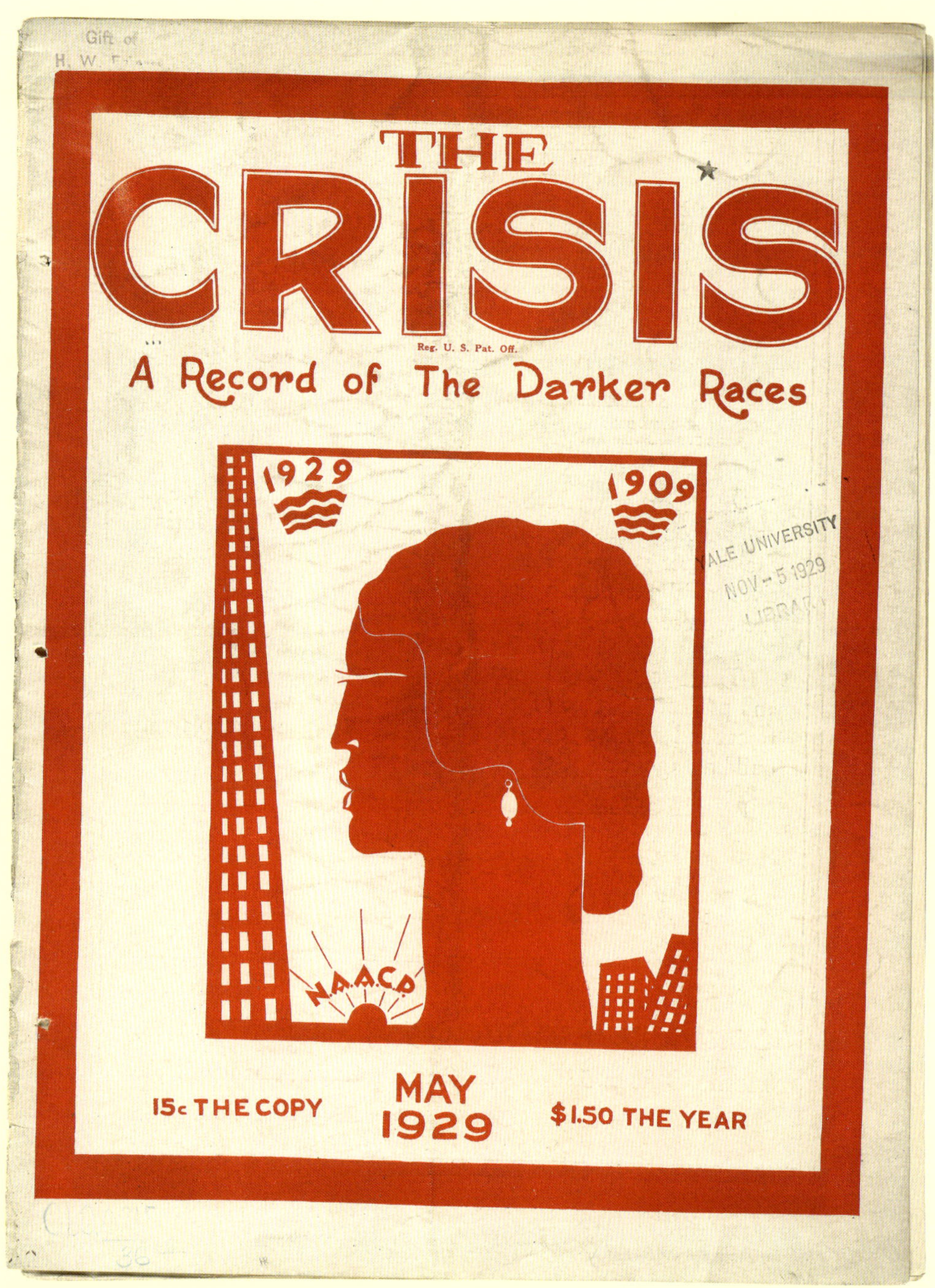

THE SKYSCRAPER FRONTIER

Anxiety about urban representation in the 1920s belonged to a broader, decades-long crisis about the city's intelligibility.[13] One way to limn the depth of concern about urban space is to tether it to anxieties about the recently declared "closure" of the Western frontier. The ideology of frontier expansion, with its promises of endless access to land and unmapped spaces achieved through Native dispossession, had fueled settlers' movements westward—as well as the country's identity—for much of the previous century. With the United States now officially stretching from sea to shining sea, once Washington achieved statehood in 1889, historians and public intellectuals worried about the endurance of American exceptionalism without an active frontier driving its self-understanding.[14] In the wake of this change, the skyscraper became one potential site that the nation could transpose and revive as a new, upward conceptualization of the aspirational frontier.

FIG. 1
Aaron Douglas (American, 1899–1979). Cover of *The Crisis* 36, no. 5 (May 1929).

American ambitions of geographic expansion did not, of course, end with the settlement of the continental United States. President Theodore Roosevelt's imperialist policies in the Philippines, Cuba, and Panama in the early twentieth century proved almost immediately that the country's investment in horizontal spatial conquest was far from dead. And yet, as America established itself from coast to coast through conquest, figures like Roosevelt worried about how domestic attitudes toward space would begin to shift from one of infinite plenitude to one of enclosure, limitation, and maintenance. When the president implored the nation in 1903 to leave the Grand Canyon "as it is," seeking its preservation for and from man so it could remain "the one great sight which every American should see," he failed to account for the ways that changing spatial, technological, imperial, and aesthetic practices were altering the very character of Americans' sight itself.[15] The skyscraper would not only come to usurp the Grand Canyon as an iconic American symbol—it would also change the ways in which "every American should see," full stop. Many would seek to make sense of how these spatial and perceptual changes were altering mythologies about the essence of Americanness.

Roosevelt hazarded his own answer five years later in a 1908 speech at the Corcoran Gallery of Art in Washington, DC, in which he grappled with the possibilities for a new urban picturesque. Delivered during the final months of his eight-year presidency, Roosevelt's speech questioned whether the industrial cityscape—the new engine of American exceptionalism—could ever present as powerful a picture or as enticing an ideology as its frontier predecessor. Narrating how the American people "conquered a continent," "laced it with railways," and "dotted it with cities," Roosevelt stepped back to appreciate the "marvellous [*sic*] artistic effects" produced by recent industrial growth, if "quite unconsciously."[16] He then anointed the skyscraper the next great innovator in the schema of national development, anticipating that "some day people will realize that one effect of the 'sky-scraper' in New York" has been "to produce a city of singularly imposing type and of unexampled picturesque." The agent of this realization, Roosevelt prophecied, would be a "great artist" who had "yet to arise" but would one day "bring before our eyes the powerful irregular sky-line of the great city at sunset, or in the noon-day brightness, and, above all, at night, when the lights flash from the dark, mountainous mass of buildings, from the stately bridges that span the East River, and from the myriad craft that blaze as they ply to and fro across the waters."

By placing the skyscraper within a broader chronology of American spatial aesthetics, Roosevelt folded this architecture into a coherent system of national representation. His narrative lays out a smoother geographic trajectory of nationhood than was ever actually the case, granting the United States a clear linear progression from continental domination to urbanization. Within this picture of progress, the skyscraper emerges as the logical next step in the technological seeding of the land, its verticality downplayed to better synthesize its development within older horizontal frameworks of settlement. Roosevelt further assimilated the skyscraper into a frontier lineage by assigning natural characteristics to this newer form. He described New York in terms of the "mountainous mass" of its "irregular sky-line," rendering its jagged architectural silhouette in the imagery of peaks and crags. Sunlight, stone, and water became Roosevelt's requisite framing devices for viewing the city, naturalizing the "imposing type" of the skyscraper and the city surrounding it. Roosevelt recast New York not as an alien and alienating space, as others claimed, but as a vibrant, new frontier rooted in the cycle of endless Anglo-American conquest that had begun all over again, if in more vertical terms.[17]

Draping the skyscraper in frontier tropes had another desired effect for Roosevelt and others like him seeking to bring the city into order: it helped cleanse the

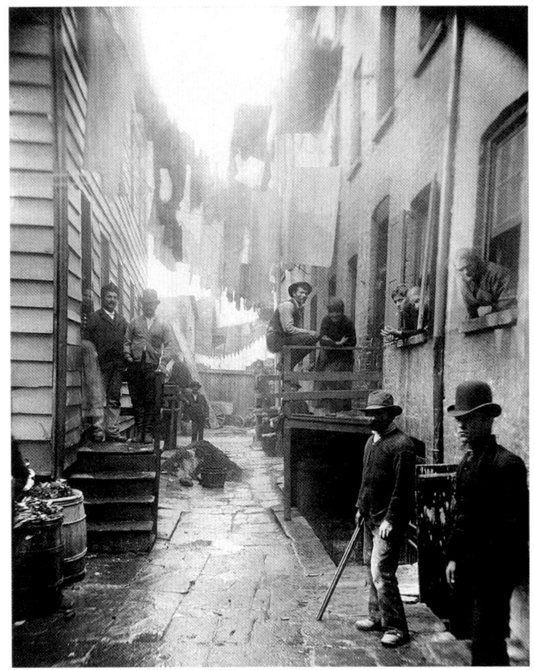

skyscraper of its correlation with the racial disorder also associated with urban space at the time. City boosters, for example, wielded frontier imagery at the turn of the century as a tactic for countering New York's connections to mass immigration, as historian Angela Blake has explained, making the city more approachable for a burgeoning class of white domestic tourists.[18] Roosevelt invoked the unpeopled vista of the eastern industrial frontier, while at the same time heralding the photographer and reformer Jacob August Riis, whose popular images of New York revealed the living conditions of the urban poor—primarily crumbling old tenements that stood in striking contrast to the era's new, gleaming commercial skyscrapers (see fig. 2).[19] Roosevelt was largely sympathetic to the reformist efforts of Riis, whom he cited as "the most useful citizen of New York."[20] And yet, Roosevelt's representation of the city omits any reference to the teeming streets and ethnic enclaves Riis had publicly documented. Just as popular nineteenth-century paintings of empty Western landscapes obscured the presence of Native peoples, Roosevelt's vision of the cityscape served the white settler-colonialist legacy he was most keen to preserve while allowing the industrial miracles of American ingenuity to shine alone, freed from the messy, huddled ethnic masses also staking a claim to New York's "material achievements"—a choice later echoed in O'Keeffe's renderings of skyscrapers isolated from the populations with which they shared space.

Despite Roosevelt's efforts to empty the cityscape of its troublesome populace in his 1908 speech, he remained uncertain of when the skyscrapered cityscape might come into its own as a representable vista. His urban meditation ends with a call for the messianic appearance of an artist to complete the aesthetic synthesis of the lost frontier and this emerging industrial space. Given Roosevelt's obsession with masculinity in both his self-presentation and his theorizations of the nation's virile past, we can assume he did not picture a woman when calling for a "great artist" to wrestle the "irregular sky-line of the great city" into a capturable form. But in some ways, O'Keeffe was exactly whom Roosevelt sought—someone who cut her teeth pictorially on the prairies and cities of the Midwest, the open sky of Texas, and the churning waters of Maine before turning her eye and hand to scaling the verticality of New York City. It is even less likely that Roosevelt envisioned this "great artist" as Black, and yet Aaron Douglas, too, had a spatial and aesthetic pedigree fitting the bill. A son of Topeka, Kansas, Douglas shuttled between the Midwestern locales of Nebraska, Minnesota, and Missouri before making his way to New York City in 1925 with a desire to render its angularity and energy anew.[21] Unknowingly answering Roosevelt's call, Douglas and O'Keeffe each fashioned themselves as manifestations of his prophecy while interrogating and dismantling his aesthetic mandates for urban representation along the way.

FIG. 2
Jacob August Riis (American, born Denmark, 1849–1914). *Bandits' Roost, 59 ½ Mulberry Street*, 1888, printed 1958. Gelatin silver print; 48.7 × 39.4 cm (19 3⁄16 × 15 ½ in.). The Museum of Modern Art, New York, gift of the Museum of the City of New York, 326.1959.

DOUGLAS AND O'KEEFFE IN CONVERSATION

Despite their differences in race, gender, audience, and medium, Douglas and O'Keeffe took respective approaches to urban representation in the 1920s that feel dynamically conversant. Consider their shared interest in rendering the city at night, returning once more to Roosevelt's divinatory call for a great artist to represent New York: such a figure

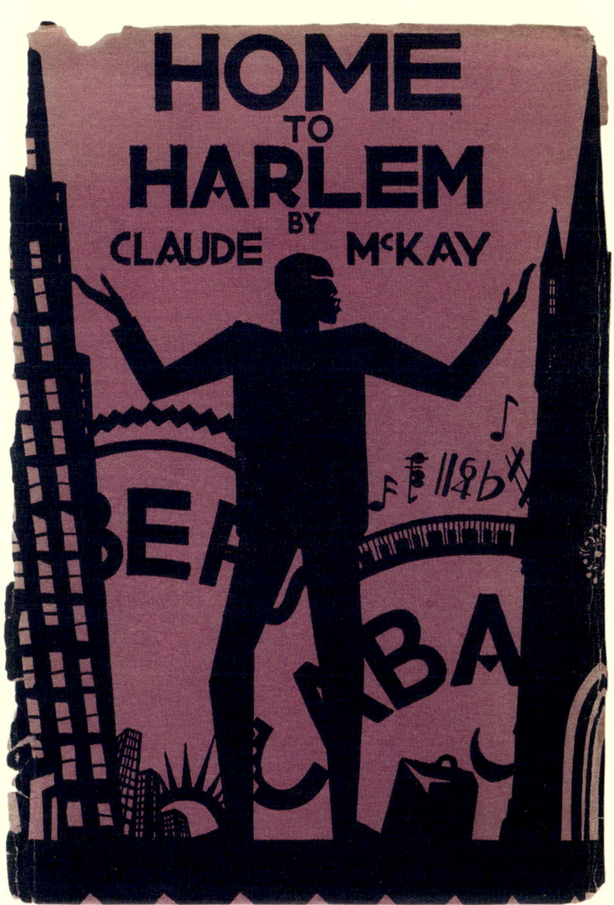

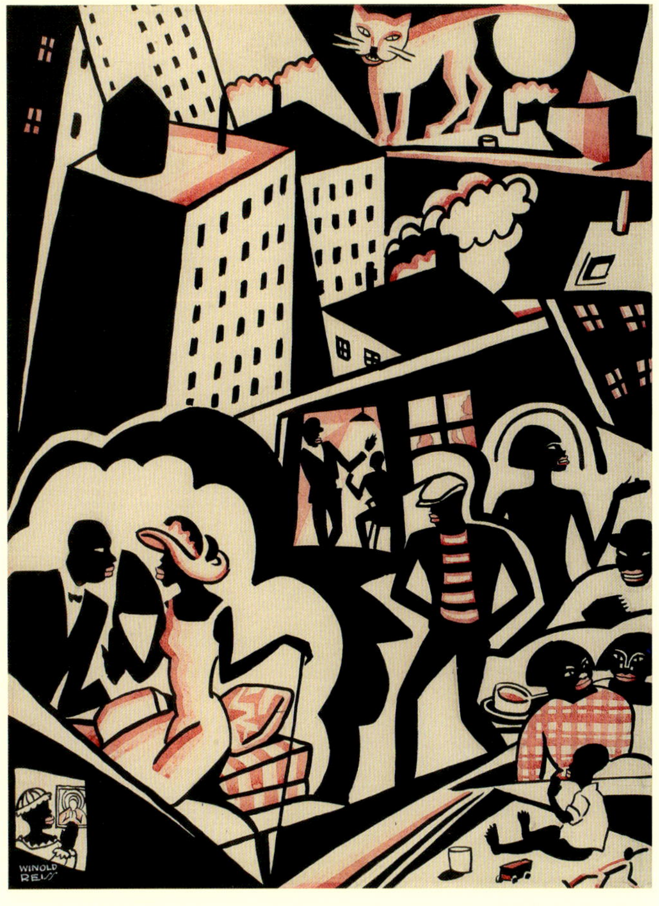

would be able to represent the city "above all, at night, when the lights flash from the dark, mountainous mass of buildings."[22] Whereas the skyscraper might favor the mountainous masses of the Western frontier in daylight, the chasm between these landscapes was most pronounced at night when the city's manmade sources of illumination increasingly outshone the moonlight. The city at night appears prominently in the work of both Douglas and O'Keeffe from the late 1920s, in pictures and canvases cloaked in blackness—if different shades and types—a choice distinguishing their oeuvres from other urban painters at the time.

Douglas would become best known for the mystical murals and friezes he completed in the 1930s and 1940s, but he first made his name in 1920s New York as an illustrator, creating distinctive cityscape covers for some of the most prominent literary works of the Harlem Renaissance. In these early works, largely produced using a pared-down color palette of two or three hues, the time of day can be hard to pinpoint. The glowing skyscraper windows in some and the occasional small crescent moon in the corners of others—such as his cover for Claude McKay's novel *Home to Harlem* (fig. 3)—help to subtly signal their nighttime settings. Some of Douglas's first night scenes play explicitly with the association between Black life and nightlife in an era when the club and cabaret scenes in New York City—and especially in Harlem—were all the rage. His earliest works borrow from his teacher Winold Reiss's stylized renderings of Black Harlem as a nighttime space indebted to jazz aesthetics in which people, buildings, and public space came alive (see fig. 4).

But Douglas grew less interested in identifiable nightscapes over time as his silhouetted images began to look the same, whether illuminated by sun, moon, or streetlights, emphasizing the timelessness of his scenes over their situatedness despite their modern trappings. As Susan Earle pointed out, Douglas's work from this period is notable for its commitment to public accessibility—circulating largely in mass publications—and

FIG. 3
Douglas. Dust jacket of Claude McKay, *Home to Harlem* (New York: Harper and Brothers, 1928).

FIG. 4
Winold Reiss (German, 1886–1953). *Harlem at Night*, 1924. Ink on paper; 50.8 × 38.1 cm (20 × 15 in.). Collection of Renate Reiss.

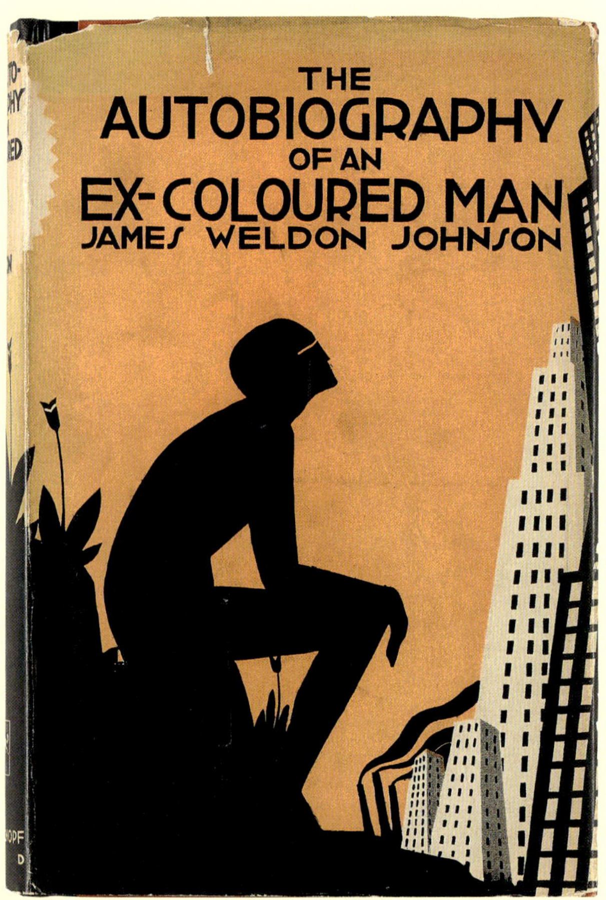

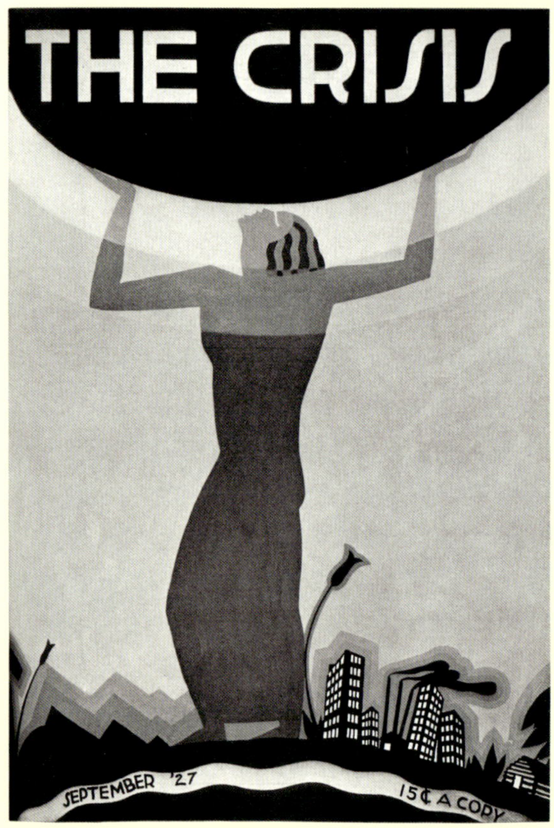

collaboration, as Douglas worked with artists and editors to produce images that evoke specific texts and themes.[23] In this spirit, his work rarely represents a locatable point of view or even a single moment in time (see fig. 5) but evokes instead the striving yet melancholic mood of Black modernity developing over eons. The indeterminacy between night and day in these works attunes viewers to the transhistorical spirit of Black urban life defying plottable time. In the age of what his contemporary Alain Locke termed "the New Negro," Douglas framed Blackness as more than a style or passing fascination, counter to what many white critics predicted at the height of the Harlem Renaissance. Instead, Douglas represented Black presence as a continuous driver of aesthetic, industrial, philosophical, and spiritual life from the mythic past up through the skyscrapered present. Whereas O'Keeffe moved deeper over the course of her career toward investigating the intricacies of light and space in specific places, Douglas moved toward generality in order to insist on the continuity of Black presence across time and space, a presence frequently diminished in both the visual and historical records in which he intervened.

Douglas's restricted color palette in this period further evokes the openness of time, mood, and space in his work. Although he often used electric oranges, deep reds, and hazy grays as contrasting background shades, Douglas most regularly called upon a single, unifying shade of black to render a host of forms—human, natural, and architectural. On the cover illustration he created for Claude McKay's 1928 novel *Home to Harlem*, for instance, silhouetted renderings share the same deep shade of black, unifying the appearance of bodies and buildings. Blackness here is both racial—the figure at the center of the image is African American, rendered in a shade darker than any person—and atmospheric, producing a fusion between Black figures and urban modernity often dismissed or denied in the period. Even when working in grayscale, as Douglas did in his September 1927 cover for the National Association for the Advancement of Colored People's magazine, *The Crisis* (fig. 6), his dwarfed skyscrapers glow as if

FIG. 5
Douglas. Dust jacket of James Weldon Johnson, *Autobiography of an Ex-Coloured Man* (New York: A. A. Knopf, 1927).

FIG. 6
Douglas. *The Burden of Black Womanhood*, 1927. Cover of *The Crisis* 34, no. 7 (Sept. 1927).

illuminated at night, while the large figure of a Black woman rises above these structures to hold up a glowing orb, which could represent either the sun or the moon. Douglas ultimately allowed for the connection between Black life and skyscrapers to become newly visible in his cityscapes as he often enlarged his Black figures to rival the steel structures they graze and touch, recentering Blackness within modernity writ large.

Whereas Douglas's images represent the collective dream space of Black modernity, O'Keeffe's cityscapes conjure the ways the city's changing built environment was making the vision of grounded individuals appear spectacular and, at times, even surreal. Rather than use indeterminacy to conjure a quasi-allegorical mood of a people as Douglas did, O'Keeffe depicted sensorial challenges to determinacy as experienced by a lone city dweller. Although O'Keeffe painted a few daytime cityscapes—most famously *The Shelton with Sunspots, N.Y.* (pl. 12)—many of her most iconic images of New York depict it at night. In paintings such as *New York Street with Moon* (pl. 1), *City Night* (pl. 21), *Radiator Building—Night, New York* (pl. 16), *Ritz Tower* (pl. 17), and *New York, Night* (pl. 62), the moon competes with or is eclipsed by streetlights, stoplights, spotlights, billboards, and lit-up windows that float, glow, and almost blink. In many of these works, smoke and clouds blur indistinguishably, eerily lit in blues, whites, and greens that just as easily conjure the Northern Lights as the smoggy urban sky. Never simplistically dark, O'Keeffe's nighttime paintings render the city scenes, often eerie, in a broad spectrum of colors. Bronzes, reds, blues, and the whitish-yellow of two glowing spheres dominate *New York Street with Moon*, whereas the sky and buildings in *City Night*, made a year later, appear so bright that, without the insertion of a few twinkling stars, the scene could be mistaken for being set during the day. O'Keeffe captured how artificial light changed the ways the city looked at night but also understood how the shadows of ever-rising skyscrapers could make it appear as though night was descending at any time of day. O'Keeffe painted a city with little respect for circadian rhythms, depicting the blurry perceptual line between night and day, darkness and light, being remade by an increasingly monumental urbanity. If Douglas's images "confront" the skyscraper's "impersonal edifices" with monumental, eons-spanning visions of Blackness, as Richard Powell noted, O'Keeffe's quietly marvel at the noirish wonder of the growing city as she saw it—a potentially powerful statement of its own given the position of critics who undercut her talents, peers most interested in her as a vessel of white femininity, and nativists calling for aggrieved solidarity in a city "swarmed" by "prolific aliens." O'Keeffe painted the city from the perspective of an autonomous individual, locating its strange beauty not in its people but in its structures , which were, in turn, changing how and what people saw.[24]

For both Douglas and O'Keeffe, blackness proved essential to their new visions—Douglas using a single shade of black to render bodies and buildings alike, and O'Keeffe using richly varied shades of the color in her paintings of this period. *Radiator Building—Night, New York* and *Black Abstraction* (fig. 7)—both painted in 1927—show her ability in wielding chromatic blackness with dimension and depth. Although Stieglitz frequently associated O'Keeffe with a "special white aura," and Marsden Hartley, an artist in Stieglitz's circle, described her as "impaled with a white consciousness"—comments reflecting her agility with chromatic whiteness as well as each man's investment in her as an ideal of racial whiteness—O'Keeffe's work from the late 1920s attests to her equally powerful interest and skill in representing chromatic blackness.[25] O'Keeffe's agile approach to blackness in her cityscapes is further highlighted when placed

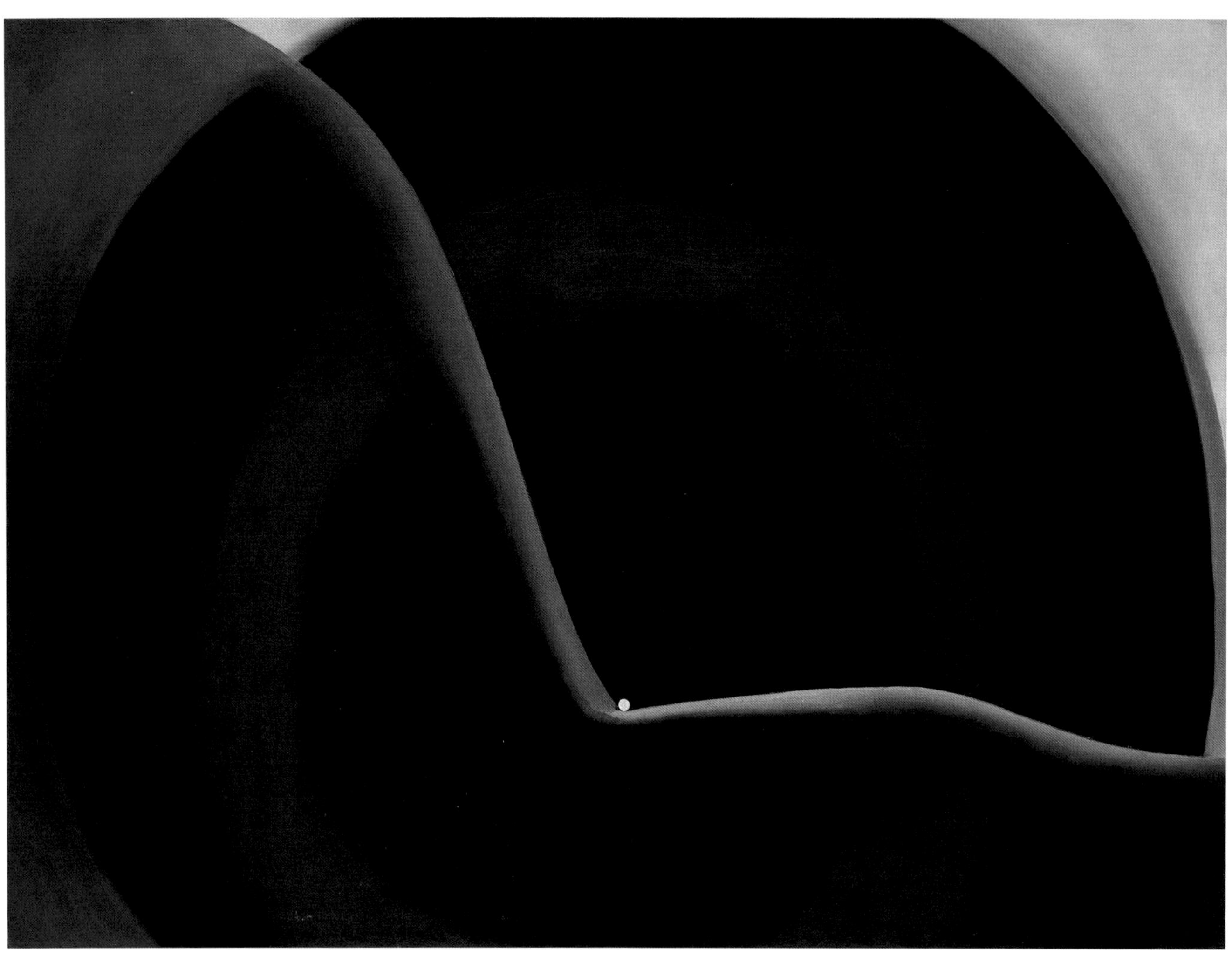

FIG. 7
Georgia O'Keeffe (American, 1887–1986). *Black Abstraction*, 1927. Oil on canvas; 76.2 × 102.2 cm (30 × 40 ¼ in.). The Metropolitan Museum of Art, New York, Alfred Stieglitz Collection, 1969, 69.278.2.

alongside a much later work by artist Kerry James Marshall, ever the student—and critic—of the art historical canon. In Marshall's 2015 painting *Untitled (Policeman)* (fig. 8), a Black policeman dominates the canvas, pictured in hues of blue and black enriched by glowing streetlights that surround him. Almost a century prior, O'Keeffe deployed a similar palette of blacks, blues, and glowing whites and yellows in her painting *City Night*, rendering a different black monolith with the same kind of soft monumentality. In addition to sharing color schemes, Marshall's painting demonstrates a "meditative eloquence and quiet unresolvedness," as one critic described it, that rhymes with the tone of O'Keeffe's work.[26] The main subjects in each painting—the black skyscraper in O'Keeffe's and the Black policeman in Marshall's—evoke like qualities of solitude, complexity, and unmoving presence that refuse to cohere into a judgment about said subject. Both artists wielded blackness in darkness to produce tonally and chromatically conversant portraits of modernity, each pointing to the era's doubts and contradictions in times of perceptual and social tumult.[27] This connection between Marshall and O'Keeffe, moreover, highlights the dialogue between O'Keeffe's and Douglas's capture of the simultaneous awe and disquiet of urban perception.

Flatness is another tool Douglas and O'Keeffe leveraged to represent urban space. Douglas most notably committed to two-dimensionality in his embrace of the silhouette. As he explained of this choice, "I tried to keep my forms very stark and geometric with my main emphasis on the human body," resulting in what he described as a "simplified and abstract" style evoking "the starkness of the old spirituals" while simultaneously "painting modern."[28] African American culture and jazz scholar Robert O'Meally described Douglas's style as "a play of liquid smoothness and jagged texturation"

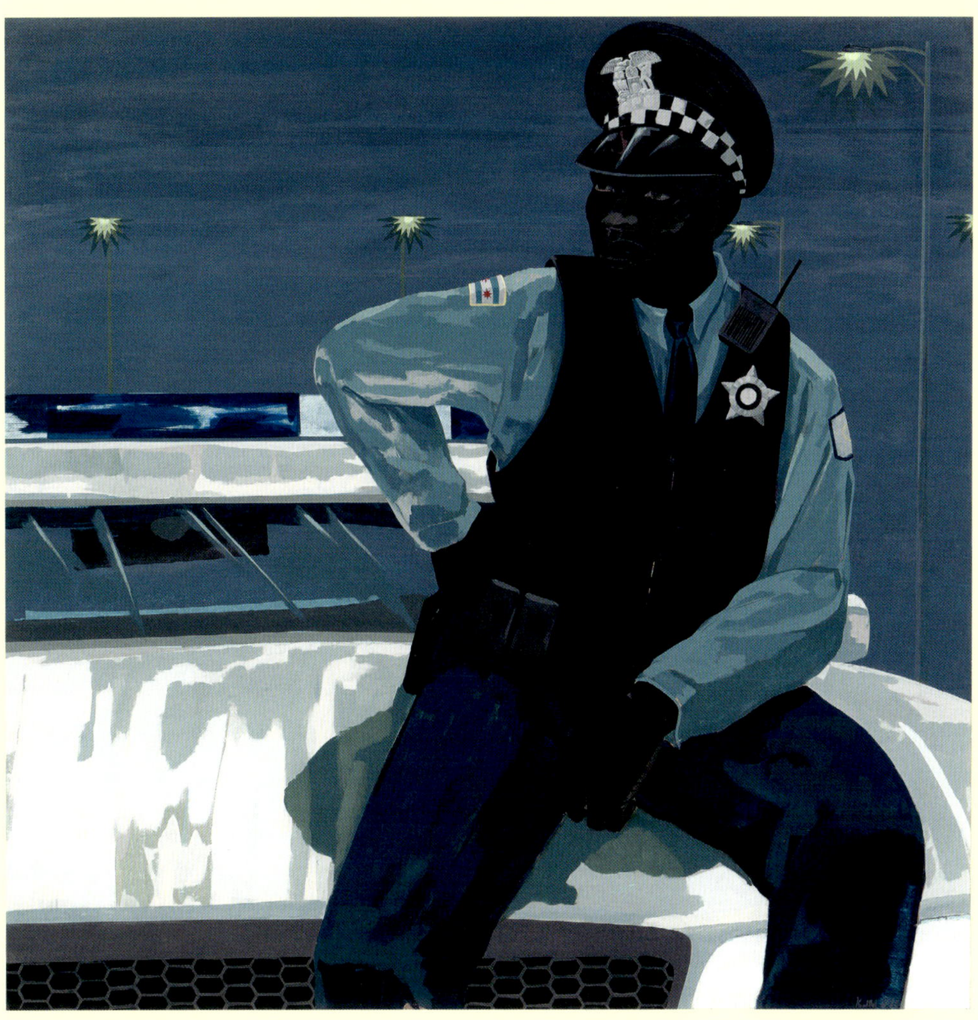

combining a "modernist assertion of the flatness of the picture plane" in dialogue with Pablo Picasso, Henri Matisse, and Georges Braque but also with the traditional arts of Africa, Asia, the Pacific Islands, and Greece.[29] His figures' jagged flatness creates the appearance of continuous movement, physical and existential in nature, as they seem to either dance across the pictorial plane or lose themselves in a meditative stillness amid a world moving all around them.[30] At times O'Keeffe's approach to the picture plane also conjures flatness, if less directly than Douglas. The straight-on perspective through which she captured the Radiator Building in 1927 mimics depth through the layering of flat rectangles.[31] In charcoal drawings (see pls. 13–14) and paintings such as *East River from the Shelton, No. III* (pl. 55), the city appears as an array of piled shapes. In more vertically oriented pieces such as *City Night* and *A Street* (pl. 15), she emphasized the canyon-like heights of skyscrapers forming the city's cavernous walls and framing pedestrians' visual access to the open sky above.

In contrast to several contemporary artists of this period who embraced flatness in the wake of Cubism, O'Keeffe and Douglas developed approaches to two-dimensionality that fail to be attributed to this movement's influence alone. They each proved less interested in assembling a scene from multiple simultaneous perspectives and more in rendering the angularity of a single viewpoint, as O'Keeffe did, or evoking a sleek modernity that was also mythic and timeless, like Douglas. The spiritual sublimity each artist conjured in their cityscapes feels deeply auratic and, at times, forlorn, as a counterpoint to the dense overwhelmingness stressed by other artists painting the city. Portraying New York as it felt and with the forms of sight it enabled, Douglas and O'Keeffe departed from literalism while never obscuring the city's grounded materiality

FIG. 8

Kerry James Marshall (American, b. 1955). *Untitled (Policeman)*, 2015. Acrylic on PVC panel with plexiglass frame; 152.4 × 152.4 cm (60 × 60 in.). The Museum of Modern Art, New York, gift of Mimi Haas in honor of Marie-Josée Kravis, 8.2016.

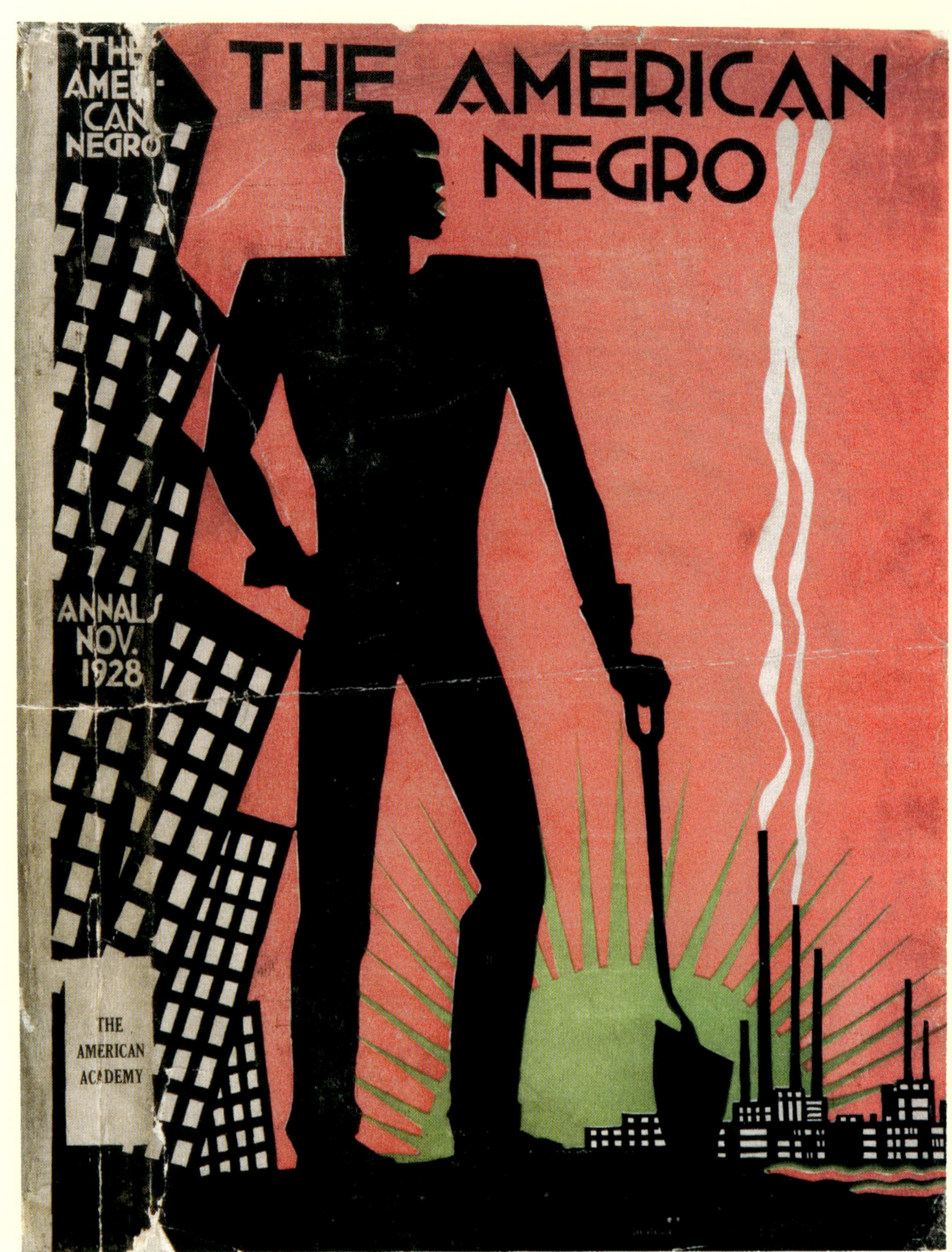

FIG. 9
Douglas. Cover of Clyde L. King, *The American Negro: The Annals* (Philadelphia: American Academy of Political and Social Sciences, 1928).

by centering either the new steel structures (O'Keeffe) or newly migrated bodies (Douglas) central to its sublimity.

O'Keeffe and Douglas parted ways, significantly, in their rendering of the human figure itself within these conditions. Black bodies not only appear prominently in Douglas's images but also often overwhelm the neighboring steel structures, swallowing up and demanding space within the city (see fig. 9). Douglas may not have felt he had the luxury to ignore the body in his images of New York given the lynchings and race riots erupting across urban and rural space alike in the 1920s.[32] In O'Keeffe's New Yorks, not only are people absent but her seemingly neutral view of the world has led many critics to assign the camera credit for her eye, as is famously the case with *The Shelton with Sunspots, N.Y.*[33] She created work from the perspective of the human observer, but the human is never what we observe in her cityscapes.[34]

We can understand O'Keeffe's approach in at least two ways. One is to interpret her disinterest in human figures as a sign of evading the urban—and increasingly ethnic—masses, whom figures like Lothrop Stoddard feared would doom the white

metropolitan to categorical extinction.[35] Just as earlier frontier landscapes of the Americas removed or diminished Indigenous presences, we might approach O'Keeffe's cityscapes as similarly occluding the changing face of New York—a city where, by 1910, more than three-fourths of inhabitants were either immigrants or had a foreign-born parent and whose Black population grew forty percent between 1910 and 1930.[36] This reading situates O'Keeffe within the nationalist—and nativist—aesthetic project that Roosevelt called for in 1908. But in reading O'Keeffe after Douglas, her decision to create cityscapes devoid of people also illuminates a strategy for capturing how these buildings made one see and feel, rather than how they made one feel seen. In contrast to efforts at the time to claim O'Keeffe as being "impaled with a white consciousness," the vision of the city she offered us appears, at times, intensely autonomous, unattributable to any community beyond herself (take the red neon sign spelling out "Alfred Stieglitz" in *Radiator Building—Night, New York* [see fig. 10, pl. 16]); at others, she depicted the vantage point of any urban dweller, as in *New York Street with Moon*, uninterested in rendering *white* consciousness but, rather, an emerging *urban* consciousness trying to make sense of how the city was transforming consciousness itself and, by extension, the ability to register difference from within the city. Instead of reading her New York paintings as keeping the masses just out of the pictorial frame—all the better to celebrate an unsullied urban sublimity—we might understand these works as an attempt to study the architecture that newly framed how race could show up in a changing city where night and day, Black and white, flatness and depth were proving harder to distinguish from one another. Aaron Douglas and Georgia O'Keeffe, each through the radical reorganization of New York's landscape and population unfolding around them, interrogated not just what one might see differently but how one could see at all in a city where "impossible ideas" were increasingly becoming real.

FIG. 10
Detail of *Radiator Building—Night, New York*, 1927 (pl. 16).

NOTES

1. Georgia O'Keeffe, *Georgia O'Keeffe* (New York: Viking Press, 1976), n.p., opp. pl. 17.

2. Ibid.

3. Ibid., n.p., opp. pl. 18.

4. See, for instance, Peter R. Kalb, *High Drama: The New York Skyscrapers of Georgia O'Keeffe and Margaret Bourke-White* (New York: Midmarch Arts Press, 2003).

5. For three examples see Kalb, *High Drama*; Lisa Mintz Messinger, *Georgia O'Keeffe* (New York: Thames and Hudson, 2001); and Randall R. Griffey, "Reconsidering the 'Soil': The Stieglitz Circle, the Regionalists and Cultural Eugenics in the Twenties," in *Youth and Beauty: Art of the Twentieth Century*, ed. Teresa A. Carbone (New York: Skira Rizzoli Publications, in association with the Brooklyn Museum, 2011), 245–77.

6. Lothrop Stoddard, *The Rising Tide of Color against White World-Supremacy* (New York: Charles Scribner's Sons, 1922), 165.

7. See Adrienne Brown, *The Black Skyscraper: Architecture and the Perception of Race* (Baltimore: Johns Hopkins University Press, 2017).

8. The question of who counted as white in this period—as well as how to define race more broadly—was a fraught one. As Matthew Frye Jacobson noted: "The contest over whiteness—its definition, its internal hierarchies, its proper boundaries, and its rightful claimants has been fairly untidy." Those considered white later in the twentieth century, including Eastern Europeans and the Irish, were less firmly identified as such in the earlier decades. Matthew Frye Jacobson, *Whiteness of a Different Color: European Immigrants and the Alchemy of Race* (Cambridge, MA: Harvard University Press, 1998), 6.

9. Douglas and O'Keeffe would more certainly have encountered one another decades later at Fisk University, to whom O'Keeffe bequeathed a portion of Stieglitz's art collection in 1949 and where Douglas taught from the mid-1940s until his 1966 retirement. It is also possible they crossed paths years prior in Manhattan, where movement between the city's Black and white arts scenes was largely brokered by Carl Van Vechten—a writer, photographer, and inveterate socialite who was close to both artists. It was Van Vechten who encouraged O'Keeffe to eventually leave part of Stieglitz's collection to Fisk University.

10. For more on the relationship between Douglas and Van Vechten, see Amy Helene Kirschke, *Aaron Douglas: Art, Race, and The Harlem Renaissance* (Jackson: University Press of Mississippi, 1995); and Richard J. Powell, *Black Art and Culture in the 20th Century* (New York: Thames and Hudson, 1997). For the relationship between O'Keeffe and Van Vechten, see Roxana Robinson, *Georgia O'Keeffe: A Life*, expand. ed. (New York: Harper and Row, 1989; Waltham, MA: Brandeis University, 2020). Harlem Renaissance writer Jean Toomer is another possible bridge between them. O'Keeffe met Toomer in the early 1920s, and the two had an intense and likely intimate connection that unfolded over the next ten years. Douglas's connection to Toomer was more spiritual in nature, with Toomer introducing Douglas to the teachings of Russian Armenian mystic G. I. Gurdjieff, whose work they would study together. See Amanda Mehsima Licato, "The Shared Journeys of Jean Toomer and Georgia O'Keeffe," *Yale Program in the History of Book* (blog), bookhistory.yale.edu/blog/shared-journeys-jean-toomer-and-georgia-okeeffe.

11. Richard J. Powell, "Paint That Thing! Aaron Douglas's Call to Modernism," *American Studies* 49, nos. 1–2 (Spring–Summer 2008): 108.

12. Ibid.

13. For many in the early twentieth century, as literary critic Enda Duffy described, "space ceased to be credibly representable." Duffy pointed to the work of European modernist writers such as Marcel Proust and James Joyce who became obsessed with time as a refuge from spatial chaos, but we might just as readily claim the painterly movements of Expressionism, Surrealism, and Regionalism as having similar aims. Enda Duffy, *The Speed Handbook: Velocity, Pleasure, Modernism* (Durham, NC: Duke University Press, 2009), 102–3.

14. Frederick Jackson Turner's 1893 history, "The Significance of the Frontier in American History," most notably attributed American ingenuity, egalitarianism, and intelligence to a process of Western conquest he believed had enabled American settlers to fully break with the moribund cultures of Europe and craft an original mode of selfhood. For a version of Turner's history, see "The Significance of the Frontier in American History (1893)," American Historical Association, historians.org/about-aha-and-membership/aha-history-and-archives/historical-archives/the-significance-of-the-frontier-in-american-history-(1893).

15. Theodore Roosevelt, *Presidential Addresses and State Papers: February 19, 1902, to May 13, 1903*, vol. 1 (Whitefish, MT: Kessinger Publishing, 2006), 370. Roosevelt made this speech at the Grand Canyon on May 6, 1903.

16. Theodore Roosevelt, *Presidential Addresses and State Papers*, vol. 8 (New York: Review of Reviews Company, 1910), 2009. Subsequent quotations in this paragraph come from the same source.

17. Despite Roosevelt's confident rhetoric of American progress, his speech nonetheless reveals his niggling concern that national space was not as legible or knowable as it once was. We can see this in his suggestion that urban beauty emerges "quite unconsciously" and only "incidentally" produces "marvelous artistic effects" as happenstance. Space, and aesthetics more broadly, no longer seem to have locatable agents in his scenario; the picturesqueness of the industrialized cityscape is best understood as a kind of pleasing accident to be parsed only after the fact. Ibid.

18. Angela Blake, *How New York Became American, 1890–1924* (Baltimore: Johns Hopkins University Press, 2006).

19. Jacob Riis, *How the Other Half Lives* (New York: Charles Scribner's Sons, 1890).

20. Theodore Roosevelt, "Reform through Social Work," in *American Ideals and Other Essays, Social and Political*, vol. 2 (1898; New York: Charles Scribner's Sons, 1906), 200.

21. For more on Douglas's Midwestern roots, see Susan Earle, "Harlem, Modernism and Beyond: Aaron Douglas and His Role in Art/History," in *Aaron Douglas: African American Modernist*, ed. Susan Earle, exh. cat. (Lawrence: Spencer Museum of Art, University of Kansas; New Haven, CT: Yale University Press, 2007), 5–52.

22. Roosevelt, *Presidential Addresses and State Papers* (1910), 2010.

23. Earle, "Harlem, Modernism and Beyond," 12.

24. This reading is in line with Lauren Kroiz's argument in "Leaving the Body: The Empty Spaces of American Modernism," in which she reframed "the vision of a standardized, productive, clean city" O'Keeffe and others produced in this period as a form of utopianism, as "depopulated scenes operated to prioritize and enact unity in an era of racial tension, participating in the tumultuous reinvention of New York." Katherine M. Bourguignon, Lauren Kroiz, and Leo G. Mazow, eds., *America's Cool Modernism: O'Keeffe to Hopper*, exh. cat. (Oxford, UK: Ashmolean Museum, 2018), 67.

25. Cited in Marta Ruiz del Árbol, ed., *Georgia O'Keeffe*, exh. cat. (Madrid: Museo Nacional Thyssen Bornemisza, 2021), 168. For more on the Stieglitz circle's fetishization of whiteness, see Camara Dia Holloway, "Lovechild: Stieglitz, O'Keeffe, and the Birth of American Modernism," *Prospects* 30 (Oct. 2005): 395–432; and Griffey, "Reconsidering the 'Soil,'" 245–77.

26. *MoMA Highlights: 375 Works from The Museum of Modern Art, New York* (New York: Museum of Modern Art, 2019).

27. O'Keeffe would notably come to render Black skin very differently from how she depicted dark buildings, as demonstrated in the tender browns in her 1940s portrait series of artist Beauford Delaney. But in her cityscapes, we find O'Keeffe exploring the expressive possibilities of chromatic blackness in ways that speak to her interest in its variability and possibility, even if she turned away from representing people of any color in her work from this period.

28. Quoted in Robert G. O'Meally, "The Flat Plane, the Jagged Edge: Aaron Douglas's Musical Art," *American Studies* 49, nos. 1–2 (Spring–Summer 2008): 28.

29. O'Meally, "The Flat Plane," 29.

30. Ibid, 30–31.

31. Elizabeth Duvert described O'Keeffe's rendering of the Radiator Building as "a vertical silhouette." Elizabeth Duvert, "Georgia O'Keeffe's *Radiator Building*: Icon of Glamorous Gotham," *Places* 2, no. 2 (1984): 16.

32. This is not to say that all Black painters in this period foregrounded the body. Take Lauren Kroiz's focus on several images from Jacob Lawerence's Migration Series in which "bodies are exceptionally absent . . . but have left their traces." Kroiz, "Leaving the Body," 57.

33. For a complication of this interpretation, see p32n32 of this volume.

34. Peter Kalb wrote of her cityscapes, "O'Keeffe did not eschew context entirely. . . . The riverbanks never intimate the contents of Manhattan Island," before noting that her "resistance to overt content" resulted in "a narrative of isolation that informs O'Keeffe's image of the city and an understanding of her relationship to it." Kalb, *High Drama*, 17–18.

35. As Sascha T. Scott assessed, "O'Keeffe's art is often understood as transcending—instead of being tethered to—the social and political context in which she worked." "Georgia O'Keeffe's Hawai'i?: Decolonizing the History of American Modernism," *American Art* 34, no. 2 (Summer 2020): 27. Scott primarily focused on O'Keeffe's representations of Hawai'i with respect to the island's history of colonialism and noted the work that a few have done in relationship to O'Keeffe's New Mexico paintings, but the same could be said of her cityscapes.

36. Library Congress, "U.S. History Primary Source Timeline," loc.gov/classroom-materials/united-states-history-primary-source-timeline/progressive-era-to-new-era-1900-1929/immigrants-in-progressive-era/; and Robert E. Weir, *Workers in America: A Historical Encyclopedia* (Santa Barbara, CA: ABC-Clio, 2013), 311.

(RE)FRAMING THE VIEW

Lisa Volpe

Georgia O'Keeffe's *Chrysler Building from the Window of the Waldorf Astoria, New York* (pl. 40) is a striking, atmospheric photograph. The Chrysler Building rises elegantly from the bottom edge of the image, reaching far above the surrounding architecture. The artist contained the view with a dark window frame sloping diagonally across the top of the composition and a sheer window curtain hanging at top left, its gauzy appearance matching the hazy city sky. O'Keeffe carefully foregrounded these interior elements to enclose the exterior view. Taken in 1960, the photograph is an apt entry point into a fuller understanding of O'Keeffe's art: interior and exterior, organic and inorganic, these juxtaposed forms create a view of the city that reaffirms key aspects of the artistic vision O'Keeffe honed in New York City in the 1920s and developed throughout her career.

O'Keeffe was no stranger to photography. Her early years are captured in family photographs and travel snapshots, and in later decades the enigmatic painter's portrait was taken by numerous artists, including her husband, photography impresario Alfred Stieglitz. This intimate experience notwithstanding, she did not begin her own photographic practice until later in life.[1] O'Keeffe was in her late sixties when a friend, the photographer Todd Webb, visited her in Abiquiu, New Mexico, and started teaching her how to photograph (see fig. 1). Webb wrote in a 1956 letter, "I am giving her a few lessons with the Leica and she will probably get one. Funny, but she knows nothing of the operation of a camera. She sees well of course and seems to have a sense of the photographic eye."[2] O'Keeffe also marked the occasion in a letter, writing, "[Todd Webb] is trying to teach me to use a Leica camera that I seem to resist but . . . I want to use for records."[3] Although O'Keeffe appreciated photography as an art form, she did not use the camera to produce artworks.[4] Instead she utilized it as a tool to record and reassess the world around her.

O'Keeffe's 409 extant photographic images reflect the subjective passions, formal concerns, and physical foundations that run throughout her entire body of work while also capturing the world she saw: her Abiquiu home and environs; her dogs; her travels to New York, Glen Canyon in Utah, Japan, and more, as well as her close circle of friends. The photographs give further insights into her artistic process, the serial imagery especially revealing her artistic eye. Although singular examples exist, most of the artist's photographs cohere into groups depicting the same subject shot from different positions or at different times of the day or year. O'Keeffe perceived her surroundings as an array of shapes and forms that she could arrange to produce different emphases. Small compositional changes between images illuminate O'Keeffe's constant search for the ideal composition and for greater clarity of expression. No two photographs are perfectly alike. As records of what she saw, how she moved, and how her artistic mind organized and reorganized her compositions, the artist's photographic output reveals her tireless reconsideration of the world.

Only recently attributed to O'Keeffe, her photographs may be some of the most fruitful objects for investigating her artistic practice. Comparing them with her better-known paintings and drawings highlights central aspects of her work across her career. O'Keeffe utilized the same formal approaches no matter the time, medium, or subject. "For me Texas is the same wonderful thing that oceans and the highest mountains are," she emphasized, equating her approach in Texas in the late 1910s to her work in New Mexico after 1929.[5] Analysis of O'Keeffe's photographs—although they were not made

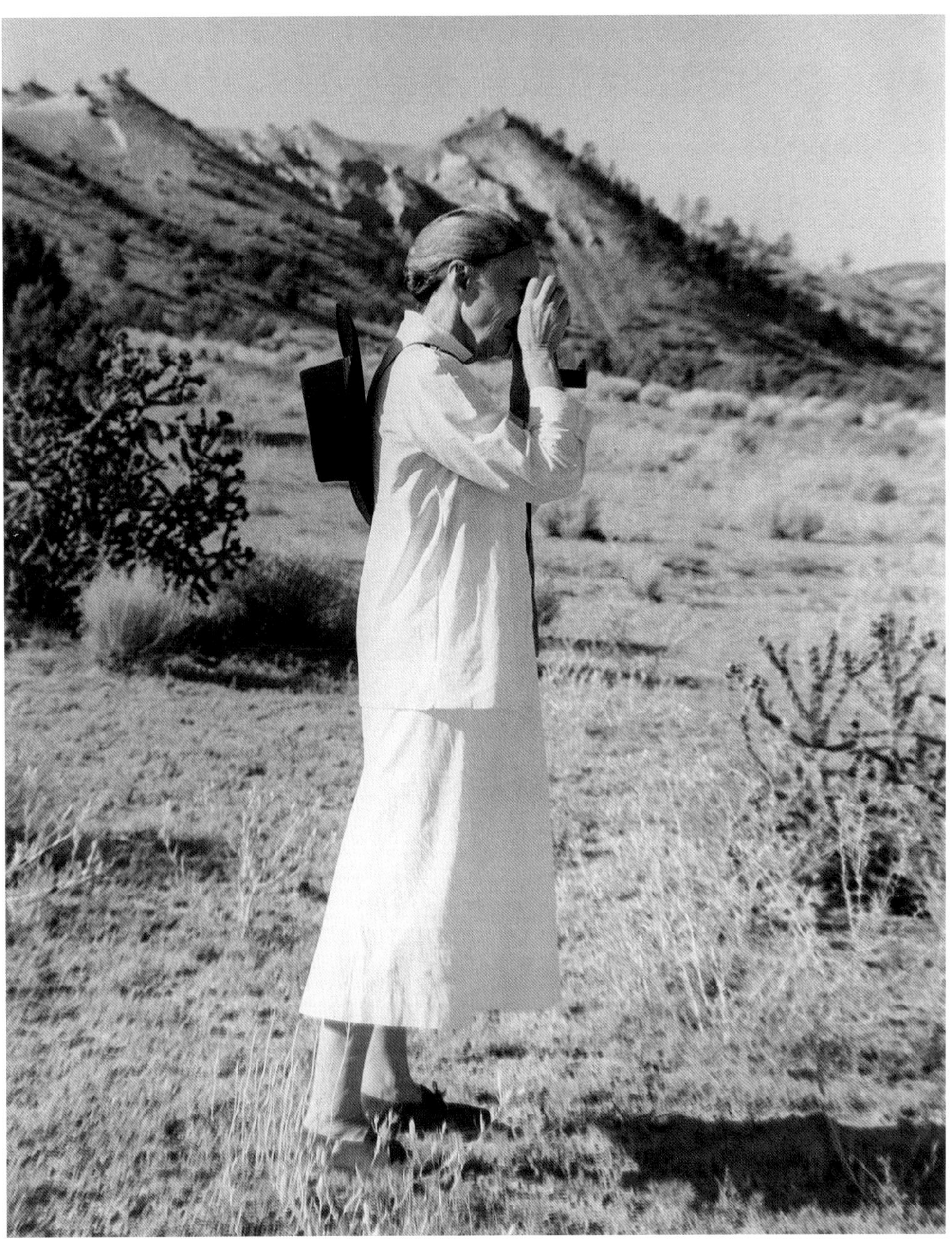

until the 1950s and 1960s—can thus help illuminate the artist's process of moving, looking, and creating compositions as she emerged as a major modernist figure in New York in the 1920s. This investigation, arising from *Chrysler Building from the Window of the Waldorf Astoria, New York*, identifies the constellation of similar subjects and formal choices in O'Keeffe's oeuvre, draws a clear distinction between her work in photography and that of Stieglitz, and considers her stylistic and expressive emphases as they relate to her physicality. What emerges is a clearer picture of O'Keeffe's particular approach to modernism as it developed during her time in New York and continued throughout her career.

In the deluge of scholarship on the artist, the words *O'Keeffe* and *photography* used in proximity typically conjure the specter of Stieglitz. The recent attribution of O'Keeffe's photographs affords an opportunity to study them and to demonstrate the particularities of her photographic output and broader artistic perspective. Stieglitz made his first portrait of O'Keeffe in 1917, at the beginning of their romantic relationship, and over the next twenty years, he photographed her more than three hundred times. Due in large part to Stieglitz's prolific portrait project and his outsized legacy in the American art world, historians have assumed that O'Keeffe's relationship to

FIG. 1
Todd Webb (American, 1905–2000). *Georgia O'Keeffe with Camera*, 1958. Gelatin silver print; sheet: 23.7 × 19.1 cm (9 5/16 × 7 1/2 in.). Georgia O'Keeffe Museum, Gift of The Georgia O'Keeffe Foundation, 2006.6.981.

photography was that of a sitter, assistant, or spectator—in short, a passive position; O'Keeffe, however, played an integral role in much of Stieglitz's lauded work in the medium. She designed and hung photographic exhibitions, met independently with photographers to discuss their work, wrote about photography as an art, advised and oversaw the formation of a photography department at the Museum of Modern Art, New York, and, after Stieglitz's death, she selected his key set of work. From the outset of her own photographic practice, the records O'Keeffe made with her camera reflected her own strong sense of the medium without any true resemblance to Stieglitz's images.

Yet it is not only O'Keeffe's photography that has suffered from the lasting comparison with Stieglitz's work but also her early artwork from the decades when they lived and worked together. Although O'Keeffe was producing and selling major works in the 1920s and emerged in the national consciousness as an influential modernist artist, this recognition was deeply entangled with references to Stieglitz. Her history as a member of Stieglitz's circle and his promotion and interpretation of her early work (as her gallerist and dealer) further blurred the line between their artistic perspectives. O'Keeffe's friend and fellow artist Rebecca Strand argued that writers too often applied their critiques of Stieglitz's art to O'Keeffe's work.[6] Writing in 1923, Strand correctly identified the flaw in explaining O'Keeffe's paintings through Stieglitz's photographs—anticipating the decades-long problem of subsequent scholarship's intertwined analysis.

The interpretation of O'Keeffe's New York paintings as derivatives of Stieglitz's views of the city is typified by Sarah Whitaker Peters's analysis from 1991. "The central subject of O'Keeffe's cityscapes is the skyscraper, seen from quintessentially photographic vantage points and angles," wrote Peters, continuing, "The design . . . appears to have been 'adapted' from one of Stieglitz's best-known photographs, *The Flatiron Building*."[7] Peters characterized O'Keeffe as a passive apprentice, even proposing that "she look[ed] into the ground glass of Stieglitz's large-format camera as well as his prints" to create her own paintings of the East River.[8] She added, "We might also ask whether O'Keeffe's use of color was ever inspired by the preternaturally bright image reflected on the camera's viewing screen."[9] Throughout her investigation, Peters credited nearly every element of O'Keeffe's work to Stieglitz's superior photographic vision.

Muddied criticism aside, comparing and contrasting O'Keeffe's and Stieglitz's photographic works and practices does help delineate her approach to New York City specifically and to modern art more broadly. Analyzing O'Keeffe's *Chrysler Building from the Window of the Waldorf Astoria, New York* and the New York views Stieglitz captured from his window, such as *From the Shelton, New York (Room 3003), Looking Southeast* (pl. 81), reveals much about their work, bringing the differences between O'Keeffe's and Stieglitz's artistic perspectives into clear focus.

FRAMES OF MIND

There is a fundamental divide between O'Keeffe's and Stieglitz's photographic practices. Unlike Stieglitz, who considered photographs works of fine art to be refined and finalized, O'Keeffe had no interest in creating an "art print." Instead she used the camera as a tool for looking, focusing solely on the image as a record. She took quick, rough photographs and was happy with enlarged contact sheets, test prints, Polaroids, and even drugstore prints. *Chrysler Building from the Window of the Waldorf Astoria, New York* is a small 3 15⁄16-by-2 11⁄16-inch print that Webb printed on Kodak Medalist F, a single-weight paper he used for test prints of his own work. O'Keeffe also did not concern herself with paper types or printing and was evidently pleased with the quick print. The verso of the Chrysler Building photograph shows minor skinning on all four corners, evidence that it was taped to a surface at some point, a rough rather than precious treatment of the print. Stieglitz believed that a large portion of the artistry of photography involved creating prints in the darkroom, and he labored over various versions of single negatives, claiming each was a unique work of art: "What might seem duplicates . . . are in reality different methods of printing from one and the same negative and as such become significant prints each with its own individuality."[10] Despite her familiarity with the darkroom, having helped Stieglitz spot his prints during their summers at Lake George, O'Keeffe was focused on the photographic image rather than the photographic print.

Just as their photographic oeuvres indicate two different minds at work, O'Keeffe's and Stieglitz's methods of composing an image were strikingly different. Many of Stieglitz's works imply an omniscient, untethered perspective that seems to float above the ground. In his New York photographs taken from various windows, apartment buildings and skyscrapers rush toward the top of the compositions, whereas the ground from which they spring is rarely visible. *From the Shelton, New York (Room 3003), Looking Southeast*, for example, presents the quilt-like geometry of New York's buildings. From this angle the pedestrian-filled streets are fully out of view, and the city blocks are reduced to a rhythmic geometry, as diagonal forms stretch from one end of the photographic frame to the other. Only the river and sky provide relief from the unending density, two threads of gray across the top third of the photograph. There is no grounding element, no indication of where the camera was placed or where the photographer stood. Stieglitz's preference for an omniscient, untethered view is not surprising considering his infamous temperament, which bordered on godlike. Art historian Wanda Corn described his "megalomania," saying, "He was a man of enormous self-confidence and ego" who prided himself on his detachment from "the vulgarities of the modern world."[11] *From "Room 303"—(Intimate Gallery)—New York* (pl. 83) is an additional step removed from the realities of the world: Stieglitz turned his camera counterclockwise to take the photograph, then rotated the print clockwise so that the bottom-right corner points downward. This movement cast the frame at an angle but correctly oriented the subject, further abstracting the view and ungrounding the perspective. The untethered buildings appear as mere forms against the print's skewed geometry. There is no true left or right, top or bottom, only the abstract relation of shapes.

O'Keeffe's abstraction, by contrast, offers a perspective in which the viewer understands their physical relationship to the scene. She emphasized both the physical reality of seeing and the physical reality of the city's human element in her work, labeling her painting output "my New Yorks." *Chrysler Building from the Window of the Waldorf Astoria, New York* situates viewers within a room, the relatable scale of the window framing the city outside. Similarly, her paintings of New York feature streetlamps and boats hazy from water spray, human-scaled objects that enable viewers to understand their relative position. *Shelton Hotel, N.Y., No. I* (pl. 11) presents a specific, grounded vision of the Shelton taken from Lexington Avenue. As the hotel lifts skyward, two buildings frame it on each side. Foregrounding the physical experience of the city, O'Keeffe rendered views only achieved by straining to spy the tops of buildings, awkwardly tilting the head back while standing on a crowded street. Her photograph of the Seagram Building (pl. 39), made decades later, again reflects this approach. O'Keeffe snapped the photograph with the camera's lens angled almost vertically, capturing a craned-neck view. The image relies on O'Keeffe's invisible presence, which places the viewer's body in relation to not only the impressive height of the structure but also its massive, dominating footprint at street level—the physical relationship between the subject and the implied body are perceptible.

One shared aspect of O'Keeffe's and Stieglitz's photographs—seriality—is also illuminating due to the artists' differing purposes for this multiplicity. Stieglitz asserted that artistic truth could only be achieved through a large number of images considered as a whole: "I had in mind to do one hundred different phases of New York—to do them as supremely well as they could be done," he wrote.[12] Shooting from the windows of An American Place, the Shelton, and more, he added to his serial study of New York City, capturing changing visions of the urban landscape. Even reprints of the same negative, produced over time, contributed to the greater whole. Similarly, in his hundreds of portraits of O'Keeffe, he aimed to "record a single person throughout life, in many moods and many forms."[13] Only together could these varied photographs capture the changeability of his subject and form a singular portrait. Changeability was not only something Stieglitz aimed to capture in his work but was also an essential trait of his ethos. His friend and associate Herbert J. Seligmann recalled, "At supper in the Hotel Shelton I said to Stieglitz that some-one [*sic*] might begin an essay upon him by saying that no statement could be made about him which could not with perfect truth be contradicted. Stieglitz replied that of everything he felt, he felt the opposite also to be true."[14] O'Keeffe also commented on this, "He thought aloud and his opinion about anything in the morning might be quite different by afternoon, so that people quoting him might make contradictory statements."[15] Truth, for Stieglitz, was relative, and change was inevitable. In his assessment, one of the effects of modernity was a fragmented, evolving sense of self. Thus, the truth of a subject could only be captured through multiple works of art created over a period of time.

Far from believing *quantity* was the key to revelation, O'Keeffe created series in a continual search for the *one* formal combination that would fully express the truth of her feelings. In the 1920s she produced multiple visions of the New York cityscape, which she described saying, "One can't paint New York as it is, but rather as it is felt."[16] Revisiting subjects again and again, O'Keeffe eliminated details, flattened space, and simplified her compositions, working toward the harmonious formal relations that would best convey her subjective experience. The dozen photographs of the *salita* door in her Abiquiu courtyard join twenty-three paintings and drawings of the same location (see figs. 2–3). "I'm always trying to paint that door—I never quite get it," O'Keeffe wrote, "It's a curse—the way I feel I must continually go on with that door."[17] In her pursuit of the ideal expression, O'Keeffe often destroyed work that she felt was unsuitable. Her assistants recall burning finished canvases in the courtyards of her Abiquiu home. "I'm a careless mother—most of [my works] have little interest for me after they are made," she noted.[18] In her photography, she selected specific negatives for Webb to print, choosing to produce only the best combinations of forms out of her many reframed captures.

In developing their modernist styles, O'Keeffe and Stieglitz approached the connection between formal abstraction and subject matter in novel ways. Both artists believed formal harmony was a primary mode of expression, but Stieglitz saw subject matter as a means to an end, while O'Keeffe upheld content as the foundation of her work. Stieglitz once described his iconic photograph *The Steerage* (fig. 4) by saying, "I

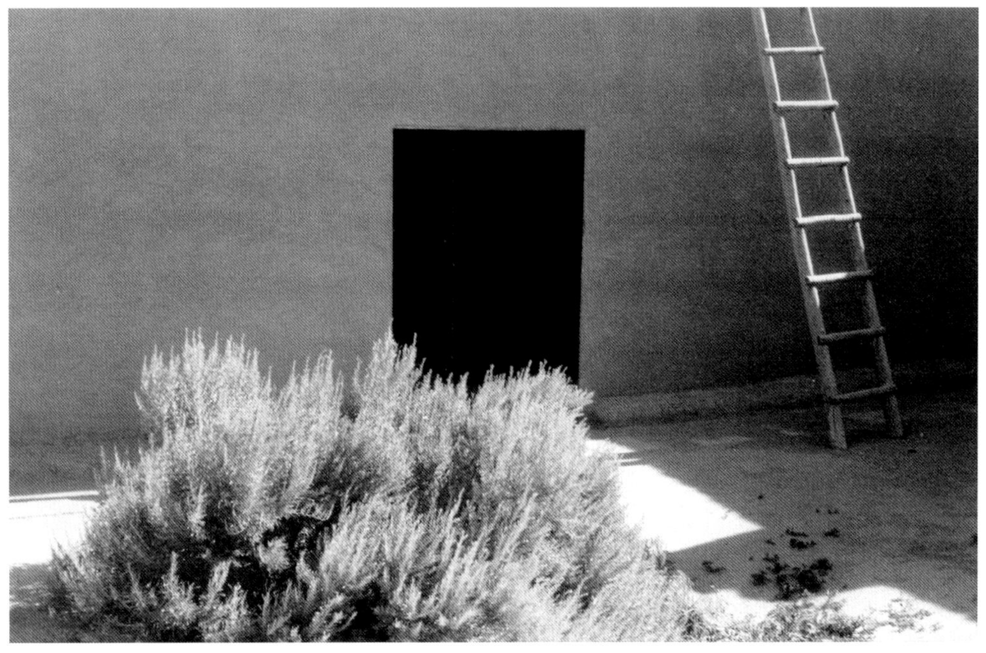

saw shapes related to each other. I saw a picture of shapes and underlying that the feeling I had about life."[19] Minimizing his subject, he claimed to not recognize the crowd of ship passengers at all, rather only the shapes they formed within the composition. Speaking about his *Equivalents* series (see fig. 5), he asserted that his choice of subject was based on a desire to minimize the iconicity of the image: "In looking at the photographs of clouds, people seem to feel freed to think more about the actual relationships in the pictures and less about the subject matter."[20] Curator Malcolm Daniel wrote, "He made the photograph . . . to show that the content of a photograph was different than the subject."[21] Likewise, in his New York work, the atmosphere and abstract forms of the images are more important than the actual places depicted. Stieglitz sought formal harmony in order for the subject to disappear; O'Keeffe, by contrast, celebrated her subjects, using formal harmony to express the truth of her feelings about them. "You paint from your subject," she stressed.[22] As Corn noted, O'Keeffe believed that "the artists' job was to feel the vibrations of a place and translate them into an art form so that others could feel and receive them."[23] Her subjects were central, even if abstracted. O'Keeffe referred to her dedication to translating subject to form to expression as a "madness."[24]

FIG. 2
Georgia O'Keeffe (American, 1887–1986). *Salita Door, Patio*, 1956–57. Gelatin silver print; sheet: 10.2 × 15.2 cm (4 × 6 in.). Museum of Fine Arts, Boston, William Lane Collection.

FIG. 3
O'Keeffe. *My Last Door*, 1952–54. Oil on canvas; 122.6 × 213.8 cm (48 1/4 × 84 3/16 in.). Georgia O'Keeffe Museum, Gift of The Burnett Foundation, 1997.6.29.

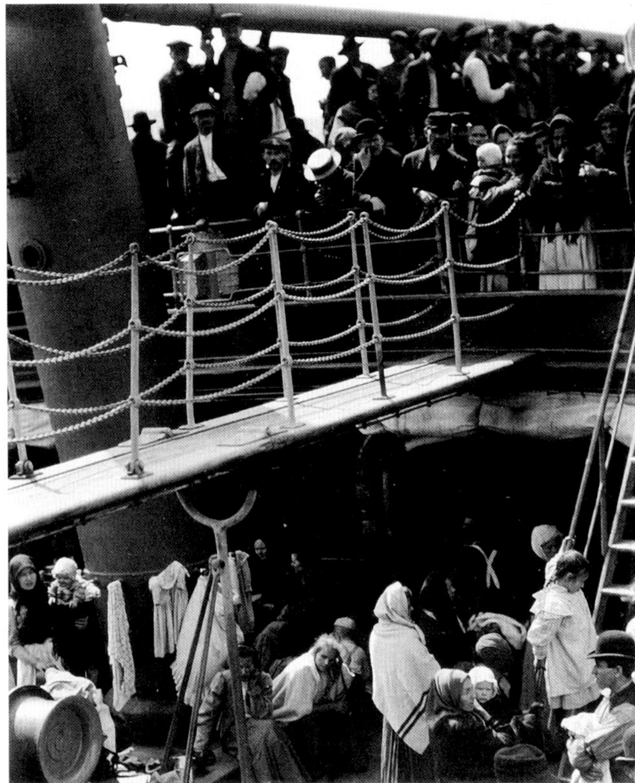

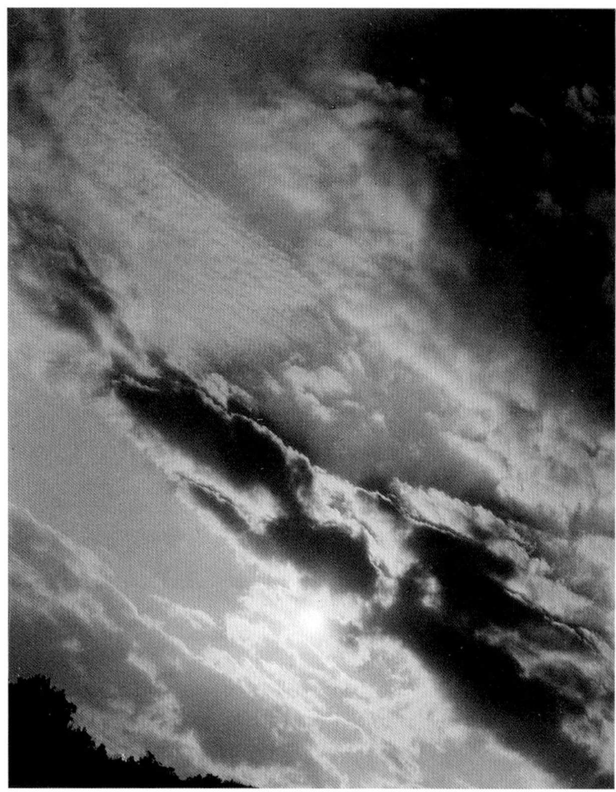

FIG. 4
Alfred Stieglitz (American, 1864–1946). *The Steerage*, 1907, printed 1920–39. Gelatin silver print; image/paper/first mount: 11 × 9.2 cm (4 3/8 × 3 5/8 in.). The Art Institute of Chicago, Alfred Stieglitz Collection, 1949.705.

FIG. 5
Stieglitz. *Equivalent*, 1923. Gelatin silver print; image: 12.2 × 9.2 cm (4 13/16 × 3 5/8 in.); paper/first mount: 12.6 × 10.1 cm (5 × 4 in.). The Art Institute of Chicago, Alfred Stieglitz Collection, 1949.795.

THE SINGULARITY OF O'KEEFFE'S ART

O'Keeffe's emphasis on personal expression is evidence of her fidelity to the teachings of Arthur Wesley Dow. First introduced to Dow's art theories while taking a course at the University of Virginia in 1912, O'Keeffe went on to study with him in the fall of 1914 at Columbia University's Teachers College. Dow's approach—which broke down the barrier between art and life—became the structure by which O'Keeffe found her singular expression. In fact, O'Keeffe referred to him as "Pa" Dow, indicating her attachment.[25] His teachings freed O'Keeffe to look beyond documentary study, as her classical art education had emphasized, and to instead seek out the most expressive balance of forms. Dow specified, "The art in your composition will lie in placing these [shapes] in good relations to each other."[26] He continued, "No work has art-value unless it reflects the personality of its author."[27] This missive drove O'Keeffe to test composition after composition, looking for the formal harmony that would signify her own point of view.

When O'Keeffe and Stieglitz moved back into the Shelton Hotel in 1925, they began producing works inspired by the view from their window, although with different artistic media, practices, and perspectives. O'Keeffe rendered the low-slung buildings crowding the East River in at least six oils and three pastels, each one an attempt to find the perfect harmony of shapes to express her feelings. They recall Dow's challenge to his students to draw a landscape and to "enclose it in a rectangle, to make a horizontal picture or a vertical . . . to balance the drawing by making less foreground, or more sky, to change the masses."[28] More than forty years after her lessons with Dow, O'Keeffe picked up a camera and utilized these same exercises. Changing orientation, moving around the scene, and adjusting her camera angle, she used successive captures to explore the formal relationships of elements within the frame. In some photographs, her compositions echo the paintings and drawings she produced years—or decades—earlier. *Chrysler Building from the Window of the Waldorf Astoria, New York* recalls many of the same formal elements seen in O'Keeffe's 1920s drawings of New York: the stacked buildings at the right and bottom of the composition, an organic element at upper left (see pl. 43), and the dominating spire of a skyscraper (see pl. 47).

A similar reframing is evident in her East River series. Each work presents a slightly shifted perspective and, thus, a different arrangement of shapes. The painting *East River No. 1* (pl. 52) is dominated by a hazy sky. A dark chain of indiscernable buildings obscures the near shore. At center a singular, large smokestack crosses the plane of the river, its top aligned with the far shore. The pastel *East River with Sun* (pl. 53) presents a similar vision, yet O'Keeffe again shifted the view to show a different configuration of forms. A haze once again dominates the upper register of the composition, but here the smokestack sits lower and to the right, crossing the expanse of water but not quite reaching the far shore.

Although O'Keeffe's commitment to reframing was rooted in Dow's teachings, her artistic treatment of light and shade is a testament to her unique form of abstract expression. Dow considered light and shade "mere fleeting effects or accidents."[29] O'Keeffe saw them as essential elements. In many works—whether on paper or canvas or in photographs—she gave formal weight to dapples of light and dark shadows. *East River with Sun* demonstrates her abstraction of light into shape. The sun is surrounded by a corona, an ethereal effect rendered as clearly as the smokestacks below. At the center of the composition, the shadows cast by buildings on the far side of the river are solid, rectangular forms creeping into the watery space. Her later photographs exemplify this formal transformation. Photographing a roofless room in Abiquiu, O'Keeffe captured the shadows cast by the *latillas* (fig. 6), the black spires creeping down the walls and across the bare floor as distinct shapes. In the graphite rendering of the same scene (fig. 7), she outlined the shadows as well as the wooden vigas and door in the same way, giving both shadow and form equal treatment and mass.

Another compositional device O'Keeffe used throughout her career is the window frame. As a different type of reframing, it helped advance the subjectivity of her work. The artist first played with this approach in a painting of the Palo Duro Canyon, in Texas, *No. 24—Special / No. 24* (fig. 8), enclosing a land mass with the horizontal and vertical planes of a window frame. Rendered in wavy or hazy lines that make it difficult to identify the compositional elements, the work is best compared to O'Keeffe's photograph *Road from Abiquiu* (fig. 9). Taken in New Mexico five decades later, the black-and-white Polaroid displays many of the same forms. The mesa and winding road are contained by the horizontal frame at the top and the vertical frame at the left. O'Keeffe photographed this scene out of her Abiquiu window many times in the late 1950s and 1960s, and wrote about that practice in her 1976 self-titled book:

> Two walls of my room in the Abiquiú house are glass and from one window I see the road toward Espanola, Santa Fe and the world. . . . I had made two or three snaps of it with a camera. For one of them I turned the camera at a sharp angle to get all the road. It was accidental that I made the road seem to stand up in the air, but it amused me and I began drawing and painting it as a new shape.[30]

In this excerpt, O'Keeffe introduced many of the themes tied to her rendering of windows, linking the window frame with her personal vision and her particular form of abstraction.

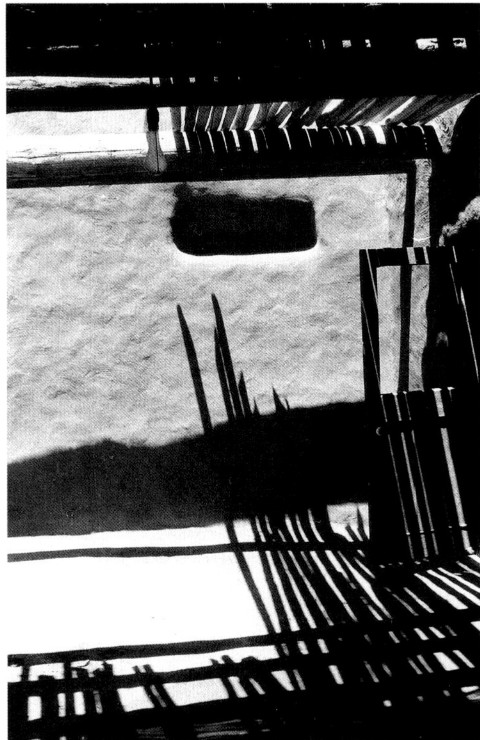

FIG. 6
O'Keeffe. *Roofless Room*, 1959 or 1960. Gelatin silver print; sheet: 9.8 × 6.7 cm (3 7/8 × 2 5/8 in.). Georgia O'Keeffe Museum, Gift of The Georgia O'Keeffe Foundation, 2006.6.1429.

FIG. 7
O'Keeffe. *Untitled (Abstraction)*, 1959–60. Graphite on paper; 33.7 × 22.5 cm (13 1/4 × 8 7/8 in.). Georgia O'Keeffe Museum, Gift of The Georgia O'Keeffe Foundation, 2006.5.302.

The 1928–29 drawing *Pink Dish and Green Leaves* (pl. 59), from O'Keeffe's East River series, and *Chrysler Building from the Window of the Waldorf Astoria, New York*, from around 1960, also include window frames. Positioning the viewer in O'Keeffe's rooms, the works give access to her private environment and offer a more direct experience of her artistic perspective and approach to absraction. In the pastel drawing, O'Keeffe incorporated both the window frame and windowsill, upon which rests a compote holding two green leaves. The window frame occupies the bottommost register of the composition, nearly obscuring the closest shore, and accentuates the central space of the river. In the photograph, the dark window frame obscures all but a few structures and encloses the hazy air. Both the pastel and the photograph feature a single building that rises above the others, its geometric form cutting into the central, negative space; in the photograph, the arced curtain softens the scene, providing a foil to the inorganic building, and in *Pink Dish and Green Leaves*, O'Keeffe used the sensual shape of the dish and fresh, curving leaf forms for the same purpose—pulling the viewer inside and emphasizing the personal space of the work.

As O'Keeffe suggested in her writing, the window frame not only delineated her personal domain but also was a means of abstraction. In each of these artworks, the window frame flattens space and allows the picture to cohere in two dimensions—another tendency O'Keeffe learned from Dow. Inspired by the stacked compositions of Japanese prints, he encouraged students to embrace the flatness of drawing paper or canvas as an element to be worked with, not against.[31] O'Keeffe sought out arrangements that created a consonant tension between two and three dimensions. In

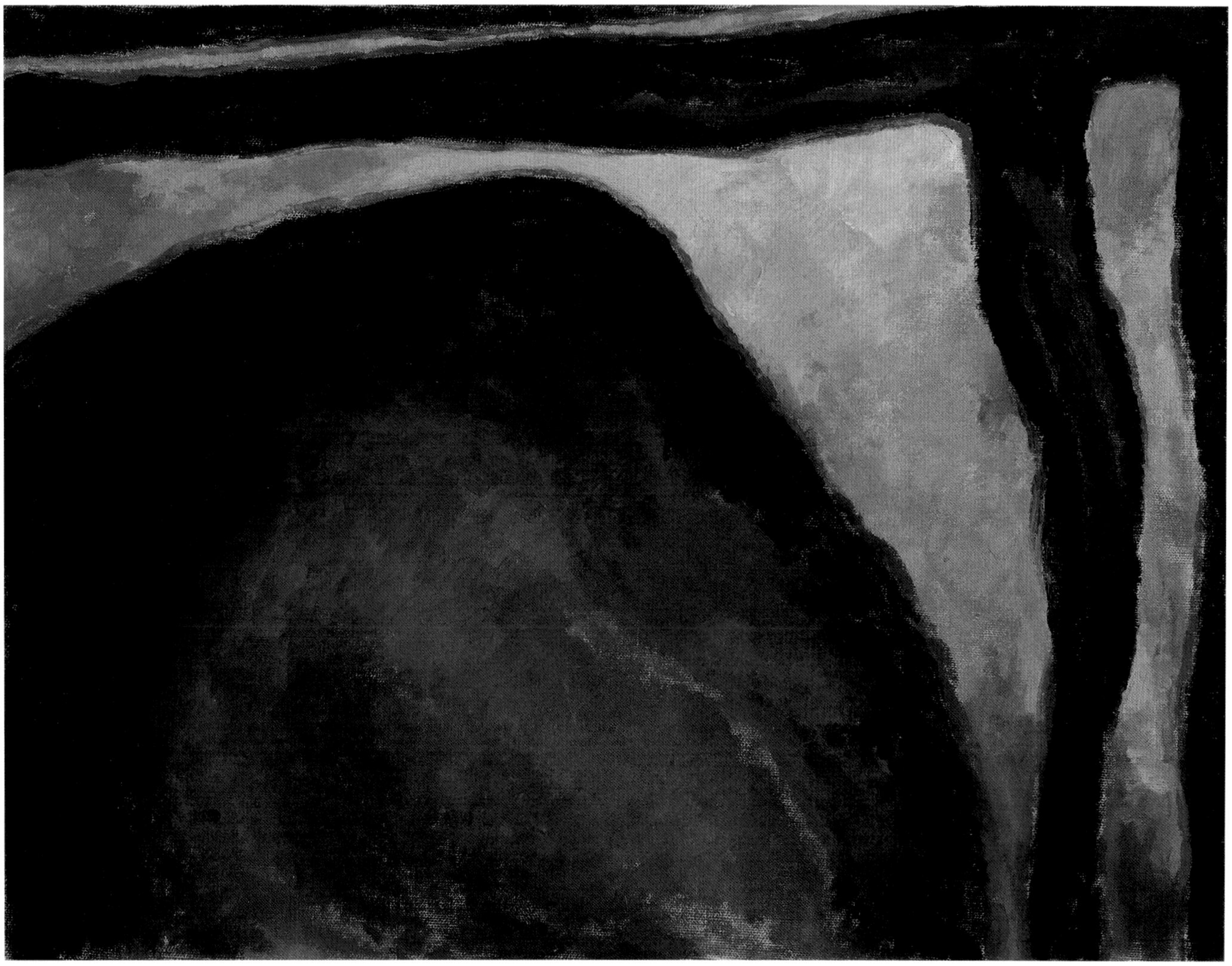

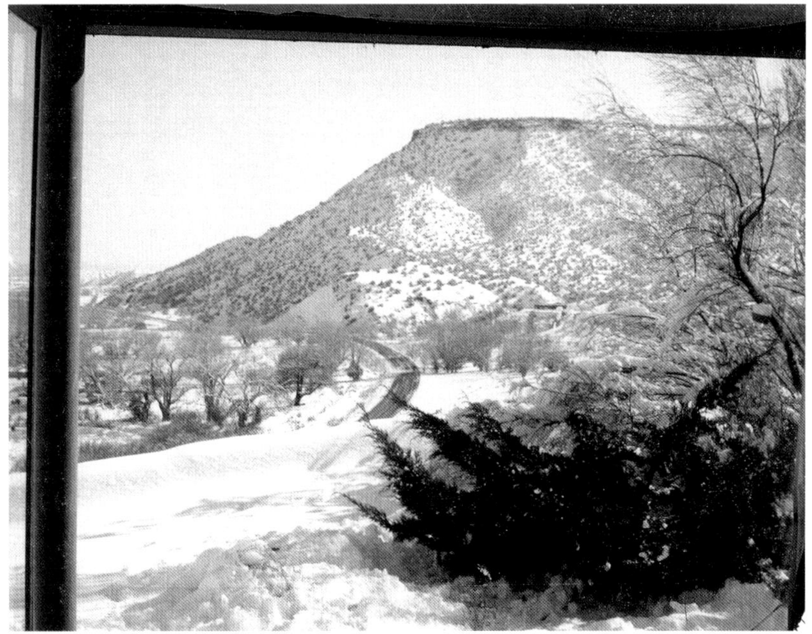

FIG. 8

O'Keeffe. *No. 24 — Special / No. 24*, 1916–17. Oil on canvas; 46.4 × 61 cm (18 ¼ × 24 in.). Georgia O'Keeffe Museum, Gift of The Georgia O'Keeffe Foundation, 2006.5.62.

FIG. 9

O'Keeffe. *Road from Abiquiu*, 1964–68. Black-and-white Polaroid; sheet: 8.6 × 10.8 cm (3 ⅜ × 4 ¼ in.). Georgia O'Keeffe Museum, 2006.6.1083.

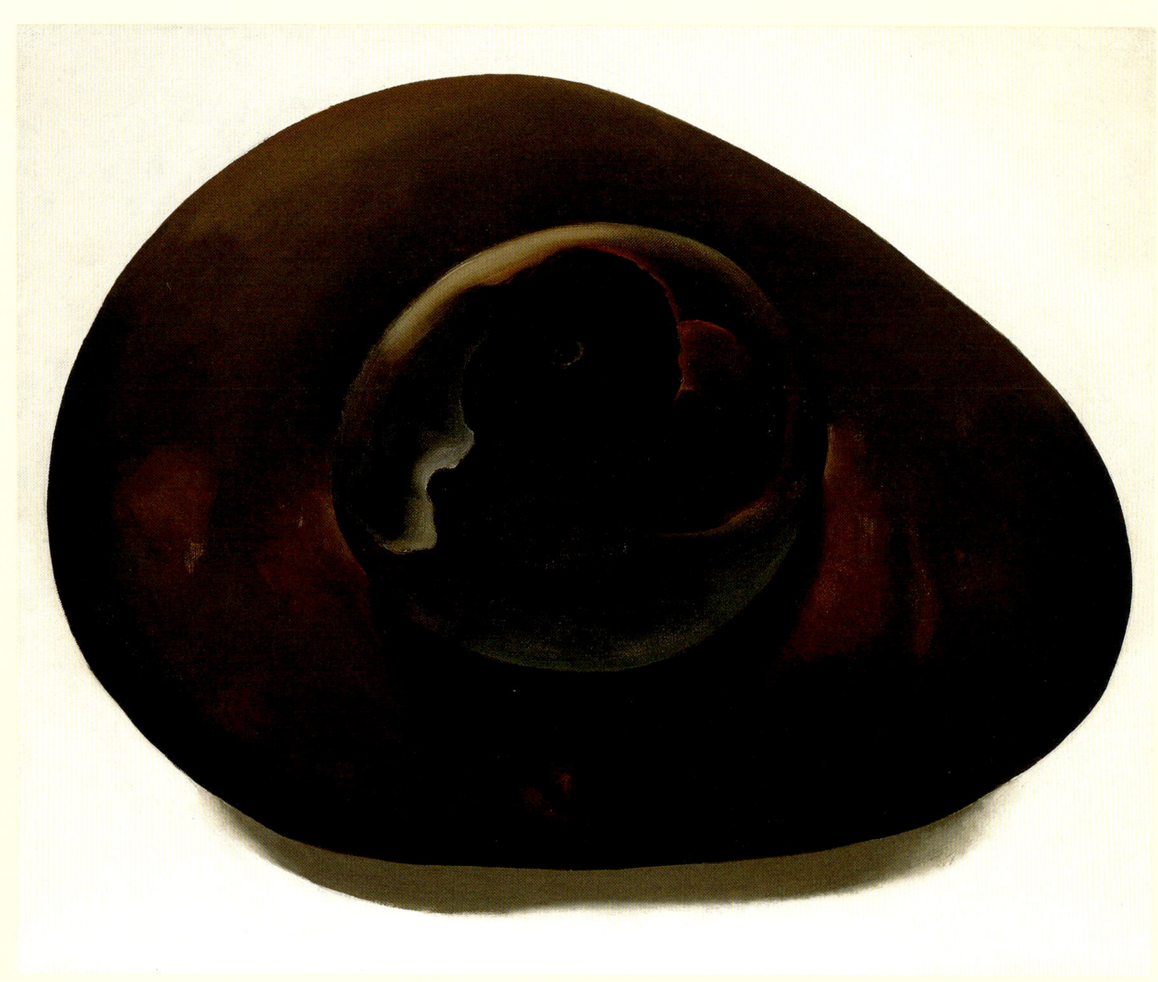

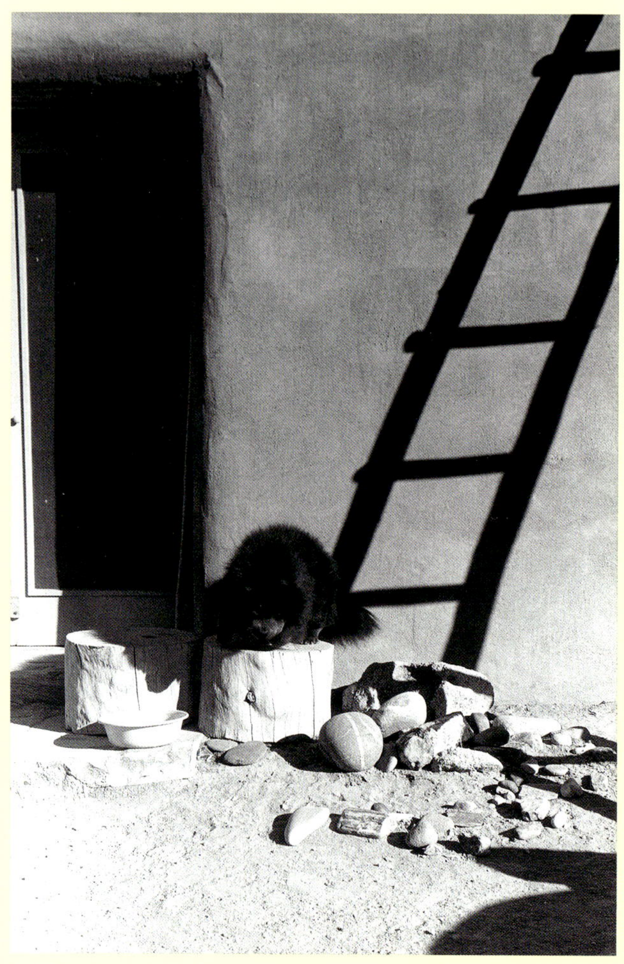

FIG. 10
O'Keeffe. *Dark Rocks*, 1938.
Oil on canvas; 40.3 × 50.2 cm
(15 7/8 × 19 3/4 in.). Museum of
Fine Arts, Houston, gift of Patricia
Barrett Carter, 98.648.

FIG. 11
O'Keeffe. *Bo II (Bo-Bo)*, 1961.
Gelatin silver print; sheet:
15.2 × 10.2 cm (6 × 4 in.).
Georgia O'Keeffe Museum,
Georgia O'Keeffe Foundation
Photographs, MS.57,
2006.6.1350.

her studies of rocks, such as *Dark Rocks* (fig. 10) and *Bo II (Bo-Bo)* (fig. 11), the juxtaposed forms, cast shadows, and bright planes render the forms weighty on the one hand, while on the other, suggest moments of negative space. Both dimensional and flat, their spatial quality is abstracted by O'Keeffe's careful composition. In *Pink Dish and Green Leaves*, the strong, dark shape of the window frame stretches from edge to edge. The heavy form establishes a maximum pictoral depth, making the hazy city beyond appear as a two-dimensional image, like a photograph or wallpaper. The same can be said for the window frame in the photograph *Chrysler Building from the Window of the Waldorf Astoria, New York*. The substantial black shape of the window frame, crossed by the hazy curtain in the foreground, makes the view outside appear as mere image.

SHARING HER EXPERIENCE

It would be a mistake to assign a greater connotative meaning to O'Keeffe's window frames; they do not stand in as a metaphor or symbol. They do, however, emphasize her subjectivity, by positioning the viewer in her space and presenting the formal relationships she perceived. Subjectivity was a theme O'Keeffe emphasized again and again in her commentary. Reflecting on the wide-ranging meanings critics assigned to her flower paintings, the artist noted, "Well—I made you take time to look at what I saw and when you took time to really notice my flower you hung all your own associations with flowers on my flower and you write about my flower as if I think and see what you think and see of the flower—and I don't."[32] The artist was put off by the sexualized interpretations of these paintings and instead asserted the importance of her personal vision: "what *I* saw."[33] This same subjectivity was at the core of O'Keeffe's work. It is a quality that drew O'Keeffe to Arthur Dove, whom Corn revealed was one of O'Keeffe's favorite artists. She admired his ability to translate for viewers what he saw and how he felt about it in his art: "He would get the feel of a particular place so completely that you'd know you'd been there."[34] O'Keeffe, too, endeavored to express what she saw and how she felt about it through a harmony of forms. With the frame, she placed the viewer in her room at the Shelton, at the Waldorf Astoria, or in her bedroom in Abiquiu. From these places, viewers stand in O'Keeffe's shoes, know her heart, and see the world as she saw it: as an arrangement of shapes awaiting her personal expression.

While the window frame device illuminates O'Keeffe's developing approach to abstraction and personal expression, the notion of reframing highlights one additional aspect of her work: physicality. These compositions foreground the physical placement of O'Keeffe's body, urging a reconsideration of her movement and position throughout her oeuvre. In every environment she inhabited, O'Keeffe made walking, looking, and considering a habit. She declared that walking was essential to her artistic vision: "I do not walk to escape, I walk to see something."[35] While walking, she aimed to frame and reframe the environment, weigh shapes and forms, test her eye, and analyze the possibilities for expression.

The physicality evident in O'Keeffe's 1920s New York artworks would not be matched until she initiated a photographic practice in the mid-1950s. In New York, the artist prowled the city streets, craning her neck from the sidewalks to frame the tallest skyscrapers. From the Shelton Hotel, she looked out left, right, and down at the river and the tightly packed buildings below. Later, the camera became an extension of her visual search. She aimed the lens this way and that, pointing it straight up at the Seagram

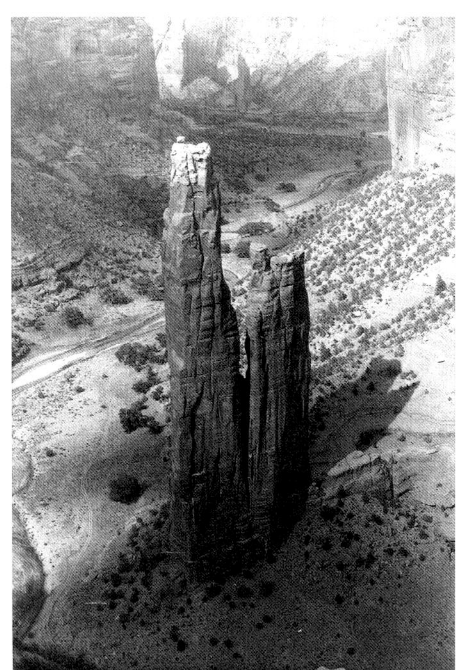

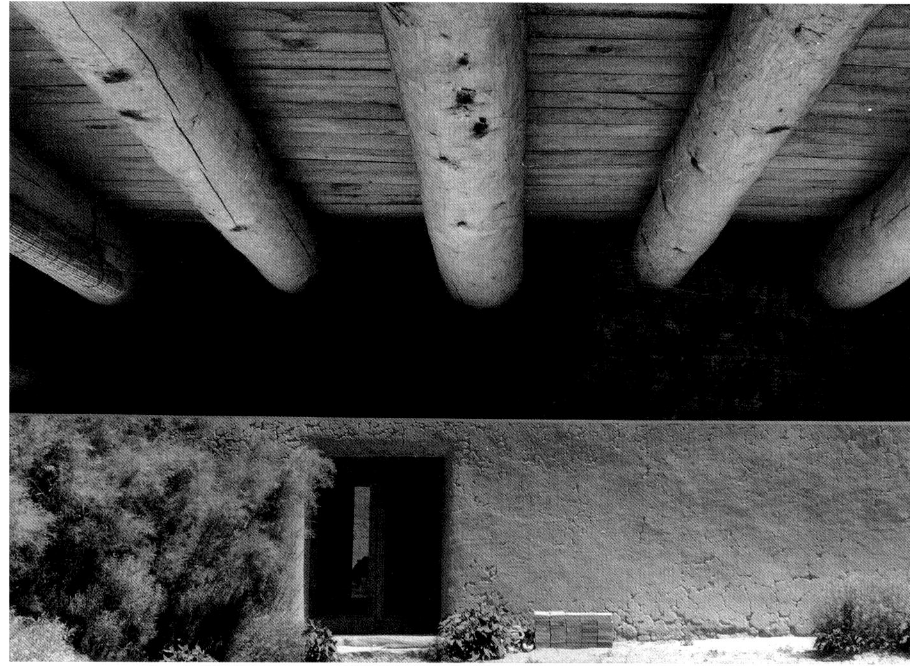

Building in New York or straight down into the bottom of Canyon de Chelly, in Arizona (see fig. 12). In her Abiquiu home, O'Keeffe moved around her central courtyard, photographing from numerous positions and angles; in another group of photographs, she raised the camera above her head to capture her garage roof and her studio door in the same frame (see fig. 13). Each combination of adobe walls, doorways, and patio space presents a new vision and a distinct point of view, while simultaneously recording her movements from frame to frame. The physical freedom of photography offered O'Keeffe the opportunity to investigate the world around her and revisit and revise its formal and expressive possibilities with ease.

The artistic vision that produced a series of New Yorks from the window of the Shelton Hotel in the 1920s was the same vision that captured the city from the Waldorf Astoria in the 1960s. Georgia O'Keeffe's artistry was unwavering throughout the decades and across media, and the recent identification of her later photographic work provides an unprecedented opportunity to reassess the artist's formative period, bringing it out from the shadow of Alfred Stieglitz and placing it firmly under her control. O'Keeffe's photographs reframe the artist's practice, point of view, and modernist vision, bringing her innovations and individuality back into focus.

FIG. 12
O'Keeffe. *Spider Rock*, July 1957. Gelatin silver print; 12.7 × 8.9 cm (5 × 3 ½ in.). Georgia O'Keeffe Museum, Georgia O'Keeffe Foundation Photographs, MS.57, 2006.6.1303.

FIG. 13
O'Keeffe. *Garage Vigas and Studio Door*, July 1956. Gelatin silver print; 11.1 × 15.9 cm (4 ⅜ × 6 ¼ in.). Georgia O'Keeffe Museum, Georgia O'Keeffe Foundation Photographs, MS.57, 2006.6.1393.

NOTES

1. Although earlier, singular snapshots are extant, the sixteen works O'Keeffe produced in 1939 during her two weeks on Maui—her "Hawaii Snaps," as she called them—represent her first concentrated photographic investigation. Again, prints can be dated between the late 1930s and the mid-1950s, but it was only in 1956 that O'Keeffe truly began a concerted photographic practice, buying two cameras and using them with regularity.
2. Todd Webb, Journal, vol. 2, July 15, 1956, Todd Webb Archive, Portland, OR.
3. Georgia O'Keeffe to Edith Evans Asbury, July 2, 1957, box 180, folder 2984, Alfred Stieglitz / Georgia O'Keeffe Archive, Yale Collection of American Literature, Beinecke Rare Book and Manuscript Library, Yale University, New Haven, CT (hereafter Stieglitz / O'Keeffe Archive, Yale).
4. O'Keeffe believed all forms of production should signify personal, artistic expression. See Georgia O'Keeffe to David McAlpin, undated, David McAlpin Letters, Georgia O'Keeffe Museum, Library and Archive, Santa Fe, NM; and Georgia O'Keeffe, interview by William Innes Homer, Sept. 21, 1972, typed notes, William Innes Homer Papers, ibid.
5. Katharine Kuh, *The Artist's Voice: Talks with Seventeen Artists* (New York: Harper and Row, 1962): 189.
6. Quoted in Carolyn Burke, *Foursome: Alfred Stieglitz, Georgia O'Keeffe, Paul Strand, Rebecca Salsbury* (New York: Alfred A. Knopf, 2019), 132.
7. Sarah Whitaker Peters, *Becoming O'Keeffe: The Early Years* (New York: Abbeville Press, 1991), 279.
8. Ibid., 289.
9. Ibid.
10. Alfred Stieglitz to Olivia Paine, May 9, 1933, Department of Prints and Drawings, Metropolitan Museum of Art, New York, cited in Weston J. Naef, *The Collection of Alfred Stieglitz: Fifty Pioneers of Modern Photography*, exh. cat. (New York: Metropolitan Museum of Art; Viking Press, 1978), 9.
11. Wanda M. Corn, *The Great American Thing: Modern Art and National Identity, 1915–1935* (Berkeley: University of California Press, 1999), 38–39.
12. Richard Whelan, ed., *Stieglitz on Photography: His Selected Essays and Notes* (New York: Aperture, 2000), 24–25.
13. Quoted in Malcolm Daniel, *Stieglitz, Steichen, Strand: Masterworks from the Metropolitan Museum of Art*, exh. cat. (New York: Metropolitan Museum of Art; New Haven, CT: Yale University Press, 2010), 22.
14. Herbert J. Seligmann, *Alfred Stieglitz Talking: Notes on Some of His Conversations, 1925–1931* (New Haven, CT: Yale University Library, 1966): 7.
15. Quoted in Lois P. Nicholson, *The Importance of Georgia O'Keeffe* (San Diego, CA: Lucent Books, 1995), 99.
16. Quoted in Blanche C. Matthias, "Georgia O'Keeffe and the Intimate Gallery: Stieglitz Showing Seven Americans," *Chicago Evening Post, Magazine of the Art World*, Mar. 2, 1926, 14.
17. Kuh, *Artist's Voice*, 190.
18. Georgia O'Keeffe and Anita Pollitzer, *Lovingly, Georgia: The Complete Correspondence of Georgia O'Keeffe and Anita Pollitzer*, ed., Clive Giboire (New York: Simon and Schuster, 1990), 31.
19. Whelan, *Stieglitz on Photography*, 195.
20. Ibid., 238.
21. Daniel, *Stieglitz, Steichen, Strand*, 22–23.
22. Kuh, *Artist's Voice*, 200.
23. Corn, *Great American Thing*, 250.
24. Georgia O'Keeffe to Alfred Stieglitz, Aug. 8, 1943, box 93, folder 1840, Stieglitz / O'Keeffe Archive, Yale.
25. Georgia O'Keeffe to Anita Pollitzer, Feb. 16, 1916, box 208, folder 3650, Stieglitz / O'Keeffe Archive, Yale.
26. Arthur Wesley Dow, *Composition: A Series of Exercises in Art Structure for the Use of Students and Teachers* (Garden City, NY: Doubleday, 1913): 47.
27. Ibid., 38.
28. Quoted in Nancy E. Green, "Arthur Wesley Dow: His Art and His Influence," in Nancy E. Green et al., *Arthur Wesley Dow (1857–1922): His Art and His Influence*, exh. cat. (New York: Spanierman Gallery, 1999), 24.
29. Dow, *Composition*, 53.
30. Georgia O'Keeffe, *Georgia O'Keeffe* (New York: Viking Press, 1976), n.p., opp. pl. 104.
31. Nanyoung Kim, "A History of Design Theory in Art Education," *Journal of Aesthetic Education* 40, no. 2 (Summer 2006): 15.
32. Quoted in Britta Benke, *Georgia O'Keeffe, 1887–1986: Flowers in the Desert* (Cologne, Germany: Taschen, 2000), 38.
33. Corn, *Great American Thing*, 250.
34. Quoted in ibid.
35. Anita Pollitzer essay draft, series VIII, Georgia O'Keeffe Correspondence, box 209, folder 3658, Stieglitz / O'Keeffe Archive, Yale.

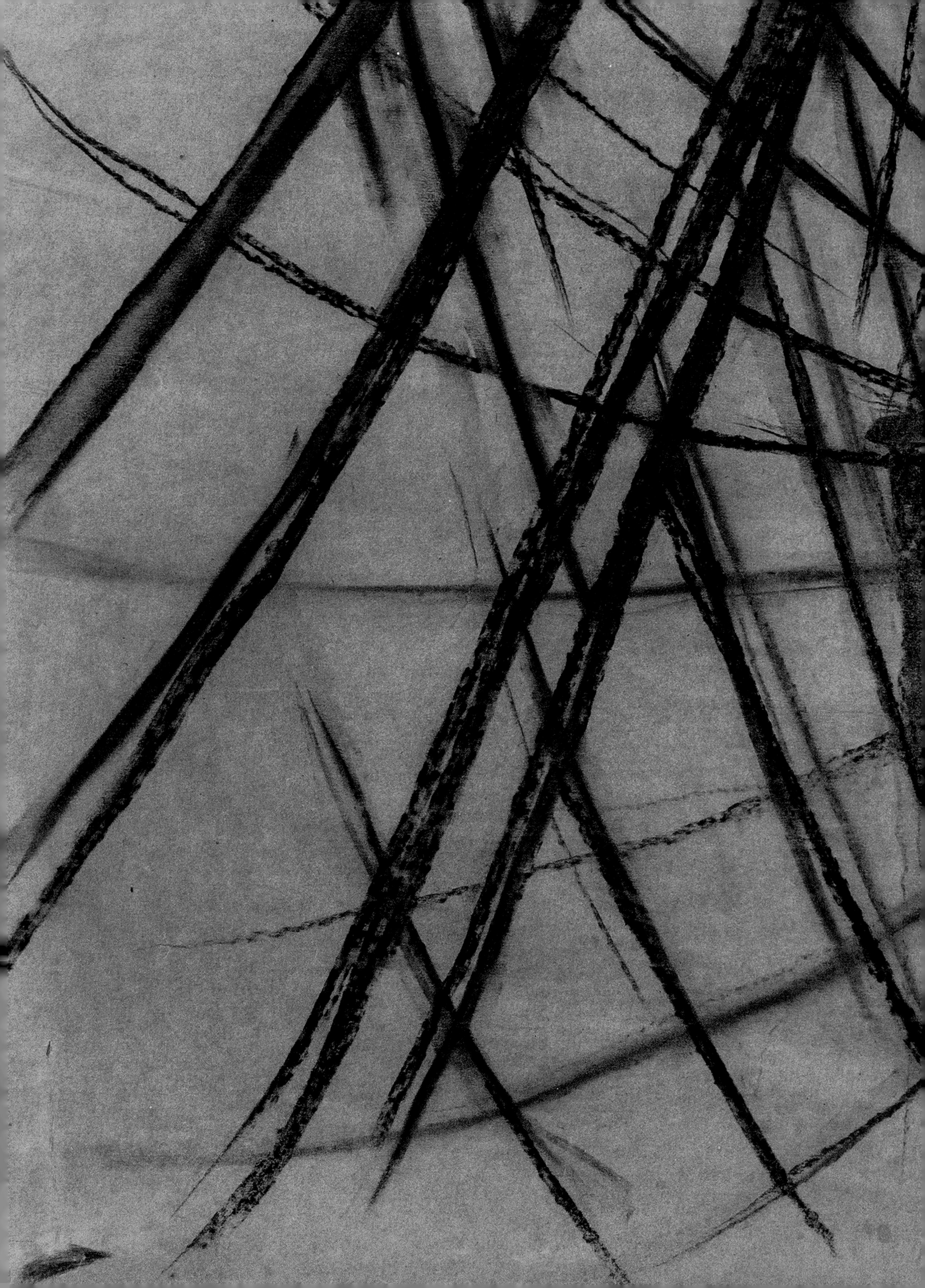

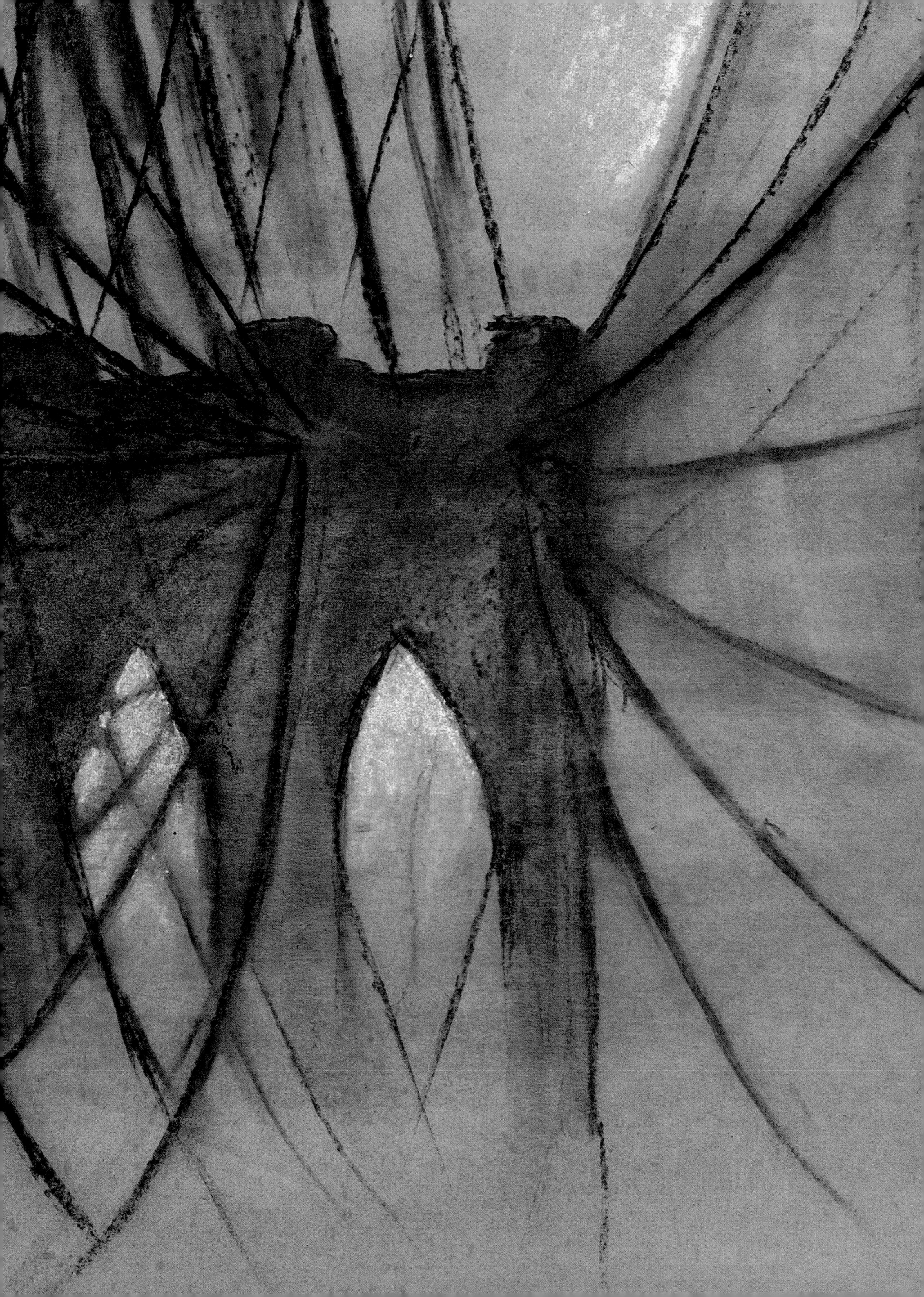

1
New York Street with Moon, 1925
Oil on canvas, mounted to Masonite

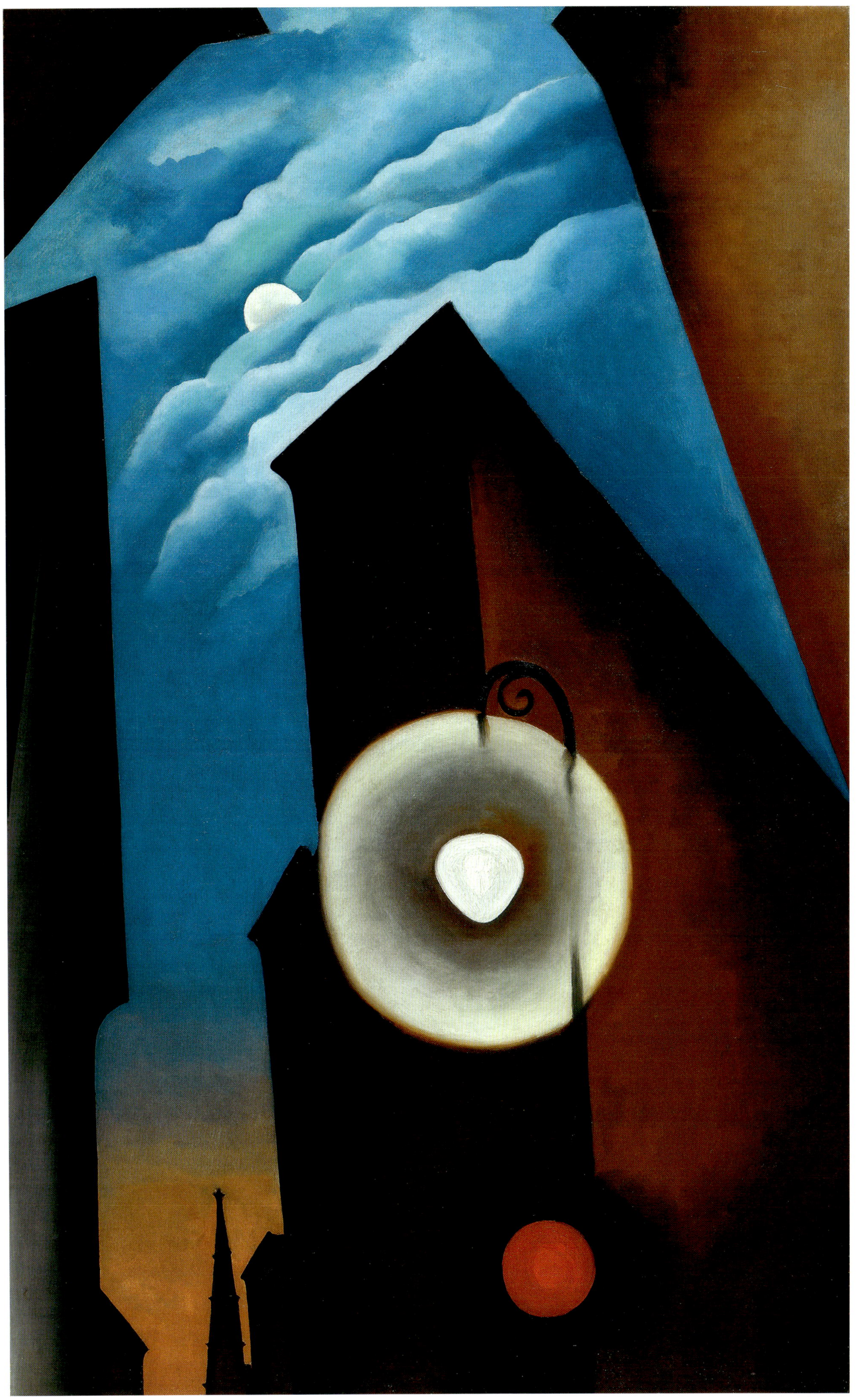

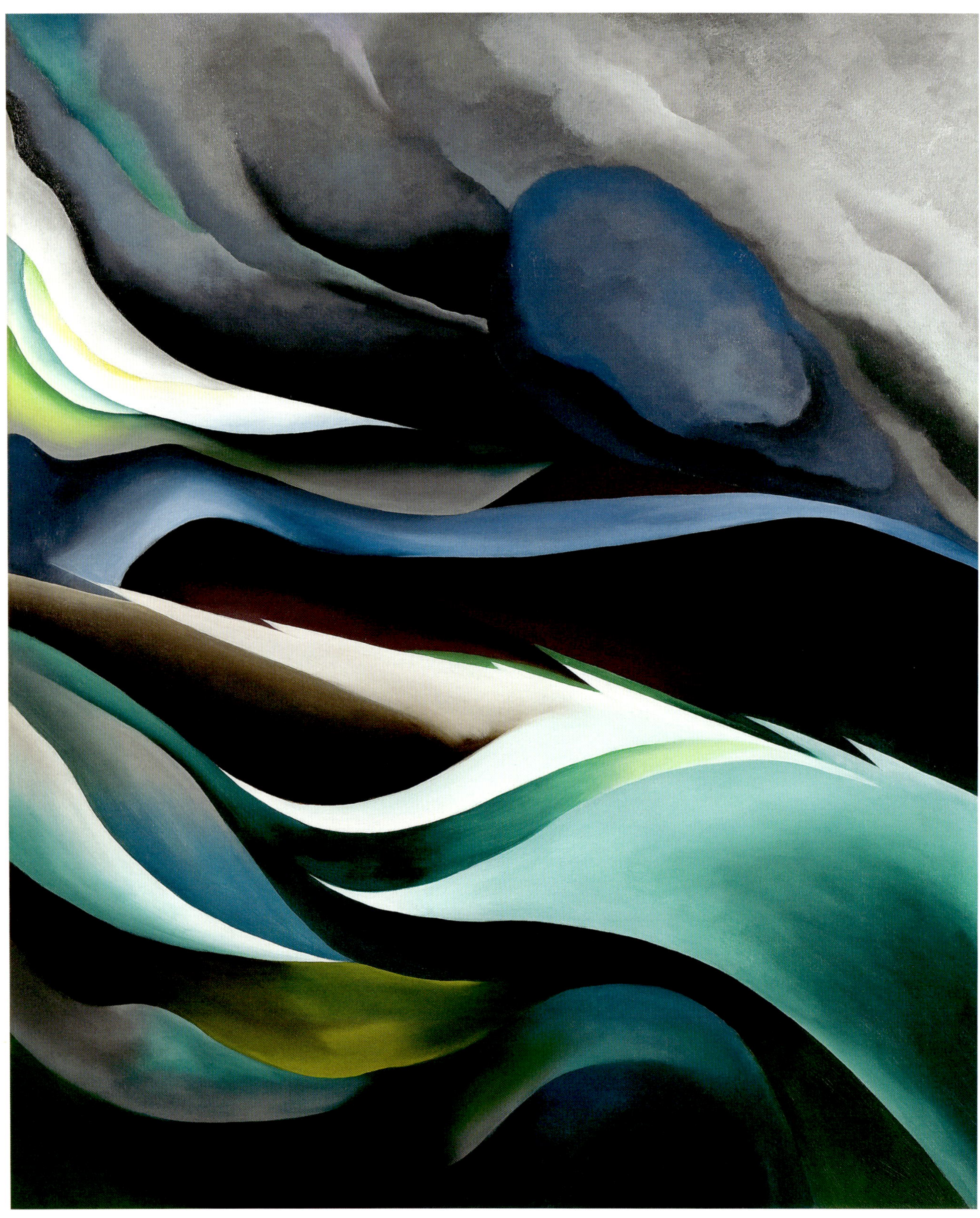

2
From the Lake No. 1, 1924
Oil on canvas

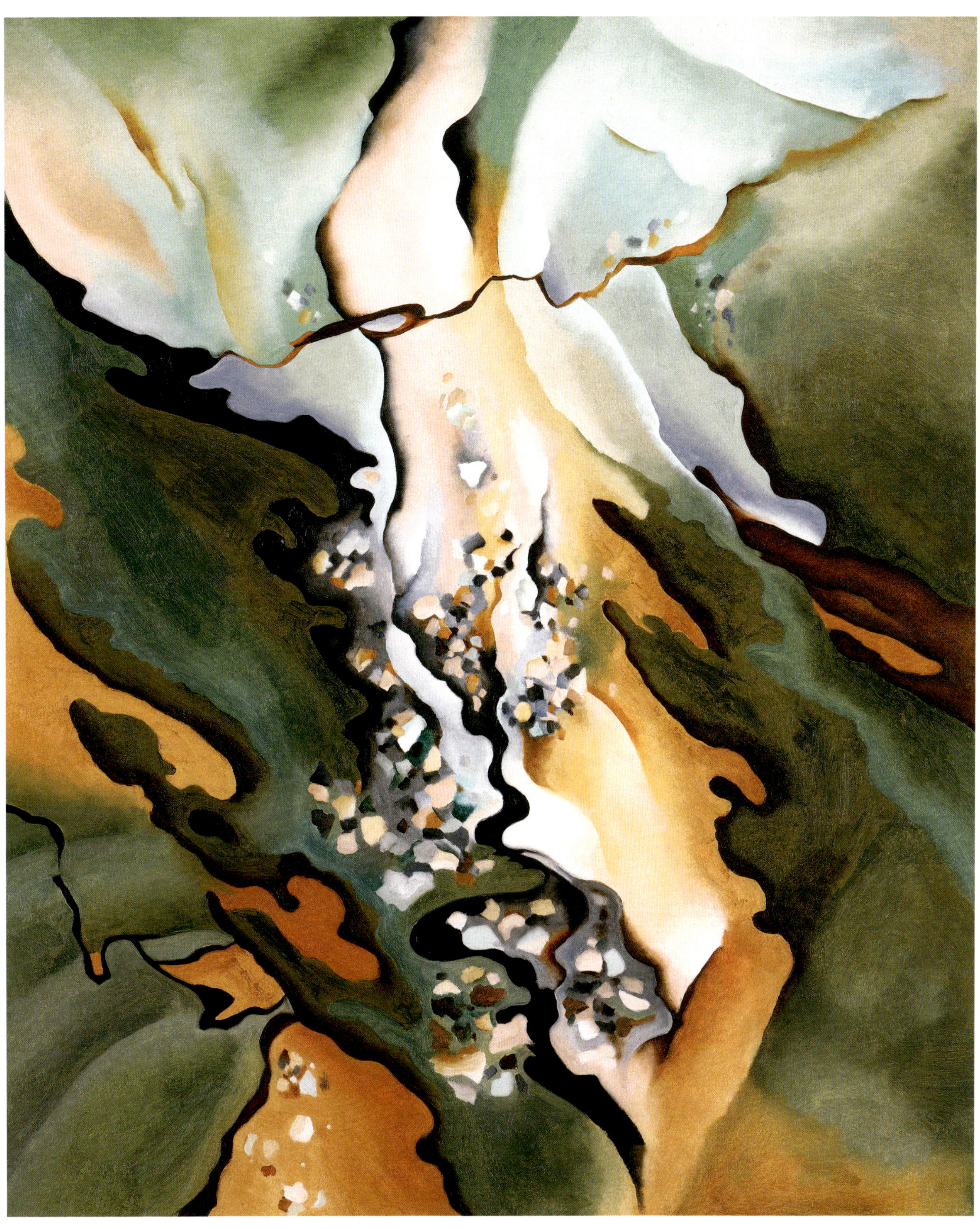

3
From the Lake No. 3, 1924
Oil on canvas

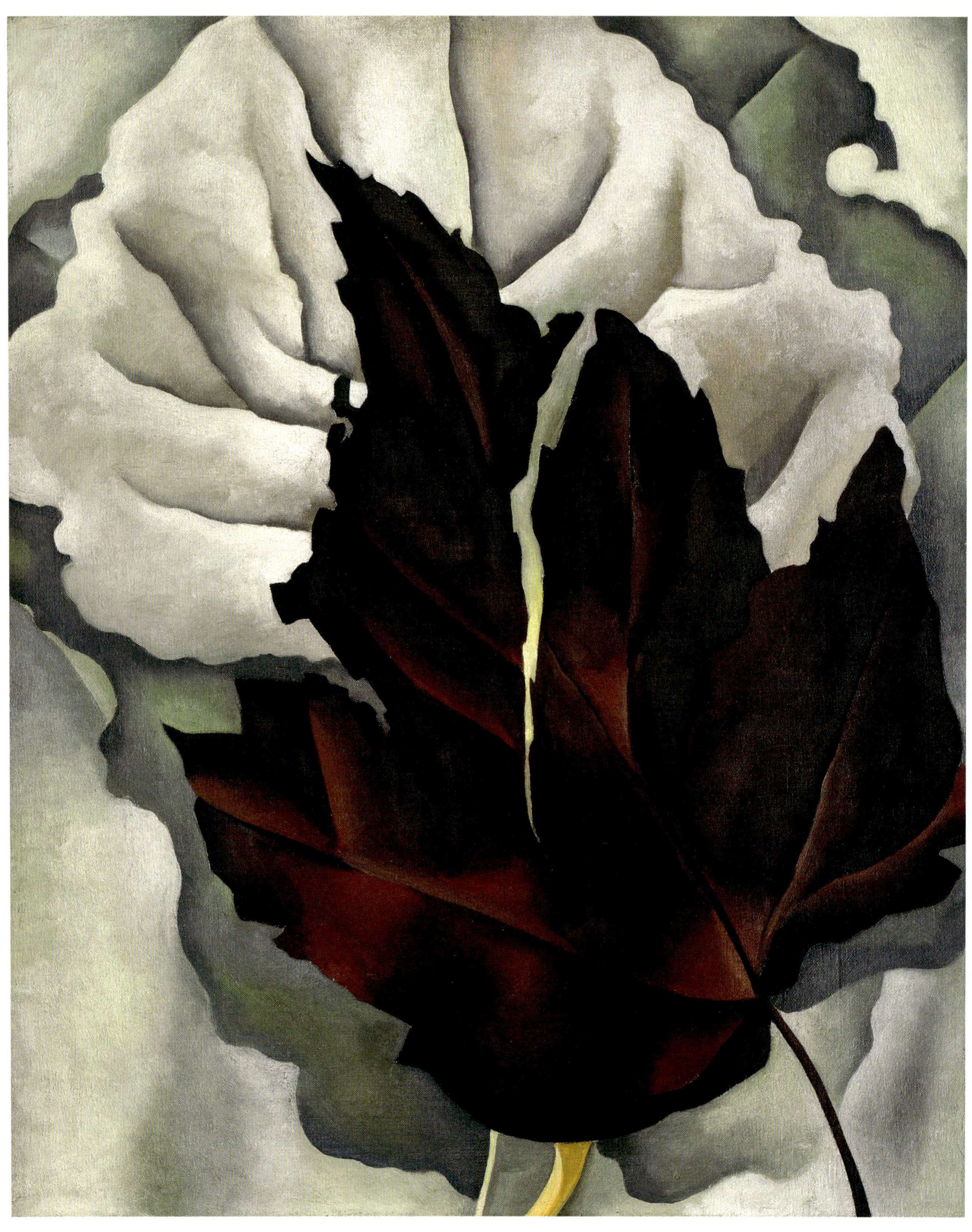

4
Pattern of Leaves, 1923
Oil on canvas

5
The Eggplant, 1924
Oil on canvas

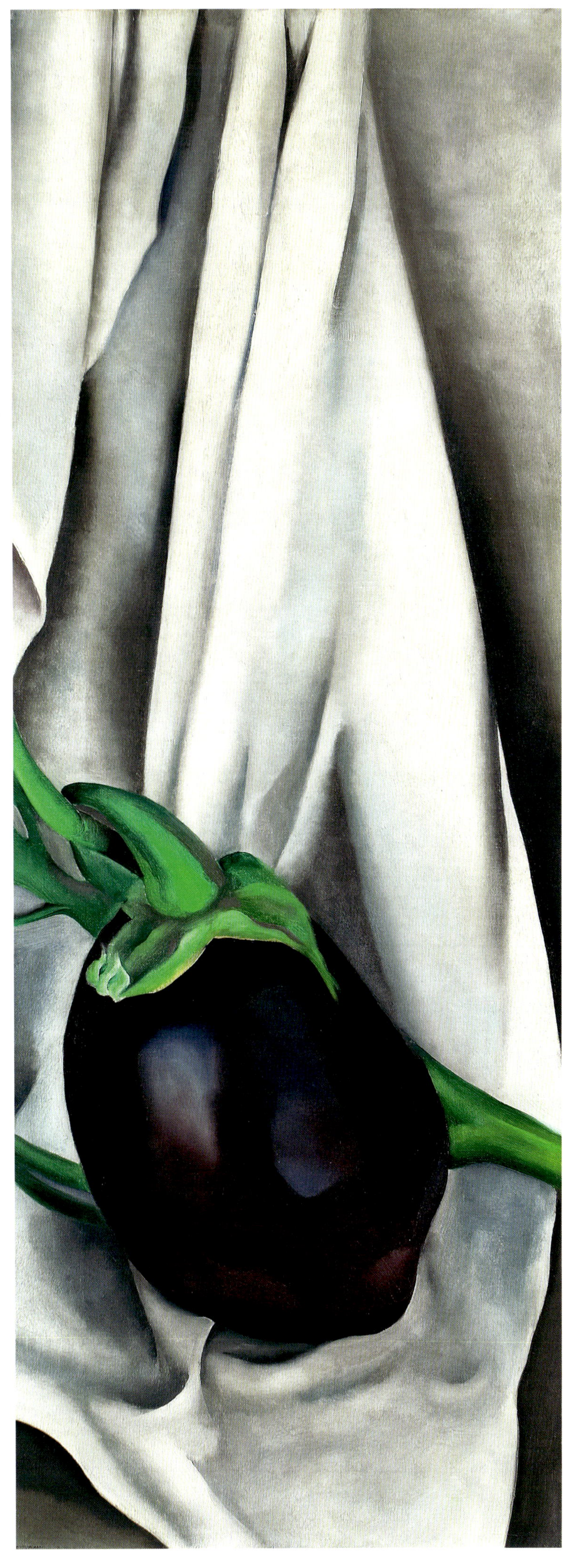

6

The Chestnut Tree – Grey, 1924

Oil on canvas

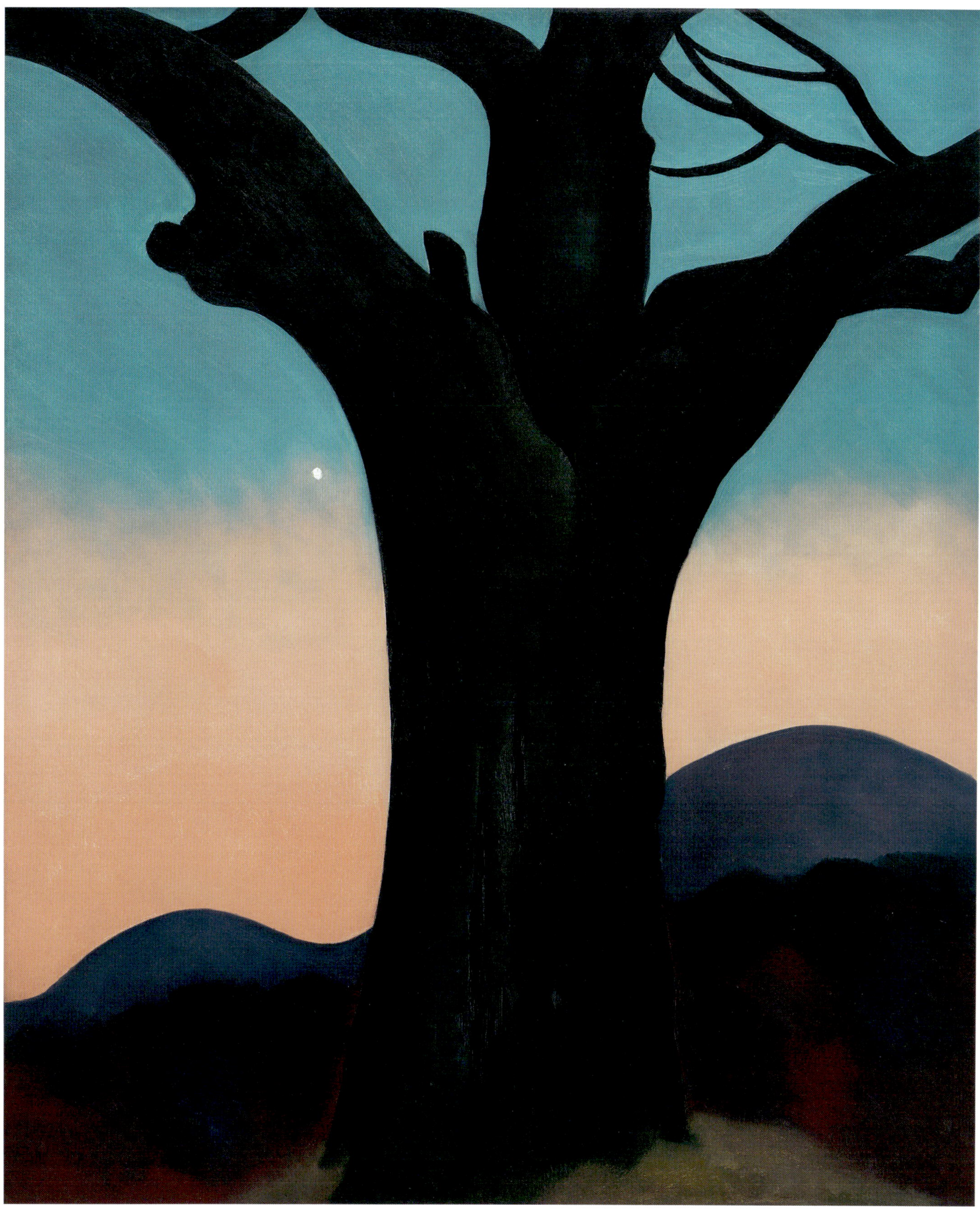

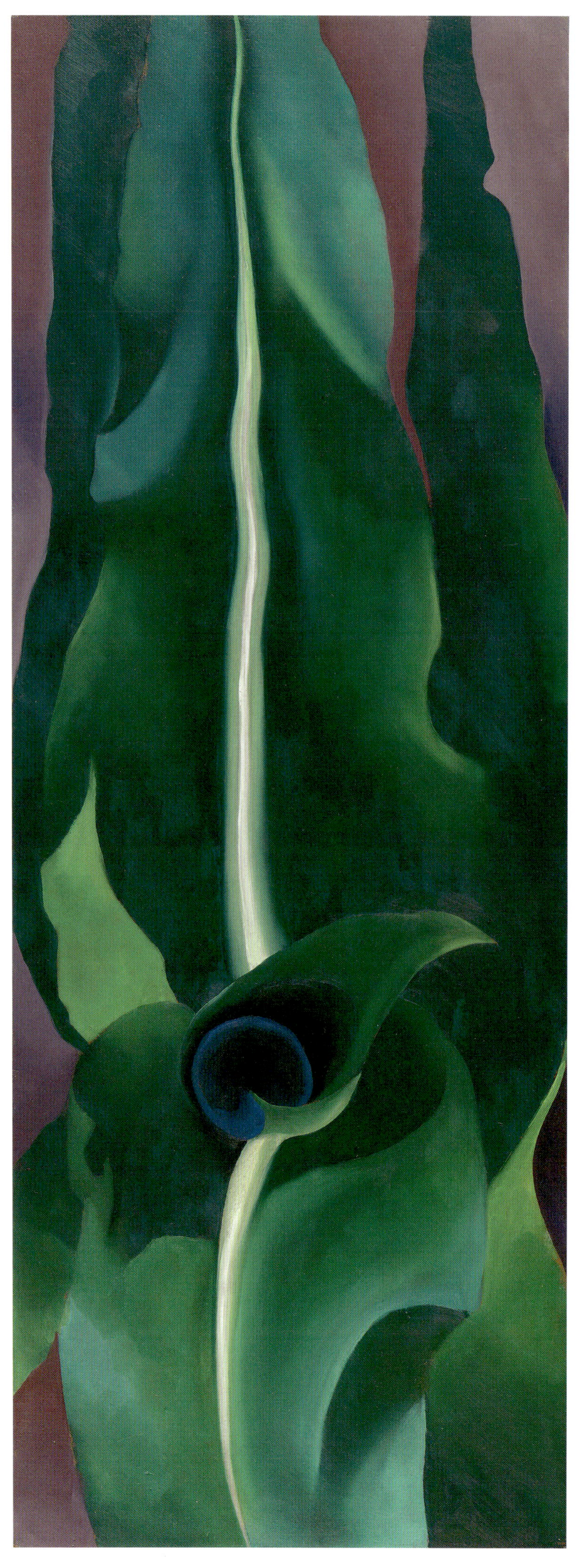

7
Corn, Dark, No. 1, 1924
Oil on wood fiberboard

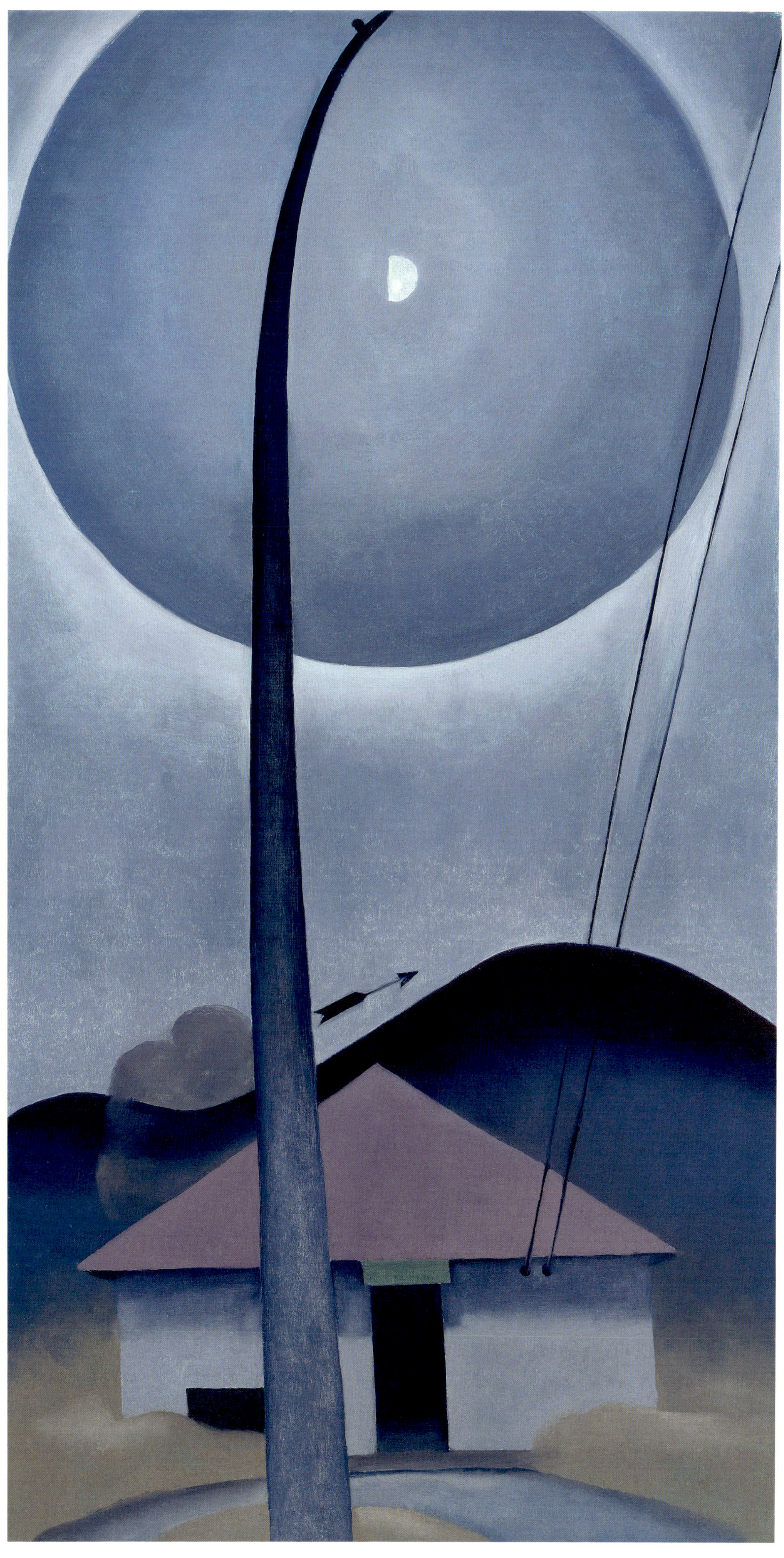

8
Flagpole, 1925
Oil on canvas

9

A Celebration, 1924
Oil on canvas

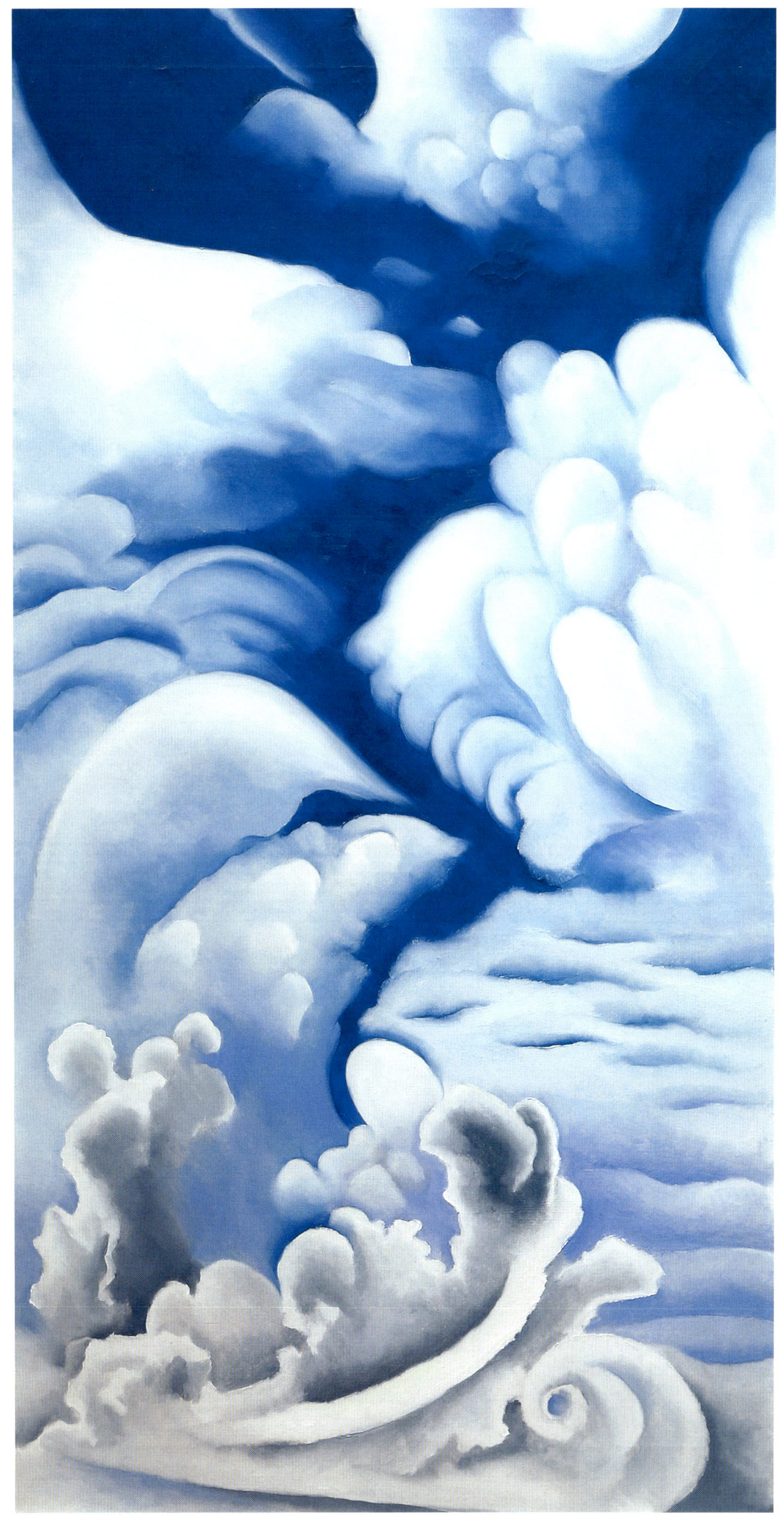

10
59th Street Studio, 1919
Oil on canvas

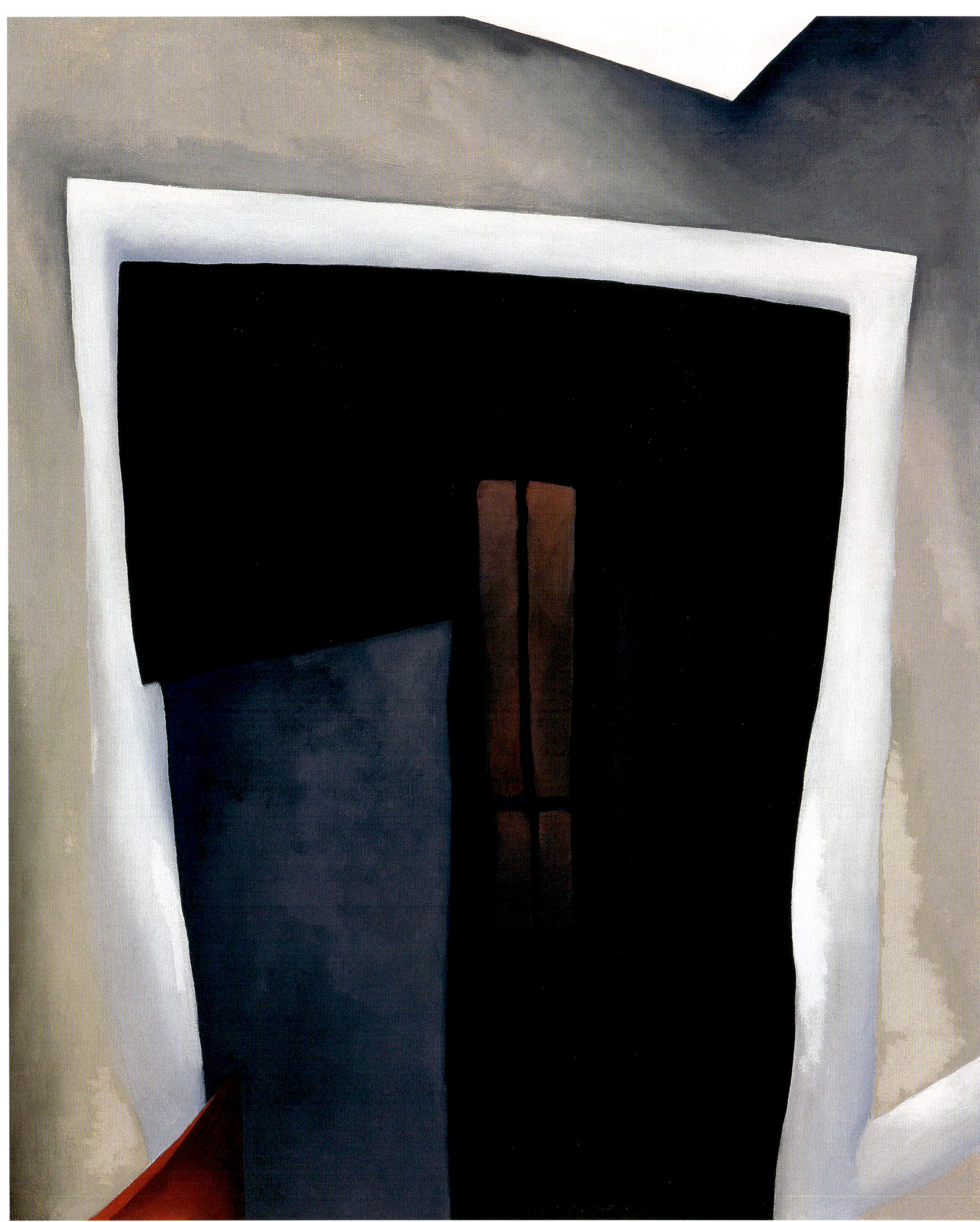

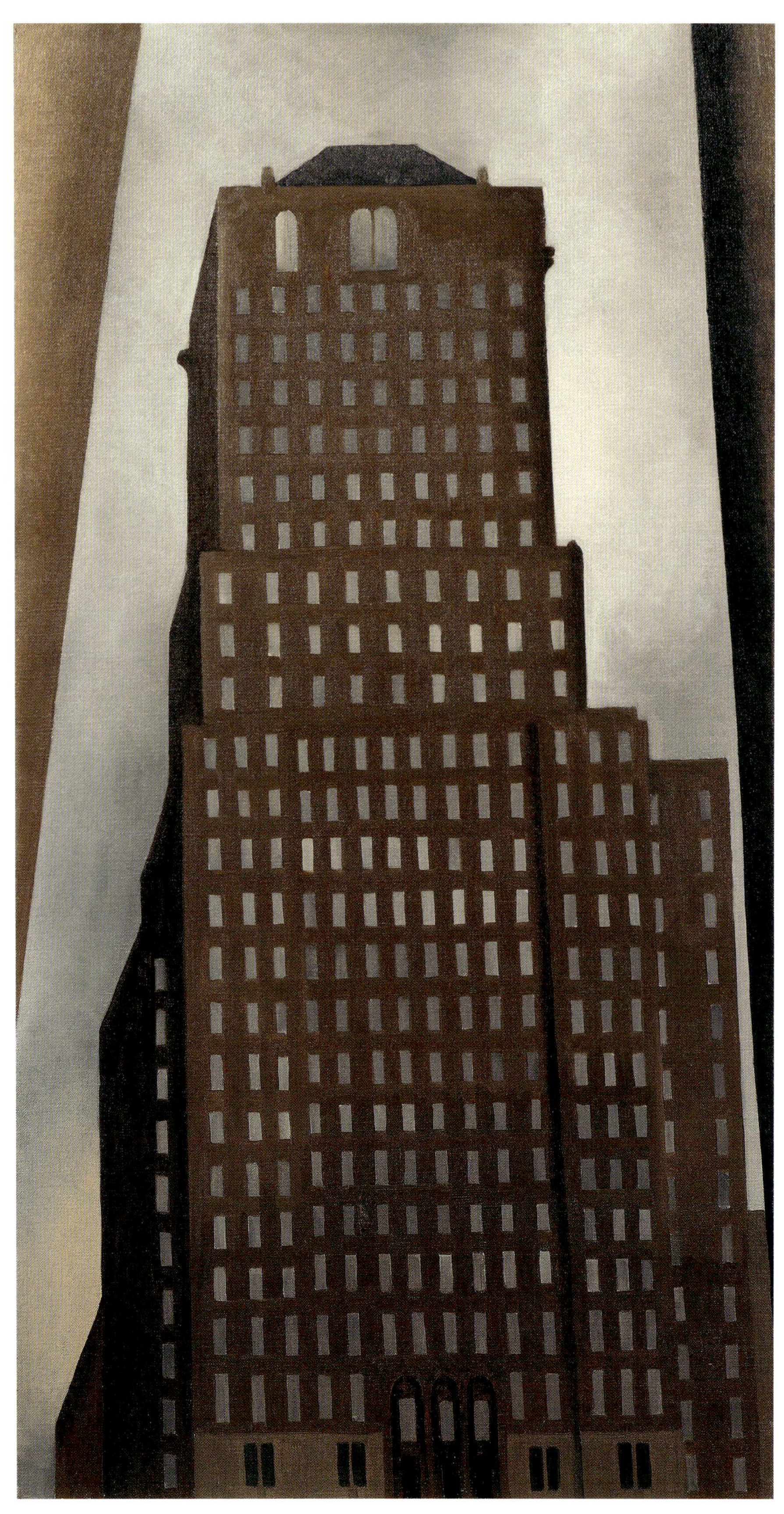

11
Shelton Hotel, N.Y., No. I, 1926
Oil on canvas

12
The Shelton with Sunspots, N.Y., 1926
Oil on canvas

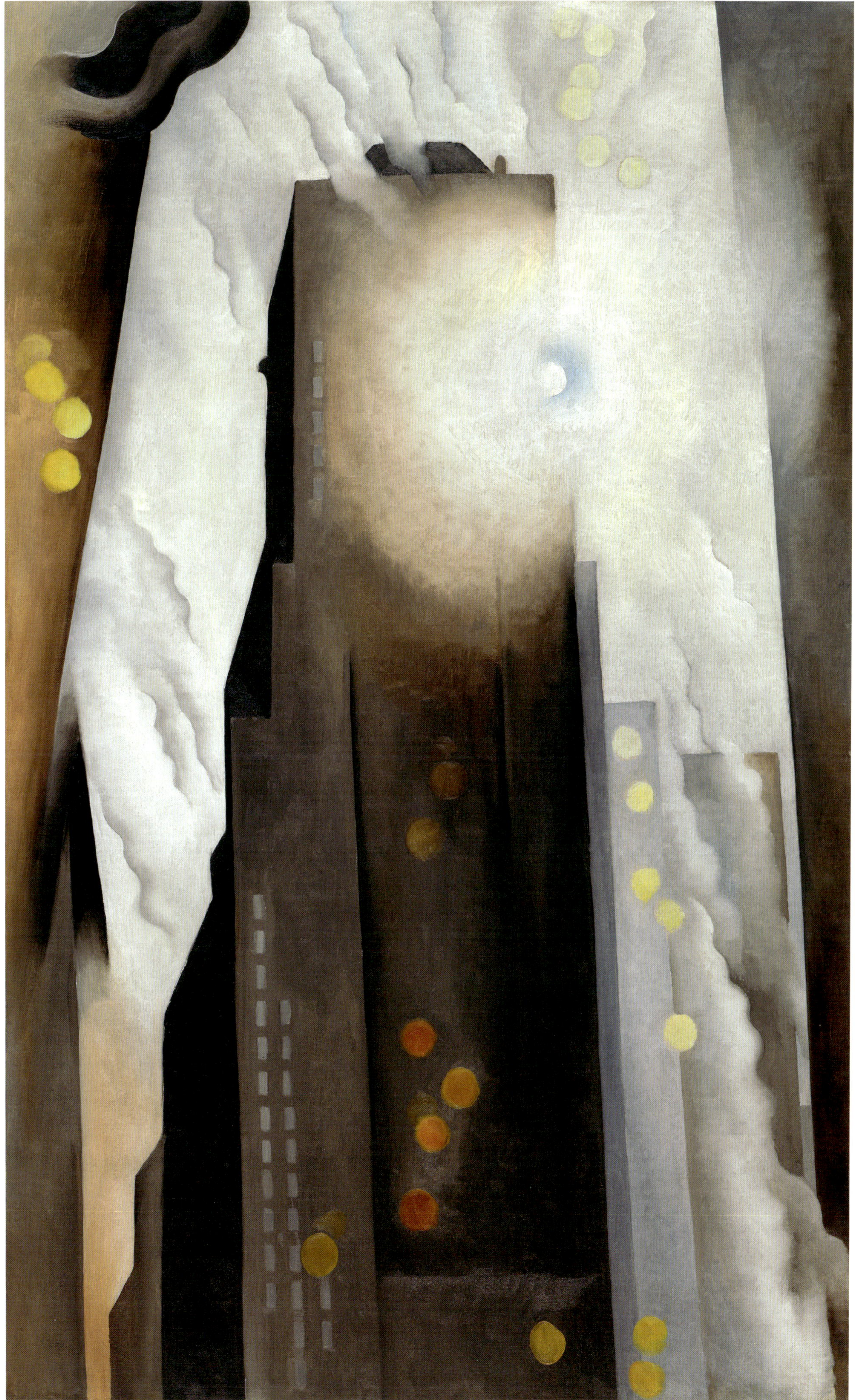

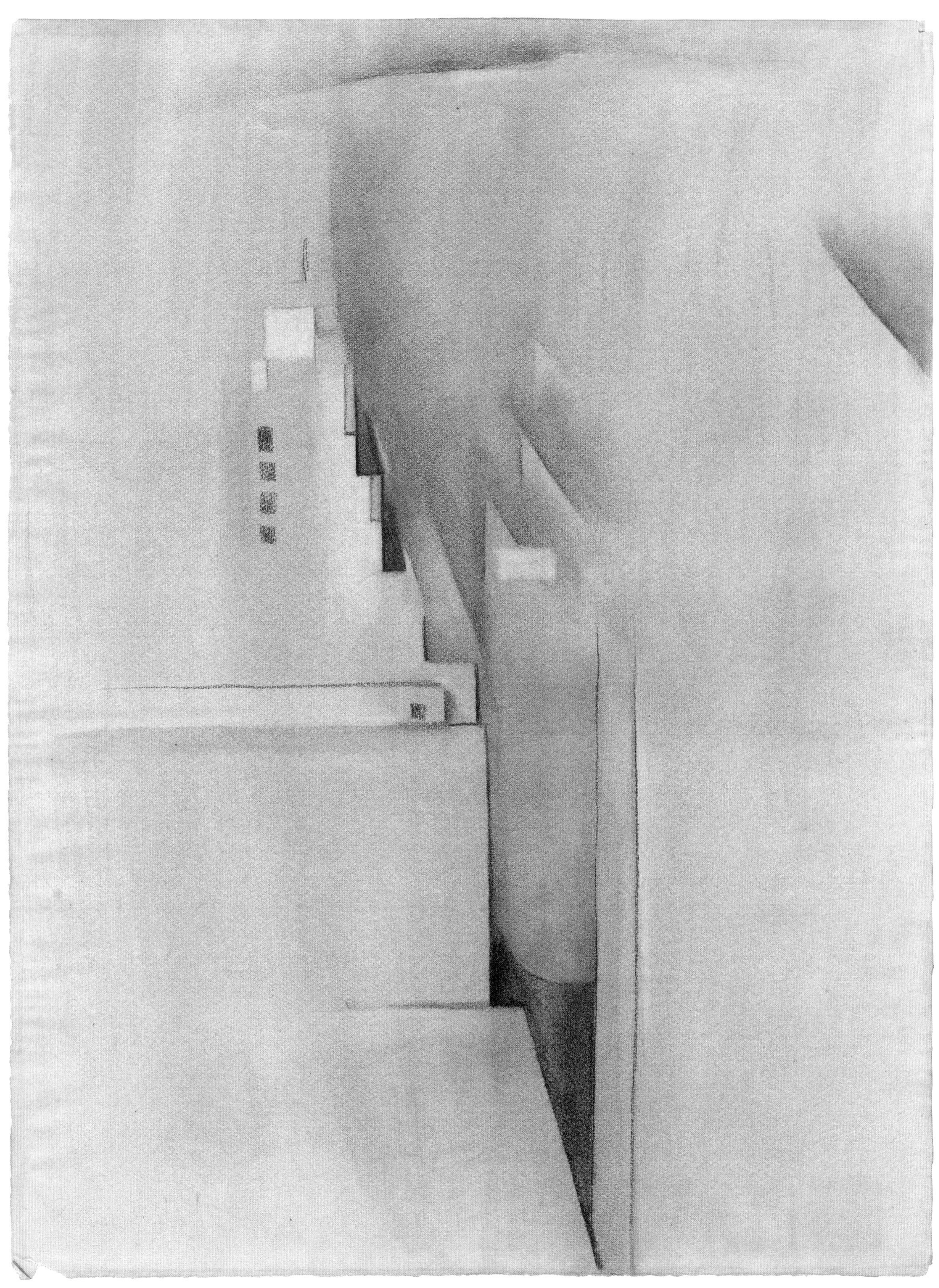

13

Untitled (New York), 1932

Charcoal on medium thick, cream, slightly textured laid paper

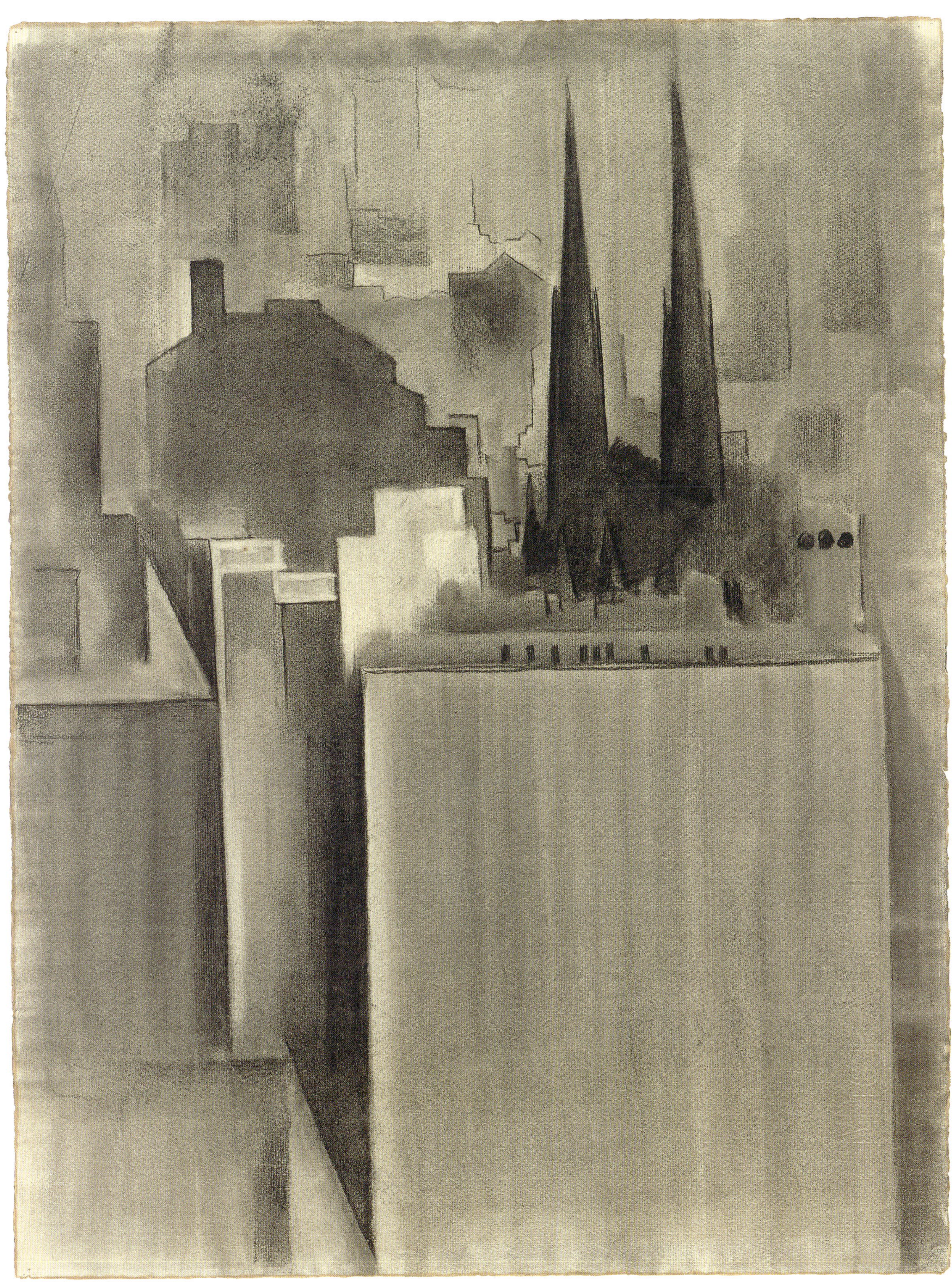

14
Untitled (New York), 1924–26
Charcoal on medium thick, cream, slightly textured laid paper

15

A Street, 1926

Oil on canvas

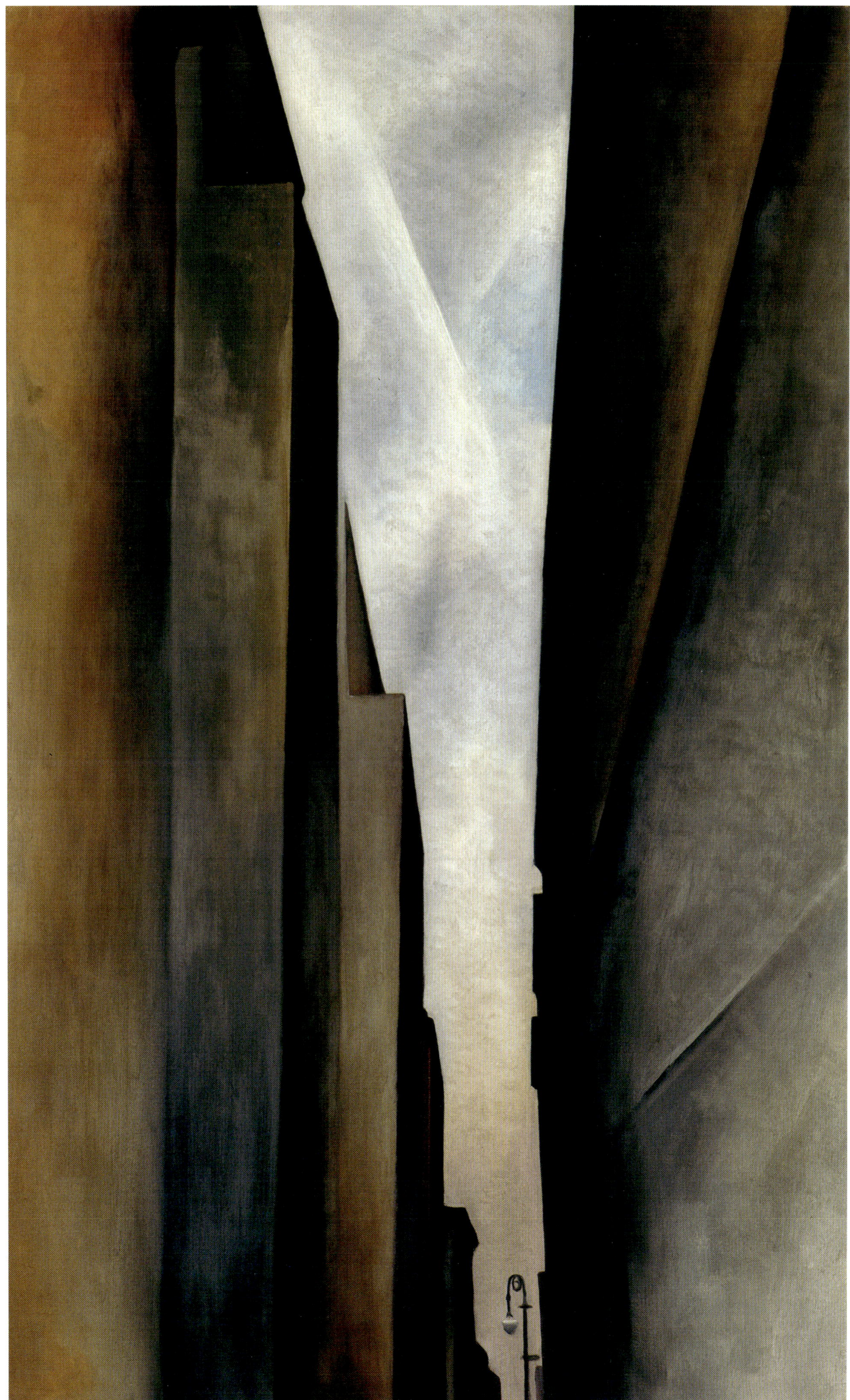

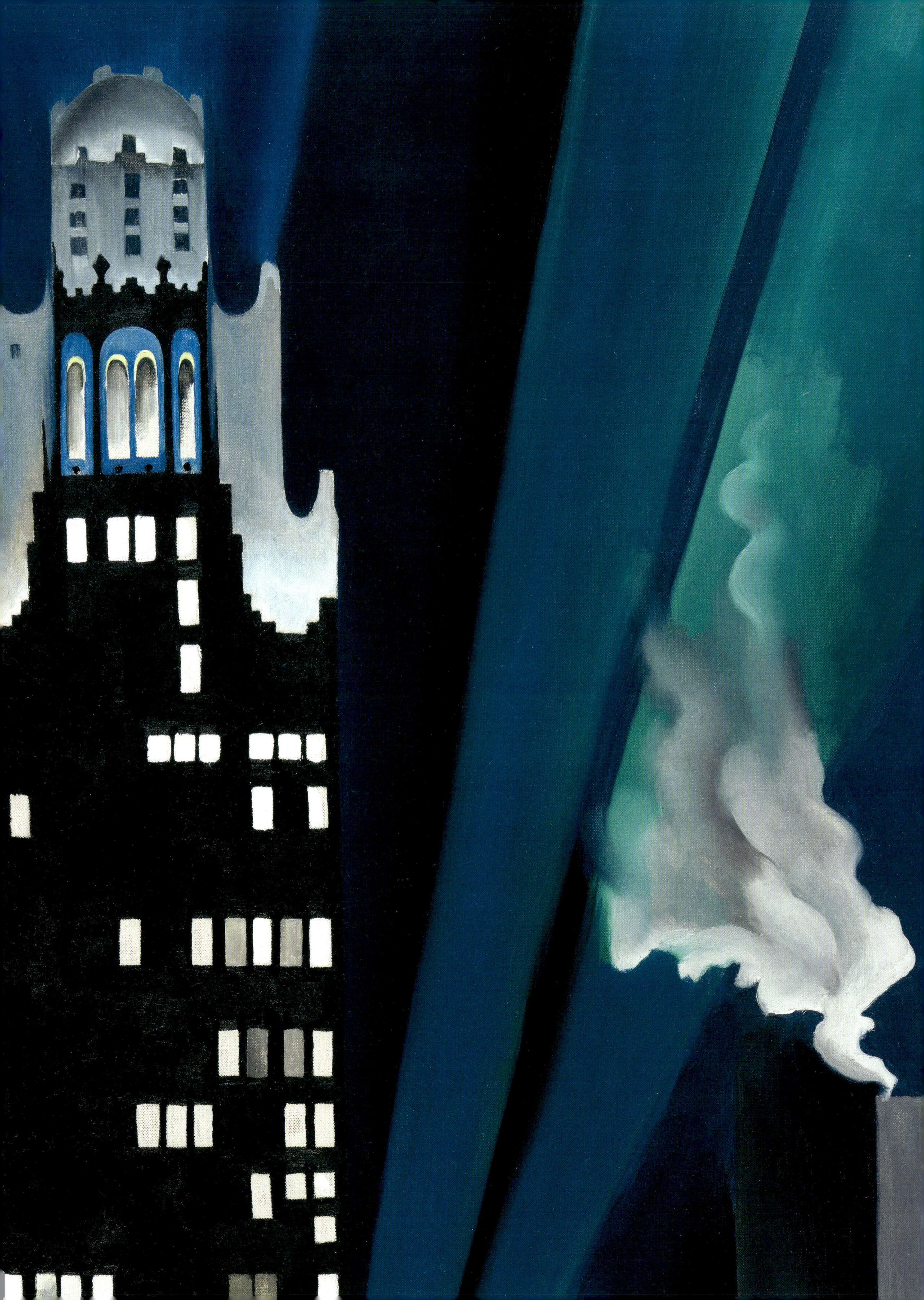

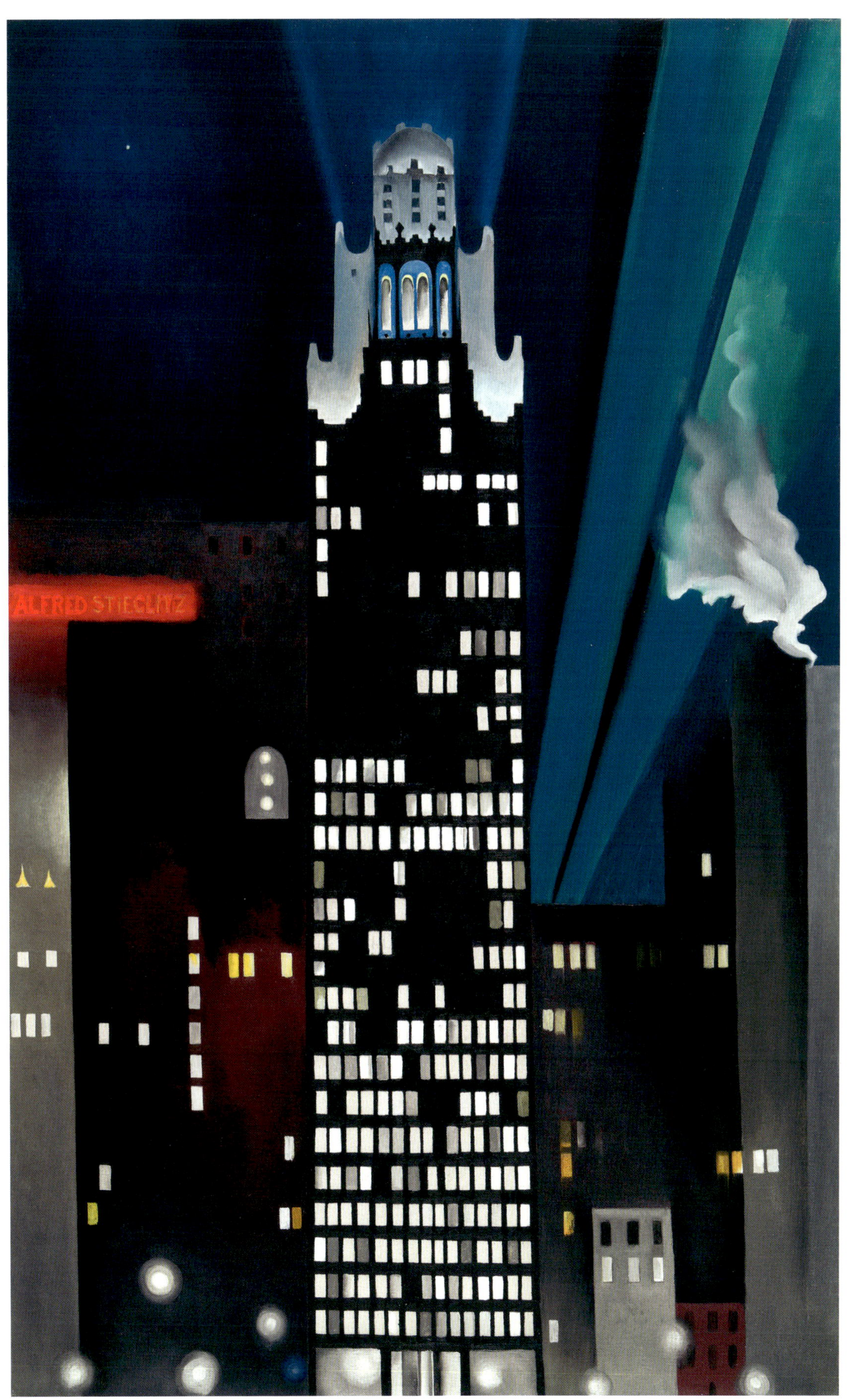

16
Radiator Building – Night, New York, 1927
Oil on canvas

17
Ritz Tower, 1928
Oil on canvas

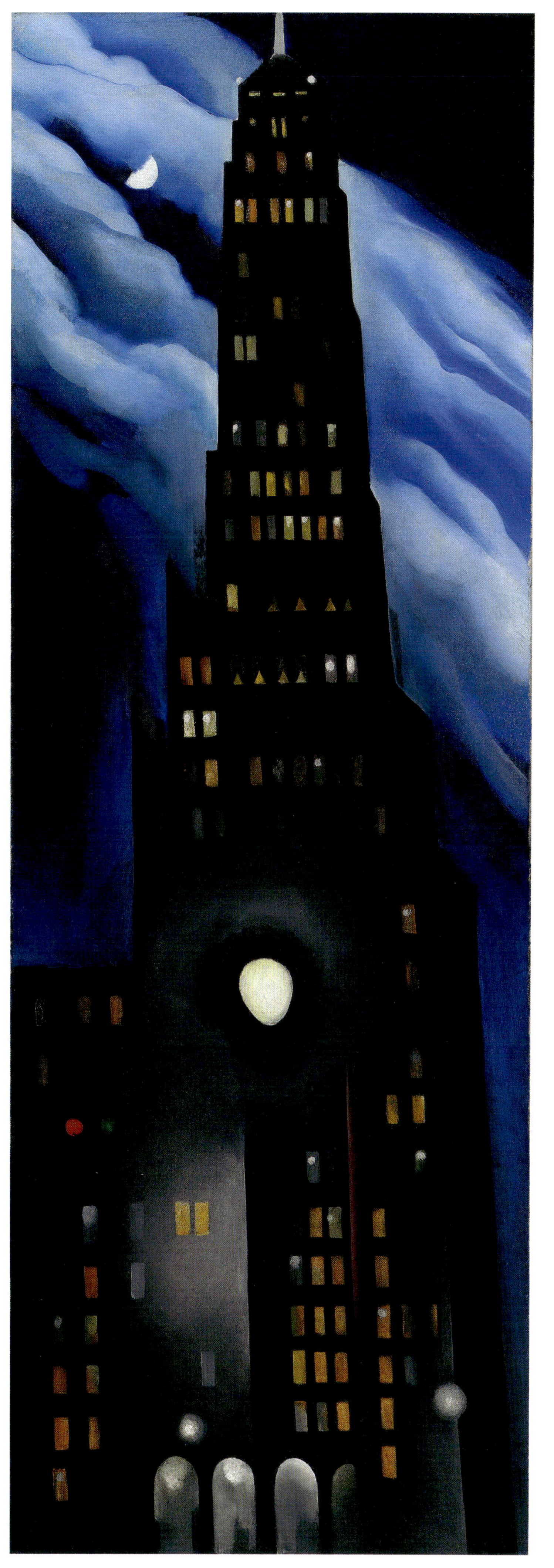

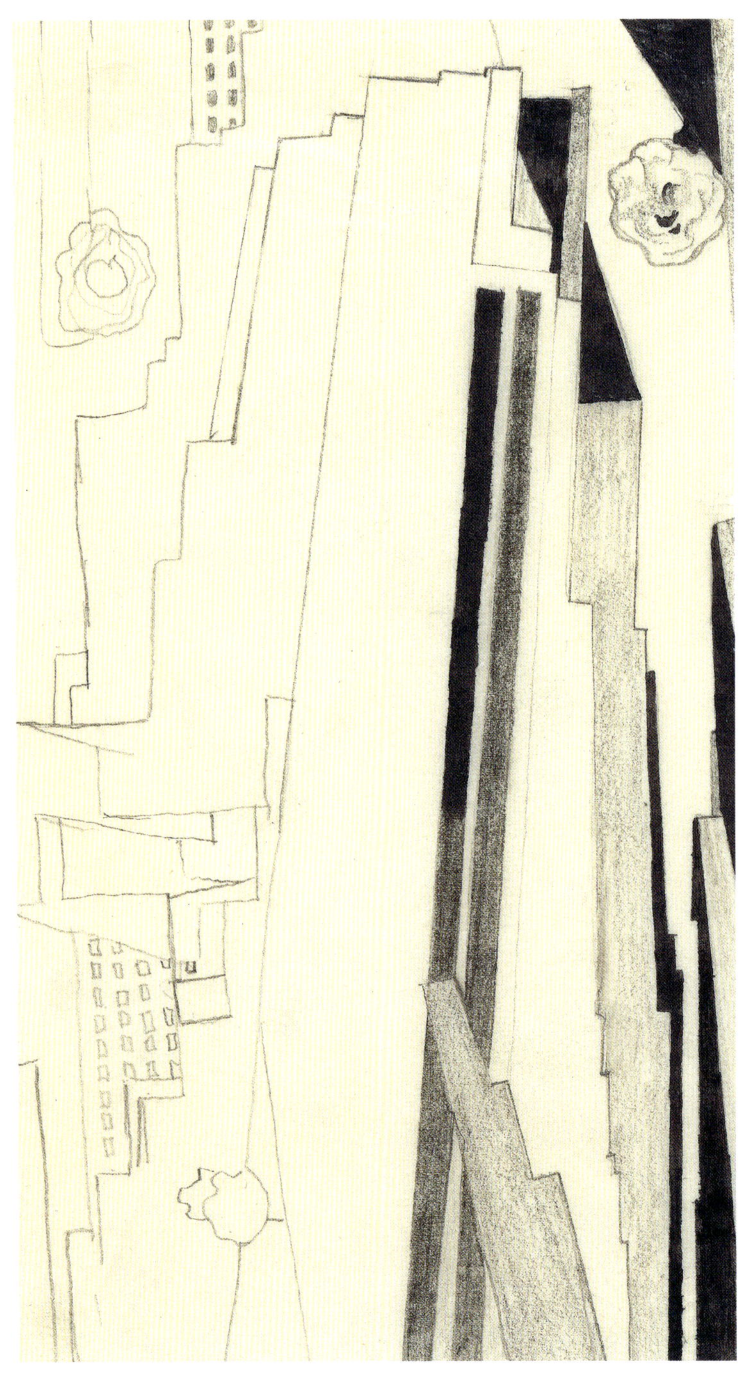

18
Untitled (Manhattan), 1932
Black ink and graphite on paper

19
Manhattan, 1932
Oil on canvas

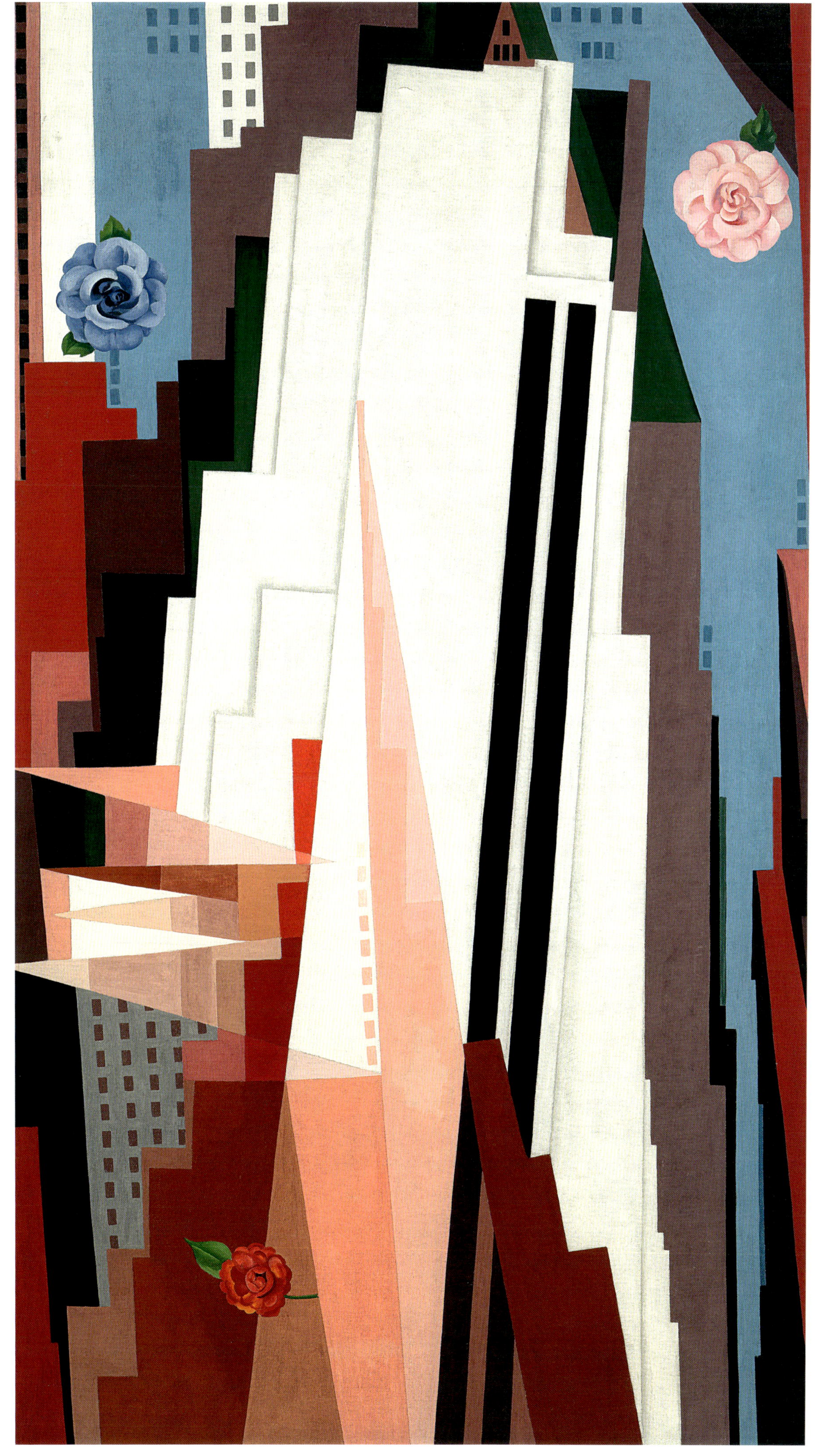

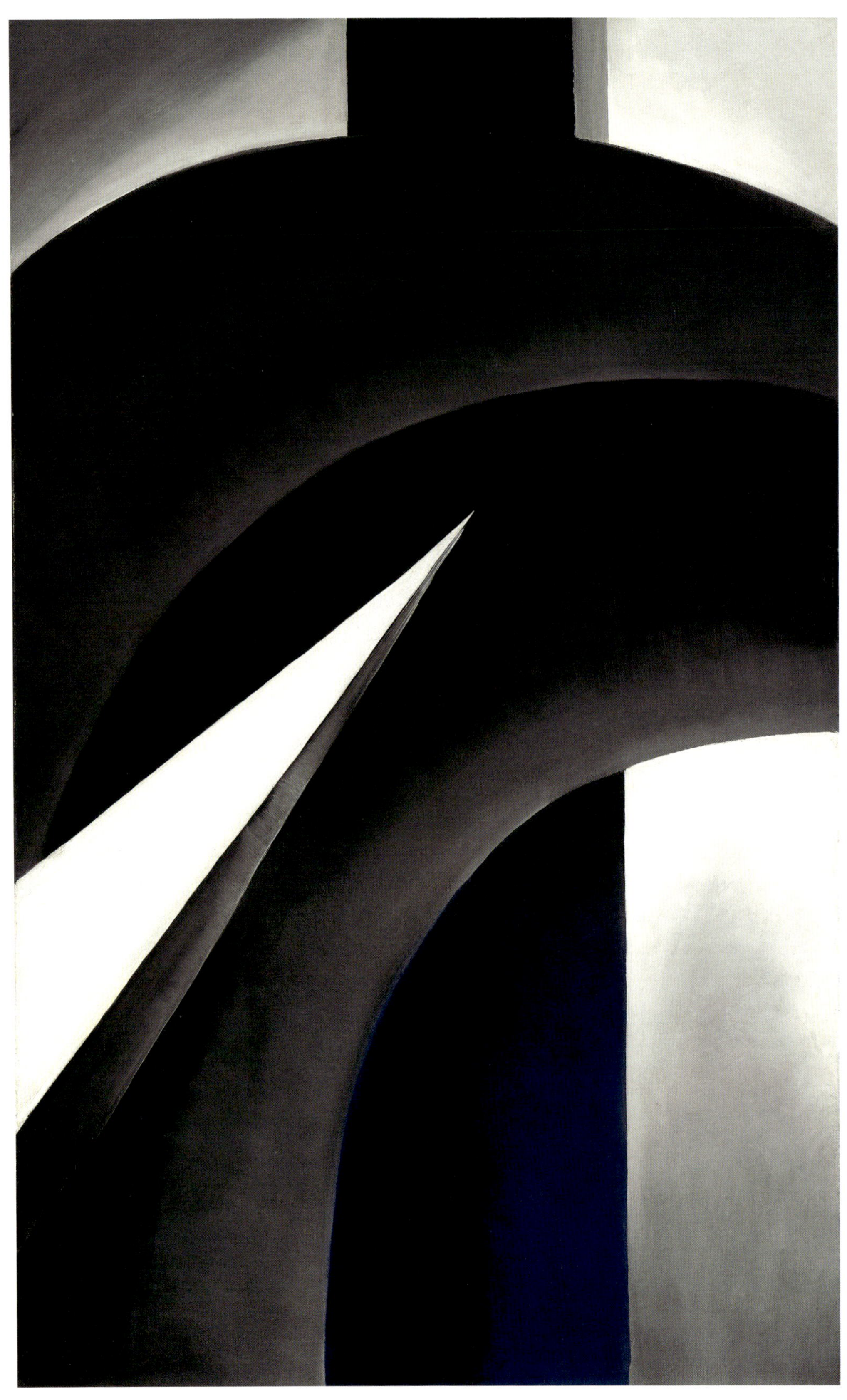

20
Black White and Blue, 1930
Oil on canvas

21
City Night, 1926
Oil on canvas

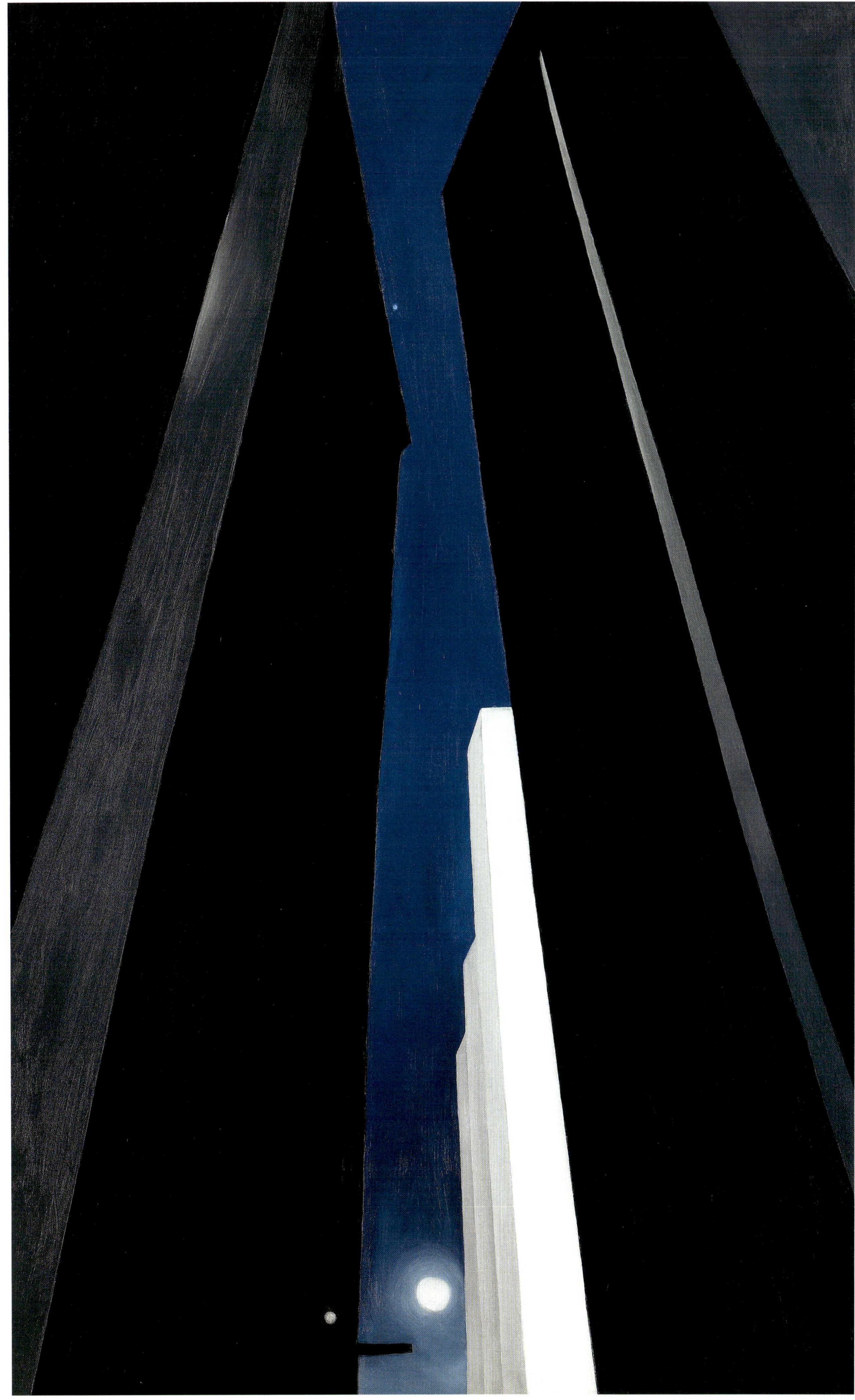

22
Black and White, 1930
Oil on canvas

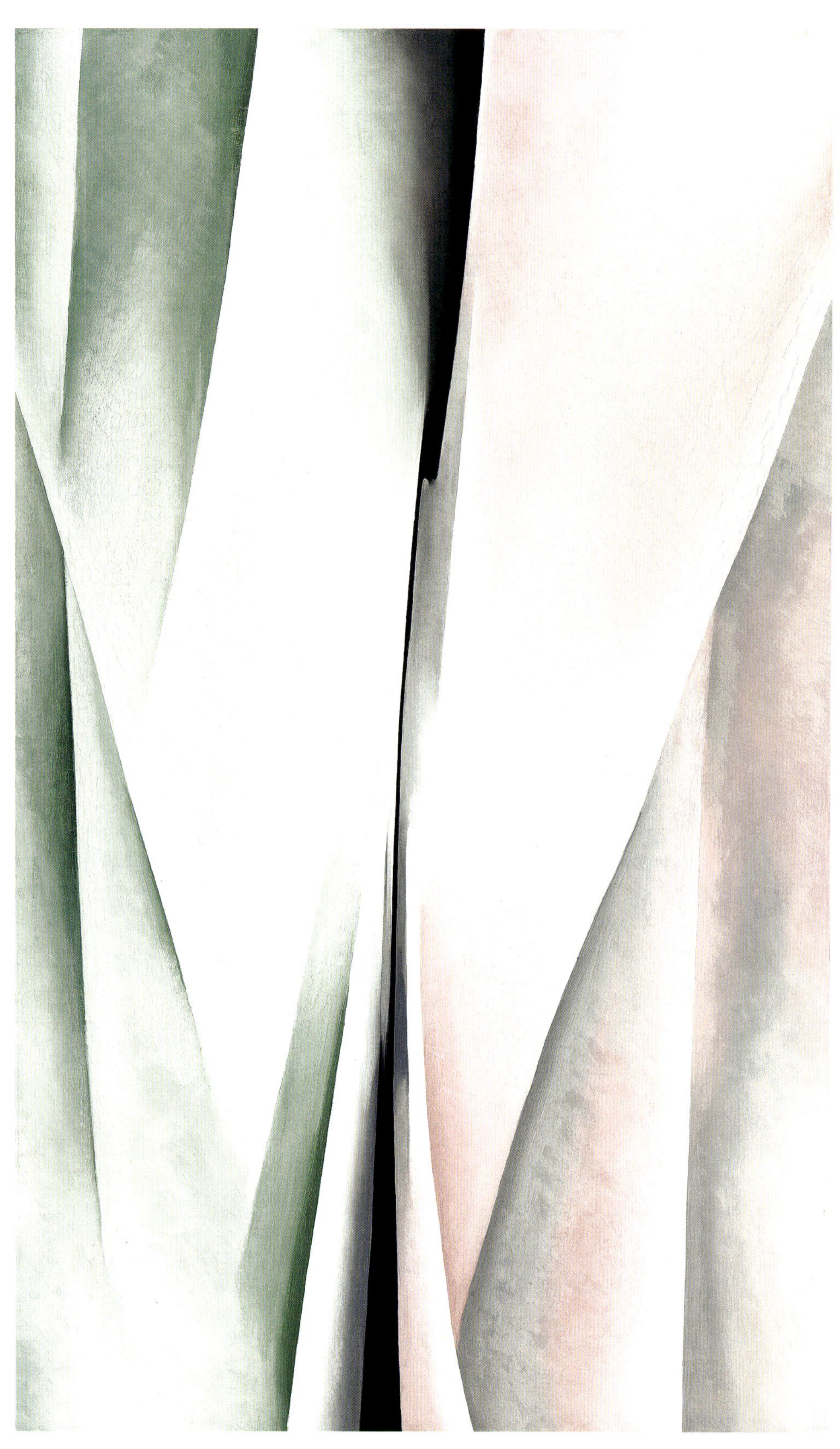

23
Abstraction, 1926
Oil on canvas

24
Line and Curve, 1927
Oil on canvas

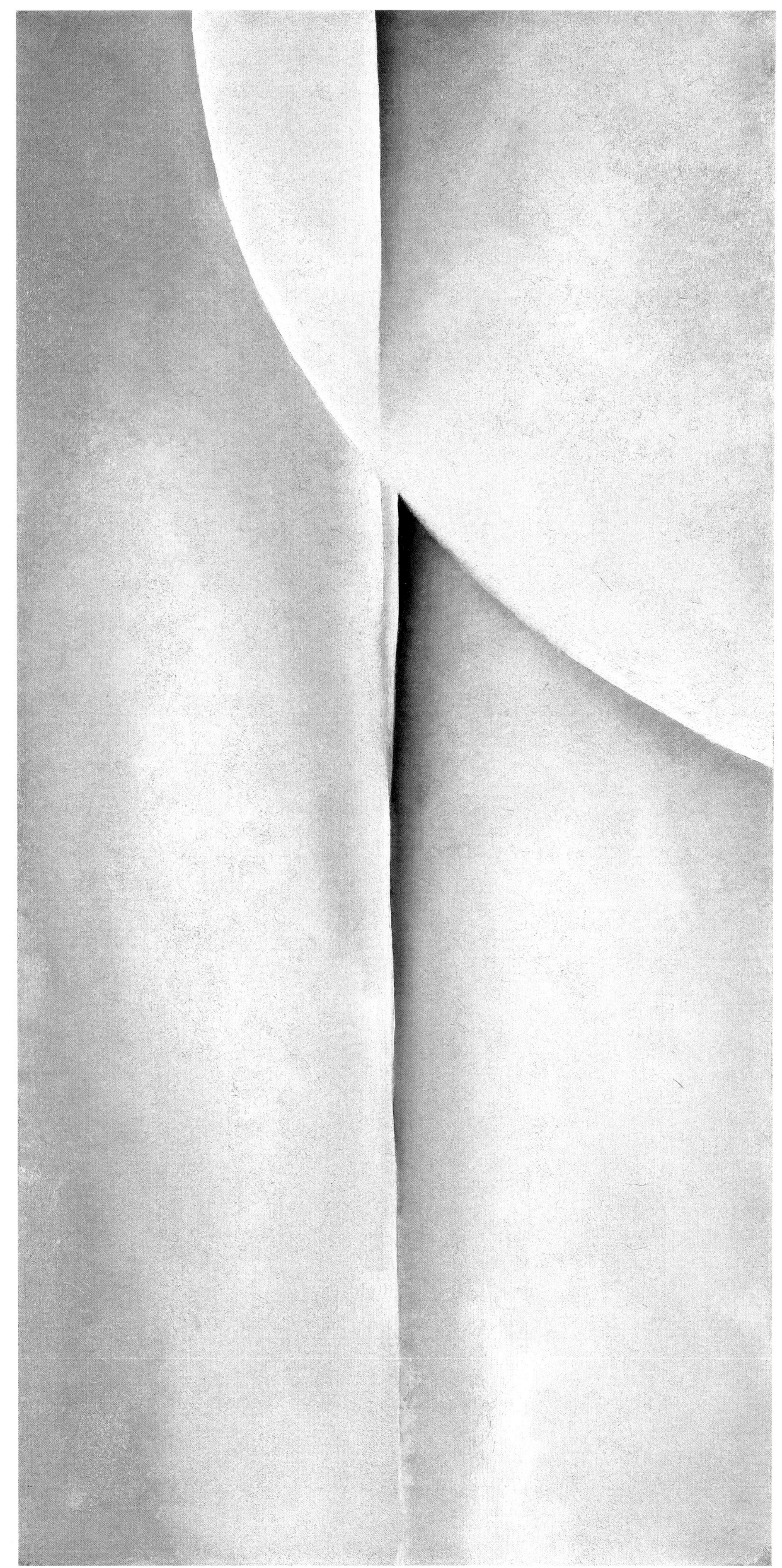

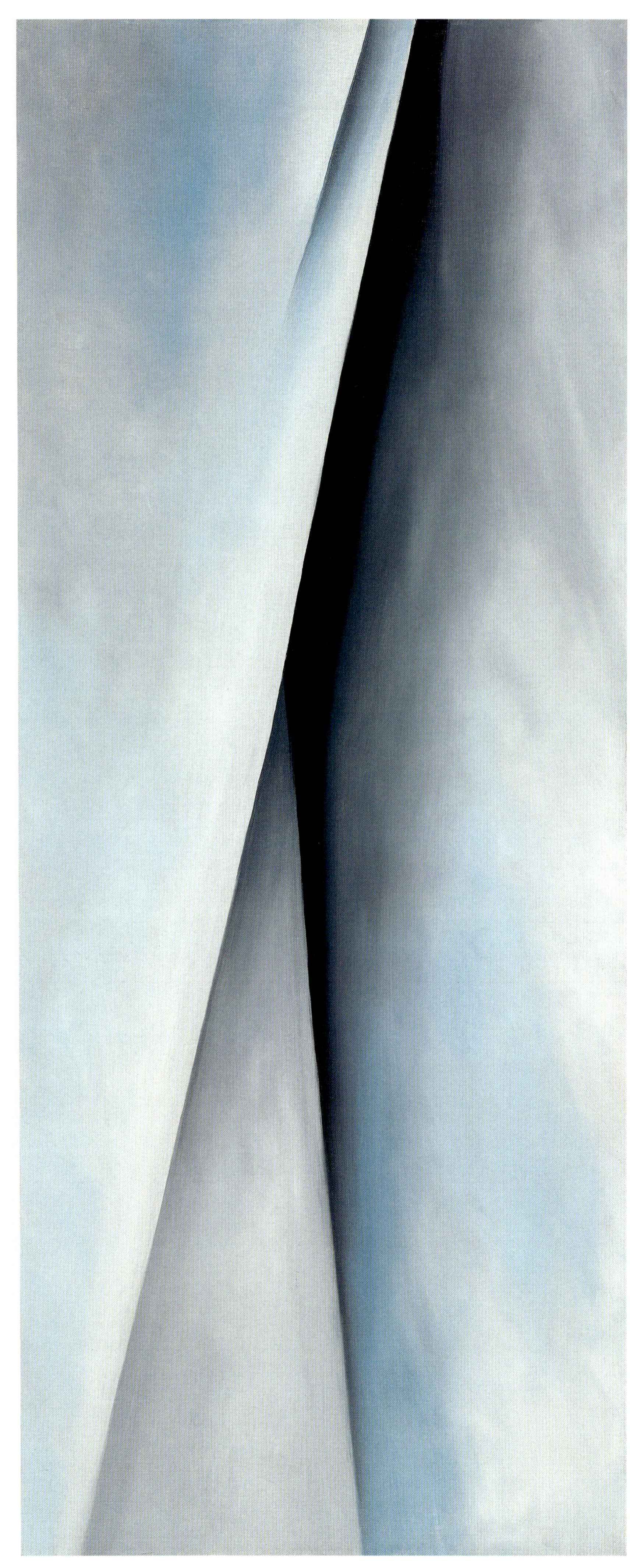

25
Abstraction White, 1927
Oil on canvas

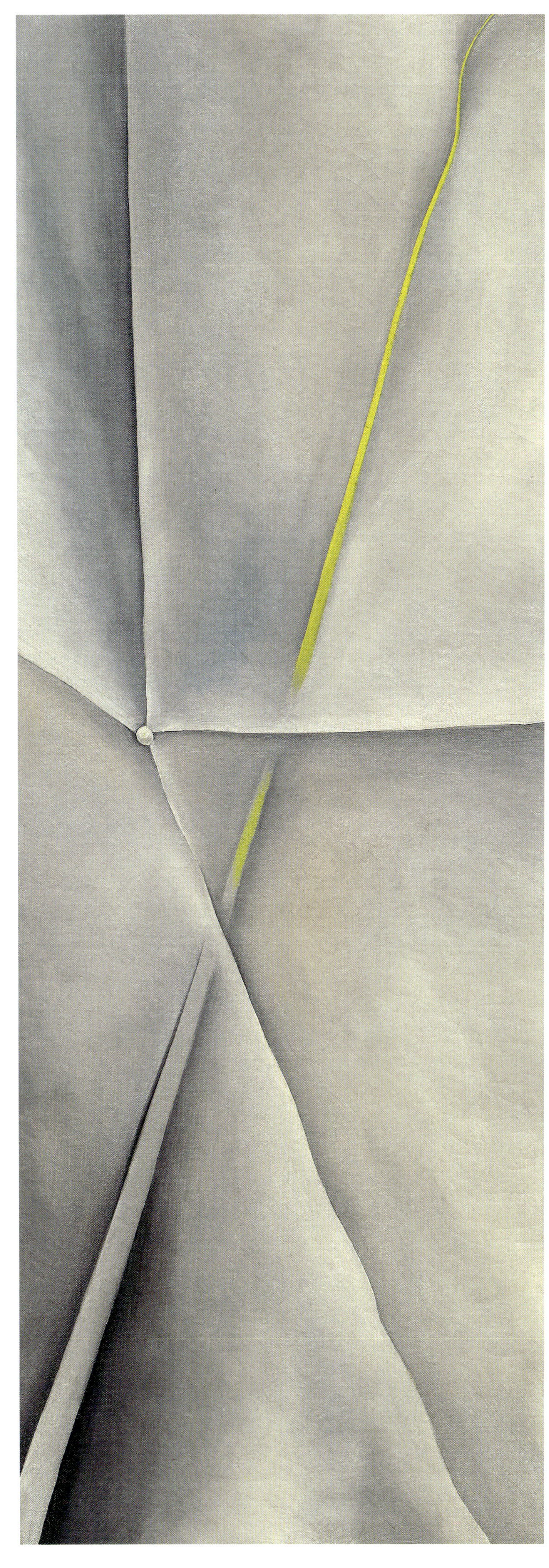

26
New York – Night (Madison Avenue), 1926
Oil on canvas

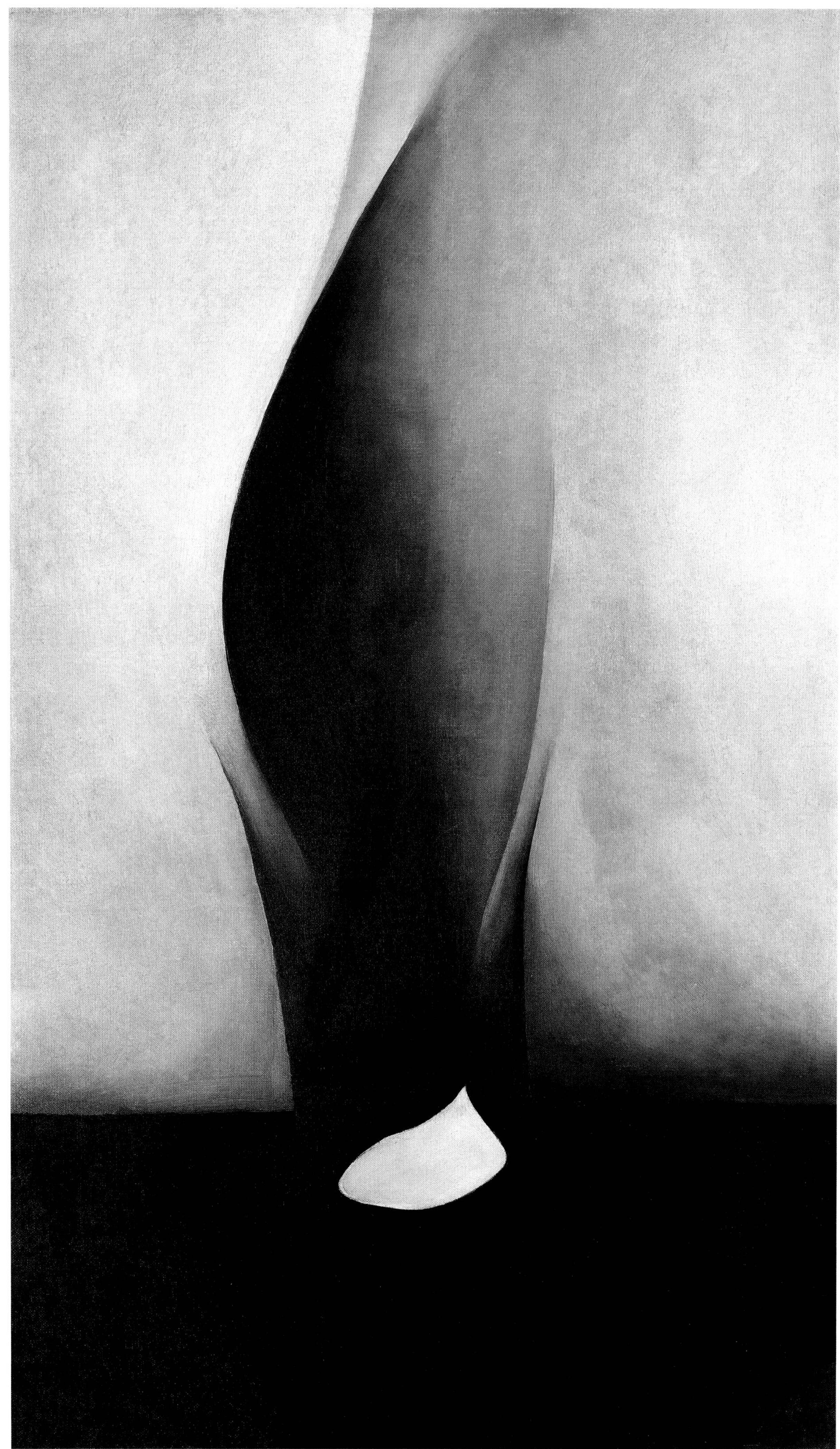

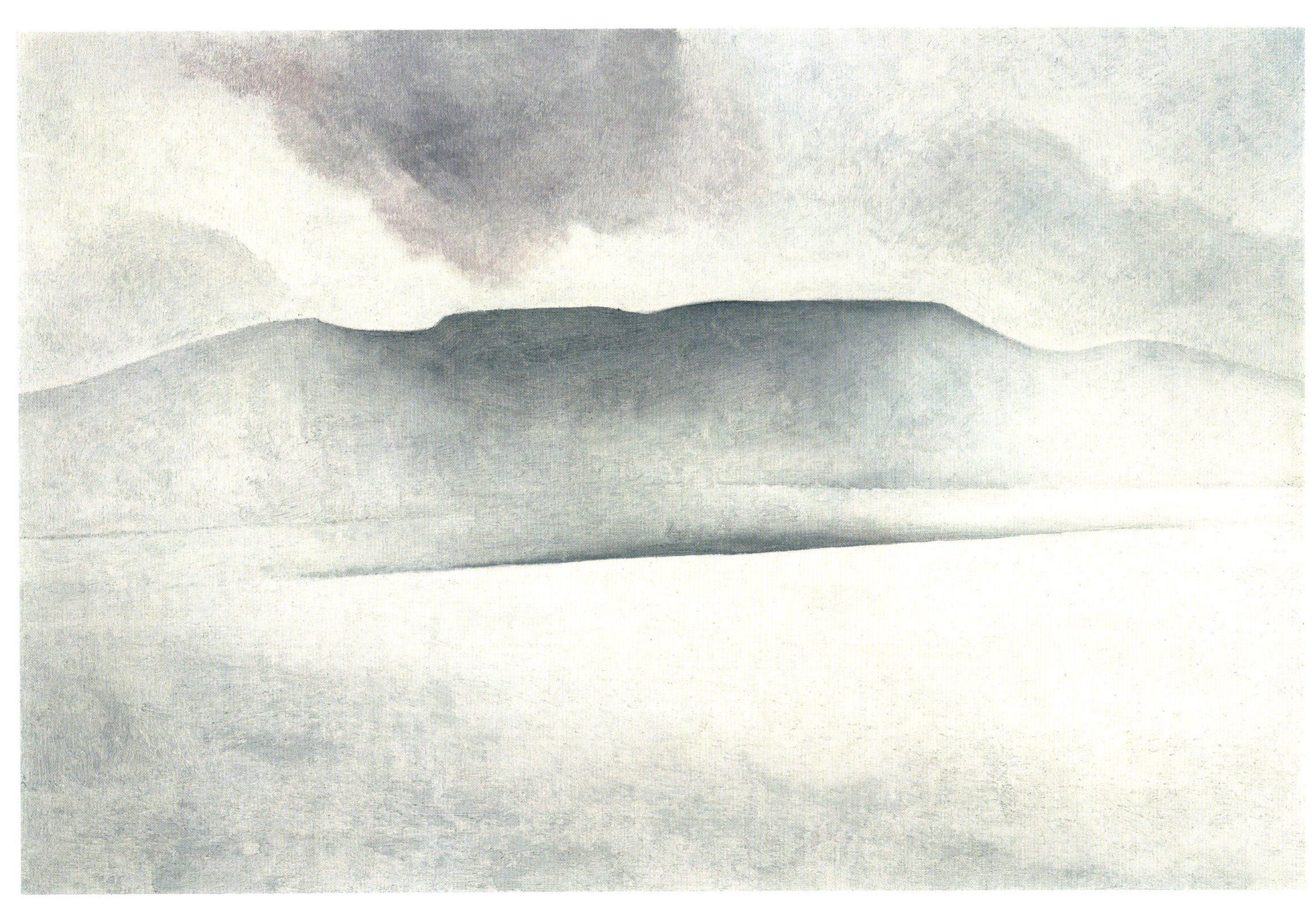

27
Shell and Old Shingle VI, 1926
Oil on canvas

28
Shell and Old Shingle No. VII, 1926
Oil on canvas

29

Slightly Open Clam Shell, 1926

Pastel on white ground on very thick gray cardboard

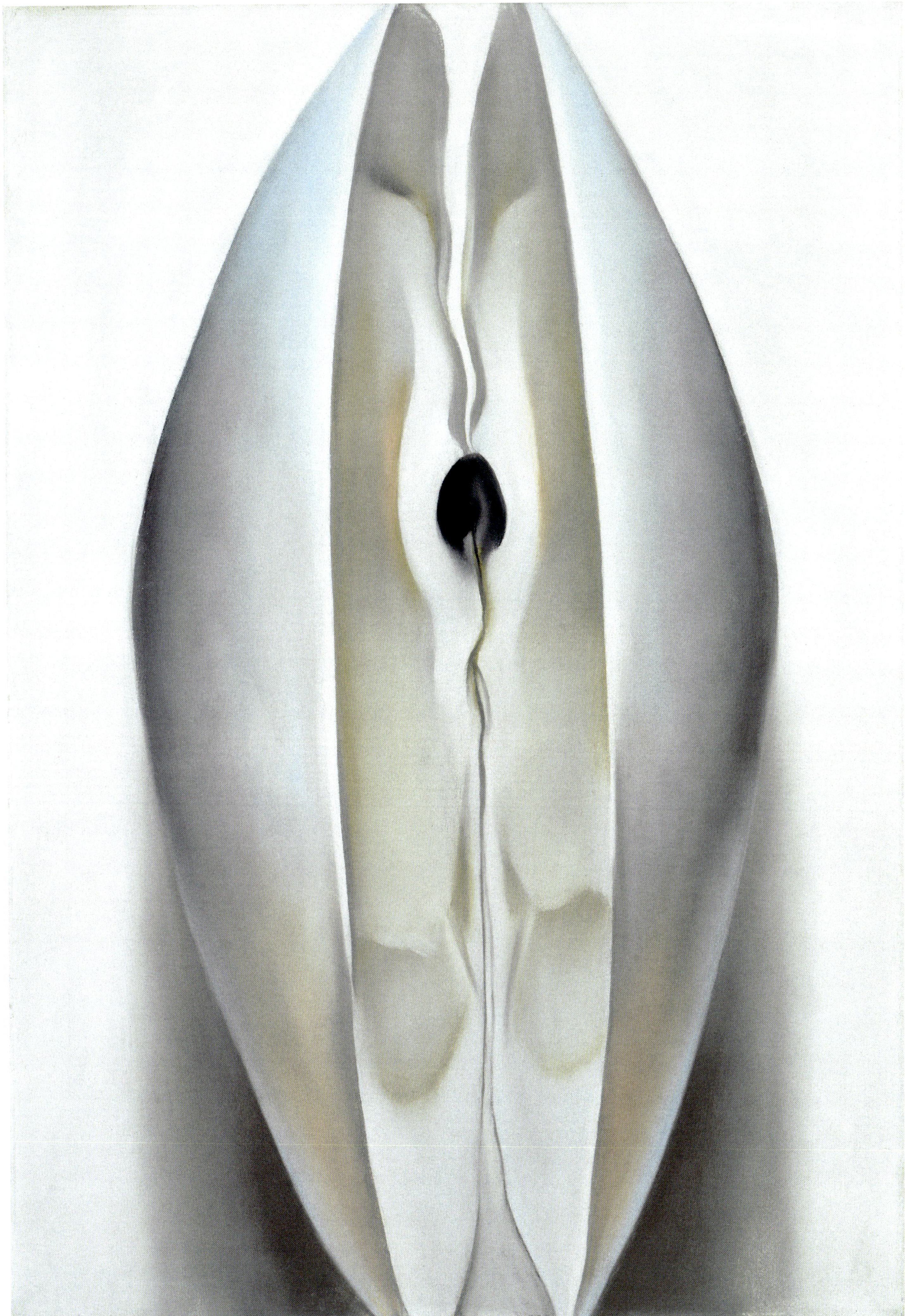

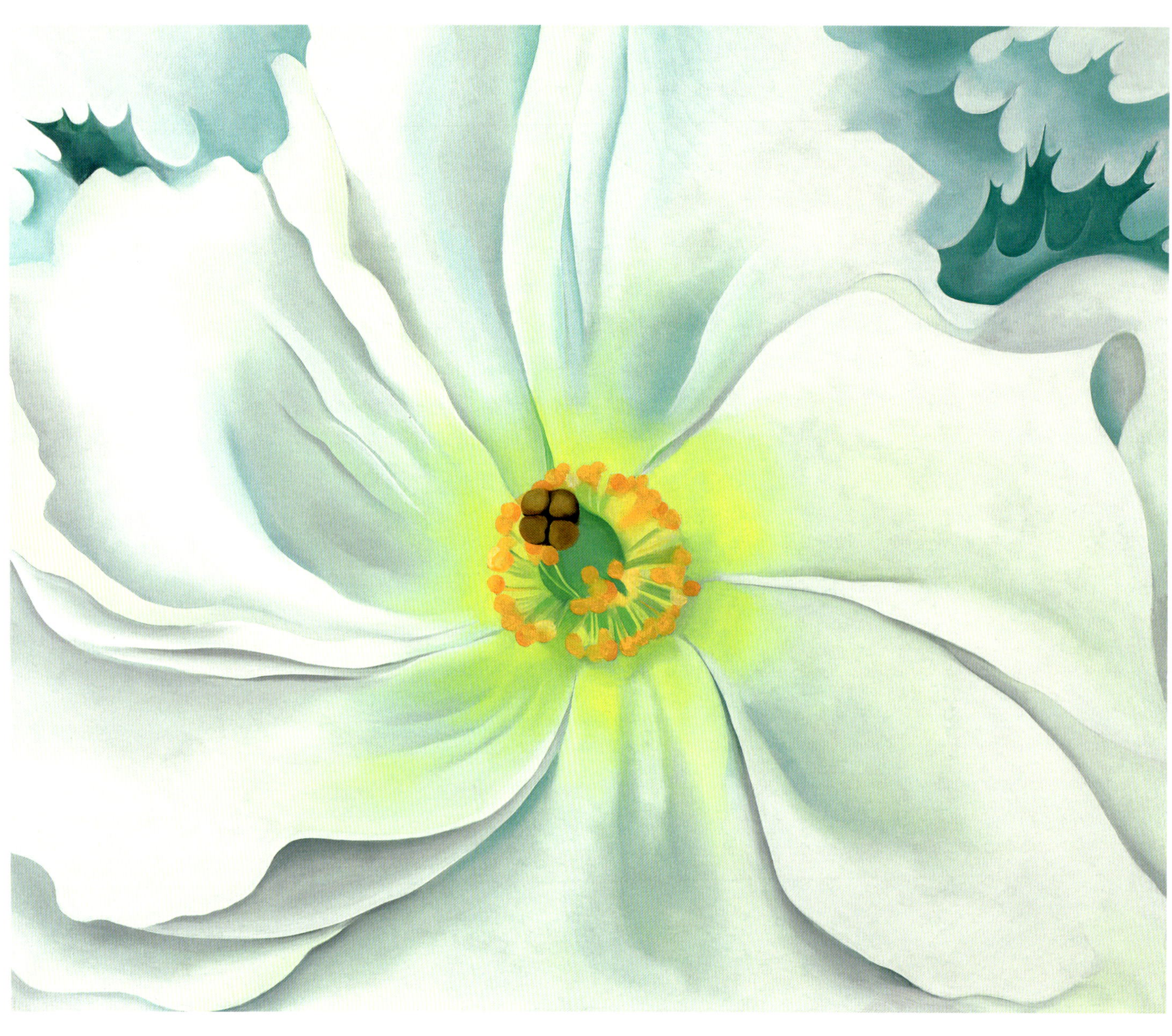

30
White Flower, 1929
Oil on canvas

31
Ballet Skirt or Electric Light (from the White Rose Motif), 1927
Oil on canvas

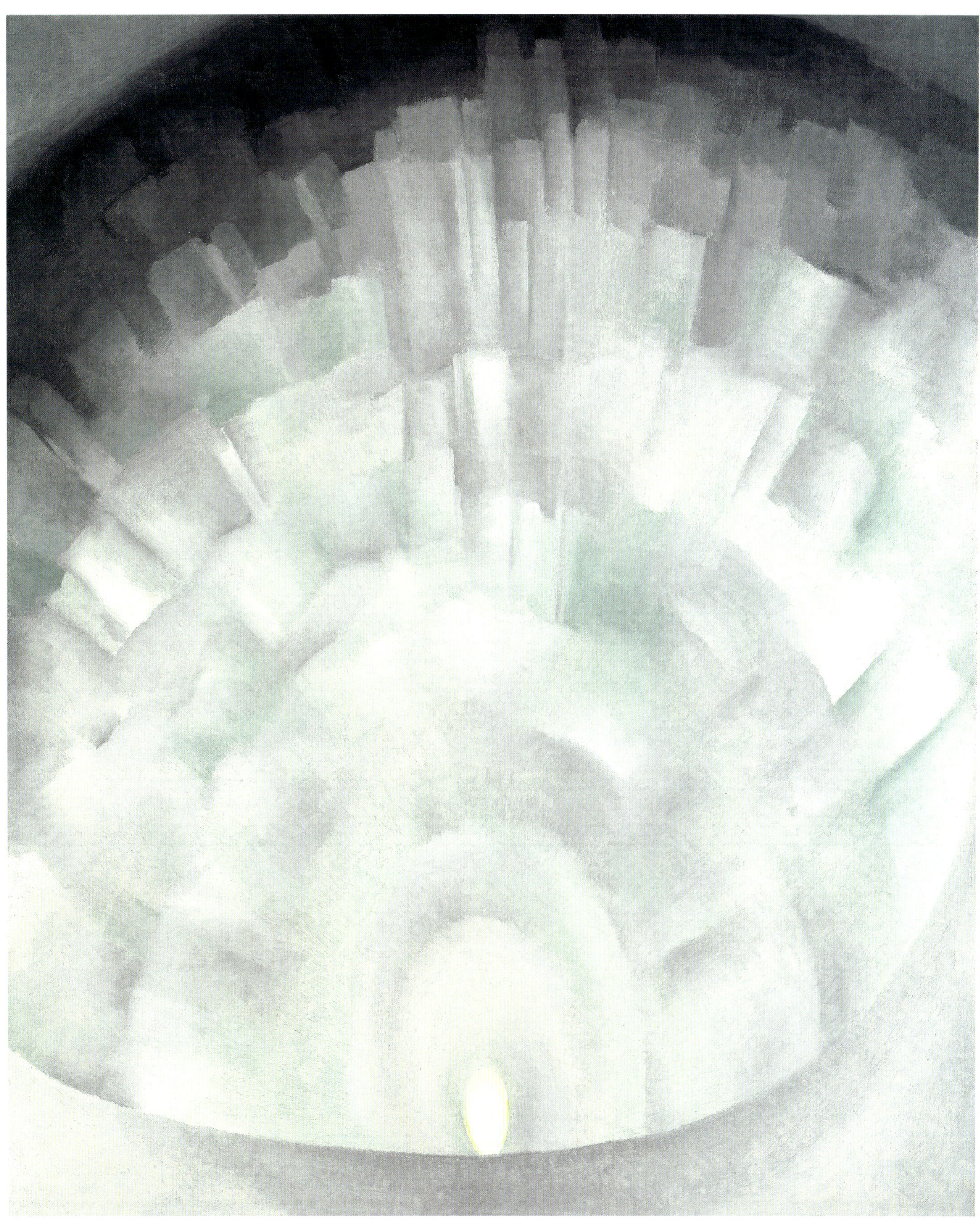

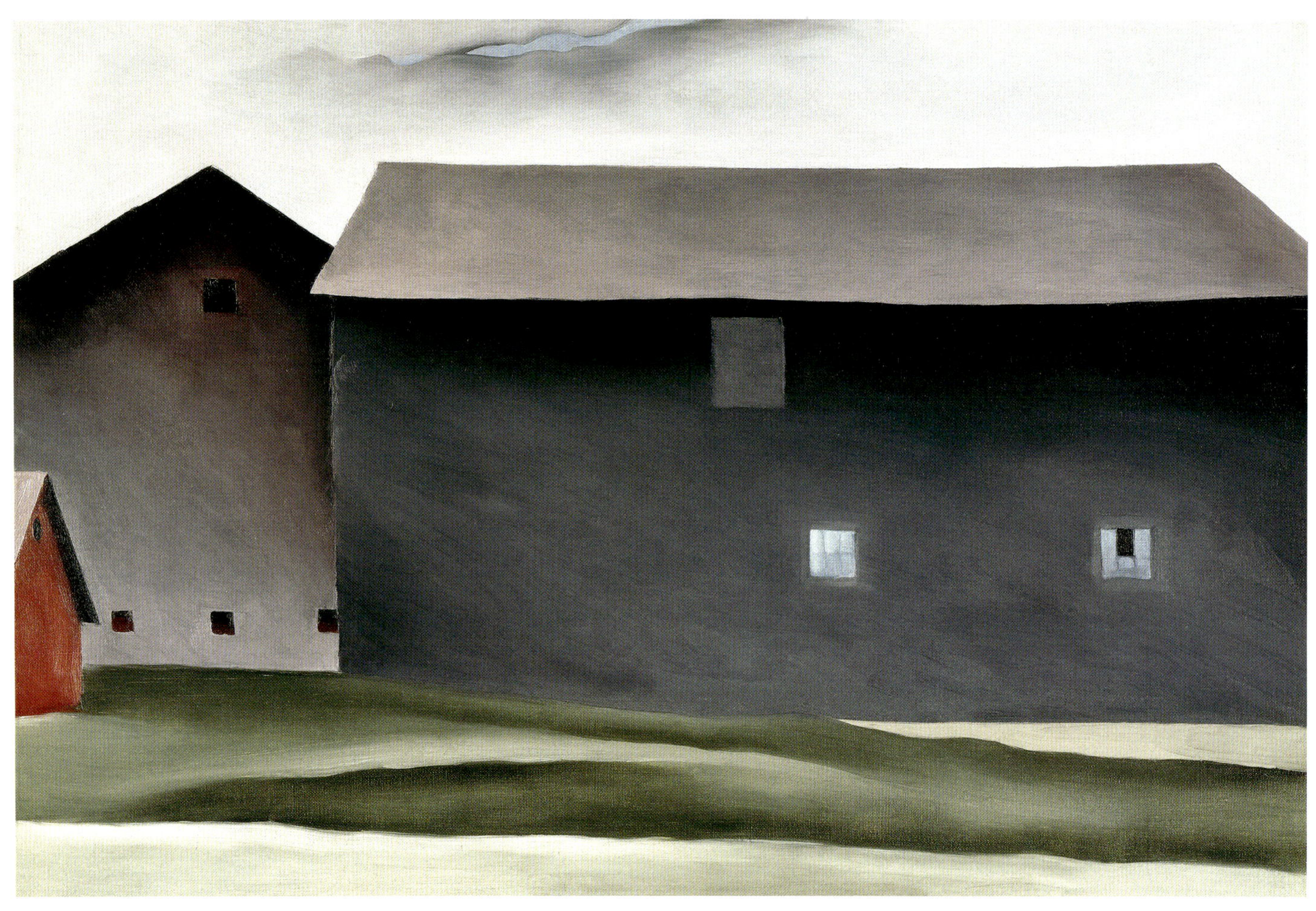

32
Lake George Barns, 1926
Oil on canvas

33
Abstraction Blue, 1927
Oil on canvas

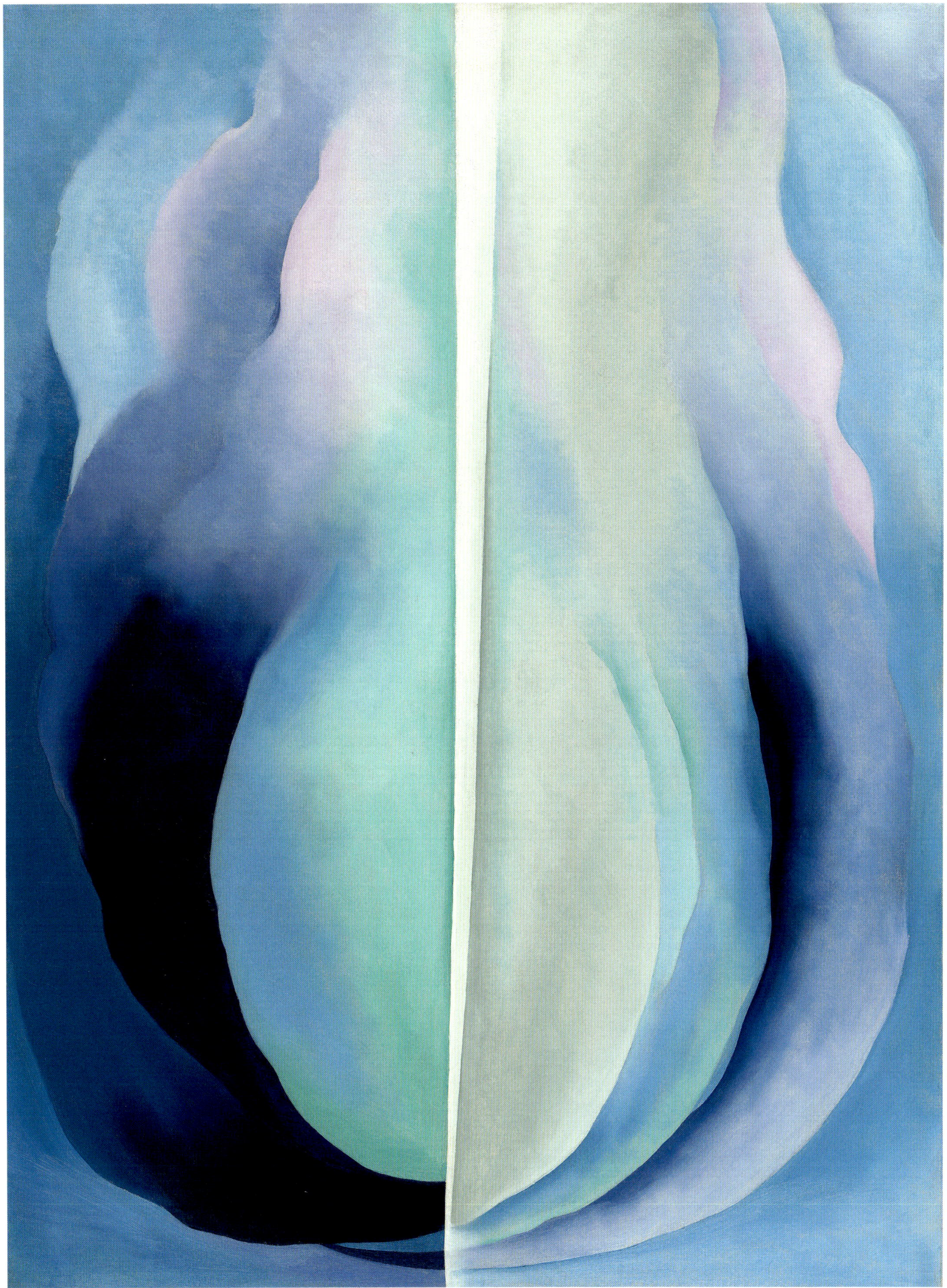

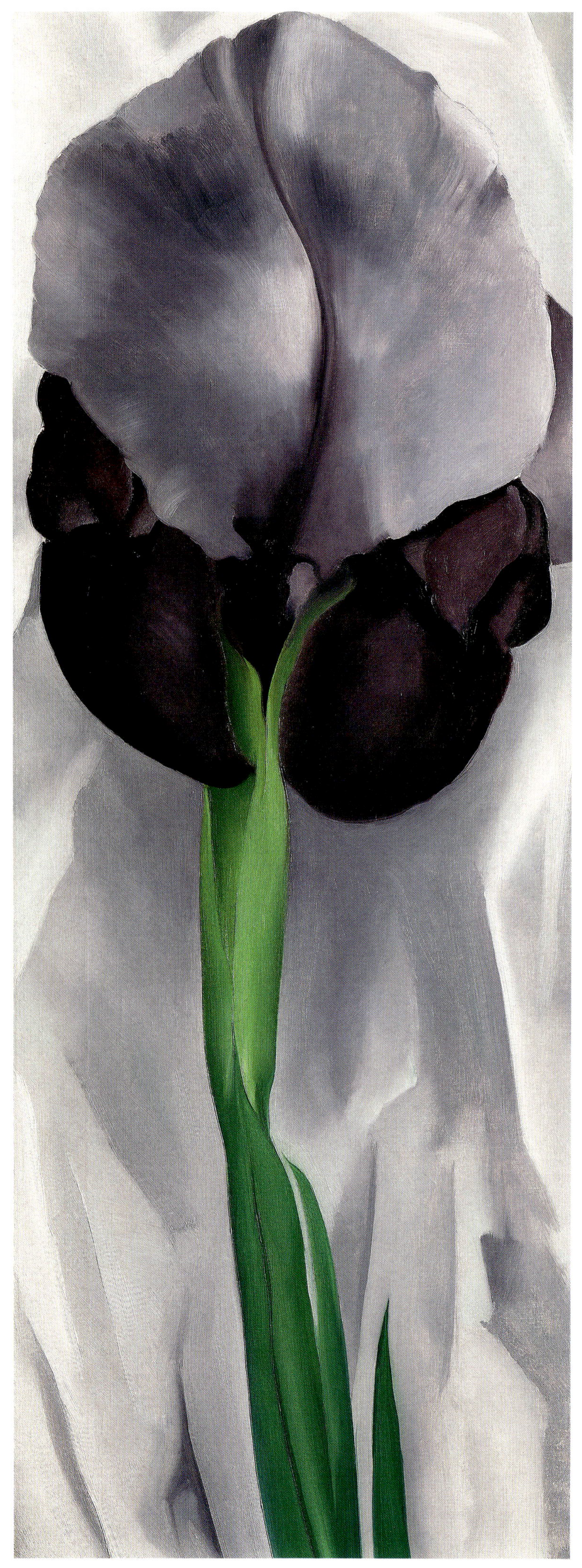

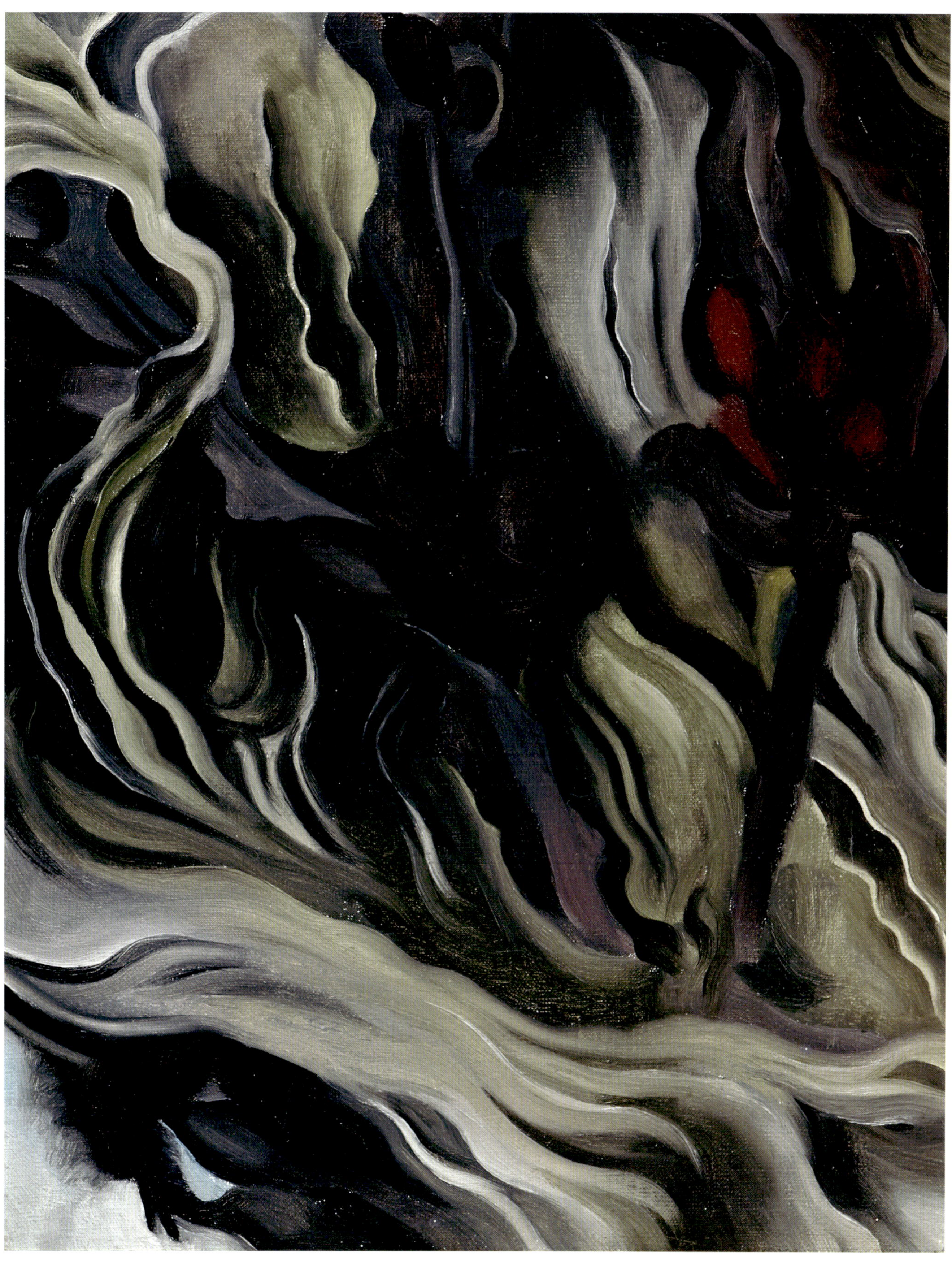

34
Dark Iris No. 1, 1927
Oil on canvas

35
Seaweed, 1927
Oil on canvas

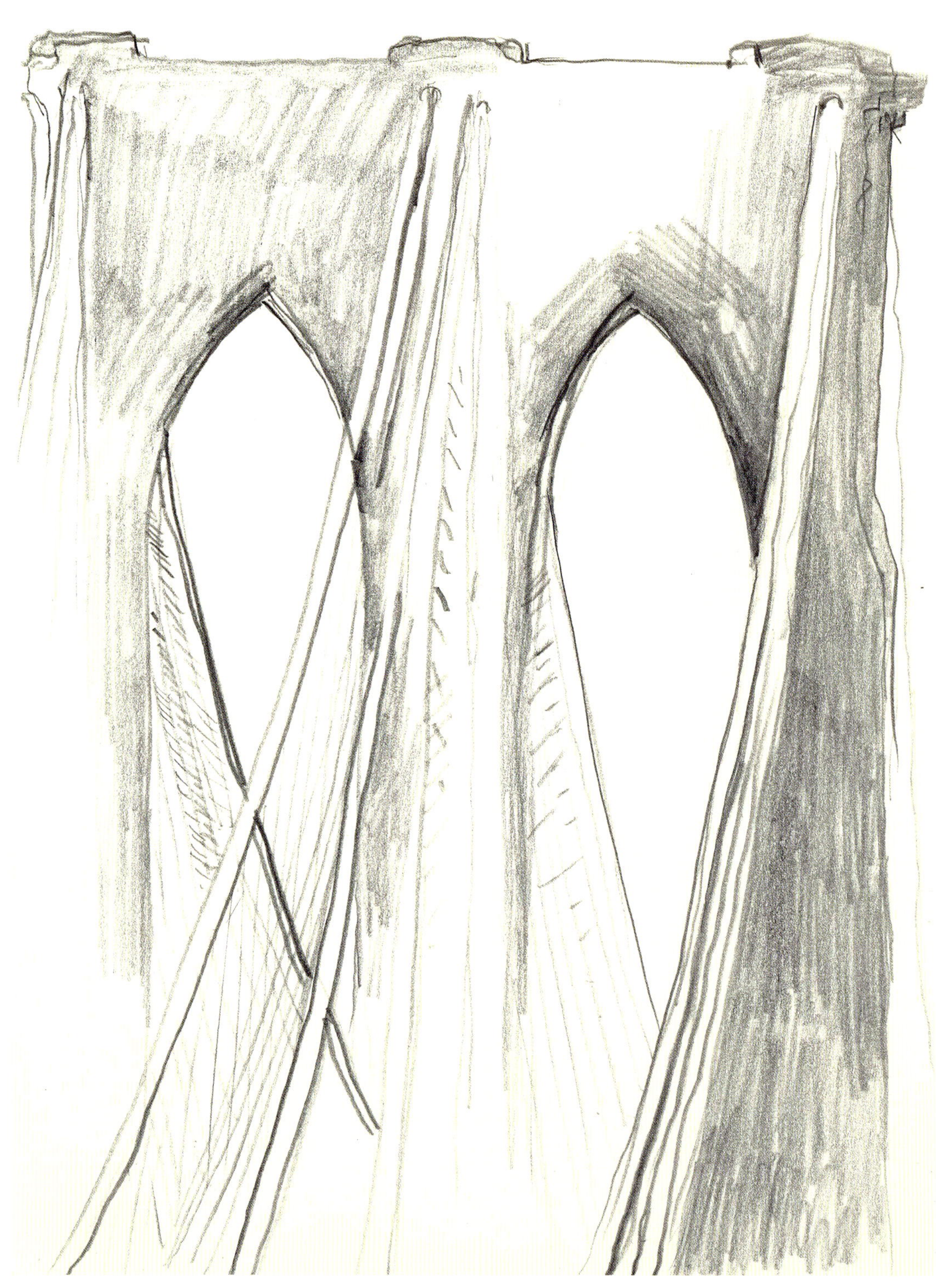

36
Untitled (Brooklyn Bridge), c. 1949
Pencil on paper

37
Brooklyn Bridge, 1949
Charcoal and black and white chalk on medium thick, brown, smooth wove paper, Kraft wrapping paper

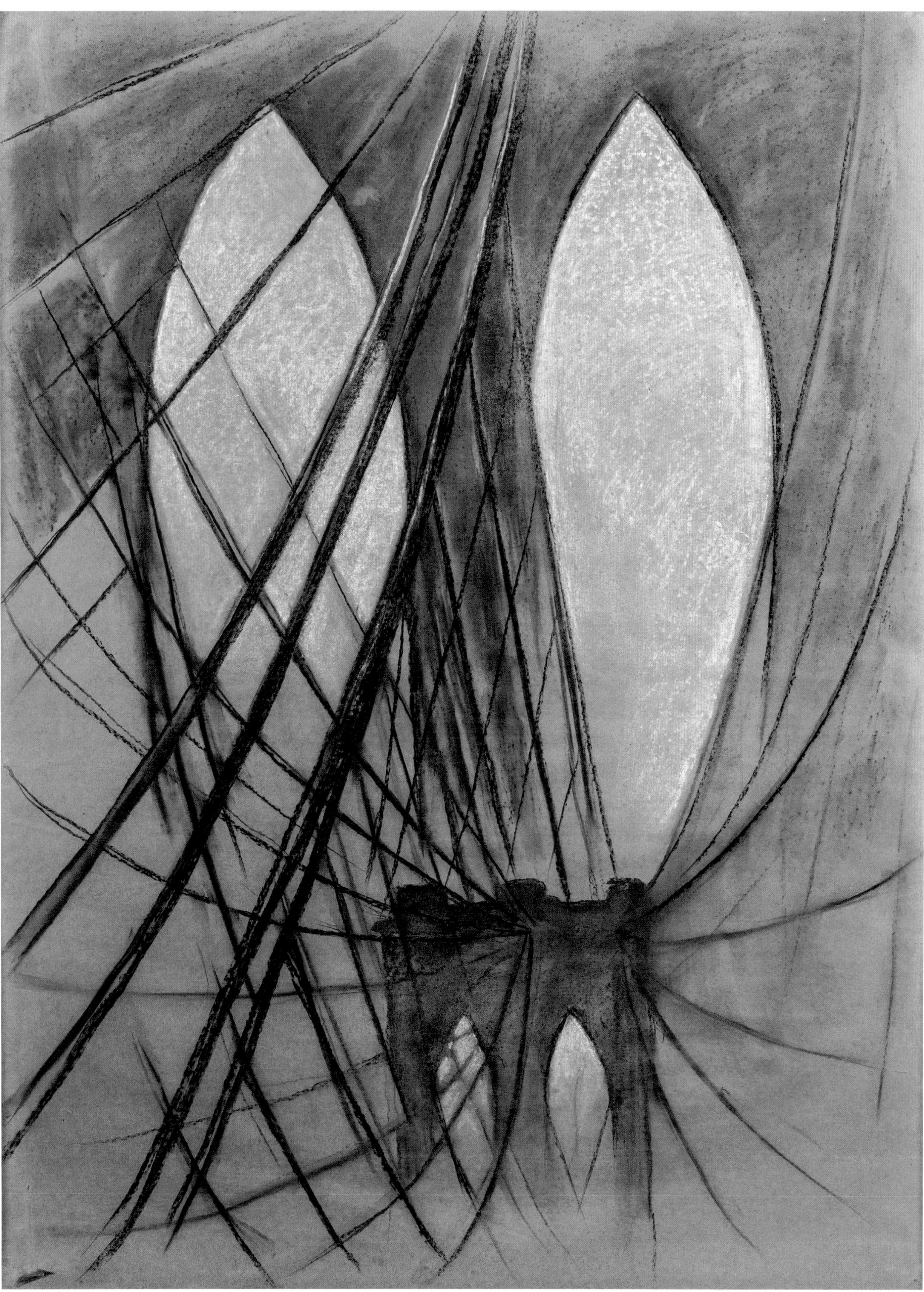

38
Brooklyn Bridge, 1949
Oil on board

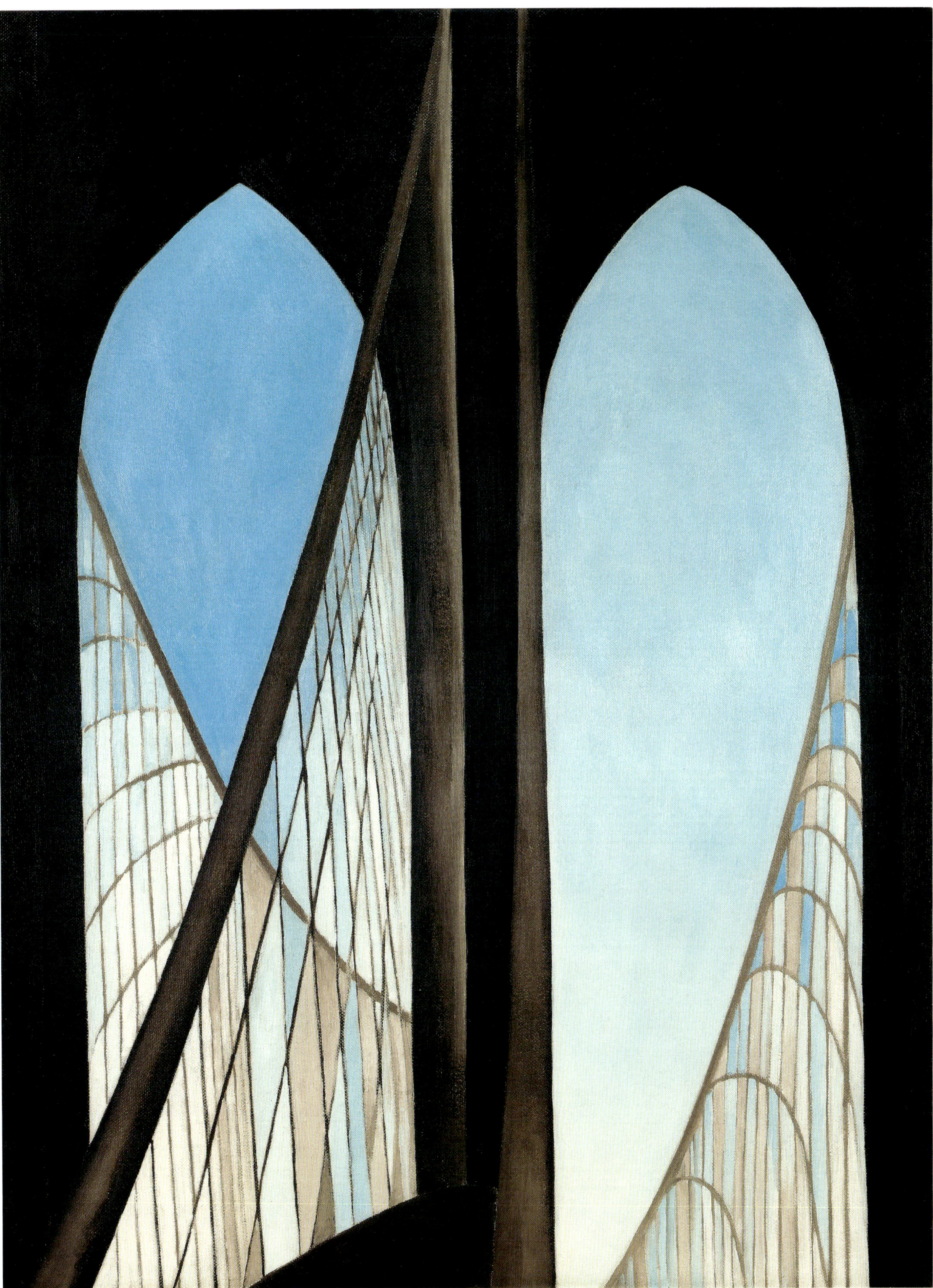

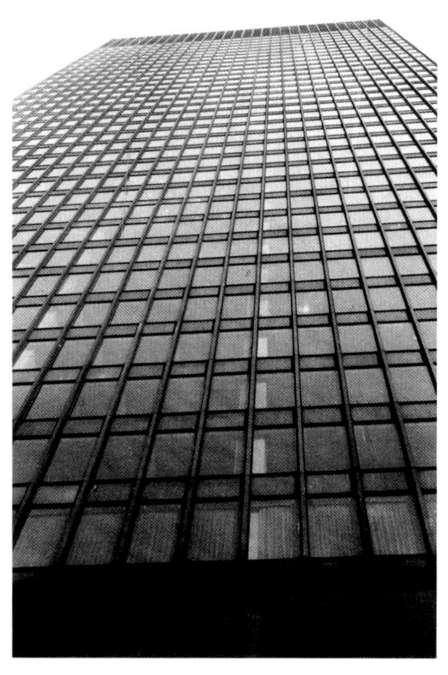

39
Seagram Building, New York, 1958–65
Gelatin silver print

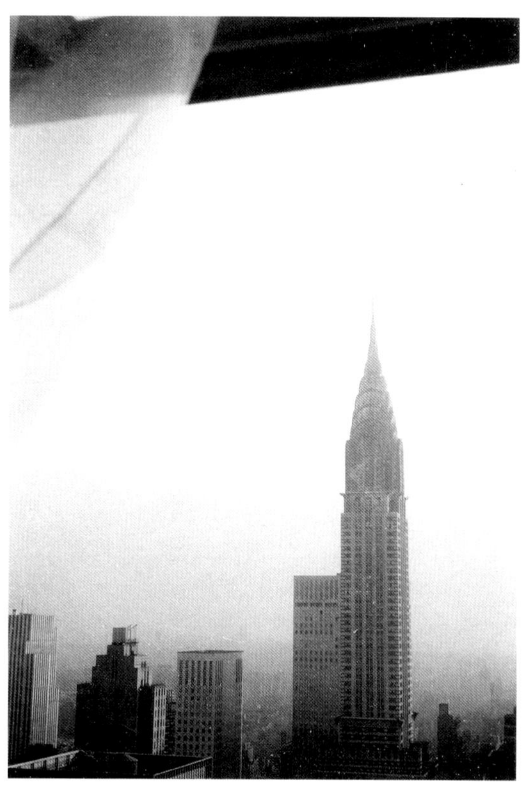

40
Chrysler Building from the Window of the Waldorf Astoria, New York, c. 1960
Gelatin silver print

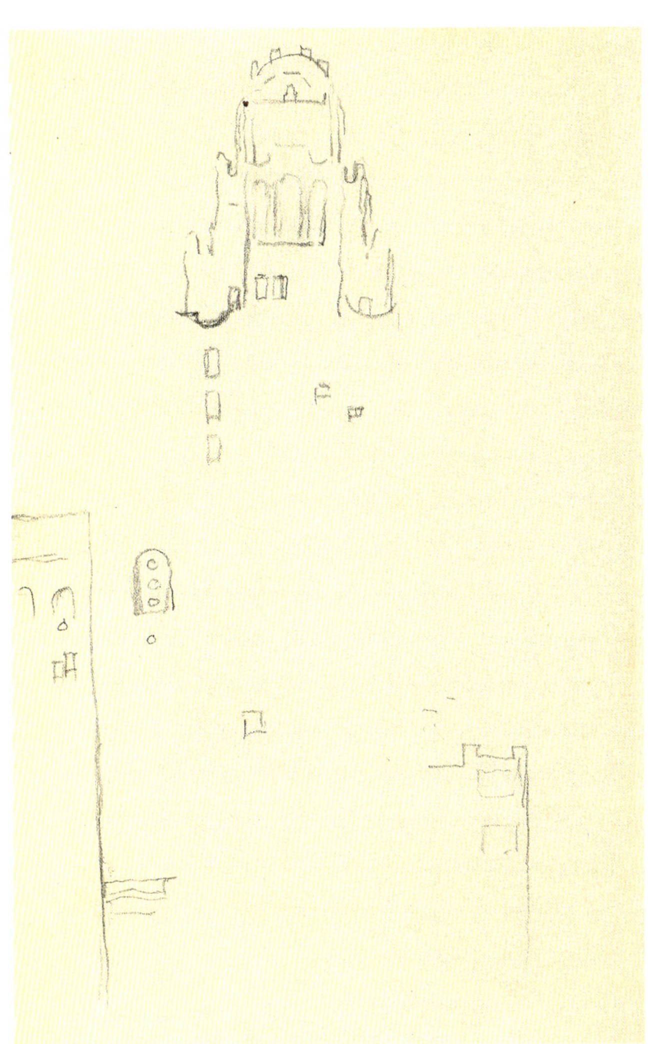

41
Untitled (Radiator Building), Pelican I Sketchbook,
1920s
Graphite on paper

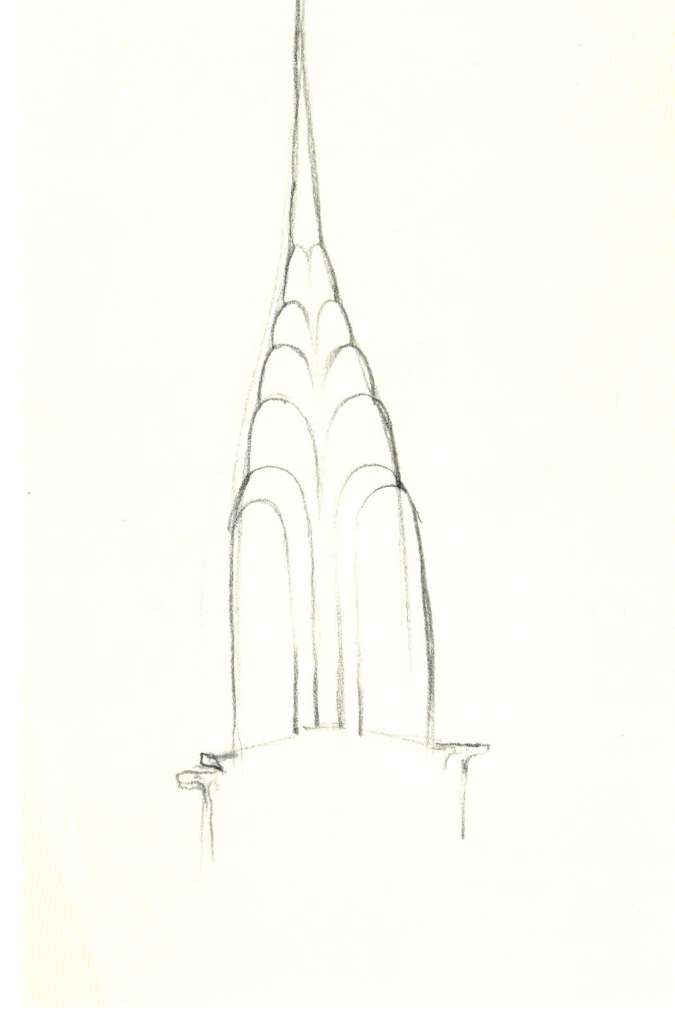

42
Untitled (Chrysler Building), Pelican I Sketchbook,
1932
Graphite on paper

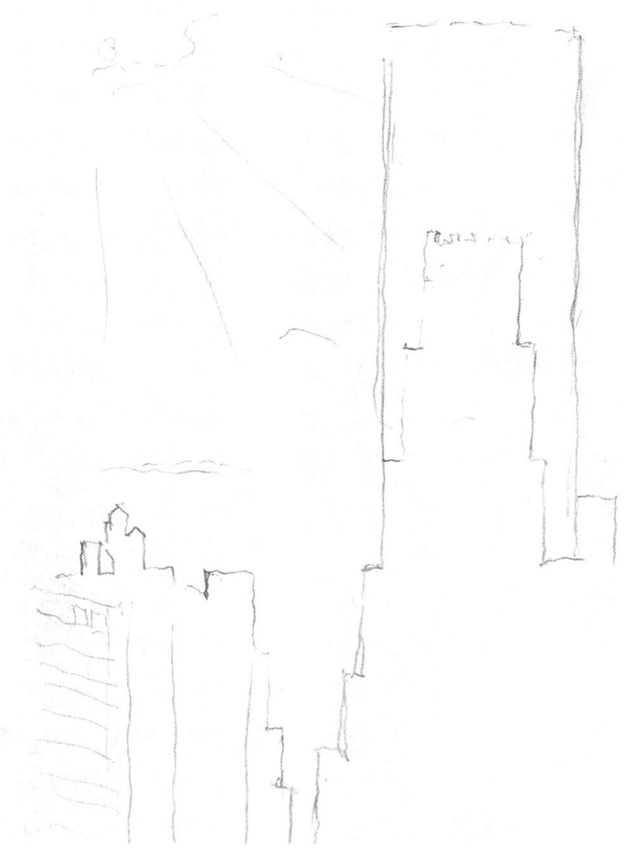

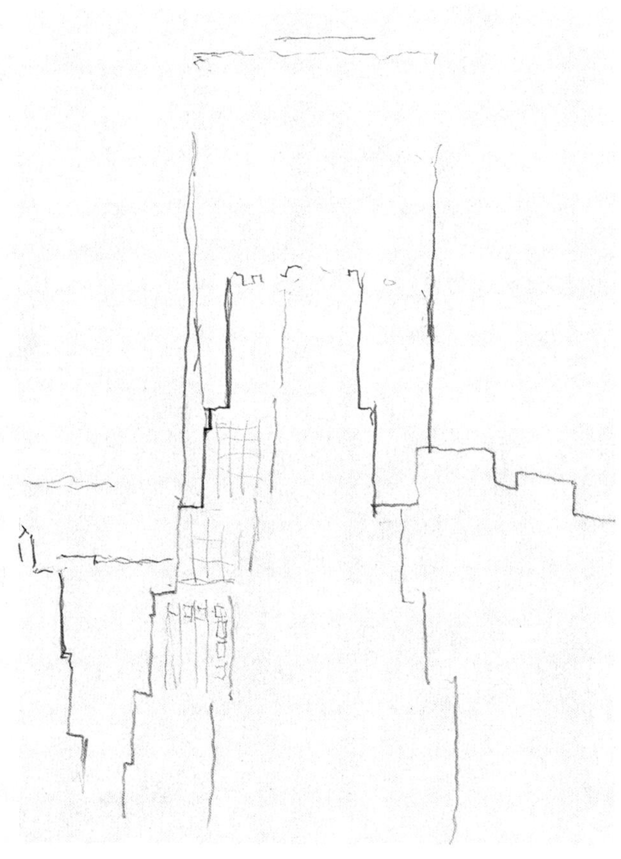

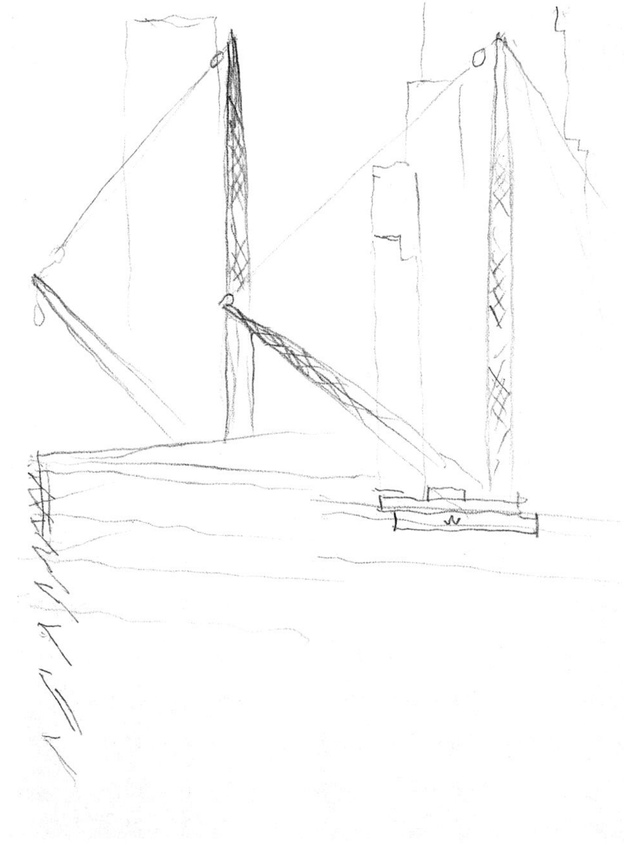

43
Untitled (New York), 1925–32
Graphite on paper

44
Untitled (New York), 1925–32
Graphite on paper

45
Untitled (New York), 1925–32
Graphite on paper

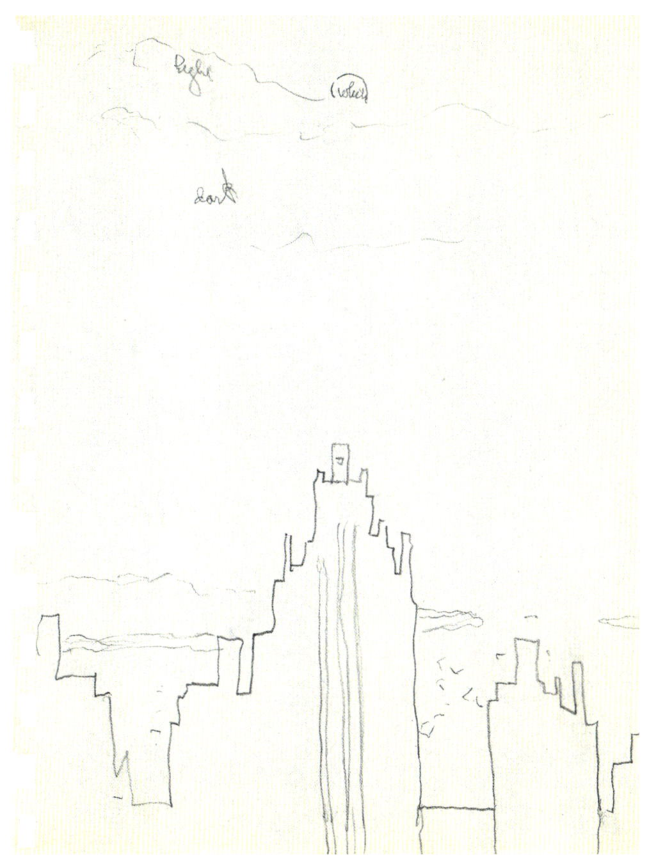

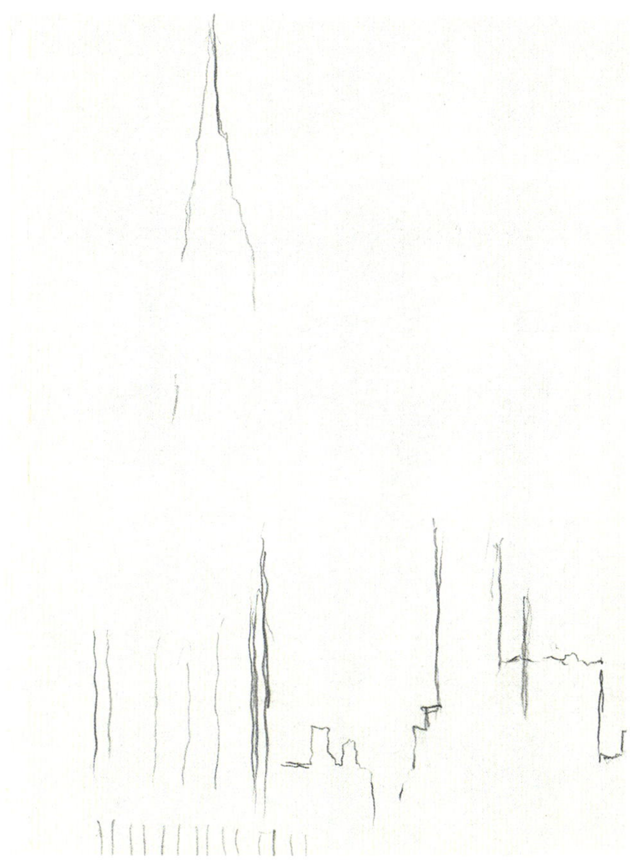

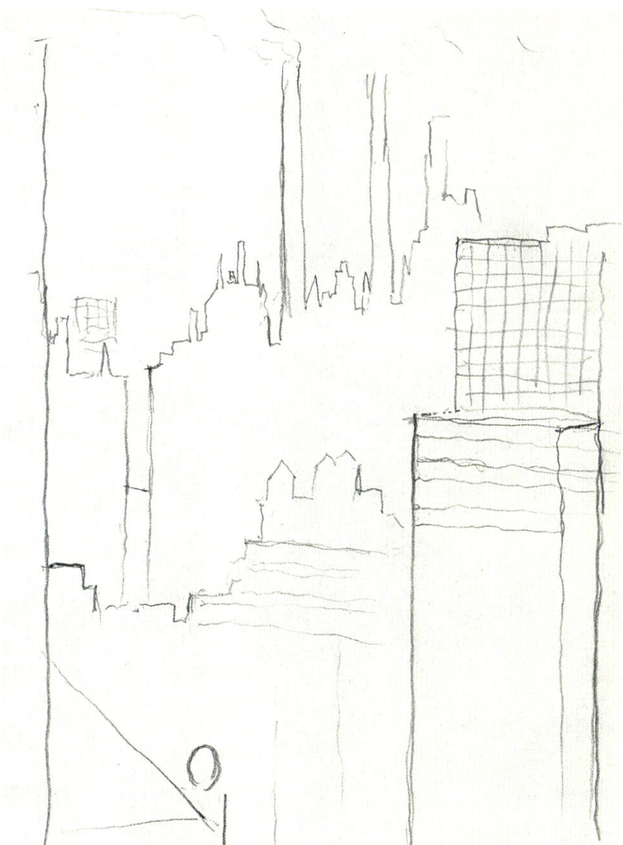

46
Untitled (New York), 1925–32
Graphite on paper

47
Untitled (New York), 1925–32
Graphite on paper

48
Untitled (New York), 1925–32
Graphite on paper

49
Untitled (New York), 1925–32
Graphite on paper

50
Untitled (New York), 1925–32
Graphite on paper

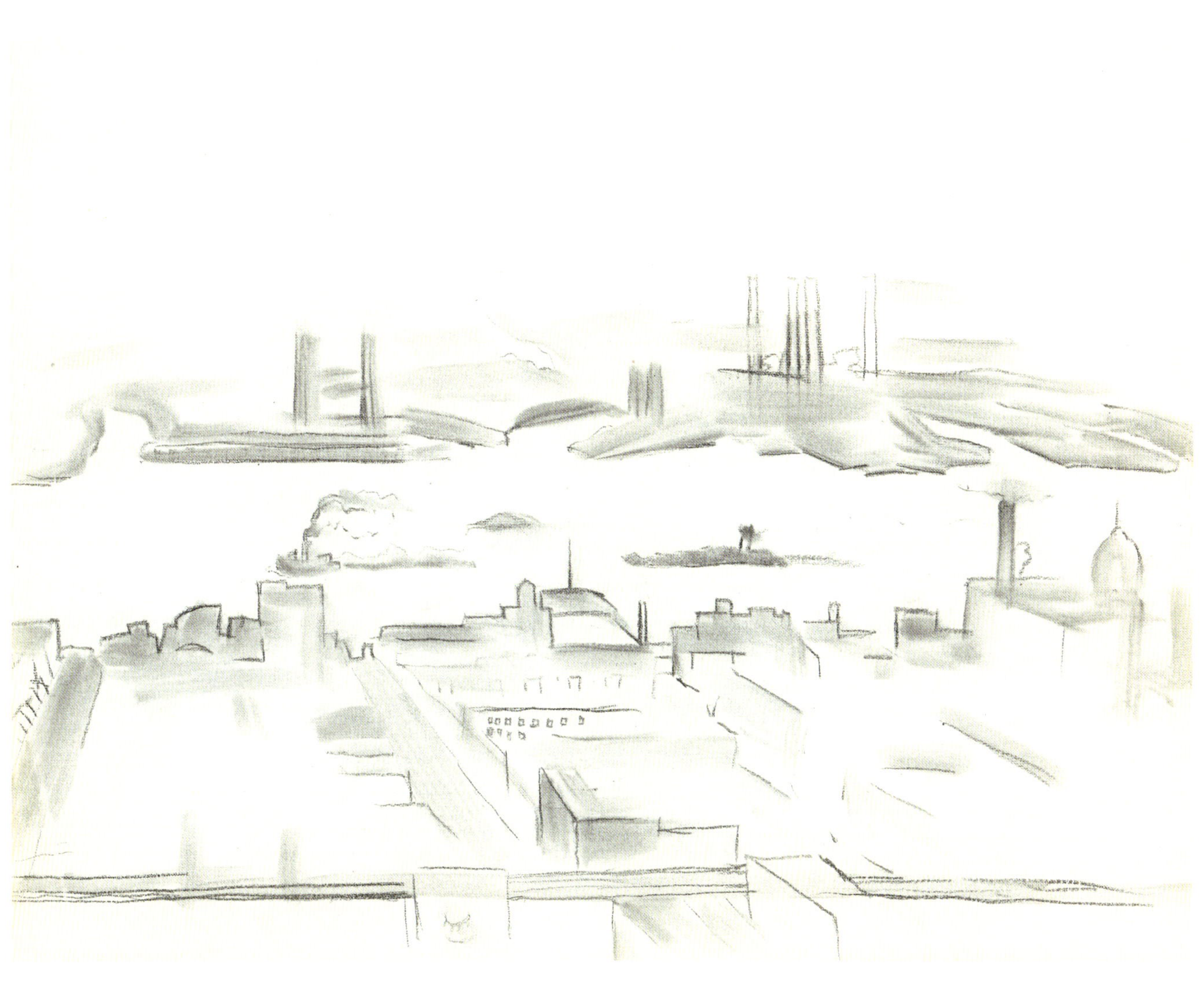

51
East River, 1932
Charcoal on paper

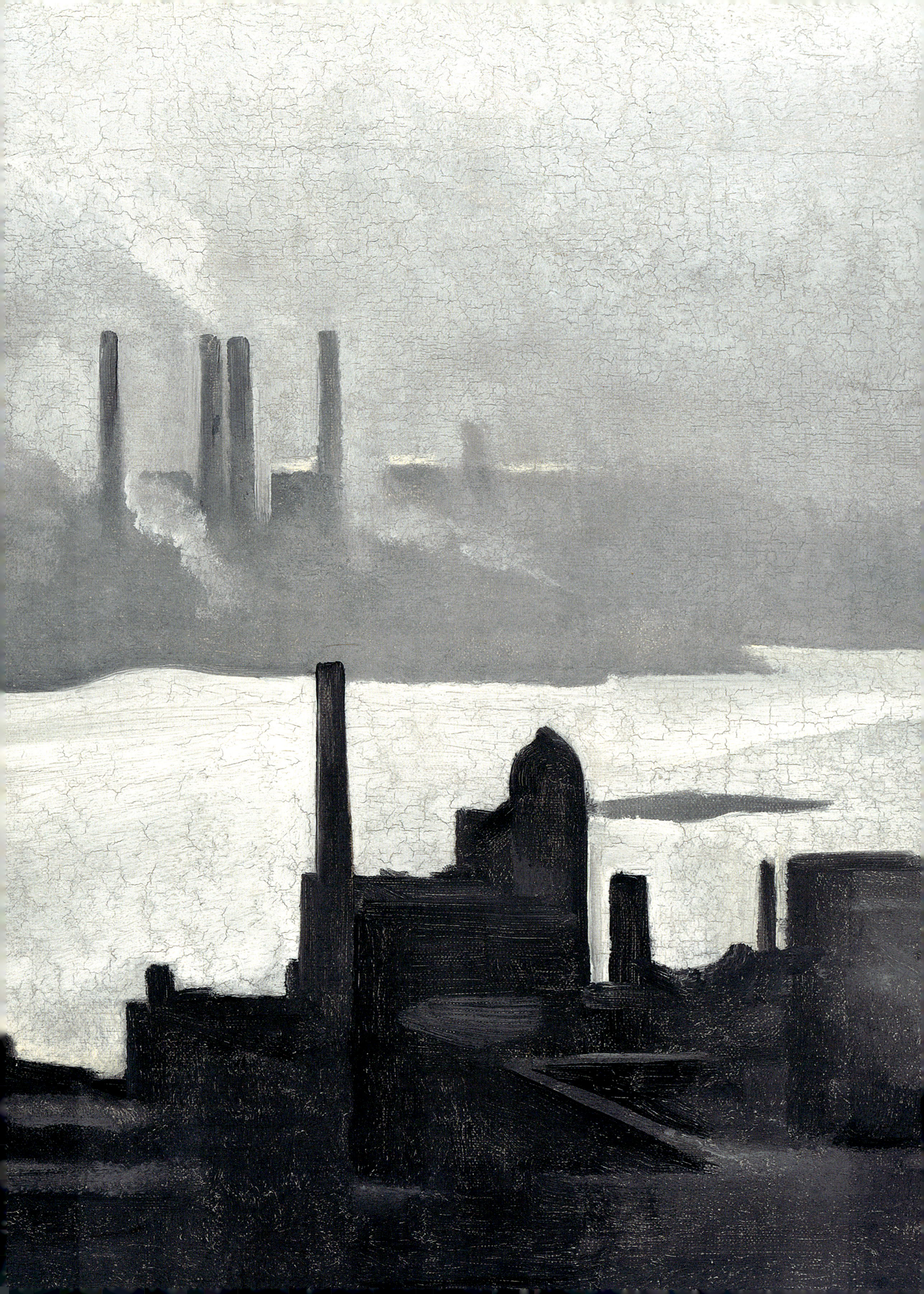

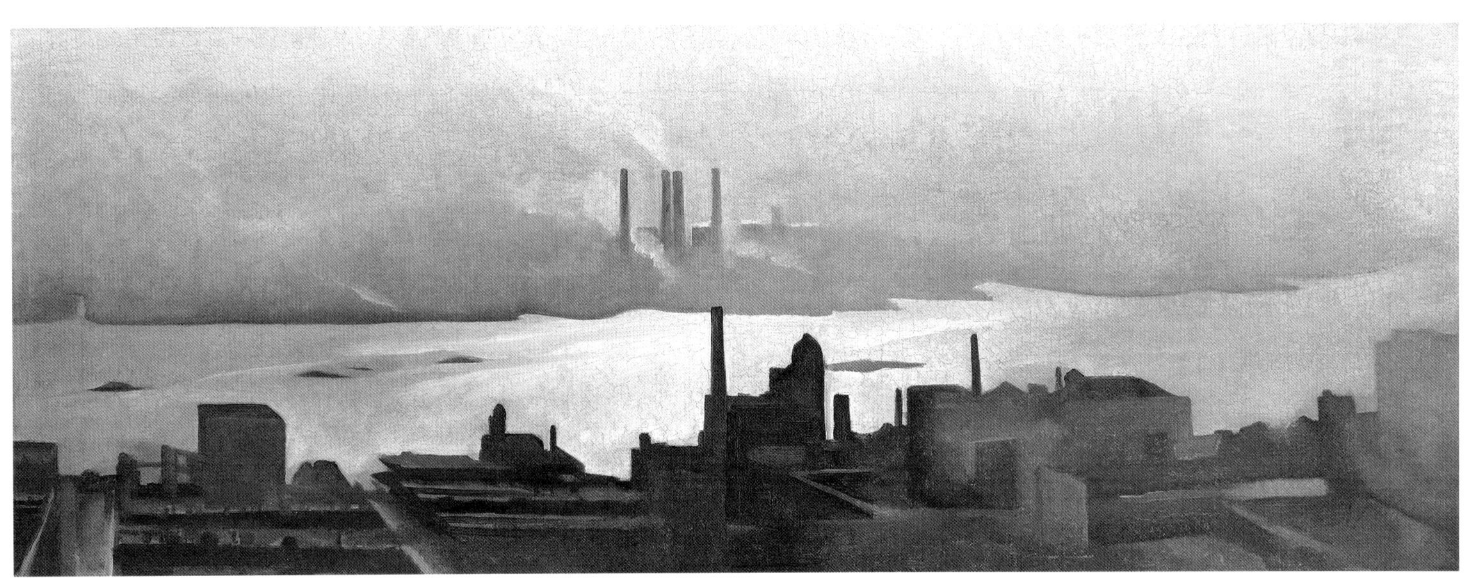

52
East River No. 1, 1926
Oil on canvas

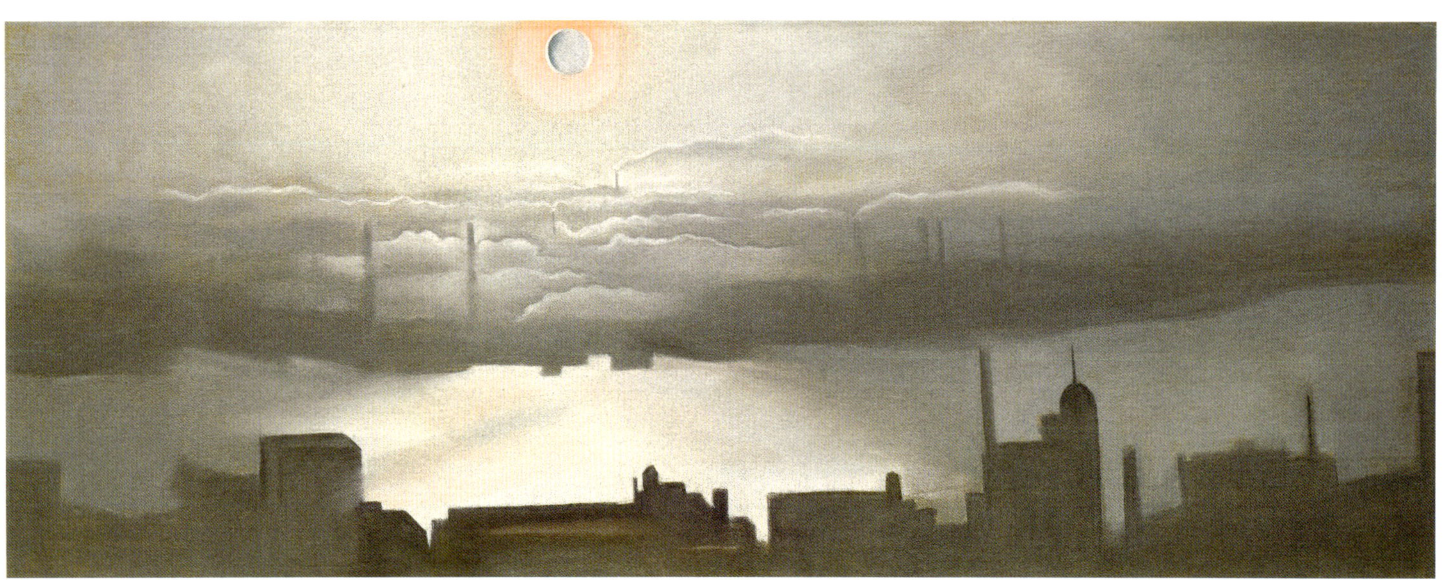

53
East River with Sun, 1926
Pastel on paper

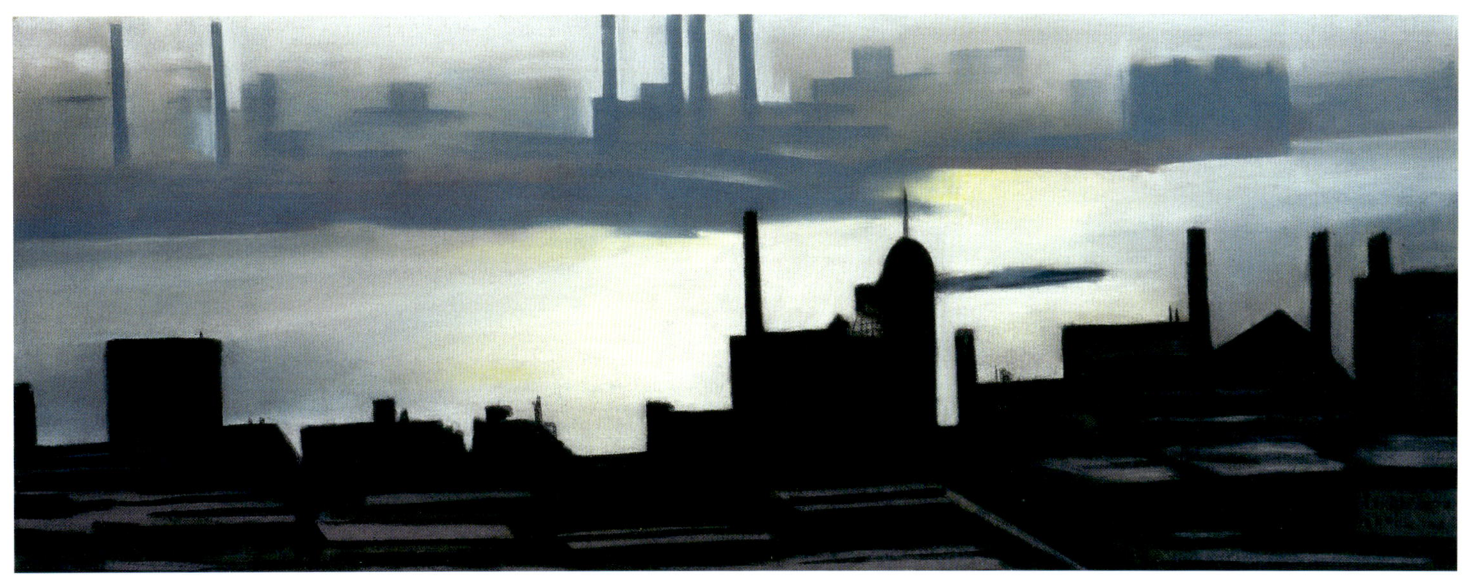

54
East River New York No. 2, 1927
Pastel on paper

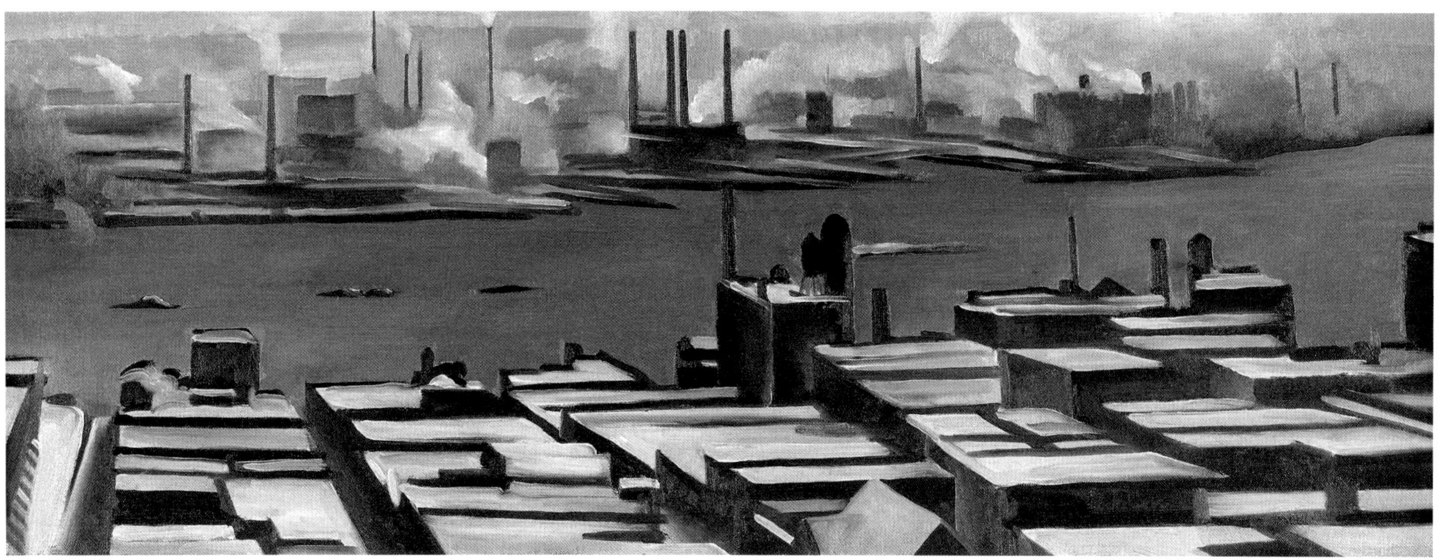

55
East River from the Shelton, No. III, 1926
Oil on canvas

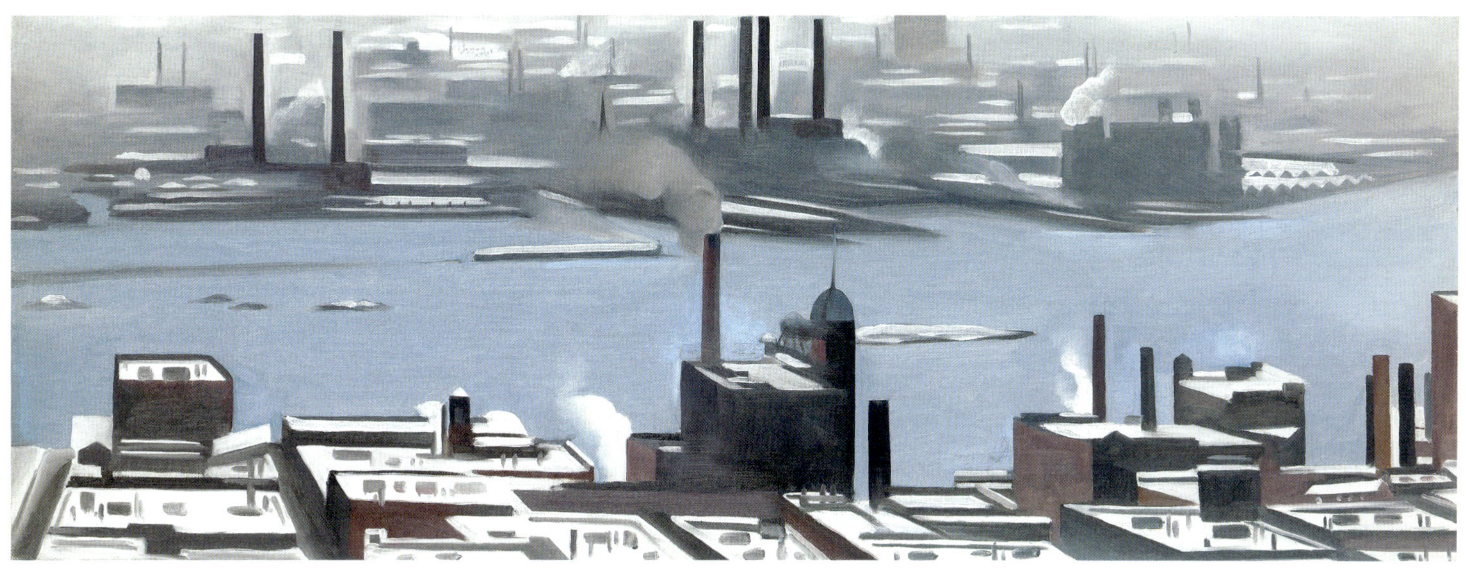

56
East River from the Shelton Hotel, 1928
Oil on canvas

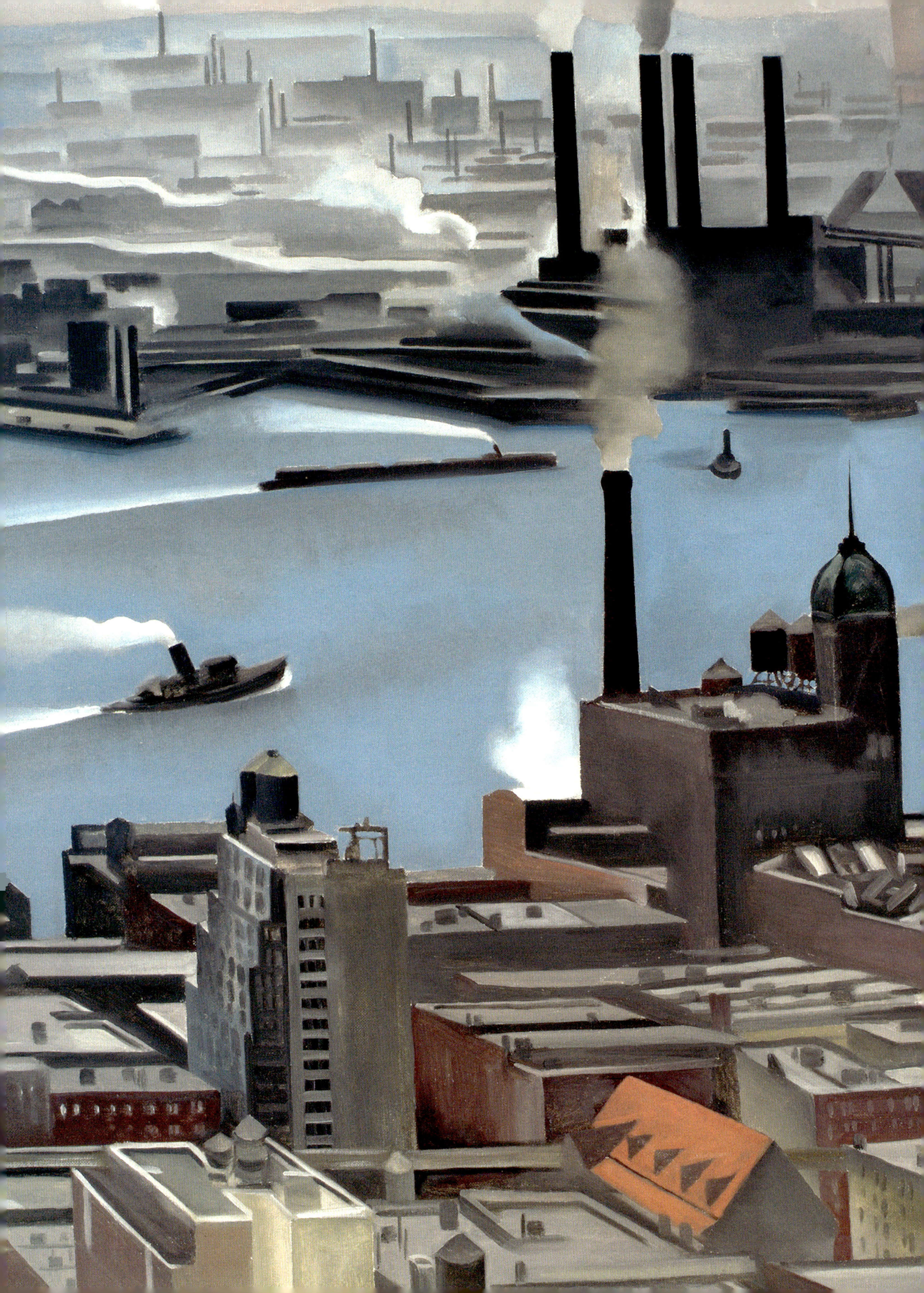

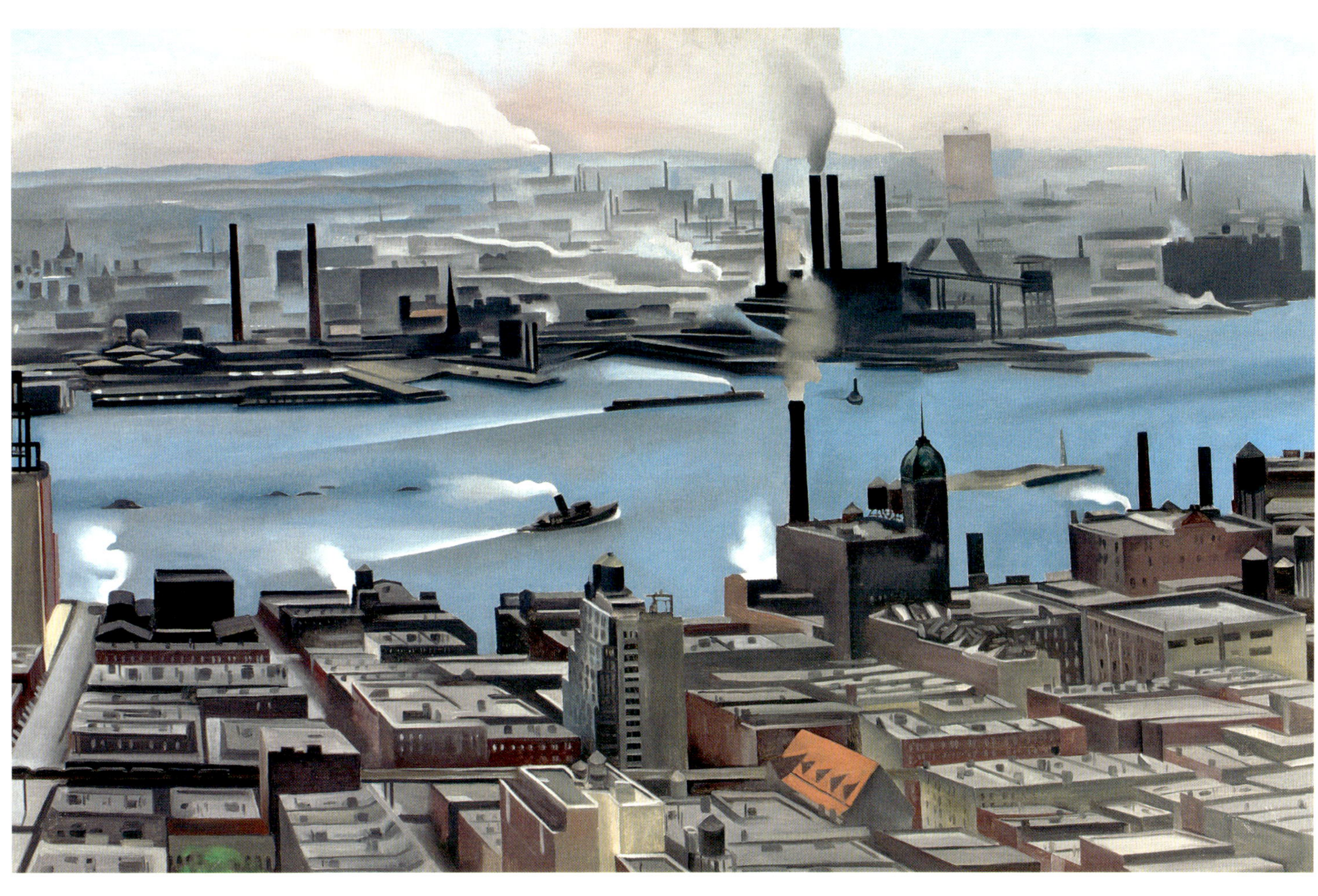

57
East River from the 30th Story of the Shelton Hotel, 1928
Oil on canvas

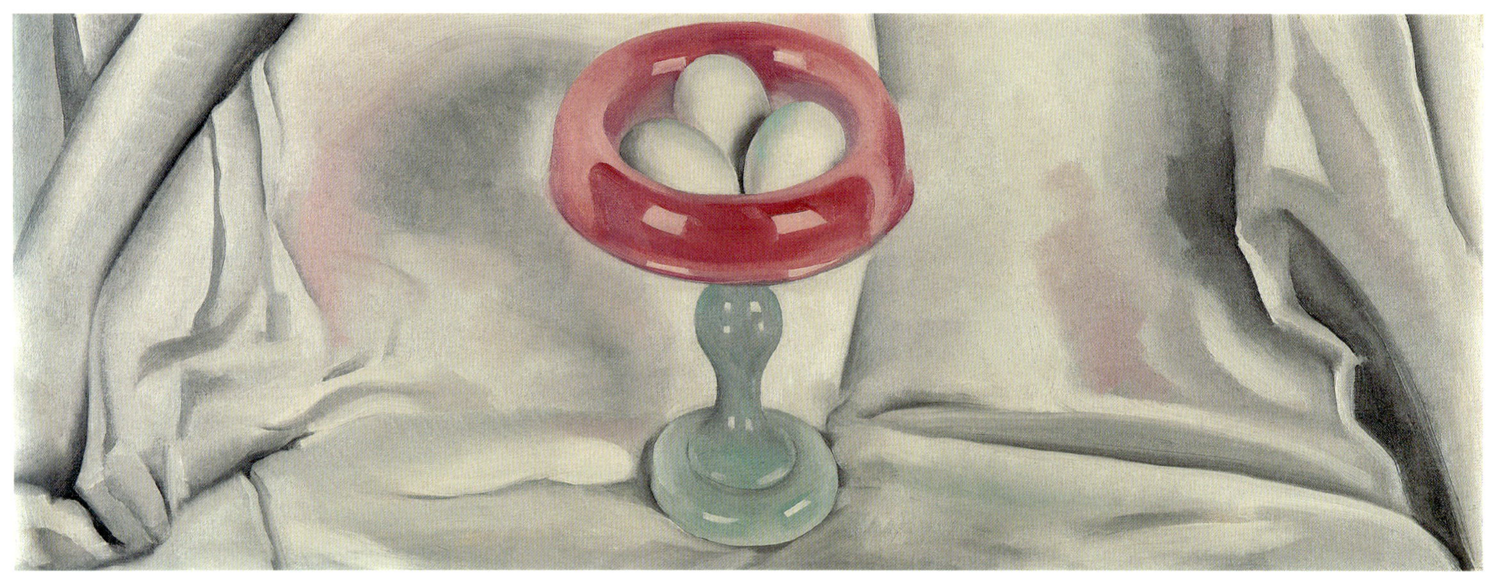

58
3 Eggs in Pink Dish, 1928–29
Oil on canvas

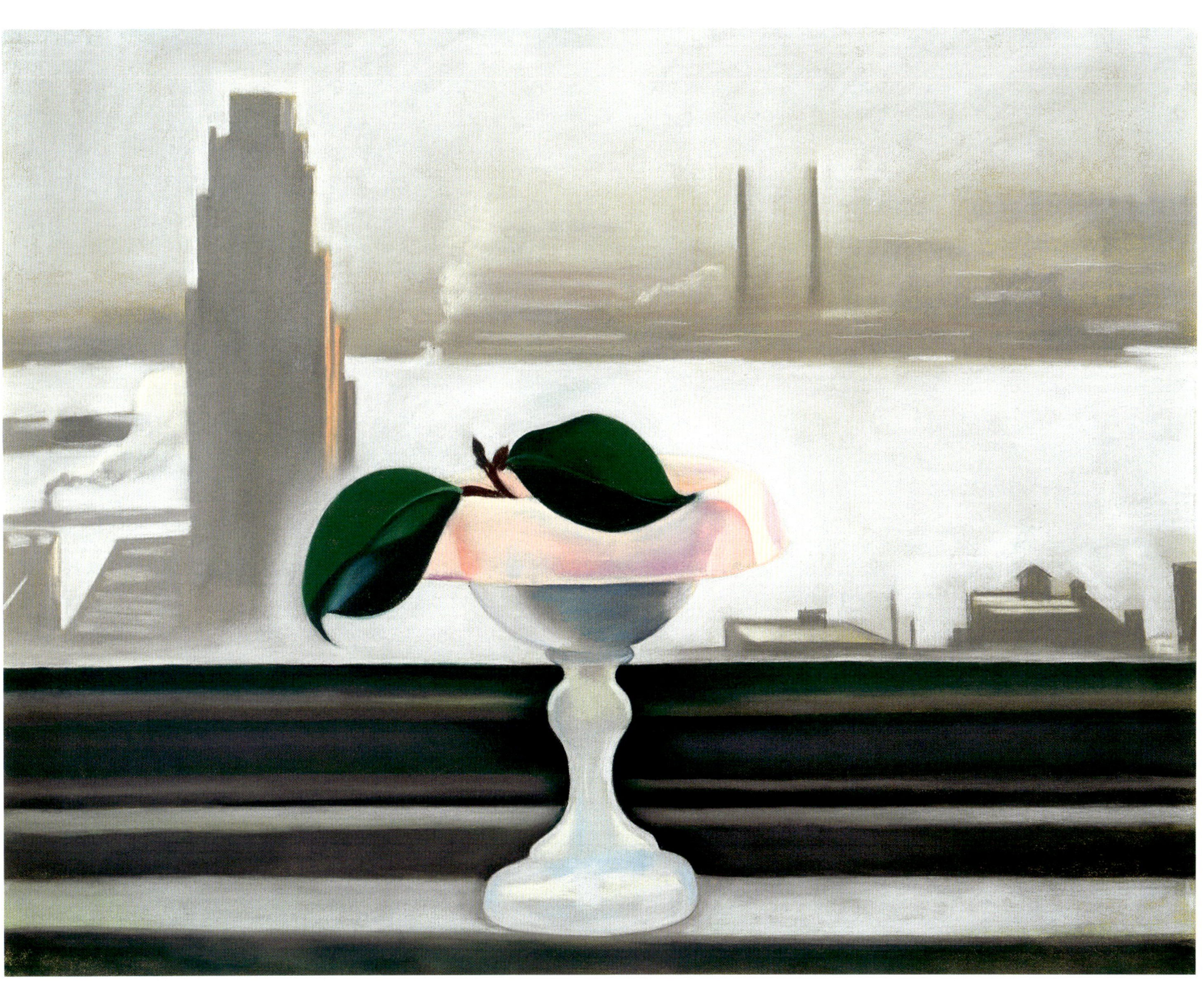

59

Pink Dish and Green Leaves, 1928–29

Pastel on board

60

East River from the Shelton (East River No. 1),
1927–28
Oil on canvas

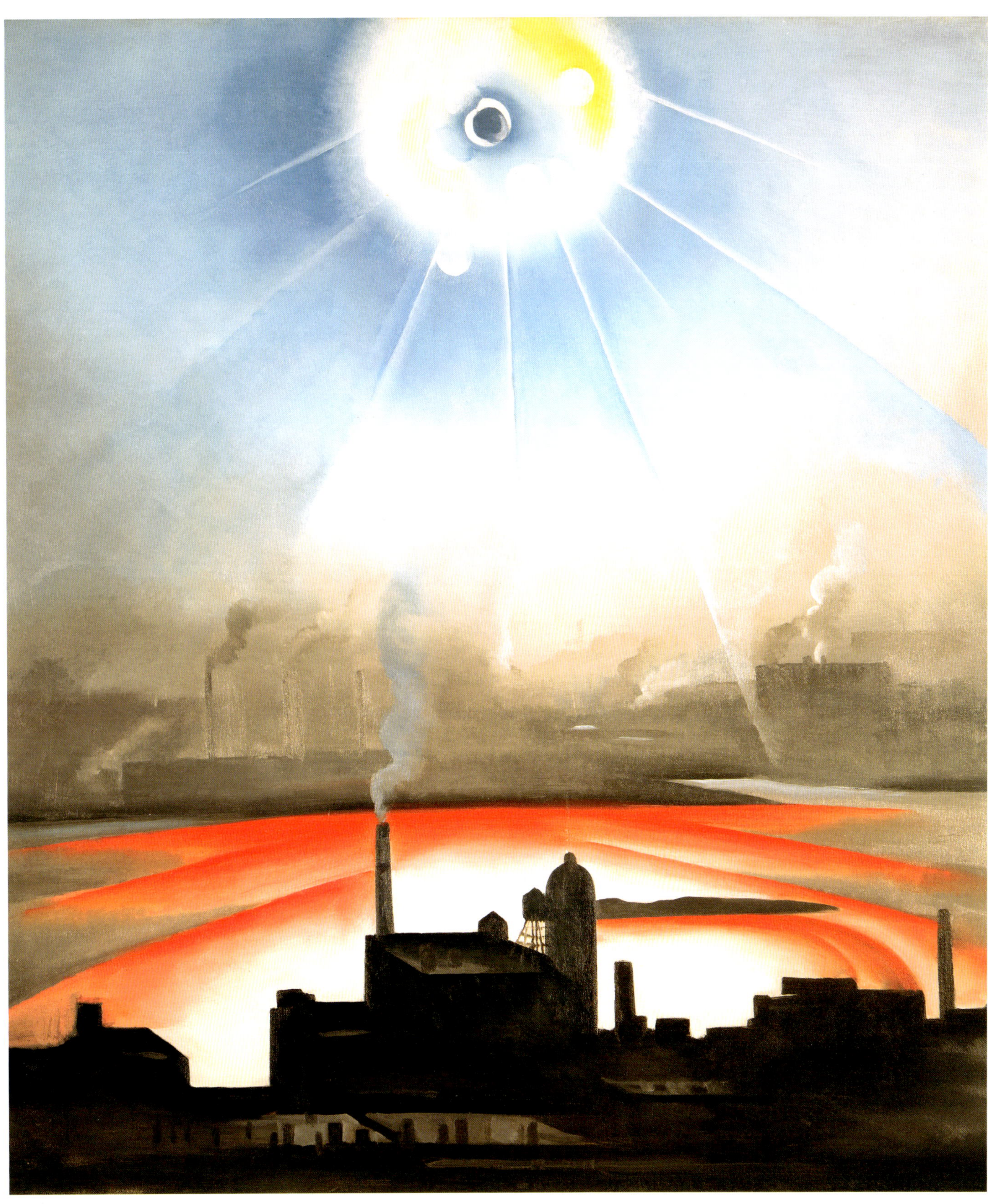

61
Black Cross, New Mexico, 1929
Oil on canvas

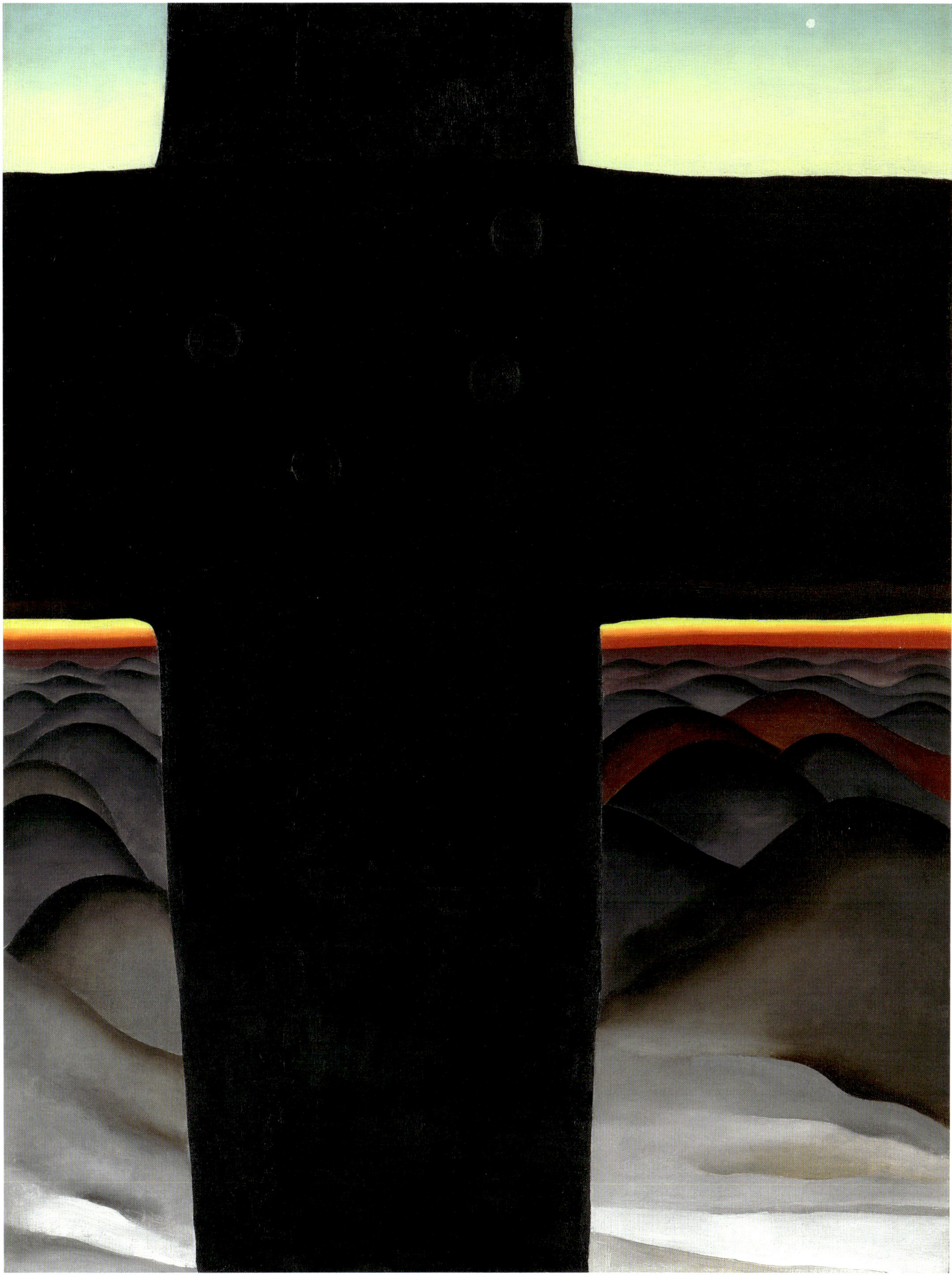

62
New York, Night, 1928–29
Oil on canvas

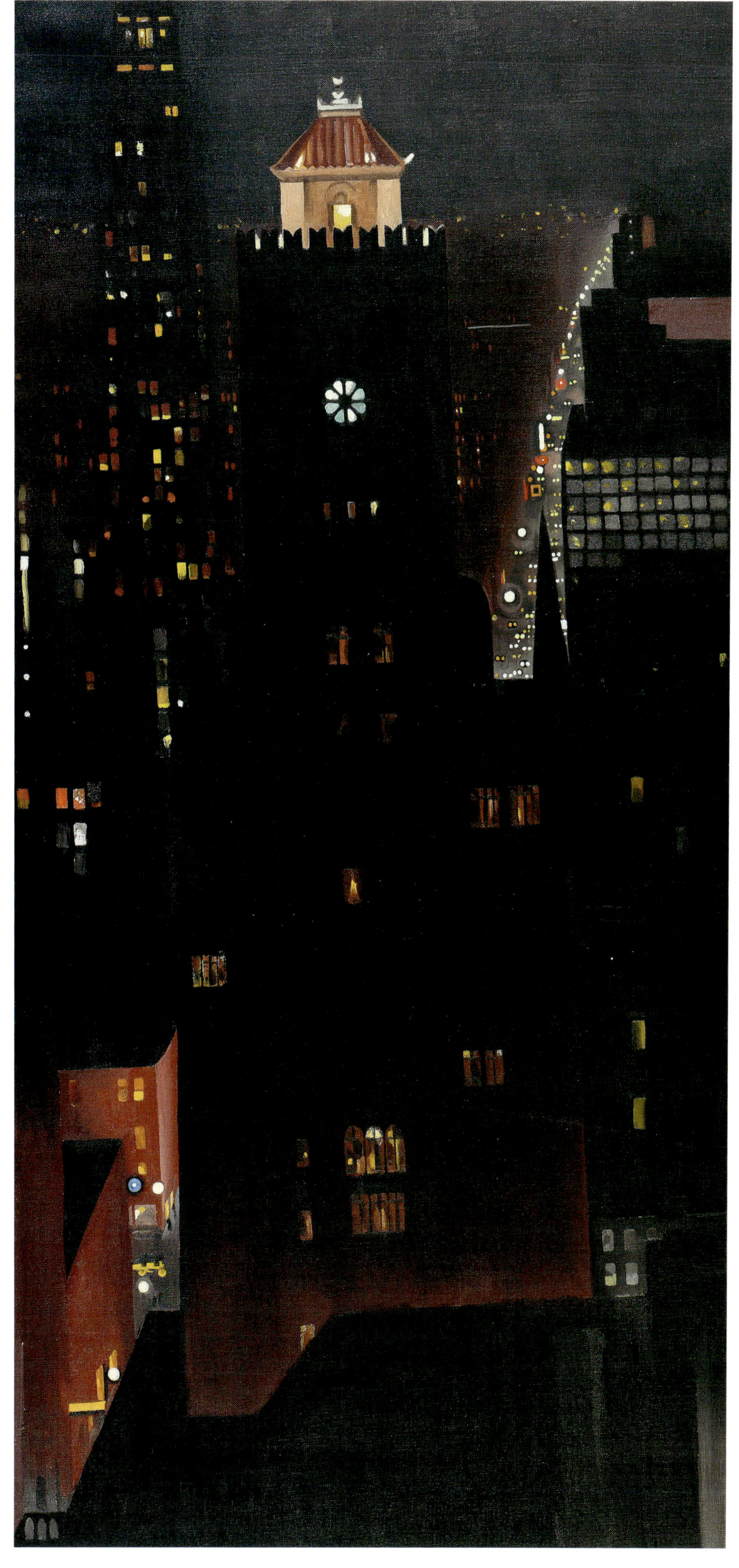

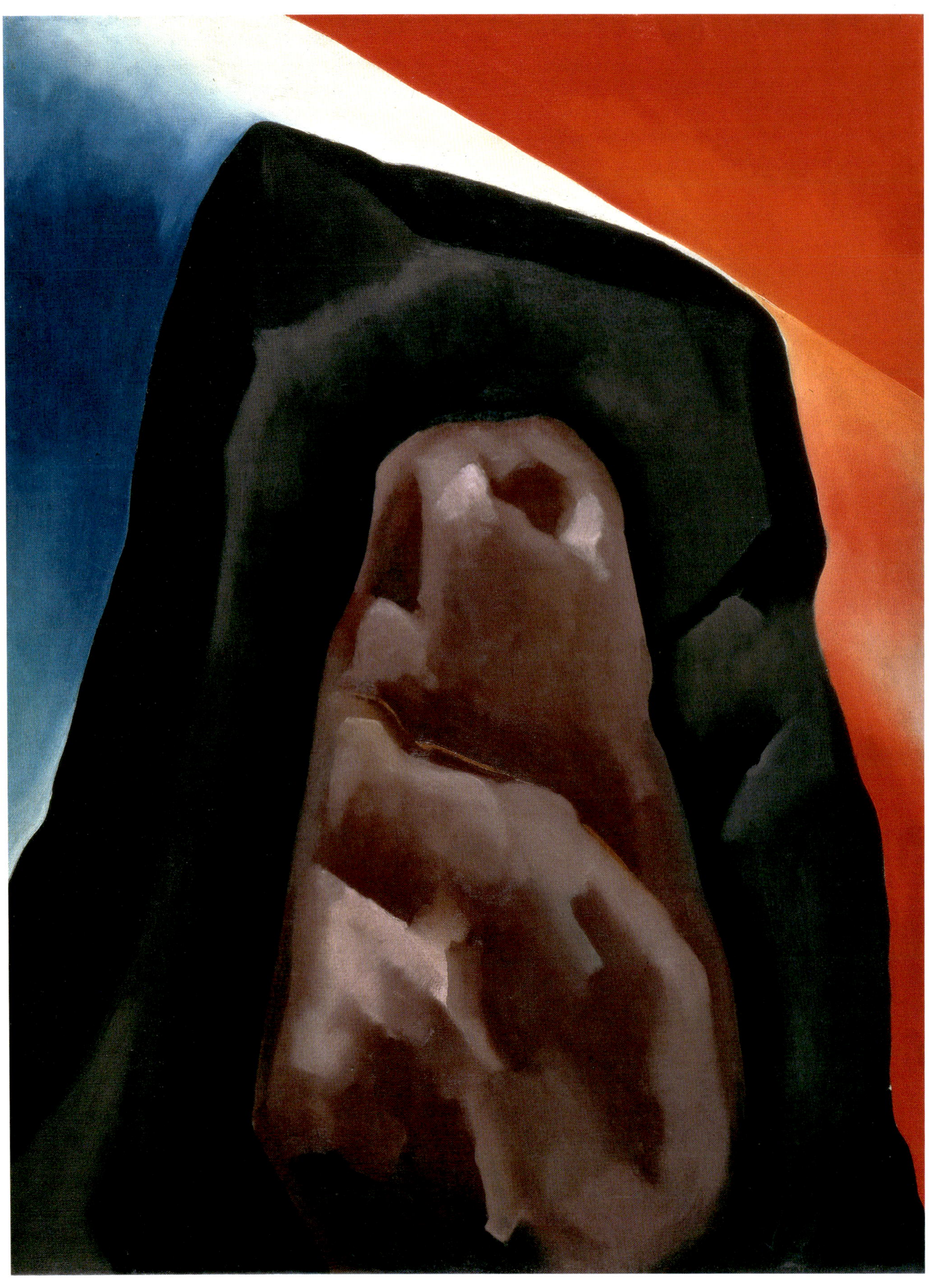

63
After a Walk Back of Mabel's, 1929
Oil on canvas

64
Dead Tree Bear Lake Taos, 1929
Oil on canvas

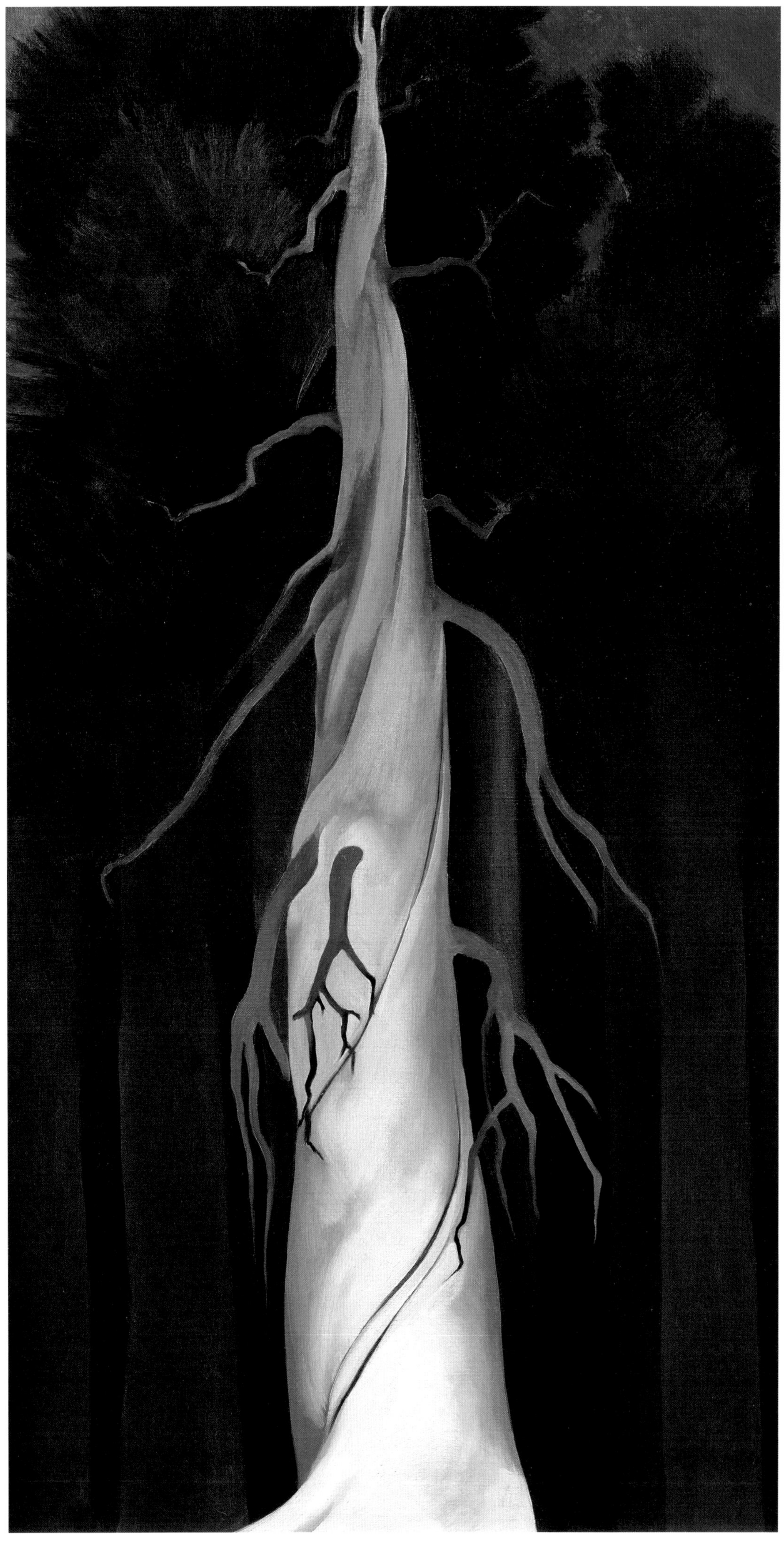

65

Farmhouse Window and Door, 1929

Oil on canvas

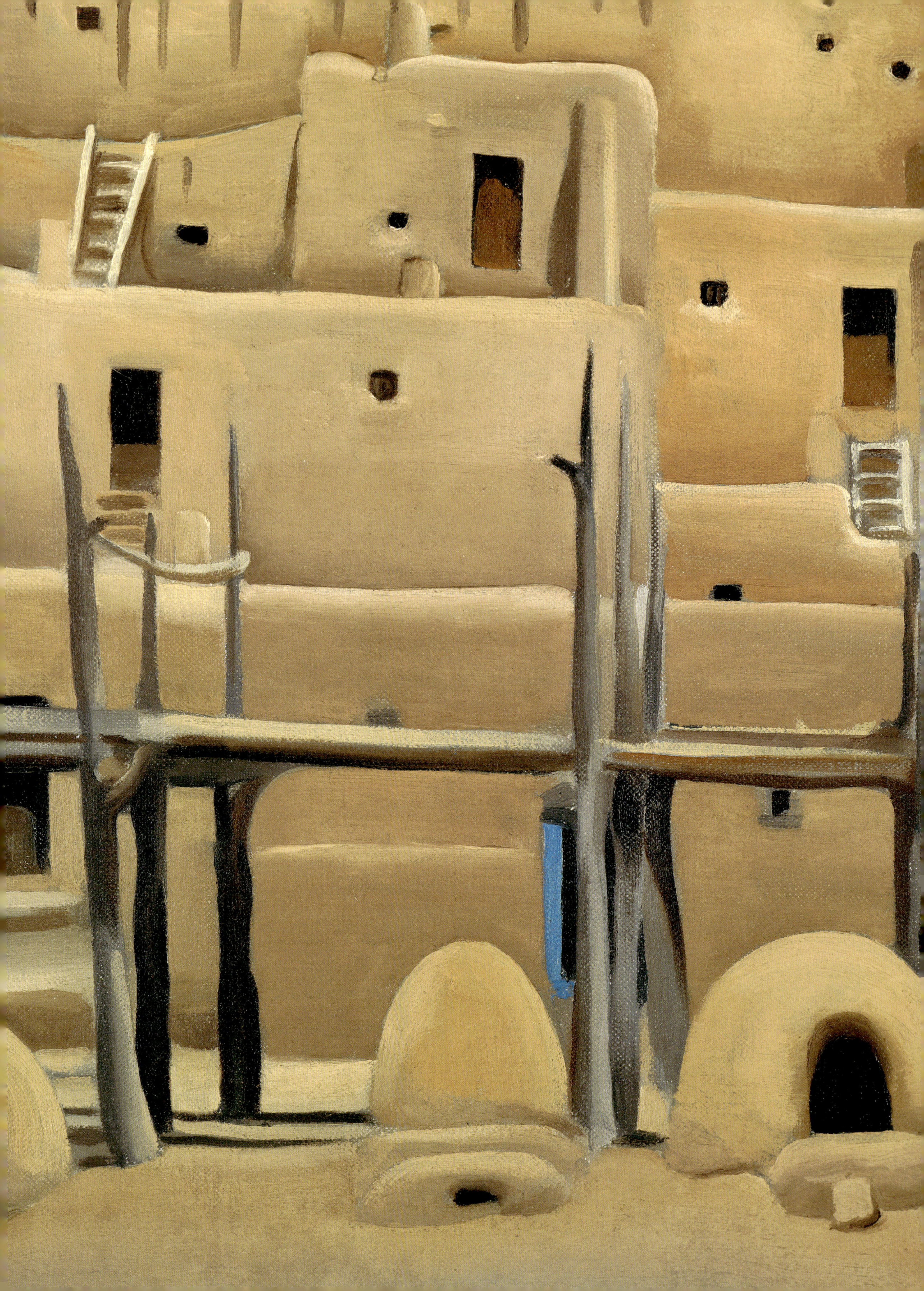

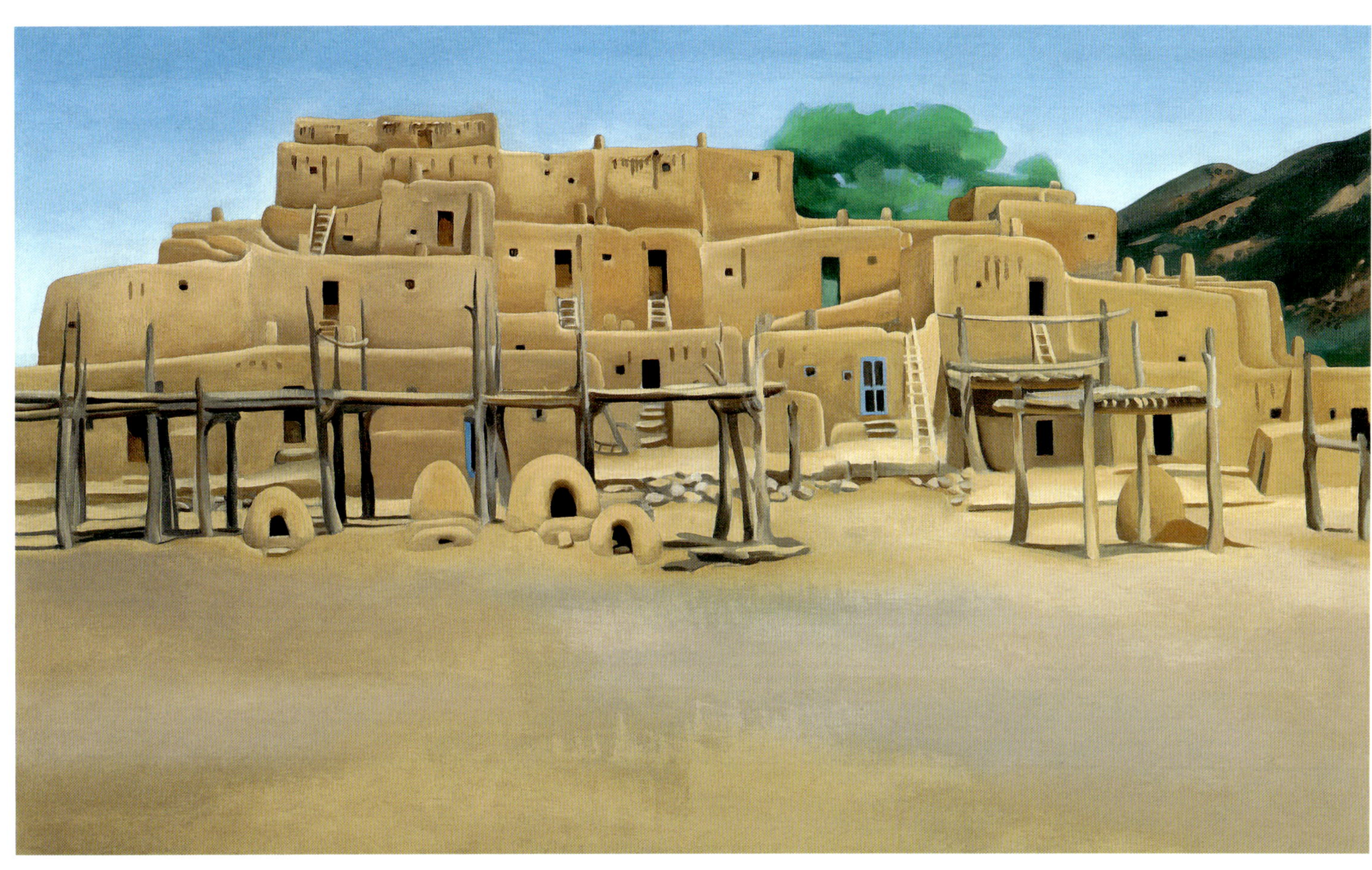

66
Taos Pueblo, 1929, reworked 1934
Oil on canvas

67

Cow's Skull with Calico Roses, 1931

Oil on canvas

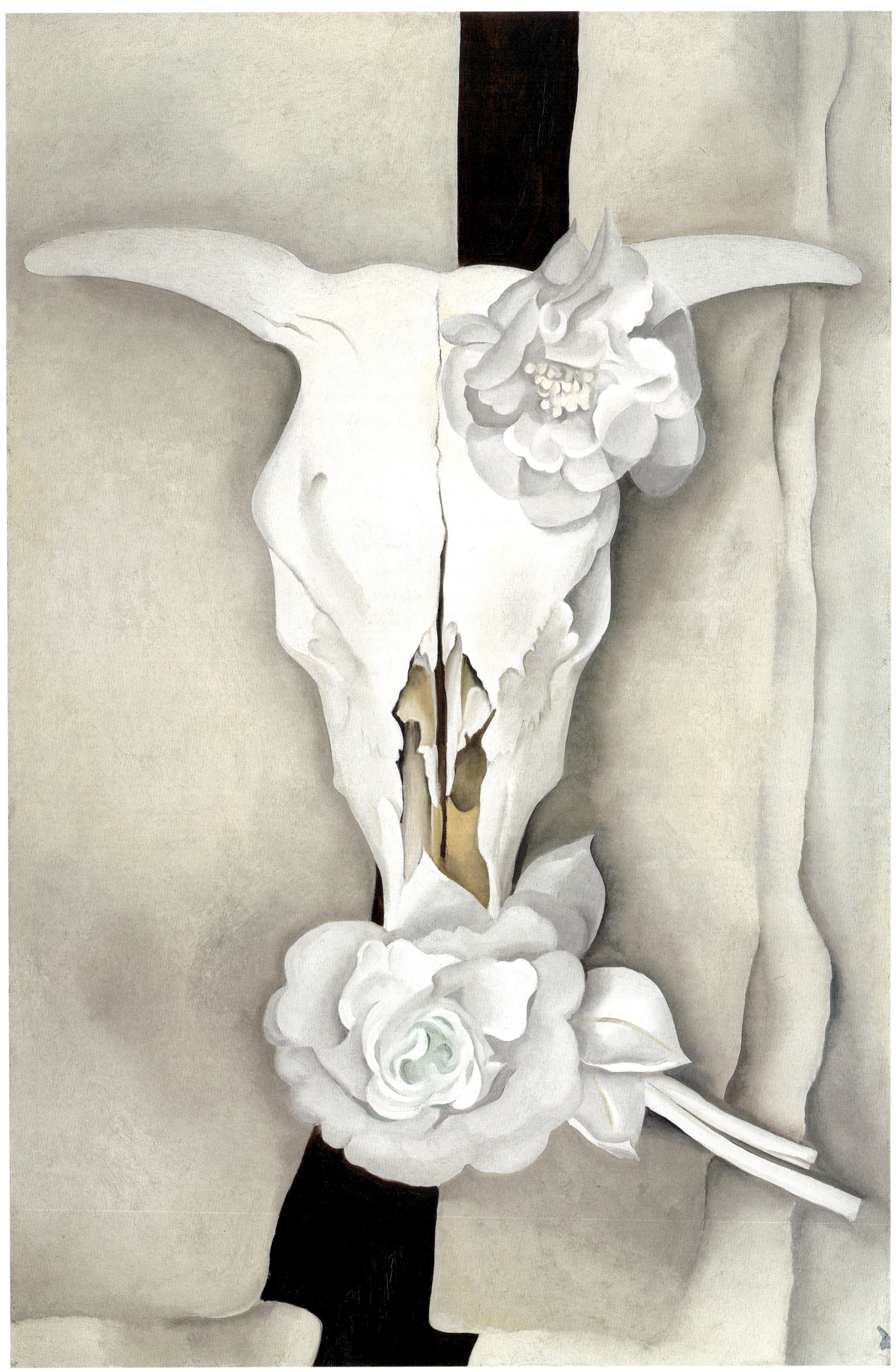

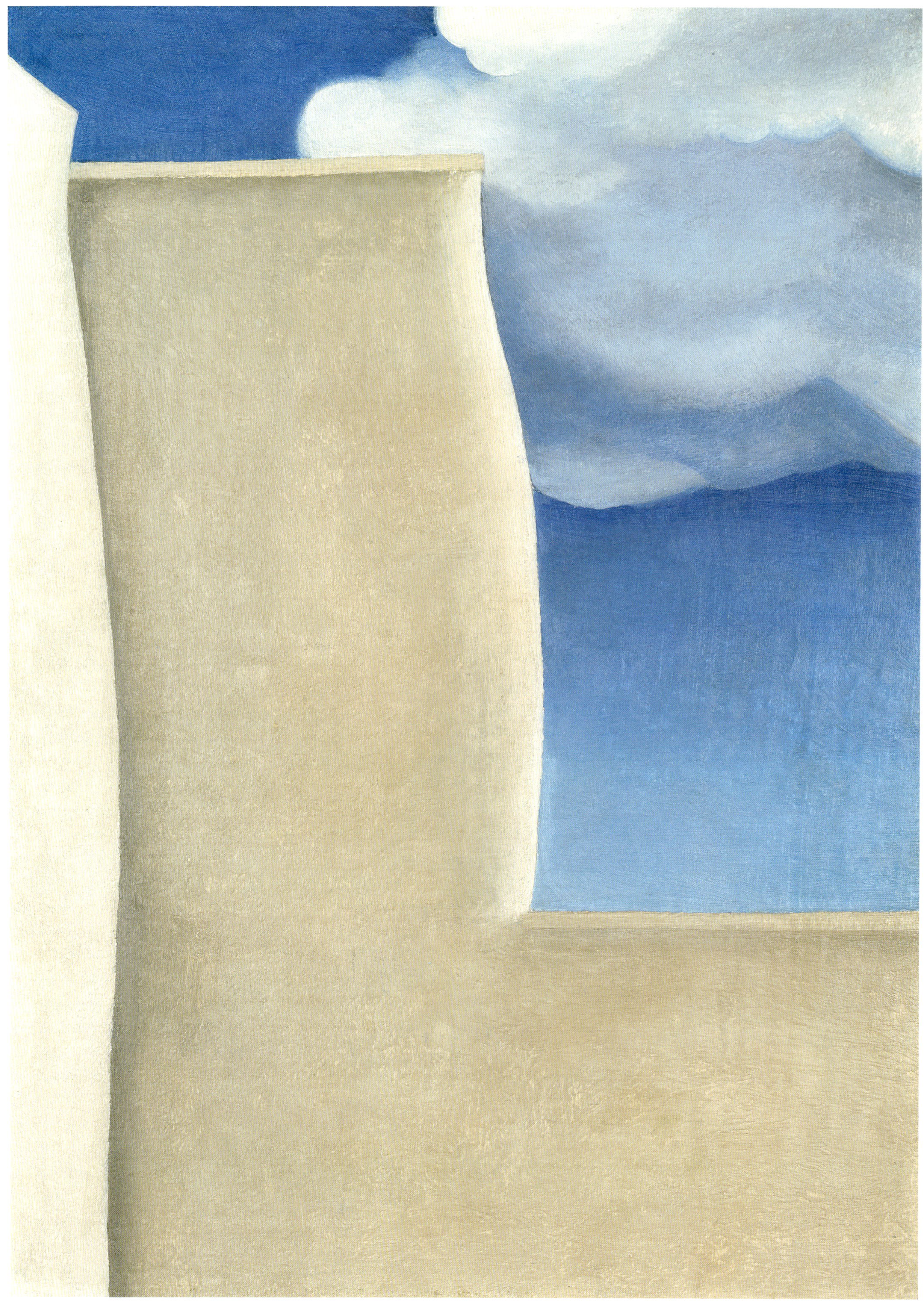

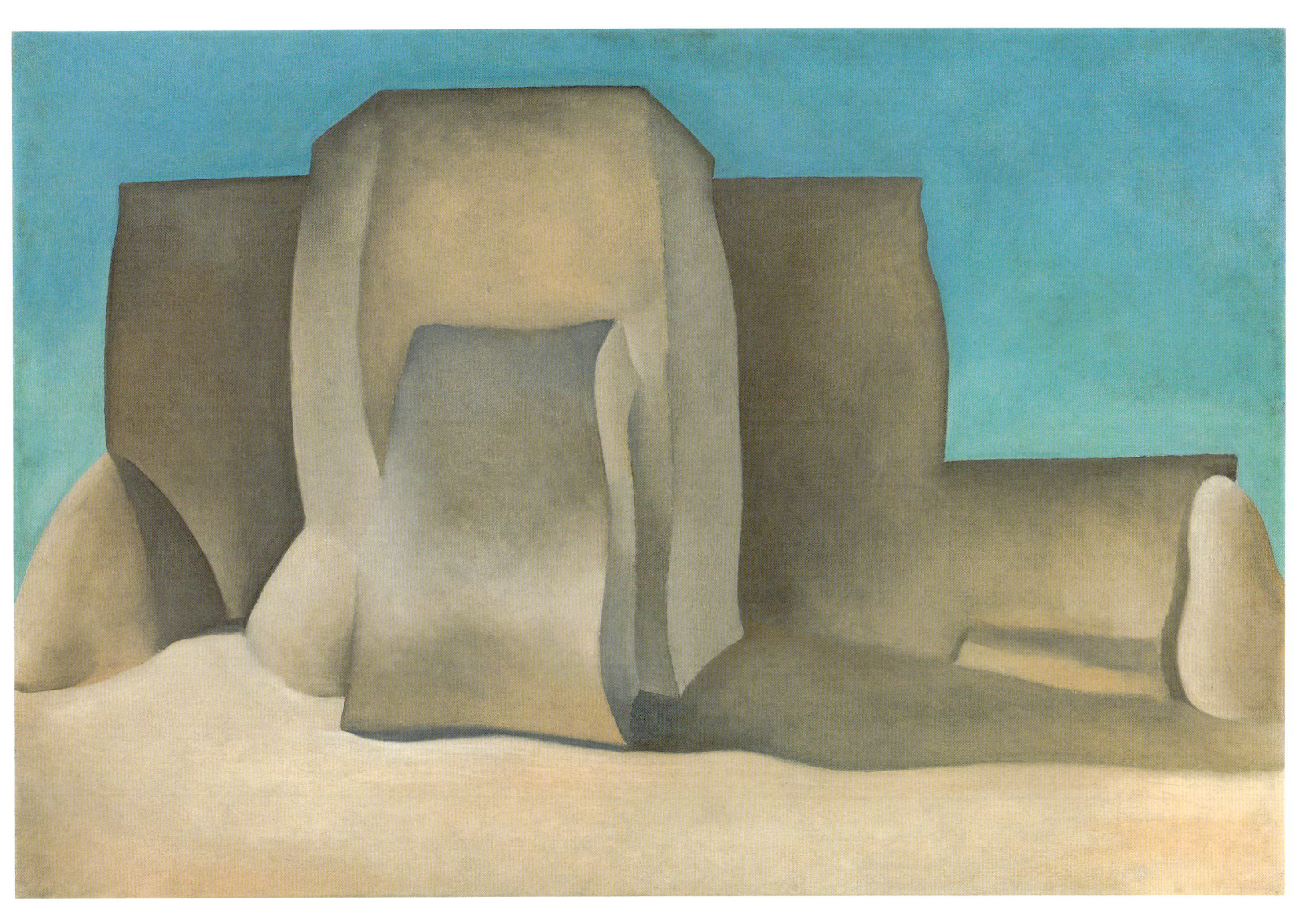

68
Ranchos Church, No. 3, 1929
Oil on canvas

69
Ranchos Church, No. II, NM, 1929
Oil on canvas

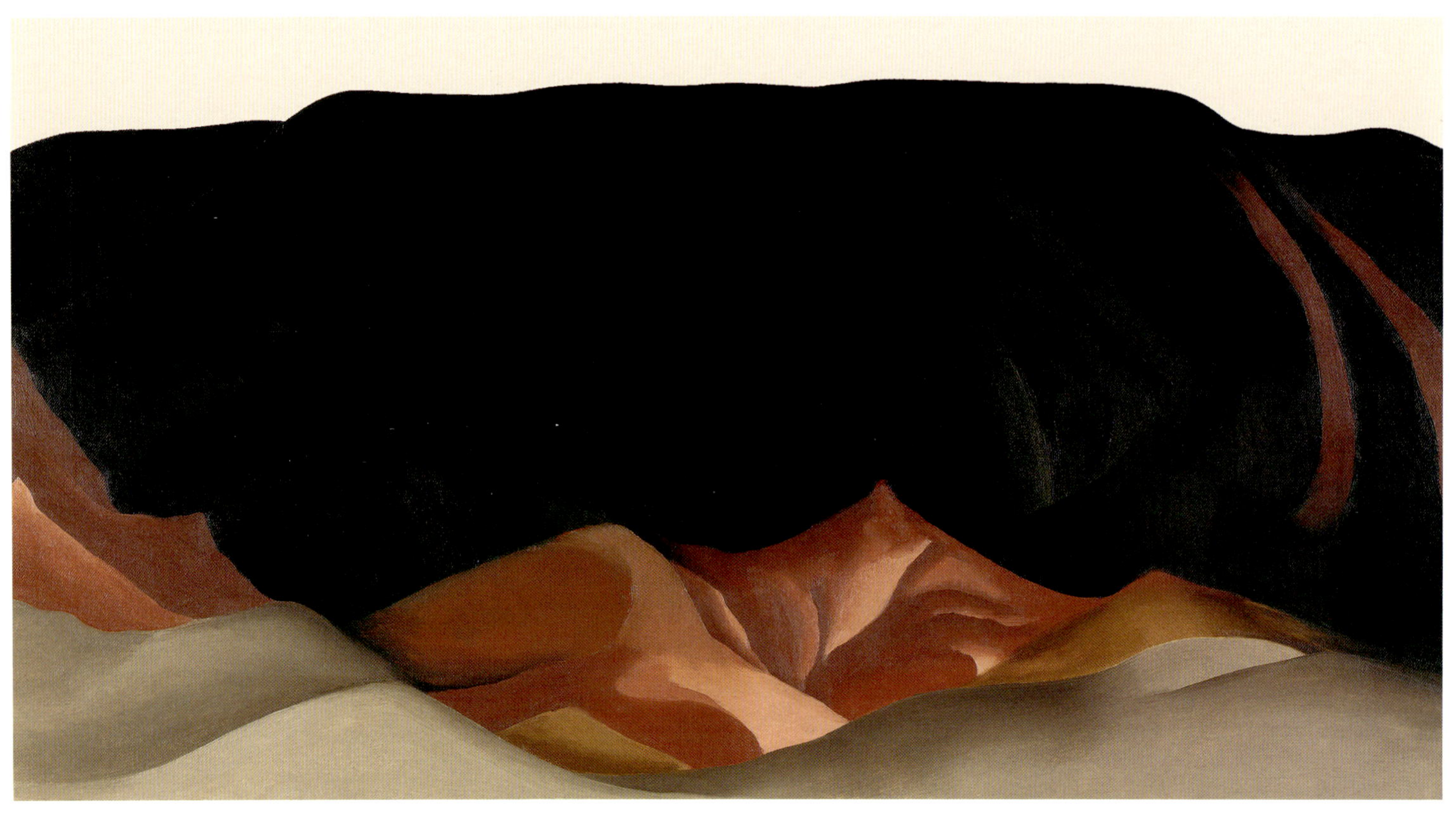

70
Dark Mesa with Pink Sky, 1930
Oil on canvas

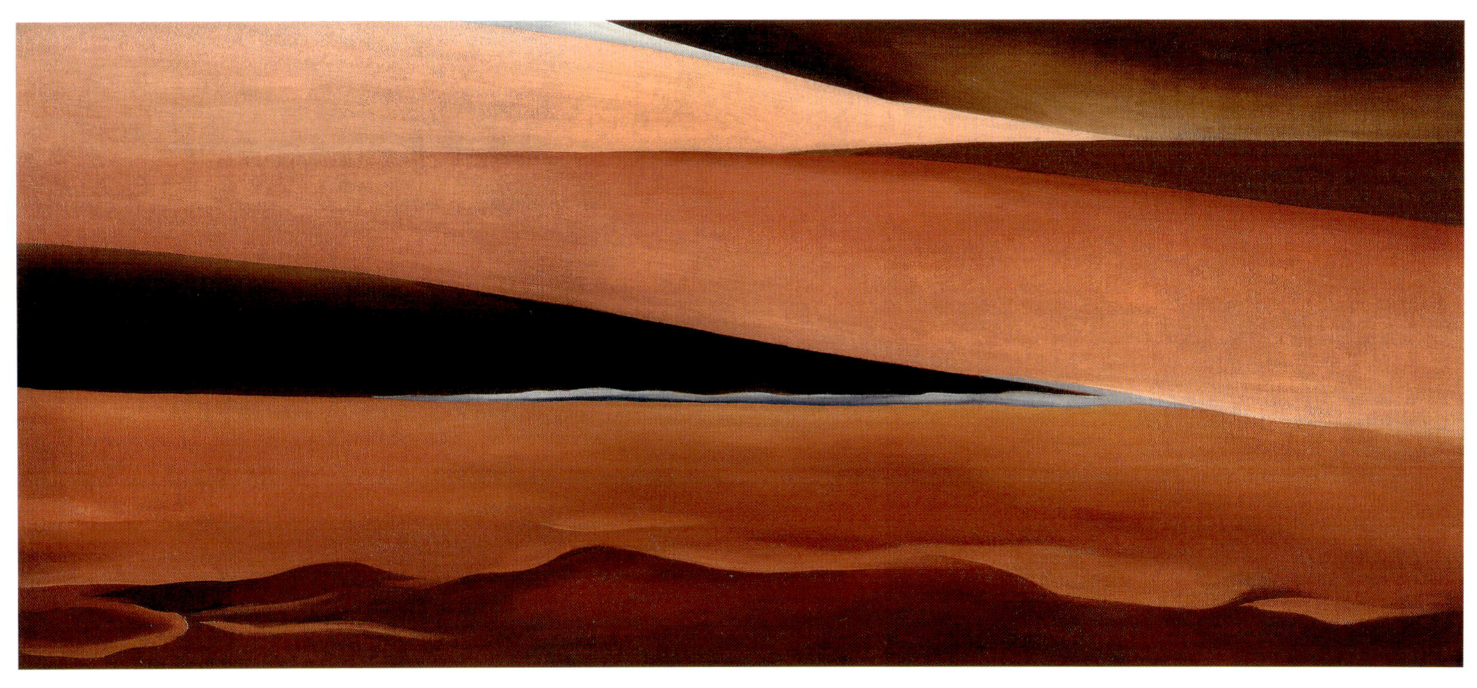

71
Desert Abstraction, 1931
Oil on canvas

72
Untitled (City Night), 1970s
Oil on canvas

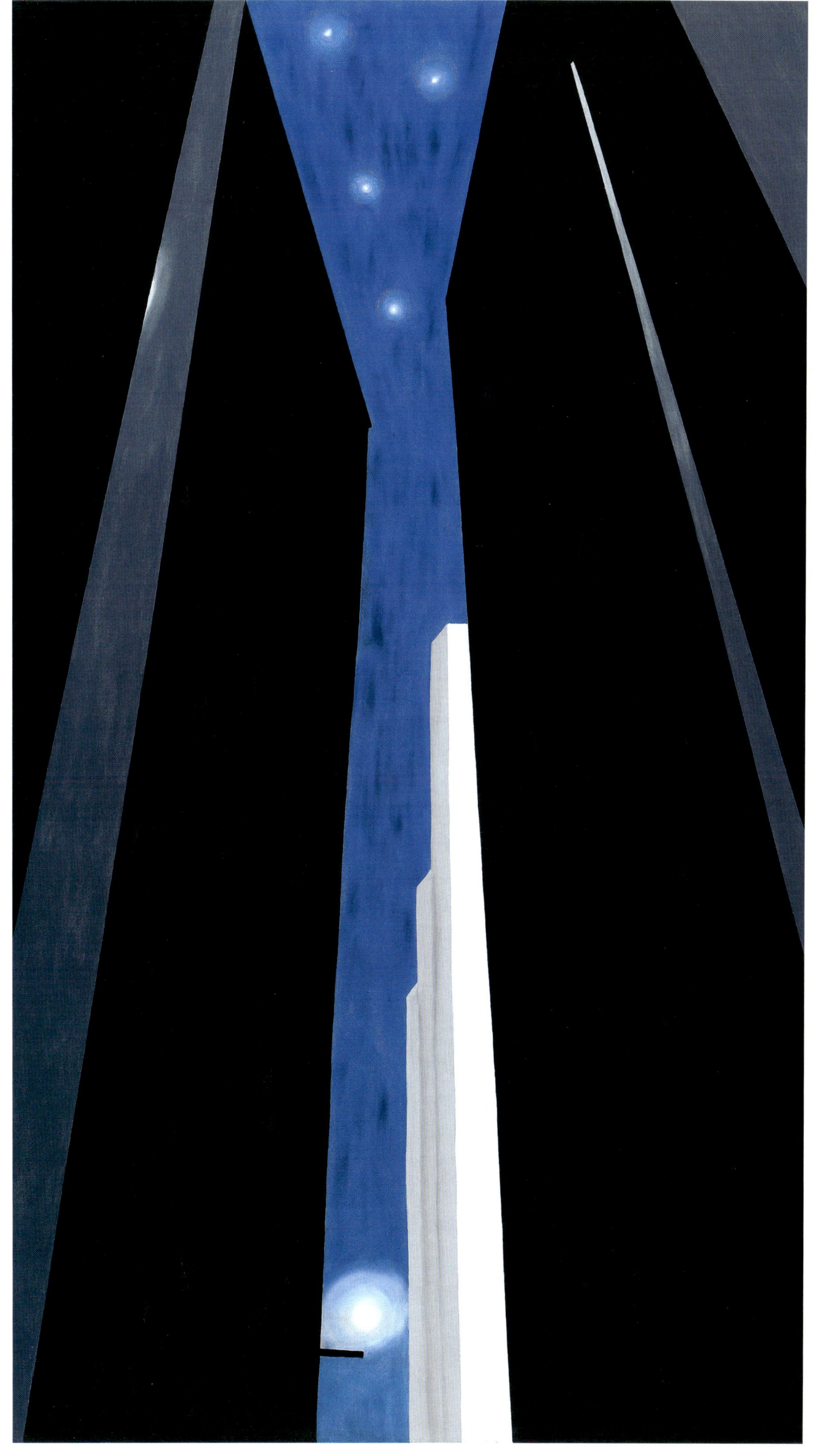

73
Alfred Stieglitz (American, 1864–1946)
Georgia O'Keeffe, 1918
Platinum print

74
Alfred Stieglitz (American, 1864–1946)
Georgia O'Keeffe, 1918
Palladium print

75
Alfred Stieglitz (American, 1864–1946)
Georgia O'Keeffe, 1918
Palladium print

76
Alfred Stieglitz (American, 1864–1946)
Georgia O'Keeffe, 1919–21
Palladium print

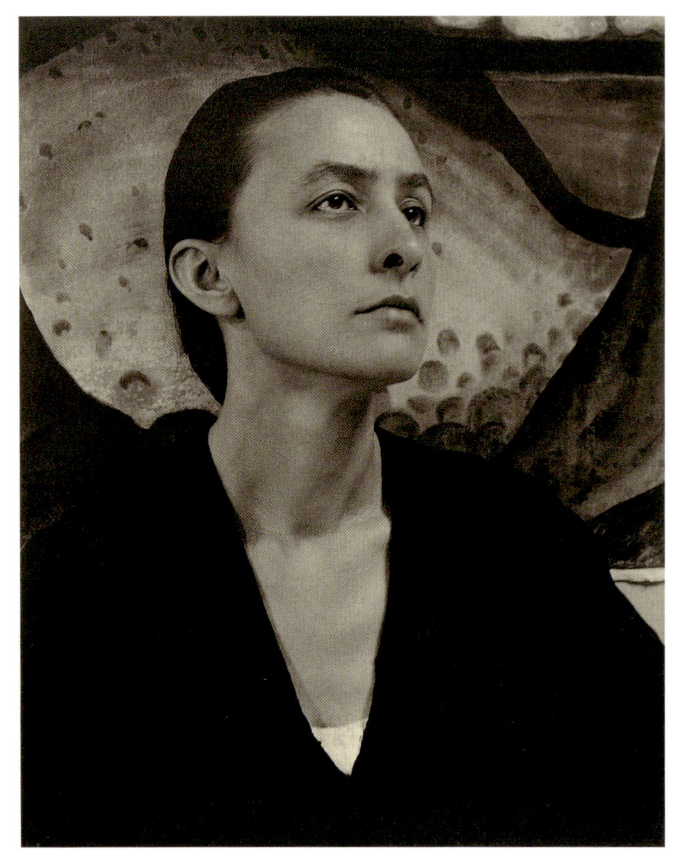

73

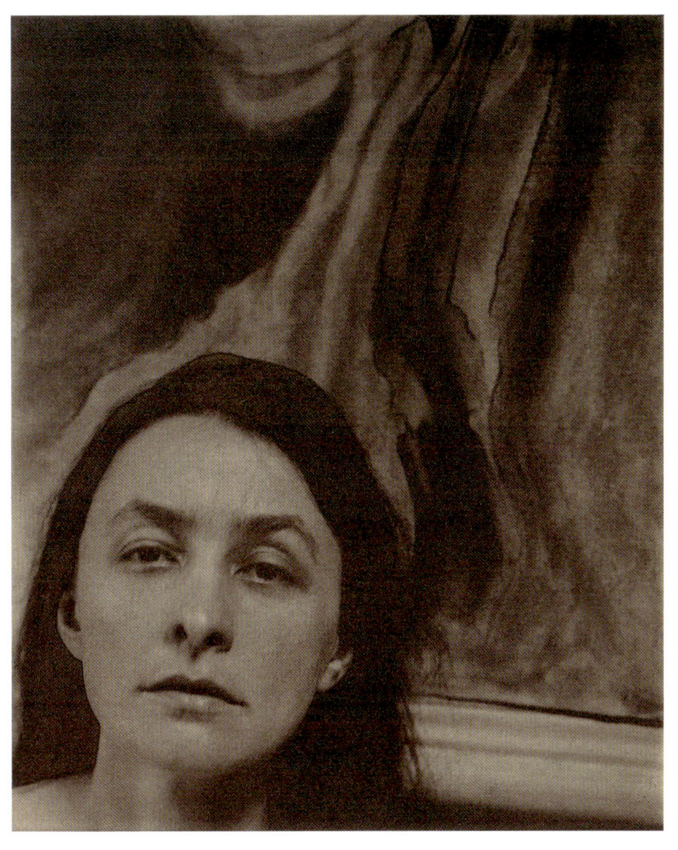

74

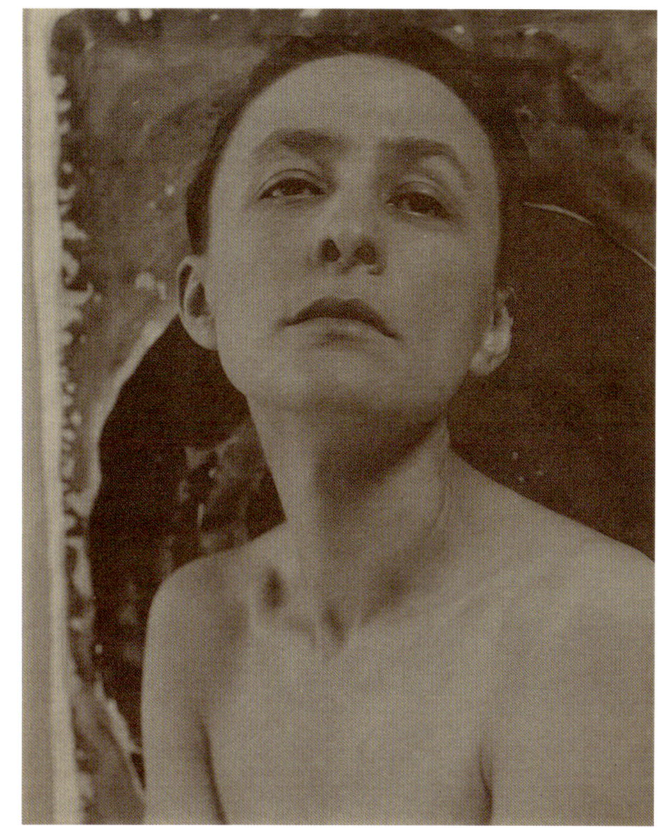

76

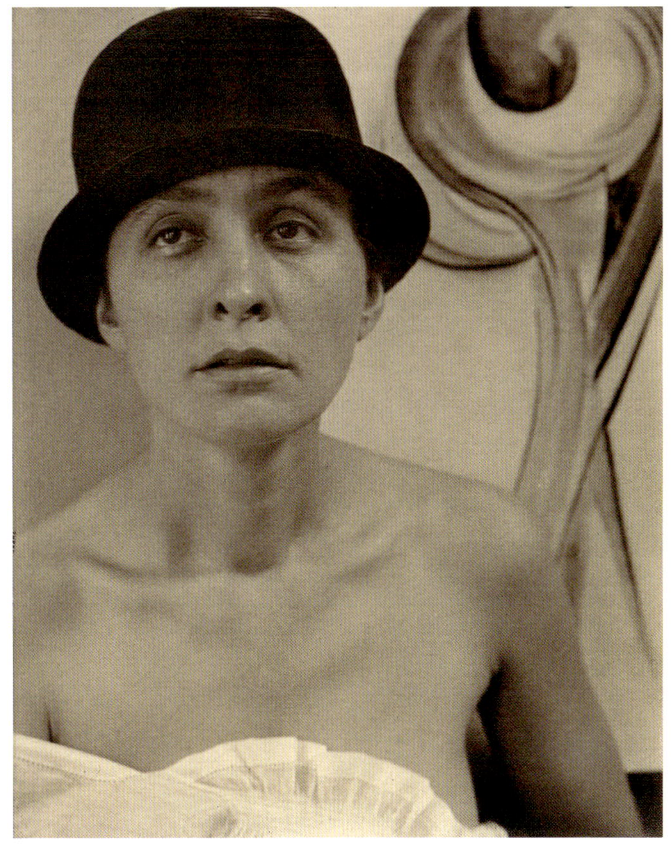

75

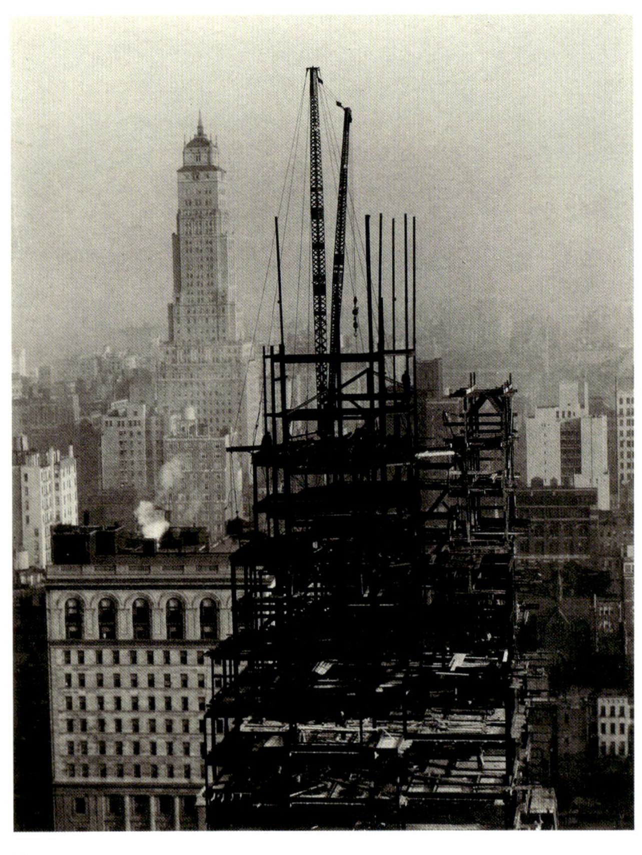

77

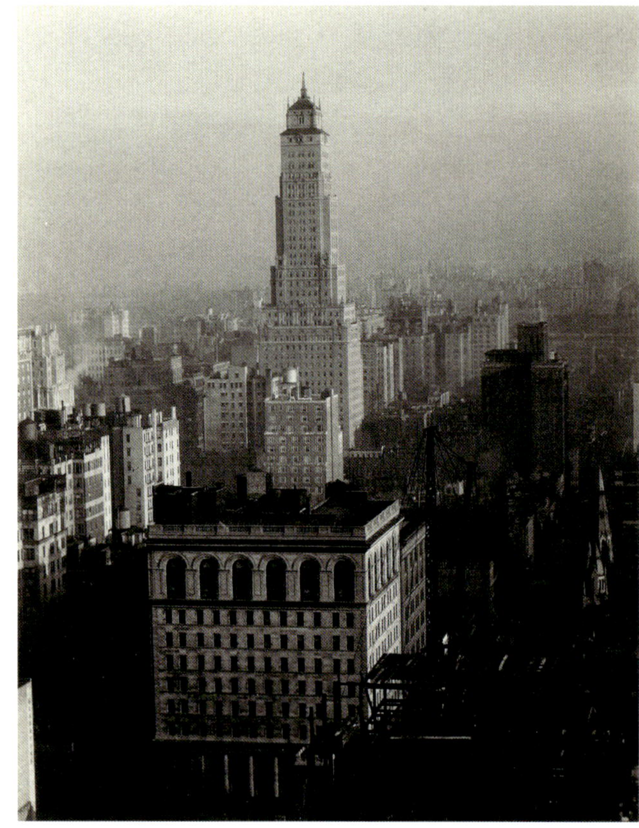

79

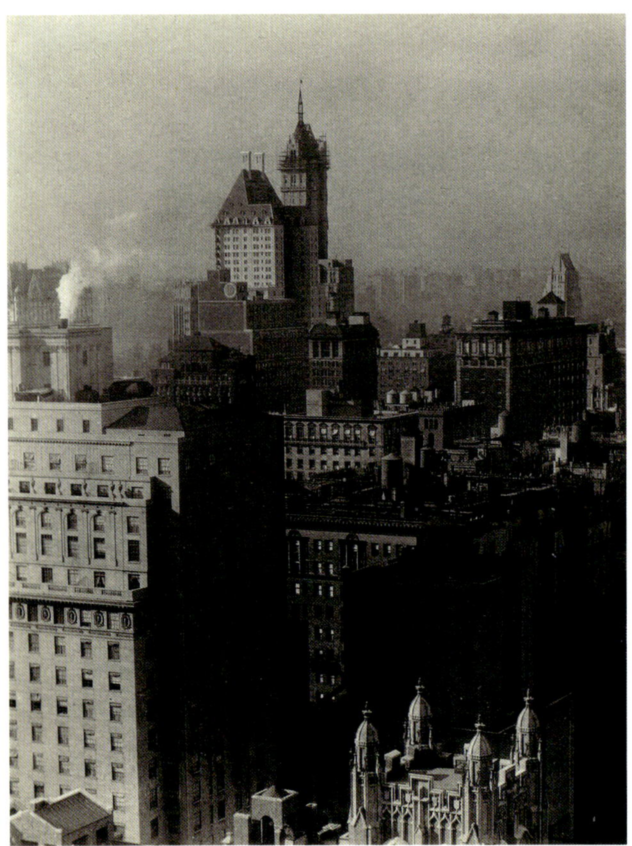

78

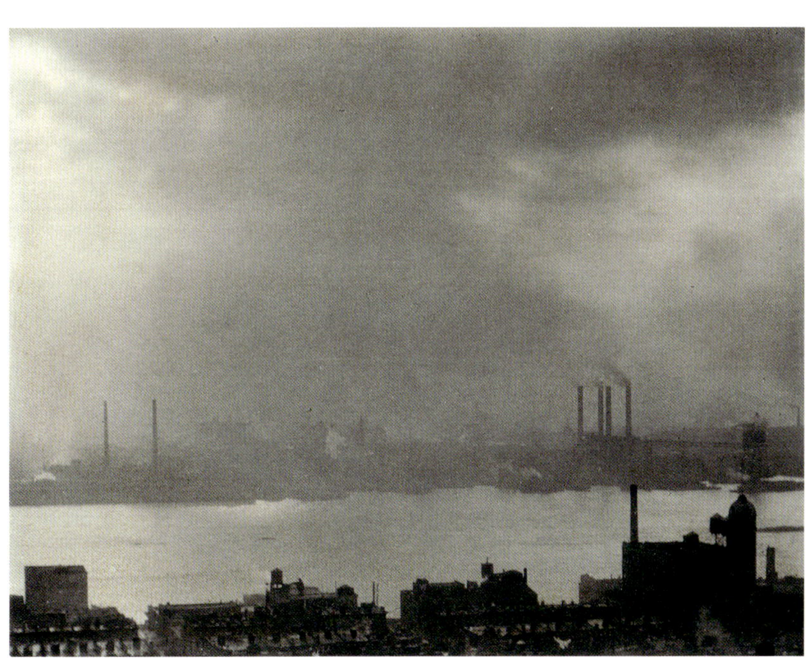

80

77
Alfred Stieglitz (American, 1864–1946)
From the Shelton, New York, 30th Floor Looking North, 1927
Gelatin silver print

78
Alfred Stieglitz (American, 1864–1946)
From Room 3003—(Looking Northwest)—The Shelton, New York, 1927
Gelatin silver print

79
Alfred Stieglitz (American, 1864–1946)
From the Shelton, New York, 30th Floor—Looking North, 1927
Gelatin silver print

80
Alfred Stieglitz (American, 1864–1946)
From the Shelton, New York, Looking East, 1926–27
Gelatin silver print

81
Alfred Stieglitz (American, 1864–1946)
From the Shelton, New York (Room 3003), Looking Southeast, 1927
Gelatin silver print

82
Alfred Stieglitz (American, 1864–1946)
From Room "3003"—The Shelton, New York, Looking Northeast, 1927
Gelatin silver print

83
Alfred Stieglitz (American, 1864–1946)
From "Room 303"—(Intimate Gallery)—New York, 1927
Gelatin silver print

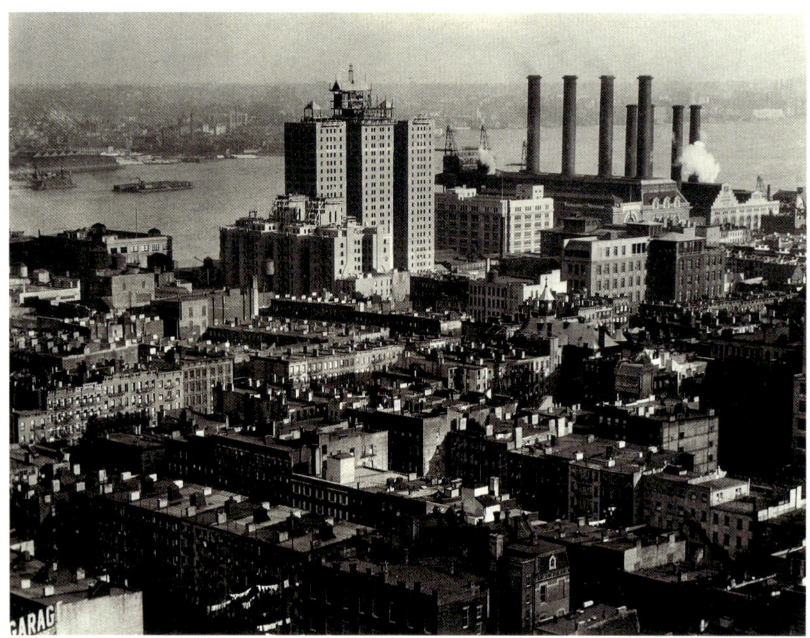

81

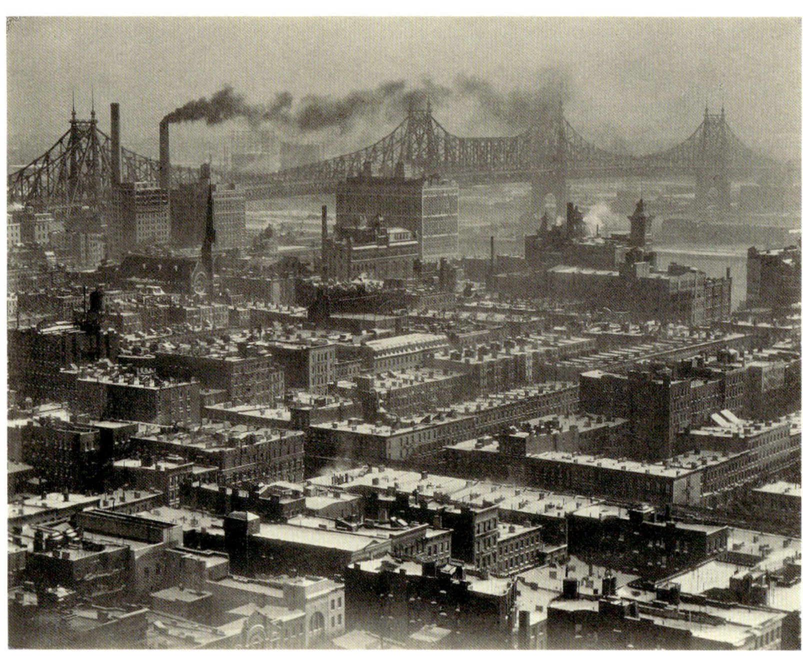

82

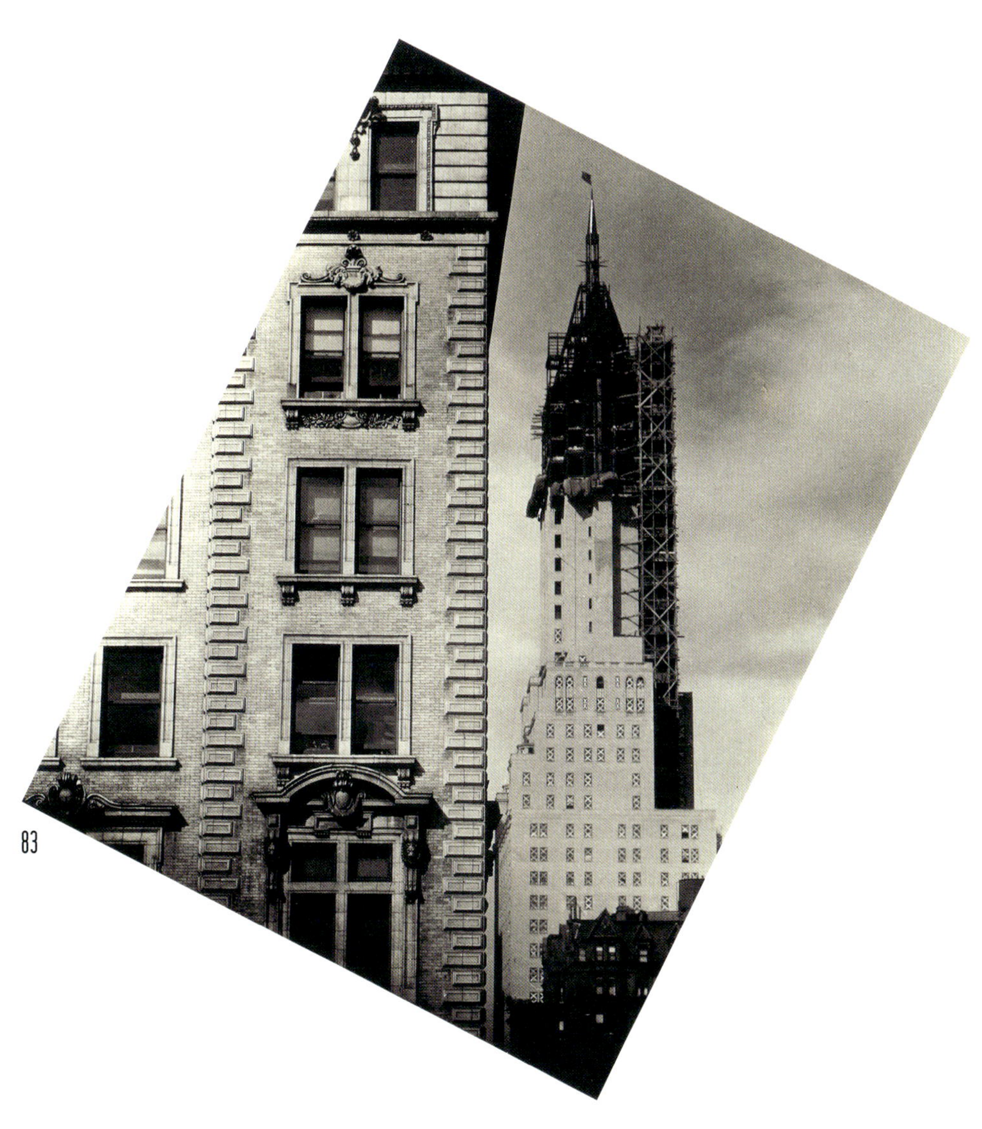

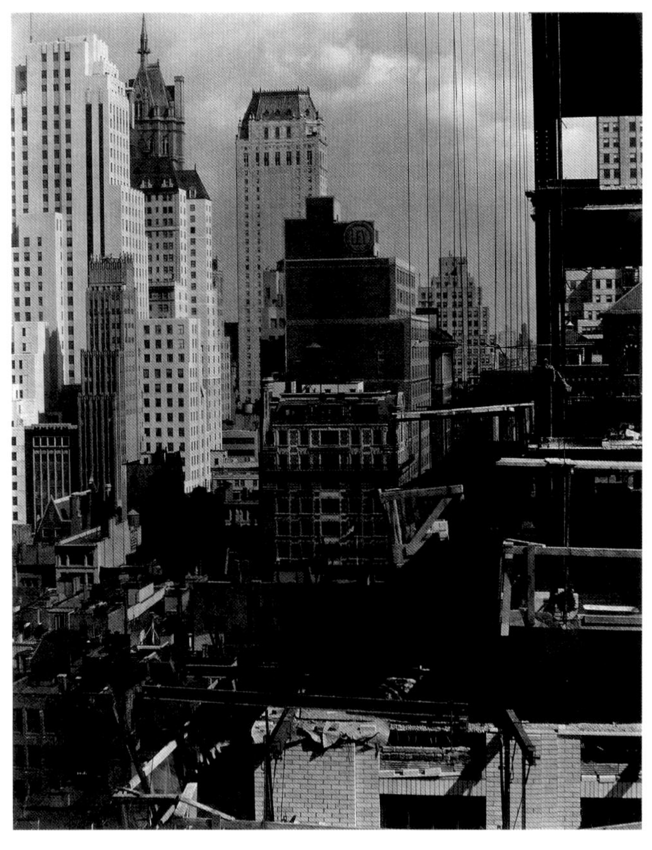

84

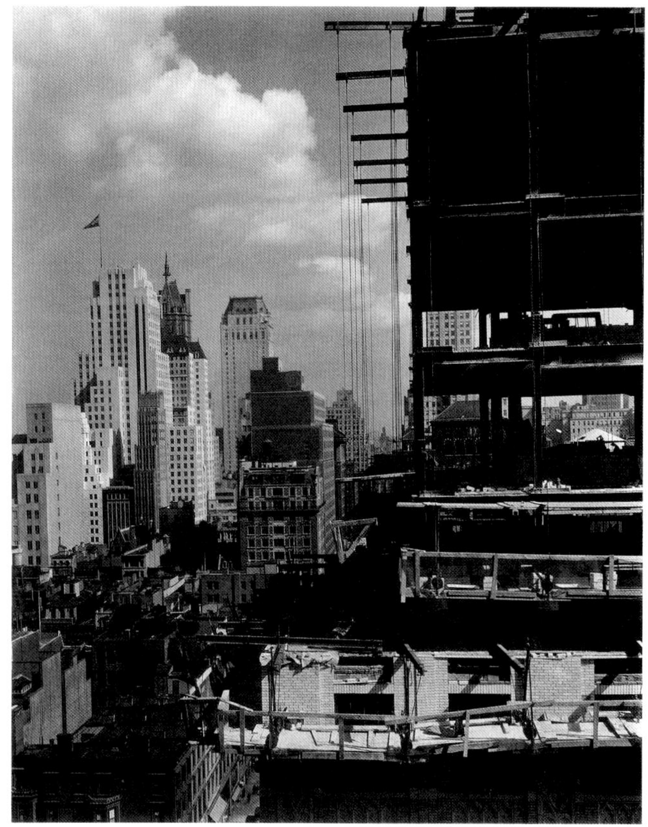

86

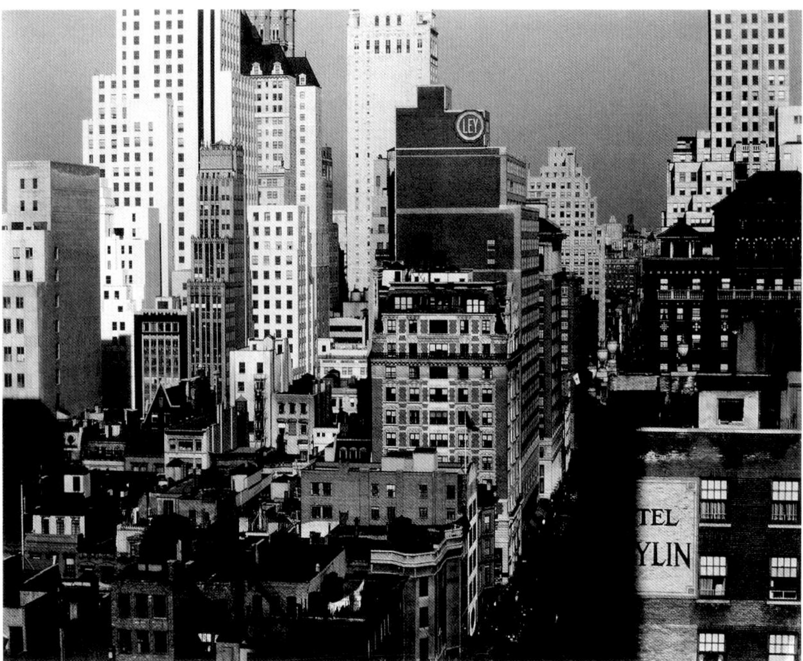

85

84
Alfred Stieglitz (American, 1864–1946)
From My Window at An American Place, North, 1931
Gelatin silver print

85
Alfred Stieglitz (American, 1864–1946)
From My Window at An American Place, North, 1930–31
Gelatin silver print

86
Alfred Stieglitz (American, 1864–1946)
From My Window at An American Place, North, 1931
Gelatin silver print

87
Alfred Stieglitz (American, 1864–1946)
From My Window at An American Place, Southwest, 1932
Gelatin silver print

88
Alfred Stieglitz (American, 1864–1946)
From My Window at An American Place, Southwest, 1932
Gelatin silver print

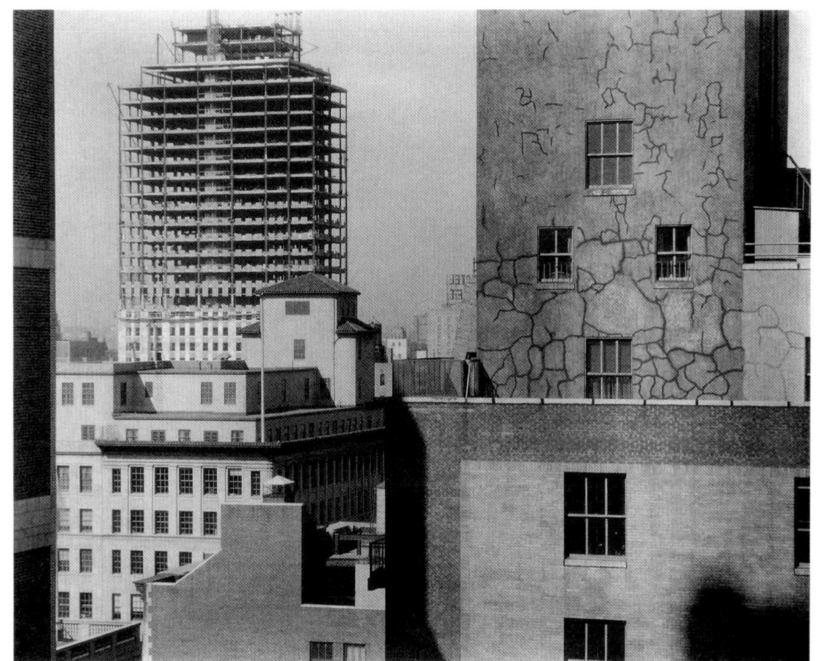

87

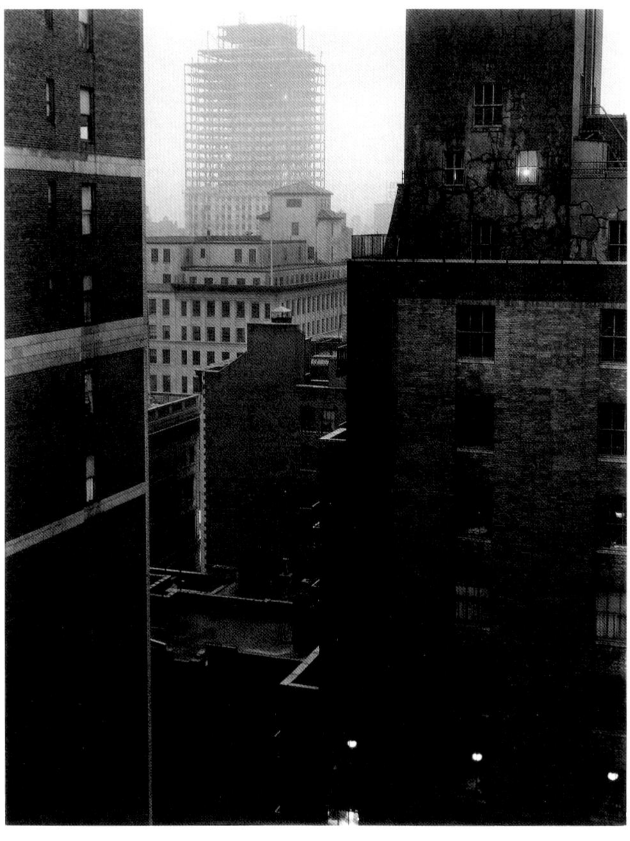

88

89
Arno Penthouse, E. 54th Street, New York, 1936–42
Gelatin silver print

90
Carl Van Vechten (American, 1880–1964)
Georgia O'Keeffe, June 5, 1936
Gelatin silver print

91
Carl Van Vechten (American, 1880–1964)
Georgia O'Keeffe, June 5, 1936
Gelatin silver print

92
Carl Van Vechten (American, 1880–1964)
Georgia O'Keeffe, June 5, 1936
Gelatin silver print

93
Carl Van Vechten (American, 1880–1964)
Georgia O'Keeffe, June 5, 1936
Gelatin silver print

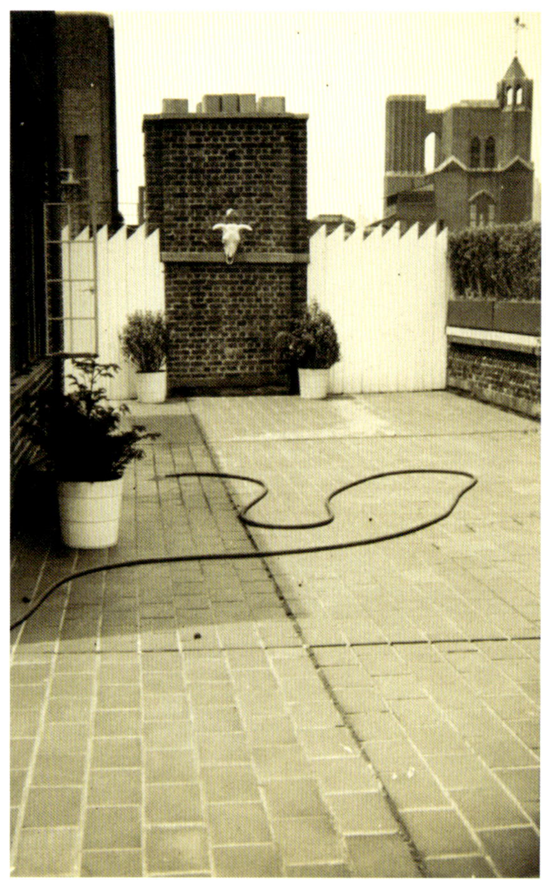

89

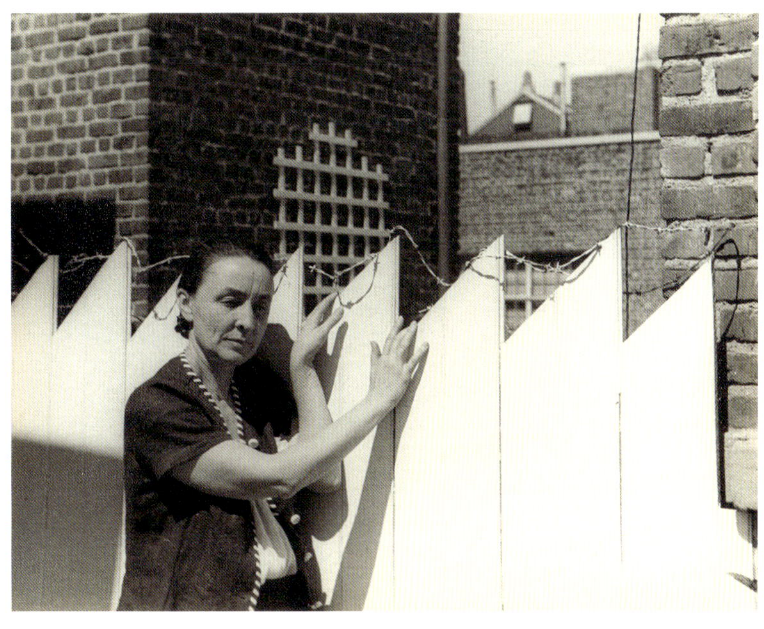
90

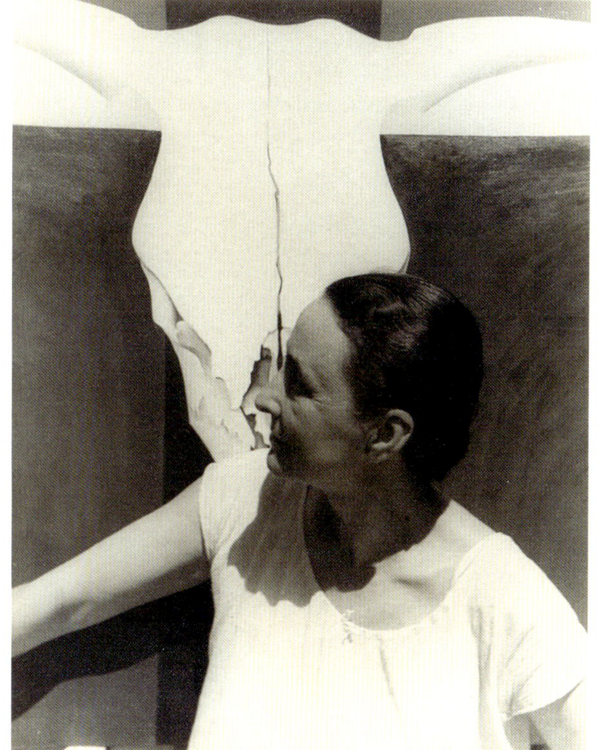
92

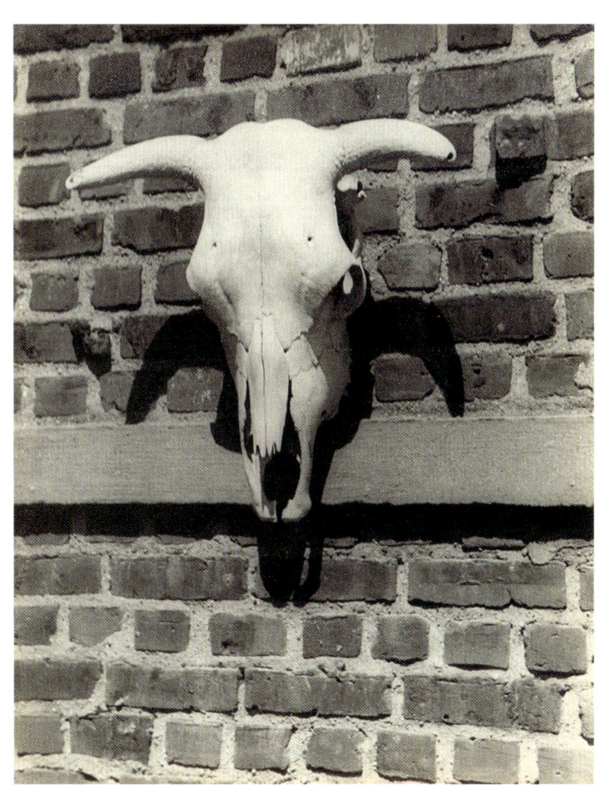
91

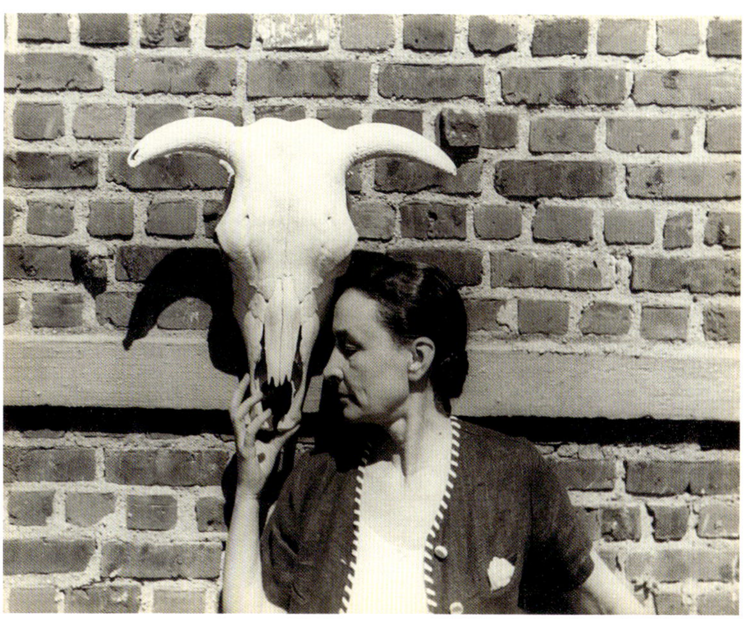
93

LIST OF PLATES

All works are by Georgia O'Keeffe (American, 1887–1986), unless otherwise noted.

The works listed here were shown at both exhibition venues, unless otherwise noted.

THE ART INSTITUTE OF CHICAGO
June 2–Sept. 22, 2024

HIGH MUSEUM OF ART, ATLANTA
Oct. 25, 2024–Feb. 16, 2025

1. *New York Street with Moon*, 1925
Oil on canvas, mounted to Masonite; 122 × 77 cm (48 1/16 × 30 3/8 in.)
Carmen Thyssen-Bornemisza Collection on loan at the Museo Nacional Thyssen-Bornemisza, CTB.1981.76

2. *From the Lake No. 1*, 1924
Oil on canvas; 91.4 × 76.2 cm (36 × 30 in.)
Purchased with funds from the Coffin Fine Arts Trust; Nathan Emory Coffin Collection of the Des Moines Art Center, 1984.3

3. *From the Lake No. 3*, 1924
Oil on canvas; 91.4 × 76.2 cm (36 × 30 in.)
Philadelphia Museum of Art: Bequest of Georgia O'Keeffe for the Alfred Stieglitz Collection, 1987

4. *Pattern of Leaves*, 1923
Oil on canvas; 56.2 × 46.1 cm (22 1/8 × 18 1/8 in.)
The Phillips Collection, Washington, DC, Acquired 1926

5. *The Eggplant*, 1924
Oil on canvas; 81.3 × 30.5 cm (32 × 12 in.)
Art Gallery of Ontario, Toronto, Donated in memory of Doris Huestis Speirs by her husband, Dr. J. Murray Speirs, 1990 (90/36)

6. *The Chestnut Tree – Grey*, 1924
Oil on canvas; 91.5 × 76.6 cm (36 × 30 1/8 in.)
Myron Kunin Collection of American Art, Minneapolis, MN

7. *Corn, Dark, No. 1*, 1924
Oil on wood fiberboard; 80.7 × 30.2 cm (31 3/4 × 11 7/8 in.)
The Metropolitan Museum of Art, New York, Alfred Stieglitz Collection, 1950, 50.234.1

8. *Flagpole*, 1925
Oil on canvas; 88.9 × 46 cm (35 × 18 1/8 in.)
Georgia O'Keeffe Museum, Gift of The Burnett Foundation and an anonymous donor, 1997.2.1

9. *A Celebration*, 1924
Oil on canvas; 88.6 × 45.8 cm (34 7/8 × 18 in.)
Seattle Art Museum, Gift of the Georgia O'Keeffe Foundation, 94.89

10. *59th Street Studio*, 1919
Oil on canvas; 88.9 × 73.7 cm (35 × 29 in.)
Private collection
(not in exhibition)

11. *Shelton Hotel, N.Y., No. I*, 1926
Oil on canvas; 81.3 × 43.1 cm (32 × 17 in.)
Private collection
(Chicago)

12. *The Shelton with Sunspots, N.Y.*, 1926
Oil on canvas; 122.6 × 76.9 cm (48 1/4 × 30 1/4 in.)
The Art Institute of Chicago, gift of Leigh B. Block, 1985.206

13. *Untitled (New York)*, 1932
Charcoal on medium thick, cream, slightly textured laid paper; 62.2 × 47 cm (24 1/2 × 18 1/2 in.)
Hirshhorn Museum and Sculpture Garden, Smithsonian Institution, bequest of Joseph H. Hirshhorn, HMSG 86.3470
(not in exhibition)

14. *Untitled (New York)*, 1924–26
Charcoal on medium thick, cream, slightly textured laid paper; 62.5 × 47.9 cm (24 5/8 × 18 7/8 in.)
Fine Arts Museums of San Francisco, Achenbach Foundation for Graphic Arts, gift of Mrs. Charlotte S. Mack, 1961.48.1

15. *A Street*, 1926
Oil on canvas; 122.2 × 75.9 cm (48 1/2 × 29 7/8 in.)
Private collection
(Atlanta)

16. *Radiator Building—Night, New York*, 1927
Oil on canvas; 121.9 × 76.2 cm (48 × 30 in.)
Alfred Stieglitz Collection, Co-owned by Fisk University, Nashville, Tennessee, and Crystal Bridges Museum of American Art, Bentonville, Arkansas, ASC.2012.73
(Chicago)

17. *Ritz Tower*, 1928
Oil on canvas; 102.2 × 35.6 cm (40 1/4 × 14 in.)
Georgia O'Keeffe Museum, Museum Purchase, 2018.14.1
(Atlanta)

18. *Untitled (Manhattan)*, 1932
Black ink and graphite on paper; 17.8 × 9.8 cm (7 × 3 7/8 in.)
Georgia O'Keeffe Museum, Gift of The Georgia O'Keeffe Foundation, 2006.5.137

19. *Manhattan*, 1932
Oil on canvas; 213.4 × 121.9 cm (84 × 48 in.)
Smithsonian American Art Museum, Gift of the Georgia O'Keeffe Foundation, 1995.3.1

20. *Black White and Blue*, 1930
Oil on canvas; 121.9 × 76.2 cm (48 × 30 in.)
National Gallery of Art, Washington, Collection of Barney A. Ebsworth, 1998.93.31

21. *City Night*, 1926
Oil on canvas; 121.9 × 76.2 cm (48 × 30 in.)
The Minneapolis Institute of Art, Gift of funds from the Regis Corporation, Mr. and Mrs. W. John Driscoll, the Beim Foundation, the Larsen Fund, and by public subscription, 80.28

22. *Black and White*, 1930
Oil on canvas; 91.4 × 61.3 cm (36 × 24 1/8 in.)
Whitney Museum of American Art; Purchase, with funds from Mr. and Mrs. R. Crosby Kemper in honor of the Museum's 50th Anniversary, 81.9

23. *Abstraction*, 1926
Oil on canvas; 76.7 × 46.4 cm (30 3/16 × 18 1/4 in.)
Whitney Museum of American Art, Purchase, with funds from Georgia O'Keeffe and by exchange, 58.43

24. *Line and Curve*, 1927
Oil on canvas; 81.2 × 41.2 cm (31 15/16 × 16 1/4 in.)
National Gallery of Art, Washington, Alfred Stieglitz Collection, Bequest of Georgia O'Keeffe, 1987.58.6

25. *Abstraction White*, 1927
Oil on canvas; 86.4 × 35.6 cm (34 × 14 in.)
Georgia O'Keeffe Museum, Gift of The Burnett Foundation, 2007.1.20

26. *New York – Night (Madison Avenue)*, 1926
Oil on canvas; 81.3 × 30.5 cm (32 × 12 in.)
Museum of Fine Arts, St. Petersburg, Florida. Gift of Charles C. & Margaret Stevenson Henderson in memory of Hunt Henderson

27. *Shell and Old Shingle VI*, 1926
Oil on canvas; 76.2 × 45.7 cm (30 × 18 in.)
Saint Louis Art Museum, Gift of Charles E. Claggett in memory of Blanche Fischel Claggett

28. *Shell and Old Shingle No. VII*, 1926
Oil on canvas; 53.3 × 81.3 cm (21 × 32 in.)
Museum of Fine Arts, Boston, Alfred Stieglitz Collection—Bequest of Georgia O'Keeffe, 1987.539

29. *Slightly Open Clam Shell*, 1926
Pastel on white ground on very thick gray cardboard; 47 × 33 cm (18 9/16 × 13 in.)
Wadsworth Atheneum Museum of Art, Hartford, CT. The Douglas Tracy Smith and Dorothy Potter Smith Fund, Purchased in honor of Elizabeth Mankin Kornhauser, Krieble Curator of American Painting and Sculpture, in gratitude for her many years of extraordinary service to the Wadsworth Atheneum Museum of Art (1983–2010)

30. *White Flower*, 1929
Oil on canvas; 76.2 × 91.5 cm (30 × 36 in.)
Cleveland Museum of Art, Hinman B. Hurlbut Collection 1930.2162

31. *Ballet Skirt or Electric Light (from the White Rose Motif)*, 1927
Oil on canvas; 91.8 × 76.2 cm (36 1/8 × 30 in.)
The Art Institute of Chicago, Alfred Stieglitz Collection, bequest of Georgia O'Keeffe, 1987.250.1

32. *Lake George Barns*, 1926
Oil on canvas; 53.9 × 81.5 × 5 cm (21 3/16 × 32 1/16 × 1 15/16 in.)
Collection Walker Art Center, Minneapolis. Gift of the T. B. Walker Foundation, 1954

33. *Abstraction Blue*, 1927
Oil on canvas; 101.6 × 76 cm (40 × 29 15/16 in.)
The Museum of Modern Art, New York. Acquired through the Helen Acheson Bequest, 1979

34. *Dark Iris No. 1*, 1927
Oil on canvas; 81.3 × 41.9 cm (32 1/16 × 16 1/2 in.)
Colorado Springs Fine Arts Center, FA 1954.4a (a,b)

35. *Seaweed*, 1927
Oil on canvas; 22.9 × 17.8 cm (9 × 7 in.)
Cantor Arts Center; Gift of the Georgia O'Keeffe Foundation, an anonymous donor, and the Committee for Art Acquisitions Fund, 1997.96

36. *Untitled (Brooklyn Bridge)*, c. 1949
Pencil on paper; 25.7 × 19.7 cm (10 1/8 × 7 13/16 in.)
Collection of Mr. Louis Bacon

37. *Brooklyn Bridge*, 1949
Charcoal and black and white chalk on medium thick, brown, smooth wove paper, Kraft wrapping paper; 101.3 × 74.9 cm (39 7/8 × 29 1/2 in.)
Elie and Sarah Hirschfeld, Promised gift to New-York Historical Society
(Chicago)

38. *Brooklyn Bridge*, 1949
Oil on board; 121.9 × 91.4 cm (48 × 36 in.)
Brooklyn Museum, bequest of Mary Childs Draper (1977), 77.11
(not in exhibition)

39. *Seagram Building, New York*, 1958–65
Gelatin silver print; 8.1 × 5.6 cm (3 3/16 × 2 3/16 in.)
Georgia O'Keeffe Museum, Gift of The Georgia O'Keeffe Foundation, 2006.6.1290

40. *Chrysler Building from the Window of the Waldorf Astoria, New York*, c. 1960
Gelatin silver print; 10.1 × 6.9 cm (3 15/16 × 2 11/16 in.)
Georgia O'Keeffe Museum, Gift of The Georgia O'Keeffe Foundation, 2006.6.1370

41. *Untitled (Radiator Building), Pelican I Sketchbook*, 1920s
Graphite on paper; 17.8 × 11. 7 cm (7 × 4 5/8 in.)
Georgia O'Keeffe Museum, Gift of The Georgia O'Keeffe Foundation, 2006.5.718c
(not in exhibition)

42. *Untitled (Chrysler Building), Pelican I Sketchbook*, 1932
Graphite on paper; 17.8 × 11.7 cm (7 × 4 5/8 in.)
Georgia O'Keeffe Museum, Gift of The Georgia O'Keeffe Foundation, 2006.5.718d
(not in exhibition)

43. *Untitled (New York)*, 1925–32
Graphite on paper; 20 × 15.2 cm (7 7/8 × 6 in.)
Georgia O'Keeffe Museum, Gift of The Georgia O'Keeffe Foundation, 2006.5.100

44. *Untitled (New York)*, 1925–32
Graphite on paper; 20 × 15.2 cm (7 7/8 × 6 in.)
Georgia O'Keeffe Museum, Gift of The Georgia O'Keeffe Foundation, 2006.5.101

45. *Untitled (New York)*, 1925–32
Graphite on paper; 20 × 15.2 cm (7 7/8 × 6 in.)
Georgia O'Keeffe Museum, Gift of The Georgia O'Keeffe Foundation, 2006.5.099

46. *Untitled (New York)*, 1925–32
Graphite on paper; 20 × 15.2 cm (7 7/8 × 6 in.)
Georgia O'Keeffe Museum, Gift of The Georgia O'Keeffe Foundation, 2006.5.102

47. *Untitled (New York)*, 1925–32
Graphite on paper; 20 × 15.2 cm (7 7/8 × 6 in.)
Georgia O'Keeffe Museum, Gift of The Georgia O'Keeffe Foundation, 2006.5.103

48. *Untitled (New York)*, 1925–32
Graphite on paper; 20 × 15.2 cm (7 7/8 × 6 in.)
Georgia O'Keeffe Museum, Gift of The Georgia O'Keeffe Foundation, 2006.5.104

49. *Untitled (New York)*, 1925–32
Graphite on paper; 15.2 × 20 cm (6 × 7 7/8 in.)
Georgia O'Keeffe Museum, Gift of The Georgia O'Keeffe Foundation, 2006.5.105

50. *Untitled (New York)*, 1925–32
Graphite on paper; 15.2 × 20 cm (6 × 7 7/8 in.)
Georgia O'Keeffe Museum, Gift of The Georgia O'Keeffe Foundation, 2006.5.106

51. *East River*, 1932
Charcoal on paper; sheet: 46.7 × 61 cm (18 3/8 × 24 in.)
Georgia O'Keeffe Museum, Gift of The Georgia O'Keeffe Foundation, 2006.5.138

52. *East River No. 1*, 1926
Oil on canvas; 30.8 × 81.6 cm (12 1/8 × 32 1/8 in.)
Wichita Art Museum, Museum purchase, Friends of the Wichita Art Museum, 1979.35

53. *East River with Sun*, 1926
Pastel on paper; 28.6 × 71.1 cm (11 1/4 × 28 in.)
Private collection
(not in exhibition)

54. *East River New York No. 2*, 1927
Pastel on paper; 28.6 × 72.4 cm (11 1/4 × 28 1/2 in.)
Private collection
(not in exhibition)

55. *East River from the Shelton, No. III*, 1926
Oil on canvas; 30.5 × 81.3 cm (12 × 32 in.)
The Frances Lehman Loeb Art Center, Vassar College, Bequest of Mrs. Arthur Schwab (Edna Bryner, '07) (1967), 67.31.1

56. *East River from the Shelton Hotel*, 1928
Oil on canvas; 30.5 × 81.3 cm (12 × 32 in.)
The Metropolitan Museum of Art, New York, Alfred Stieglitz Collection, Bequest of Georgia O'Keeffe, 1986, 1987.377.3

57. *East River from the 30th Story of the Shelton Hotel*, 1928
Oil on canvas; 76.8 × 121.9 cm (30 1⁄4 × 48 in.)
New Britain Museum of American Art, New Britain, Connecticut, Stephen B. Lawrence Fund, 1958.9

58. *3 Eggs in Pink Dish*, 1928–29
Oil on canvas; 30.5 × 81.3 cm (12 1⁄16 × 32 1⁄16 in.)
New Mexico Museum of Art, Santa Fe, gift of the Georgia O'Keeffe Estate, 1987, 1987.449.2

59. *Pink Dish and Green Leaves*, 1928–29
Pastel on board; 55.9 × 71.1 cm (22 × 28 in.)
Private collection
(Chicago)

60. *East River from the Shelton (East River No. 1)*, 1927–28
Oil on canvas; 66 × 55.8 cm (26 × 22 in.)
New Jersey State Museum Collection. Purchased by the Association for the Arts of the New Jersey State Museum with a gift from Mary Lea Johnson

61. *Black Cross, New Mexico*, 1929
Oil on canvas; 99.1 × 76.2 cm (39 × 30 in.)
The Art Institute of Chicago, Art Institute Purchase Fund, 1943.95

62. *New York, Night*, 1928–29
Oil on canvas; 101.6 × 48.3 cm (40 × 19 in.)
Sheldon Museum of Art, University of Nebraska-Lincoln, Nebraska Art Association Thomas C. Woods Memorial, N-107.1958

63. *After a Walk Back of Mabel's*, 1929
Oil on canvas; 101.6 × 76.5 cm (40 × 30 in.)
Private collection

64. *Dead Tree Bear Lake Taos*, 1929
Oil on canvas; 81.3 × 43.2 cm (32 × 17 in.)
Art Bridges
(Chicago)

65. *Farmhouse Window and Door*, 1929
Oil on canvas; 101.6 × 76.2 cm (40 × 30 in.)
The Museum of Modern Art, New York. Acquired through the Richard D. Brixey Bequest, 1945

66. *Taos Pueblo*, 1929, reworked 1934
Oil on canvas; 61 × 101.6 cm (24 × 40 in.)
Eiteljorg Museum, gift, 1987, 83.3.55

67. *Cow's Skull with Calico Roses*, 1931
Oil on canvas; 91.4 × 61 cm (36 × 24 in.)
The Art Institute of Chicago, Alfred Stieglitz Collection, gift of Georgia O'Keeffe, 1947.712

68. *Ranchos Church, No.* 3, 1929
Oil on canvas; 38.1 × 27.9 cm (15 × 11 in.)
Collection of David Warnock and Michele Speaks

69. *Ranchos Church, No. II, NM*, 1929
Oil on canvas; 61 × 91.4 cm (24 1⁄16 × 36 in.)
The Phillips Collection, Washington, DC, Acquired 1930
(Atlanta)

70. *Dark Mesa with Pink Sky*, 1930
Oil on canvas; 41.3 × 77.2 cm (16 1⁄4 × 30 3⁄8 in.)
Amon Carter Museum of American Art, Fort Worth, Texas, 1965.80

71. *Desert Abstraction*, 1931
Oil on canvas; 40 × 90.8 cm (15 3⁄4 × 35 3⁄4 in.)
New Mexico Museum of Art, Santa Fe, Gift of the Museum of New Mexico Foundation in honor of the New Mexico Museum of Art's Centennial year, 2017, 1984.336

72. *Untitled (City Night)*, 1970s
Oil on canvas; 213.6 × 122.1 cm (84 1⁄16 × 48 1⁄16 in.)
Georgia O'Keeffe Museum, Gift of The Georgia O'Keeffe Foundation, 2006.05.542

73. Alfred Stieglitz (American, 1864–1946)
Georgia O'Keeffe, 1918
Platinum print; image: 24.5 × 20.1 cm (9 11⁄16 × 7 15⁄16 in.); paper: 25.3 × 20.2 cm (10 × 8 in.)
The Art Institute of Chicago, Alfred Stieglitz Collection, 1949.755

74. Alfred Stieglitz (American, 1864–1946)
Georgia O'Keeffe, 1918
Palladium print; image: 24.4 × 20 cm (9 5⁄8 × 7 7⁄8 in.); paper: 25.2 × 20.2 cm (9 15⁄16 × 8 in.)
The Art Institute of Chicago, Alfred Stieglitz Collection, 1949.758

75. Alfred Stieglitz (American, 1864–1946)
Georgia O'Keeffe, 1918
Palladium print; image: 24.8 × 20 cm (9 13⁄16 × 7 7⁄8 in.); paper: 25.4 × 20.3 cm (10 × 8 in.)
The Art Institute of Chicago, Alfred Stieglitz Collection, 1949.750

76. Alfred Stieglitz (American, 1864–1946)
Georgia O'Keeffe, 1919–21
Palladium print; image: 24.3 × 19.4 cm (9 5⁄8 × 7 11⁄16 in.); paper: 25 × 20.3 cm (9 7⁄8 × 8 in.)
The Art Institute of Chicago, Alfred Stieglitz Collection, 1949.751

77. Alfred Stieglitz (American, 1864–1946)
From the Shelton, New York, 30th Floor Looking North, 1927
Gelatin silver print; 11.6 × 9.2 cm (4 9⁄16 × 3 5⁄8 in.)
National Gallery of Art, Washington, Alfred Stieglitz Collection, 1949.3.1196

78. Alfred Stieglitz (American, 1864–1946)
From Room 3003—(Looking Northwest)—The Shelton, New York, 1927
Gelatin silver print; 11.3 × 8.6 cm (4 7⁄16 × 3 3⁄8 in.)
National Gallery of Art, Washington, Alfred Stieglitz Collection, 1949.3.1189

79. Alfred Stieglitz (American, 1864–1946)
From the Shelton, New York, 30th Floor—Looking North, 1927
Gelatin silver print; 11.7 × 9.1 cm (4 5⁄8 × 3 9⁄16 in.)
National Gallery of Art, Washington, Alfred Stieglitz Collection, 1949.3.1195

80. Alfred Stieglitz (American, 1864–1946)
From the Shelton, New York, Looking East, 1926–27
Gelatin silver print; 9 × 11.7 cm (3 9⁄16 × 4 5⁄8 in.)
National Gallery of Art, Washington, Alfred Stieglitz Collection, 1949.3.1267

81. Alfred Stieglitz (American, 1864–1946)
From the Shelton, New York (Room 3003), Looking Southeast, 1927
Gelatin silver print; 8.8 × 11.5 cm (3 7⁄16 × 4 1⁄2 in.)
National Gallery of Art, Washington, Alfred Stieglitz Collection, 1949.3.1197
(Chicago)

82. Alfred Stieglitz (American, 1864–1946)
From Room "3003"—The Shelton, New York, Looking Northeast, 1927
Gelatin silver print; image/paper/first mount: 9.2 × 11.8 cm (3 5⁄8 × 4 11⁄16 in.); second mount: 31.9 × 25.2 cm (12 9⁄16 × 9 15⁄16 in.)
The Art Institute of Chicago, Alfred Stieglitz Collection, 1949.708

83. Alfred Stieglitz (American, 1864–1946)
From "Room 303"—(Intimate Gallery)—New York, 1927
Gelatin silver print; 11.8 × 9.2 cm (4 11/16 × 3 5/8 in.)
National Gallery of Art, Washington, Alfred Stieglitz Collection, 1949.3.1192

84. Alfred Stieglitz (American, 1864–1946)
From My Window at An American Place, North, 1931
Gelatin silver print; image/paper/first mount: 23.9 × 19 cm (9 7/16 × 7 1/2 in.); second mount: 54.6 × 41.8 cm (21 1/2 × 16 1/2 in.)
The Art Institute of Chicago, Alfred Stieglitz Collection, 1949.788

85. Alfred Stieglitz (American, 1864–1946)
From My Window at An American Place, North, 1930–31
Gelatin silver print; image/paper/first mount: 18.8 × 23.8 cm (7 7/16 × 9 3/8 in.); second mount: 22.8 × 39.5 cm (9 × 15 9/16 in.)
The Art Institute of Chicago, Alfred Stieglitz Collection, 1949.787

86. Alfred Stieglitz (American, 1864–1946)
From My Window at An American Place, North, 1931
Gelatin silver print; image/paper/first mount: 24.3 × 19.3 cm (9 5/8 × 7 5/8 in.); second mount: 56.5 × 46.6 cm (22 1/4 × 18 3/8 in.)
The Art Institute of Chicago, Alfred Stieglitz Collection, 1949.789

87. Alfred Stieglitz (American, 1864–1946)
From My Window at An American Place, Southwest, 1932
Gelatin silver print; image/paper/first mount: 19.1 × 24 cm (7 9/16 × 9 1/2 in.); second mount: 56.5 × 46.1 cm (22 1/4 × 18 3/16 in.)
The Art Institute of Chicago, Alfred Stieglitz Collection, 1949.790

88. Alfred Stieglitz (American, 1864–1946)
From My Window at An American Place, Southwest, 1932
Gelatin silver print; image/paper/first mount: 23.9 × 18.8 cm (9 7/16 × 7 7/16 in.); second mount: 55.8 × 40.2 cm (22 × 15 7/8 in.)
The Art Institute of Chicago, Alfred Stieglitz Collection, 1949.785

89. *Arno Penthouse, E. 54th Street, New York*, 1936–42
Gelatin silver print; 11.5 × 6.7 cm (4 1/2 × 2 5/8 in.)
Georgia O'Keeffe Museum, Georgia O'Keeffe Photographs, Museum Purchase, 2014.3.267

90. Carl Van Vechten (American, 1880–1964)
Georgia O'Keeffe, June 5, 1936
Gelatin silver print; image and sheet: 19.8 × 25 cm (7 13/16 × 9 13/16 in.)
Philadelphia Museum of Art: Gift of John Mark Lutz, 1965

91. Carl Van Vechten (American, 1880–1964)
Georgia O'Keeffe, June 5, 1936
Gelatin silver print; image and sheet: 24.8 × 19.5 cm (9 13/16 × 7 11/16 in.)
Philadelphia Museum of Art: Gift of John Mark Lutz, 1965

92. Carl Van Vechten (American, 1880–1964)
Georgia O'Keeffe, June 5, 1936
Gelatin silver print; image and sheet: 24.5 × 19.1 cm (9 5/8 × 7 1/2 in.)
Philadelphia Museum of Art: Gift of John Mark Lutz, 1965

93. Carl Van Vechten (American, 1880–1964)
Georgia O'Keeffe, June 5, 1936
Gelatin silver print; image and sheet: 24.5 × 19.1 cm (9 5/8 × 7 1/2 in.)
Philadelphia Museum of Art: Gift of John Mark Lutz, 1965

SELECTED BIBLIOGRAPHY

Archival Sources

Georgia O'Keeffe Museum, Library and Archive, Santa Fe, NM
- Criticism Files
- Frances O'Brien Papers Relating to Georgia O'Keeffe
- Stieglitz Circle Exhibition Ephemera
- Vertical Files

Museum of the City of New York
- Photographs Collection

New-York Historical Society
- George B. Corsa Hotel Collection

New York Public Library
- Map Division
- Mitchell Kennerley Papers, Archives and Manuscripts Division
- Photography and Prints Division

Newberry Library, Chicago
- Sherwood Anderson Papers

Yale University, Beinecke Rare Book and Manuscript Library, Yale Collection of American Literature, New Haven, CT
- Alfred Stieglitz / Georgia O'Keeffe Archive

Primary Sources

Adlow, Dorothy. "Georgia O'Keeffe." *Christian Science Monitor*, June 20, 1927, 11.

"Art: On View." *Time*, Feb. 20, 1928, 21–22.

Berman, B. Vladimir. "She Painted the Lily and Got $25,000 and Fame for Doing It!" *New York Evening Graphic Magazine Section*, May 12, 1928, 3-M.

Bragdon, Claude. "The Shelton Hotel, Arthur Loomis Harmon, Architect." *Architectural Record* 58, no. 1 (July 1925): 1–18.

Ferriss, Hugh. *The Metropolis of Tomorrow*. New York: Ives Washburn, 1929.

"Foujita's Art Is Seen in Exhibition Here." *New York Times*, Feb. 14, 1926, X12.

Hood, Raymond M. "The American Radiator Company Building, New York." *American Architect and the Architectural Review*, Nov. 19, 1924, 467–74.

"Hotel for the Bachelor Opens Its Doors to Women." *New York Times*, Oct. 12, 1924, X11.

Johns, Orrick. "What the Modish Building Will Wear." *New York Times*, Oct. 4, 1925, SM11.

Kalonyme, Louis. "In New York Galleries: Georgia O'Keeffe's Arresting Pictures." *New York Times*, Jan. 16, 1927, X10.

——. "Scaling the Peak of the Art Season." *Arts and Decoration* 26 (Mar. 1927): 57, 88, and 93.

Kotz, Mary Lynn. "A Day with Georgia O'Keeffe." *Art News* 76, no. 10 (Dec. 1977): 36–45.

Kuh, Katharine. *The Artist's Voice: Talks with Seventeen Artists*. New York: Harper and Row, 1962.

Looney, Ralph. "Georgia O'Keeffe." *Atlantic Monthly* 215, no. 4 (Apr. 1965): 106–10.

Matthias, Blanche C. "Georgia O'Keeffe and the Intimate Gallery: Stieglitz Showing Seven Americans." *Chicago Evening Post, Magazine of the Art World*, Mar. 2, 1926, 1 and 14.

O'Brien, Frances. "Americans We Like: Georgia O'Keeffe." *The Nation*, Oct. 12, 1927, 361–62.

O'Keeffe, Georgia. *Georgia O'Keeffe*. New York: Viking Press, 1976.

——. *Some Memories of Drawings*. New York: Atlantis Editions, 1974.

Reagan, Oliver, ed. *American Architecture of the Twentieth Century*. Vol 1. New York: Architectural Book Publishing, 1927.

Robertson, Howard. "'Two Splendid Skyscrapers': The Hotel Shelton and the Ritz Tower, New York." *Architect and Building News*, Jan. 21, 1927, 145–49.

Ross, Ishbel. "Bones of Desert Blaze Art Trail of Miss O'Keeffe." *New York Herald Tribune*, Dec. 29, 1931, 3.

Sabine, Lillian. "Record Price for Living Artist." *Brooklyn Sunday Eagle Magazine*, May 27, 1928, 11.

"The Shelton, a Residence for Men." *New York Times*, Mar. 2, 1924, RPA8.

T. H. R. "Georgia O'Keeffe, Artist." *Shelton Spotlight*, Apr. 24, 1926, n.p.

Secondary Sources

Brown, Adrienne. *The Black Skyscraper: Architecture and the Perception of Race*. Baltimore: Johns Hopkins University Press, 2017.

Chave, Anna C. "'Who Will Paint New York?': 'The World's New Art Center' and the Skyscraper Paintings of Georgia O'Keeffe." *American Art* 5, nos. 1–2 (Winter–Spring 1991): 86–107.

Corn, Wanda M. *The Great American Thing: Modern Art and National Identity, 1915–1935*. Berkeley: University of California Press, 1999.

——. "Painting Big—O'Keeffe's *Manhattan*." *American Art* 20, no. 2 (Summer 2006): 22–25.

——. "Telling Tales: Georgia O'Keeffe on Georgia O'Keeffe." *American Art* 23, no. 2 (Summer 2009): 54–79.

Cowart, Jack and Juan Hamilton, with Sarah Greenough. *Georgia O'Keeffe: Art and Letters*. Exh. cat. Washington, DC: National Gallery of Art, in association with Boston: New York Graphic Society Books / Little, Brown, 1987.

Duvert, Elizabeth. "Georgia O'Keeffe's *Radiator Building*: Icon of Glamorous Gotham." *Places* 2, no. 2 (Fall 1984): 3–17.

Fryd, Vivien Green. "Georgia O'Keeffe's *Radiator Building*: Gender, Sexuality, Modernism, and Urban Imagery." *Winterthur Portfolio* 35, no. 4 (Winter 2000): 269–89.

Grasso, Linda M. *Equal under the Sky: Georgia O'Keeffe and Twentieth-Century Feminism*. Albuquerque: University of New Mexico Press, 2017.

Greenough, Sarah, ed. *My Faraway One: Selected Letters of Georgia O'Keeffe and Alfred Stieglitz*. Vol. 1, *1915–1933*. New Haven, CT: Yale University Press, 2011.

Harris, Gale. *Shelton Hotel*. Landmarks Preservation Commission, Designation List 490, Nov. 22, 2016, s-media.nyc.gov/agencies/lpc/lp/2557.pdf.

Haskell, Barbara, ed. *Georgia O'Keeffe: Abstraction*. Exh. cat. New York: Whitney Museum of American Art; Washington, DC: Phillips Collection; Santa Fe: Georgia O'Keeffe Museum; New Haven, CT: Yale University Press, 2009.

Holloway, Camara Dia. "Lovechild: Stieglitz, O'Keeffe, and the Birth of American Modernism." *Prospects* 30 (2005): 395–432.

Kalb, Peter R. *High Drama: The New York Cityscapes of Georgia O'Keeffe and Margaret Bourke-White*. New York: Midmarch Arts Press, 2003.

Kroiz, Lauren. *Creative Composites: Modernism, Race, and the Stieglitz Circle*. Berkeley: University of California Press; Washington, DC: Phillips Collection, 2012.

Lynes, Barbara Buhler. *Georgia O'Keeffe: Catalogue Raisonné*. 2 vols. New Haven, CT: Yale University Press, 1999.

——. *O'Keeffe, Stieglitz, and the Critics, 1916–1929*. 1989; Chicago: University of Chicago Press, 1991.

Peters, Sarah Whitaker. *Becoming O'Keeffe: The Early Years*. 2nd ed. New York: Abbeville Press, 2001.

Robinson, Roxana. *Georgia O'Keeffe: A Life*. Expand. ed. New York: Harper and Row, 1989; Waltham, MA: Brandeis University, 2020.

Schleier, Merrill. *The Skyscraper in American Art, 1890–1931*. Ann Arbor, MI: UMI Research Press, 1986.

Scott, Sascha T. "Georgia O'Keeffe's Hawai'i?: Decolonizing the History of American Modernism." *American Art* 34, no. 2 (Summer 2020): 26–53.

Turner, Elizabeth Hutton. *Georgia O'Keeffe: The Poetry of Things*. Exh. cat. Washington, DC: Phillips Collection; New Haven, CT: Yale University Press, in association with the Dallas Museum of Art, 1999.

Volpe, Lisa, with Ariel Plotek. *Georgia O'Keeffe, Photographer*. Exh. cat. Houston: Museum of Fine Arts, Houston, in association with New Haven, CT: Yale University Press, 2021.

CONTRIBUTORS

Adrienne Brown is Associate Professor in the Departments of English and Race Diaspora and Indigeneity at the University of Chicago. She is the co-editor with Valerie Smith of *Race and Real Estate* (2015) and the author of *The Black Skyscraper: Architecture and the Perception of Race* (2017), which won the 2018 First Book Prize from the Modernist Studies Association, and *The Residential Is Racial: A Perceptual History of Mass Homeownership* (2024).

Annelise K. Madsen is the Gilda and Henry Buchbinder Associate Curator, Arts of the Americas, at the Art Institute of Chicago. She has particular interest in elevating historical women artists through museum programming, collections research, acquisitions, and scholarship. Madsen curated and authored *John Singer Sargent and Chicago's Gilded Age* (2018) and has co-curated and contributed to a number of other exhibitions and publications at the Art Institute.

Sarah Kelly Oehler is the Field-McCormick Chair and Curator, Arts of the Americas, and Vice President of Curatorial Strategy at the Art Institute of Chicago. In 2018 Oehler co-curated the critically acclaimed exhibition *Charles White: A Retrospective*. Among her numerous contributions to other exhibitions and publications is a recent essay on Georgia O'Keeffe's 1943 retrospective at the Art Institute for the digital publication *Exhibiting O'Keeffe: The Making of an American Modernist* (Georgia O'Keeffe Museum, 2023).

Sascha T. Scott is Associate Professor of art history at Syracuse University, New York, where she is also faculty in the Native American and Indigenous Studies Program. Scott is an award-winning scholar whose work on both Indigenous and settler art is framed by ethical imperatives and conceptual frameworks central to Indigenous studies. She is currently working on books about Georgia O'Keeffe and about modern Pueblo painting. The latter has been supported by grants from the NEH and NFAH.

Lisa Volpe is Curator of Photography at the Museum of Fine Arts, Houston. Among her recent publications, she authored *Georgia O'Keeffe: Photographer* (2021), which was one of two finalists for the Association of American Publishers Prose Awards, and edited *Gordon Parks: Stokely Carmichael and Black Power* (2022).

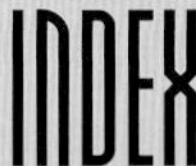

Note: page numbers in italics refer to illustrations, as do plate numbers ("pl."). Works by Georgia O'Keeffe are listed by title. Works by artists other than O'Keeffe are found under the artist's name.

PHOTOGRAPHY CREDITS

Unless otherwise noted, photographs of artworks in the collection of the Art Institute of Chicago are by Juan Molina Hernández and Robert Lifson, with postproduction by Hayley Hinsberger, and are copyrighted by the Art Institute of Chicago. Works by Georgia O'Keeffe are © Georgia O'Keeffe Museum, unless noted otherwise.

Every effort has been made to identify, contact, and acknowledge copyright holders for all reproductions; additional rights holders are encouraged to contact the Art Institute of Chicago. The following credits apply to all images in this book for which separate acknowledgment is due.

Plates

Pl. 1; pp. 72–73 (detail): © Según las indicaciones de los Titulares / Entidad de Gestión de los Derechos. Pl. 2: Photograph courtesy of Rich Sanders, Des Moines. Pls. 3, 90–93; pp. 54–55 (detail): Philadelphia Museum of Art. Pls. 4, 69: The Phillips Collection, Washington, DC. Pl. 5: Art Gallery of Ontario. Pl. 6: Minneapolis Institute of Art; Pls. 7, 56: © The Metropolitan Museum of Art; photograph: © The Metropolitan Museum of Art; image source: Art Resource, NY. Pls. 8, 10, 15, 17–18, 25, 36, 39–51, 53–54, 63, 72, 89: © Georgia O'Keeffe Museum. Pl. 9: Photograph courtesy of Mark Woods. Pl. 11; pp. 88–89 (detail): Photograph courtesy of Nathaniel Willson. Pl. 12: © Georgia O'Keeffe Museum; photograph: © The Art Institute of Chicago. Pl. 13: Hirshhorn Museum and Sculpture Garden, Smithsonian Institution. Pl. 14: Photograph by Randy Dodson, courtesy of the Fine Arts Museums of San Francisco. Pl. 16; p. 126 (detail): Crystal Bridges Museum of American Art. Pl. 19: Smithsonian American Art Museum, Washington, DC / Art Resource, NY. Pls. 20, 24, 77–81, 83: National Gallery of Art, Washington. Pl. 21: Minneapolis Institute of Art. Pls. 22–23: © Whitney Museum of American Art / Licensed by Scala / Art Resource, NY. Pl. 26: Museum of Fine Arts, St. Petersburg, Florida. Pl. 27: The Saint Louis Art Museum. Pl. 28: Photograph © 2024 Museum of Fine Arts, Boston. Pl. 29: Wadsworth Atheneum Museum of Art. Pl. 30: Courtesy of The Cleveland Museum of Art. Pl. 32: Walker Art Center. Pls. 33, 65: © The Museum of Modern Art / Licensed by SCALA / Art Resource, NY. Pl. 34: Colorado Springs Fine Art Center. Pl. 35: Cantor Arts Center. Pl. 37; pp. 104–5 (detail): New-York Historical Society. Pl. 38: Brooklyn Museum. Pl. 52; p. 160 (detail): Wichita Art Museum. Pl. 55: Frances Lehman Loeb Art Center, Vassar College, Poughkeepsie, NY / Art Resource, NY. Pl. 57; p. 166 (detail): New Britain Museum of American Art. Pls. 58, 71: New Mexico Museum of Art. Pl. 59; pp. 34–35 (detail): Photograph courtesy of Bruce M. White. Pl. 60; pp. 14–15 (detail): © New Jersey State Museum; photograph by Peter S. Jacobs. Pl. 62; p. 3 (detail): Photograph courtesy of Bill Ganzel. Pl. 64: Photograph courtesy of Roz Akin. Pl. 66; p. 180 (detail): Eiteljorg Museum. Pl. 68: Photograph courtesy of Byron Flesher. Pl. 70: © Amon Carter Museum of American Art.

Figures

P. 17, fig. 1; p. 62, fig. 6: The Phillips Collection, Washington, DC. P. 20, fig. 3; p. 45, fig. 11; p. 76, fig. 1; p. 79, fig. 3; p. 80, fig. 6: Beinecke Rare Book and Manuscript Library, Yale University, New Haven, CT. P. 22, fig. 5: Mapping Specialists. P. 23, fig. 6: New York Public Library. P. 25, fig. 8: Newberry Library, Chicago. P. 30, fig. 13; p. 46, fig. 12; p. 91, fig. 1; p. 95, fig. 3; p. 98, fig. 6; p. 98, fig. 7; p. 99, figs. 8–9: © Georgia O'Keeffe Museum. P. 37, fig. 1; p. 61, fig. 3: National Gallery of Art, Washington. P. 37, fig. 2: © Carl Van Vechten; photograph: Philadelphia Museum of Art. P. 38, fig. 3: New York Public Library / Art Resource, NY. P. 41, fig. 6: Library of Congress. P. 43, fig. 9: Addison Gallery of American Art, Phillips Academy, Andover, MA / Art Resource, NY. P. 44, fig. 10: © Whitney Museum of American Art / Licensed by Scala / Art Resource, NY. P. 47, fig. 13: p. 48, fig. 14; p. 62, fig. 5; p. 82, fig. 7: © The Metropolitan Museum of Art; photograph: © The Metropolitan Museum of Art; image source: Art Resource, NY. P. 49, fig. 15: Photograph © 2024 Museum of Fine Arts, Boston. P. 50, fig. 16: Wadsworth Atheneum Museum of Art. P. 59, fig. 2: Bettmann via Getty Images. P. 61, fig. 4: The Hood Museum of Art. P. 63, fig. 7: Derby Museum and Art Galleries, England. P. 66, fig. 10: Alamy. P. 78, fig. 2; p. 83, fig. 8: © The Museum of Modern Art / Licensed by SCALA / Art Resource, NY. P. 79, fig. 4: © Winold Reiss; photograph by Mattijs Vormer. P. 80, fig. 5: Yale University Library, New Haven, CT. P. 85, fig. 10: Crystal Bridges Museum of American Art. P. 95, fig. 2: Photograph © 2024 Museum of Fine Arts, Boston. P. 100, fig. 10: Museum of Fine Arts Houston.

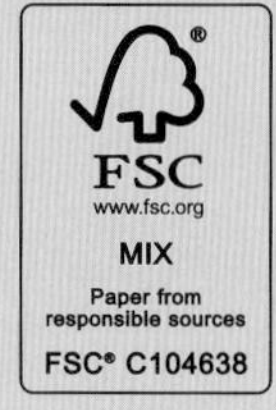

This book was made using paper and materials certified by the Forest Stewardship Council®, which ensures responsible forest management.